AF478212

Learning to Emulate the Wise

Titles in The Formation and Development of Academic Disciplines in Twentieth-Century China Series

Learning to Emulate the Wise: The Genesis of Chinese Philosophy as an Academic Discipline in Twentieth-Century China
Edited by John Makeham

Sociology and Anthropology in Twentieth-Century China: Between Universalism and Indigenism
Edited by Arif Dirlik, with Guannan Li and Hsiao-pei Yen

Transforming History: The Making of a Modern Academic Discipline in Twentieth-Century China
Edited by Brian Moloughney and Peter Zarrow

Learning to Emulate the Wise:

The Genesis of Chinese Philosophy as an Academic Discipline in Twentieth-Century China

Edited by John Makeham

The Chinese Univerity Press

Learning to Emulate the Wise:
The Genesis of Chinese Philosophy as an
Academic Discipline in Twentieth-Century China

Edited by John Makeham

ISBN: 978-962-996-478-8

THE CHINESE UNIVERSITY PRESS
The Chinese University of Hong Kong
SHA TIN, N.T., HONG KONG
Fax: +852 2603 6692
Fax: +852 2603 7355
E-mail: cup@cuhk.edu.hk
Website: www.chineseupress.com

Printed in Hong Kong

No matter whether in ancient times or modern, nor East or West, when the culture of a people reaches a certain level, then without exception the culture of that people will have a type of philosophy.

—Wang Guowei (1906)

Every philosophical system has its special spirit, its unique appearance; each age, each people, has its philosophy.

—Feng Youlan (1931)

Any cultural system has its own philosophy, otherwise it does not constitute a cultural system. Accordingly, if one acknowledges China's cultural system, then one naturally acknowledges Chinese philosophy.

—Mou Zongsan (1963)

Acknowledgments

I am grateful to all colleagues contributing to this volume; to Leigh Jenco, for constructive critical feedback on the draft Introduction; and to the two readers for the Press who provided frank and valuable advice about how to improve the volume. The sound advice of one reader, in particular, has led me to revise the order of the chapters and to make significant changes to the structure of the Introduction. I also wish to express my gratitude to the Chiang Ching-kuo Foundation for International Scholarly Exchange and to the Australian Research Council for providing grants to carry out the research underpinning this study.

—JM

Contents

Part III: The Critics' Voices

About the Series

The Formation and Development of Academic Disciplines in Twentieth-Century China

John Makeham, Series Editor

The series is the principal outcome of three annual workshops held in Canberra, Beijing and Hong Kong between 2007 and 2009 on the topic of "the Formation and Development of Academic Disciplines in Twentieth-Century China." Our aim in these workshops was to construct a historically informed multidisciplinary framework to examine the complex processes by which traditional Chinese knowledge systems and indigenous grammars of knowledge construction interacted with Western paradigms to shape the formation and development of modern academic disciplines in China. The modern disciplines were formed as intellectuals sought new roles for themselves in the context of dramatic political change. New institutions—above all academic (schools, universities) and media (newspapers, book publishing)—provided the social basis for much work on specialized disciplines from the late Qing through the Republican period. The mutual interaction of traditional Chinese and modern Western knowledge paradigms and institutional practices shaped the formation and development of modern academic disciplines in China.

Modern scholarship remains largely silent about how different domains of traditional knowledge practice responded to common challenges and the consequences of this for subsequent disciplinary developments. To what extent were new knowledge systems viewed as tools in the recovery of tradition rather than its abandonment? What were the thematics, conversations, controversies, and dominant modes of argument across these domains as they responded to the new challenges? To what extent and under what conditions did practitioners of traditional forms of learning concede authority to Western knowledge paradigms?

Specifically, we have sought to understand and analyze how traditional forms of Chinese scholarship were adapted to new knowledge paradigms; to identify the role played by indigenous "grammars" (inherited problematics and standards of rational justification) in shaping the formation of academic disciplines, and the concrete forms in which these grammars interacted with Western paradigms and concepts; to demonstrate how indigenous grammars of knowledge construction, and their ongoing complex interaction with Western paradigms, decisively influenced the formation and development of individual academic disciplines; and to examine the significance of the growing trend toward the indigenization (*bentuhua*) of knowledge systems and how it relates to broader contemporary concerns about the indigenization of knowledge in many social science and humanities disciplines.

List of Contributors

Carine Defoort is Professor in Sinology at K. U. Leuven, where she studied Sinology and Philosophy. She also studied Chinese philosophy at the National Taiwan University and at the University of Hawai'i. Her doctorate concerned the relatively unknown third-century B.C. book, *Heguanzi* [Master with the pheasant cap]. She is editor of the translation journal *Contemporary Chinese Thought* (M. E. Sharpe) and corresponding editor for Europe of *China Review International*. Her research interests lie, on the one hand, with pre-Qin and Han thought and, on the other hand, with the twentieth-century interpretation of that thought. Her publications include: *The Pheasant Cap Master (Heguanzi): A Rhetorical Reading* (Albany: SUNY Press, 1997); "Is There Such a Thing as Chinese Philosophy? Arguments of an Implicit Debate," *Philosophy East and West* 51.3 (July 2001), pp. 393–413; and "Is 'Chinese Philosophy' a Proper Name? A Response to Rein Raud," *Philosophy East and West* 56.4 (2006), pp. 625–660.

Xiaoqing Diana Lin is Associate Professor of History at Indiana University Northwest. She is currently working on an intellectual biography of Feng Youlan. Her publications include: *Peking University: Chinese Scholarship and Intellectuals, 1898–1937* (Albany: SUNY Press, 2005), and "Creating Modern Chinese Metaphysics: Feng Youlan and New Realism," *Modern China* (forthcoming).

John Makeham is Professor and Head of the Chinese Studies Department at the Australian National University. He has also held positions at Victoria University of Wellington, the University of Adelaide, National Taiwan University, and the Chinese University of Hong Kong. He is a specialist in Chinese intellectual history with a particular interest in Confucian philosophy and is editor of the Brill monograph series, Modern Chinese Philosophy. He recently published an edited volume, *Dao Companion to Neo-Confucian Philosophy* (Dordrecht and New York; Springer, 2010) and is currently preparing an annotated translation of Xiong Shili's *Xin weishi lun* [New treatise on the uniqueness of consciousness], a seminal text in twentieth-century Chinese Buddhist and Confucian philosophy.

Thierry Meynard is Professor of Philosophy in the Philosophy Department of Sun Yat-Sen University in Guangzhou, where he teaches Western philosophy, comparative philosophy, and Latin classics. He is the vice-director of the Archive for the Introduction of Western Knowledge, also at Sun Yat-Sen University.

In 2003, he obtained his PhD in Philosophy from Peking University, writing a dissertation on Liang Shuming. From 2003 to 2006, he taught philosophy at Fordham University, New York. Since 2006, he has been a member of the Macau Ricci Institute. He has authored *The Religious Philosophy of Liang Shuming* (Boston: Brill, 2010); *Confucius Sinarum Philosophus (1687): The First Translation of the Confucian Classics* (Rome: Institutum Historicum Societatis Iesu, 2011); and has edited one volume of the journal *Contemporary Chinese Thought* (M. E. Sharpe, Spring 2009), entitled *Liang Shuming's Thought and Its Reception*.

Hans-Georg Moeller is Senior Lecturer in the Philosophy Department at University College Cork in Cork, Ireland. His research focuses on Chinese and comparative philosophy and on the social theory of Niklas Luhmann. Among his book publications are: *Daoism Explained: From the Dream of the Butterfly to the Fishnet Allegory* (Chicago: Open Court, 2004); *Luhmann Explained: From Souls to Systems* (Chicago: Open Court, 2006); *The Philosophy of the Daodejing* (New York: Columbia University Press, 2006); *Daodejing (Laozi): A Complete Translation and Commentary* (Chicago: Open Court, 2007); and a treatise in defence of amorality, *The Moral Fool: A Case for Amorality* (New York: Columbia University Press, 2009).

Barry Steben is Professor at the Graduate Institute of Interpretation and Translation at Shanghai International Studies University. He has taught previously at the University of Western Ontario, the National University of Singapore, and the Chinese University of Hong Kong. He completed his PhD at the University of Toronto after doing his thesis research at the University of Tokyo on the Wang Yangming school of Confucianism in Japan. His research focuses on Sino-Japanese Confucian thought, samurai thought, and the introduction of Western thought in Japan and China in the nineteenth and early twentieth centuries. His publications include: "Nakae Tōju and the Birth of Wang Yang-ming Learning in Japan" in *Monumenta Serica* 46 (Dec. 1998), ed. Alan Chan, pp. 249–294; "Rai Sanyō's Philosophy of History and the Ideal of Imperial Restoration," *East Asian History*, No. 24 (Dec. 2002), pp. 117–170; "Wang Yangming Learning and the Path to Wisdom in the Philosophy of Ōshio Heihachirō (1793–1837)," in *Wisdom in China and the West (Chinese Philosophical Studies, XXII)*, ed. Vincent Shen and Willard Oxtoby (Washington, DC: Council for Research in Values and Philosophy, 2004), pp. 83–104; and "Ritual and the Rectification of Names in a Bi-polar Authority Field: Neo-Confucianism in the Ryukyu (Liuqiu) Kingdom," in *Crossing the Yellow Sea: Sino-Japanese Cultural Contacts, 1600–1950,* ed. Joshua A. Fogel (Norwalk, CT: EastBridge, 2007), pp. 73–98.

Yvonne Schulz Zinda is Professor of Chinese Studies at the Universität Nürnberg-Erlangen. Her Universität Hamburg PhD dissertation was on the philosopher Jin Yuelin. She has participated in projects on Chinese as a scientific language and on nationalist historiography. She is director of the project "Institutionalizing the Humanities in the PRC: The 1950s" and is currently completing a monograph on the philosophy of Jin Yuelin.

Introduction

John Makeham

When I graduated [from secondary school] our head teacher, Mr. Li Denghui, asked the students in our class about their future plans. I replied, "I want to study philosophy."

He said, "Aah, so you want to be Confucius."

—Feng Youlan[1]

This volume is an inquiry into how "Chinese philosophy" (*Zhongguo zhexue* 中國哲學) became an academic discipline in China in the early decades of the twentieth century. We seek to show how Chinese philosophy was conceived and shaped in the course of its early development. Our enquiry has been driven by a range of questions, in particular: What factors influenced this process of formation and development? What was the relationship between Chinese philosophy and traditional forms of learning in China? What role did Japanese scholarship have in its genesis? What was its relationship with European and American philosophy? What impact did models of Western learning and knowledge compartmentalization have on its formation? Who contributed to its development and how? What continued agency and relevance did the past have in the present; and to what extent were new knowledge systems viewed as tools in the recovery of tradition rather than its abandonment? Each chapter in this volume addresses one or more of these issues.

This volume is not a work of philosophy. It is a study in intellectual history, with a nod to the sociology of knowledge. Nor has our aim been to provide a comprehensive history of all the key figures involved in the development of Chinese philosophy as an academic discipline; rather we have sought to include coverage of a sufficient range of representative individuals and institutions to underscore the complexity and diversity of interests involved. As editor, I have eschewed replicating approaches found in textbook-type accounts of the history of modern Chinese philosophy. I have similarly refused to impose a unilinear, teleological trajectory on the development of modern Chinese philosophy. Instead, I have drawn on the expertise of the different contributors to demonstrate the wide range of possibilities that contributed to the academic formation of *zhexue* 哲學 and to highlight the creativity which went into its development. In the words of one of the Press's readers, "the different styles and emphases in various chapters exemplify the polyphony in *zhexue*, which, to this day, is still a discipline without a fixed identity."

This Introduction consists of two sections. The first section examines the formal processes involved in creating Chinese philosophy as an academic discipline, in order to provide a grounded historical account of how traditional categories of Chinese knowledge were "translated" into the new academic category of *zhexue*. The second section summarizes the volume's ten chapters in order to give the reader an overview of the content and scope of individual chapters. An appendix to the Introduction lists subjects offered in the Peking University Philosophy Department, 1914–1923. The volume concludes with an Epilogue, "Inner Logic, Indigenous Grammars, and the Identity of *Zhongguo zhexue*," in which I argue that the views of the scholars examined in this volume are not only of intellectual-historical significance but also throw into relief how "*Zhongguo zhexue*" is understood today.

1. Formal Processes

Forty years ago, intellectual historian Joseph Levenson famously commented: "What the West has probably done to China is to change the latter's language—what China has done to the West is to enlarge the latter's vocabulary."[2] Levenson was referring to a process that began in the decades immediately before and after 1900, through which Western disciplinary models superseded traditional schemes of knowledge classification in China. Borrowing Levenson's metaphor, it is well known that Chinese intellectuals introduced a new "language" or "grammar"—academic philosophy—into China soon after the turn of the twentieth century, subsequently leading to the institutional incorporation of the discipline "Chinese philosophy" (*Zhongguo zhexue* 中國哲學) alongside

Western philosophy. This was one of many responses to an "epistemological crisis"[3] in which China found itself in the closing decades of the Qing dynasty (1644–1911). Western philosophy provided key conceptual paradigms, vocabulary and technical terms, bibliographic categories, and even histories and periodization schemes essential to the demarcation, definition, and narration of the discipline of Chinese philosophy. This was not, however, a simple case of the blanket inscription of Western philosophy upon a Chinese *tabula rasa*. Nor was the process by which Western models of knowledge categorization were introduced into China a passive one in which the "foreign" was imposed on the "native." Rather, it was an ongoing process of negotiation and appropriation initiated and conducted by Chinese protagonists, in which traditional categories of Chinese knowledge were "translated" into the new academic category of *zhexue*. In the early years, often that process also involved Japan and Japanese scholarship, as attested by the very term for philosophy: *zhexue/ tetsugaku*.[4] What does the historical record tell us about the formal processes—nomenclature, bibliographic categorization, professionalization, and institutionalization—involved in creating Chinese philosophy as a modern discipline?

1.1 Nomenclature

In addition to various Chinese-character-based phonetic transliterations of the term "philosophy," Neo-Confucian terms such as *gewu qiongli* 格物 窮理 (to exhaust [understanding of] principles through the investigation of things) and *lixue* 理學 (principle-centered learning) had also been widely used by Jesuit scholars in China in the seventeenth century to translate the term "philosophy."[5] The earliest published account by a Chinese scholar using the term *zhexue* dates from 1887. In introducing the disciplinary divisions used at Tokyo Imperial University, Qing diplomat to Japan Huang Zunxian 黃遵憲 (1848–1905) described how that university consisted of three academic divisions, of which the Faculty of Letters (文學部) was divided into two sections (科), one of which was comprised of Philosophy (哲學), Law, and Finance. He glossed *zhexue* as being concerned with explaining "the norms of the way" (道義).[6] Liang Qichao's 梁啟超 (1873–1929) Yokohama-based periodicals, *Qingyi bao* 清 議報 (1898–1902) and *Xinmin congbao* 新民叢報 (1902–1907), also widely adopted use of the term *zhexue*. Although *zhexue* eventually became the accepted translation,[7] it was neither the first nor the only Chinese rendering of "philosophy" in the late Qing. In 1873 Protestant missionary Ernst Faber 花之安 (1839–1899) published *Deguo xuexiao lunlüe* 德國學校論略 [A brief account of Germany's schools][8] in which he introduced the courses taught in the Philosophy Faculty (*zhixue* 智學 "science of wisdom") of various European universities of the day. He identified eight sub-disciplines (*ke* 課): rhetoric (*xuehua* 學話); metaphysics (*xinglixue* 性理學), which also included logic (transcribed as *luxi* 路隙); doctrines on the soul (which included psychology and epistemology); natural sciences; theology; ethics; aesthetics; and famous philosophers.[9] Other contemporary translations included: *shenxue* 神學, *aizhixue* 愛智學, *gexue* 格學, *gezhixue* 格致學, and *lixue* 理學; the latter three could also embrace the natural sciences.[10] Writing in 1903, Wang Guowei 王國維 (1887–1927) seems to imply that 理學 would have been a more appropriate translation of "philosophy" than the term *zhexue*, but 理學 had already been adopted in Japan as a translation for the natural sciences.[11]

Although the term *zhexue* is a translation of the Western term "philosophy," its written form has historically-embedded normative connotations which are independent of meanings associated with modern Western notions of "philosophy." As a contraction of 希哲學, which, in turn, was inspired by Zhou Dunyi's 周敦頤 (1017–1073) notion of 希賢 "to emulate worthies,"[12] implicit in the concept of *zhexue* when applied to Chinese contexts are such notions as the authority invested in sages and sage-like historical figures; the normative power accorded models: human—and by correlative association—natural and cosmological; and the conviction that reading certain texts bequeathed by former sagely men affords unmediated encounters with the transformative personalities of these exceptional historical figures. The epigraph to this Introduction is one expression of this goal of emulating worthies and sages so that one might be transformed. Another is pointed out by Hans-Georg Moeller in his chapter on Feng Youlan 馮友蘭 (1895–1990) in this volume:

> It is thus not surprising that for Feng, the most philosophical philosophy does not end with conceptual analysis…. One engages in rational analysis not merely to understand reality, but, more importantly, to transform oneself into a *sheng ren* 聖人: the ideal of the wise human being that has figured so prominently throughout the history of Chinese philosophy. Philosophy is thus conceived of as a discipline that, in the end, shapes a person and opens one up to the possibility of not only knowing the world but also of integrating oneself within it, and thus becoming epistemologically and ethically wise. Feng explicitly reiterates the traditional Chinese definition of

a perfect human being: *nei sheng wai wang* 內聖外王, or "inwardly wise and outwardly kingly."

This same goal of *nei sheng wai wang* was widely espoused by the so-called New Confucian philosophers and is one reason that Feng is also sometimes classified as a New Confucian.[13]

Apropos this observation about the historically-embedded normative connotations associated with the term *zhexue*, it is instructive to reflect on Nicolas Standaert's observation that "When one talks about philosophy in China today, even about Chinese philosophy, one uses a language that is based on the Chinese adoption of Western philosophical terms."[14] Although this is undeniably true,[15] equally, in the modern context we should be mindful that the semantic fields of "philosophy" and "*zhexue*" each have their own histories and trajectories.[16]

1.2 *Bibliographic Categorization*

Bibliographic categorization provides perhaps the clearest evidence of the protracted process of negotiation and appropriation in which traditional categories of Chinese knowledge were "translated" into the new academic category of *zhexue*. Consider the example of the Dewey Decimal Classification in which Philosophy is the second of the ten bibliographic divisions. Developed in 1873 by Melvil Dewey (1851–1931), the Dewey Decimal Classification was first introduced into China in 1909.[17] The traditional Chinese bibliographic scheme consists of the Four Divisions (*sibu* 四部): classics (*jing* 經), histories (*shi* 史), masters (*zi* 子), and collected writings (*ji* 集). The most challenging of the Four Divisions to be adapted to the Dewey Decimal Code proved to be the Masters Division (*zibu* 子部), with leading Chinese bibliographers in the latter half of the 1920s describing it as the functional equivalent of an amalgam of the "philosophy, religion, social science and natural science" categories of the Dewey Decimal Classification. At the same time, other library studies professionals were still proposing ways in which sub-categories within the Masters Division could be reclassified:

> The character of the *ru*, the Mohists, and School of Names is close to that of philosophy; hence I have singled them out as philosophy and divided the category of Philosophy into Eastern and Western Philosophy. Religion and Philosophy being closely connected, I have placed them together in a combined category. Methods of Divination and Prognostication (*shushu* 術

數) … is appended after Religion. The Legalists and the Strategists mostly discuss government and models and so have been entered in the Social Science category.[18]

In addition to the Masters Division, the reclassification of the content of the Classics Division also provided resources for the new category of *zhexue*. For example, Cai Yuanpei 蔡元培 (1868–1940) wrote in 1912: "I believe that of the Fourteen Classics, *Change*, *Analects* and *Mencius* have already entered the philosophy department; *Odes* and *Erya* have already entered the literature department; and *Documents*, the three *Rites* and *Da Dai Liji* and *Spring and Autumn Annals* and its three commentaries have already entered the philosophy department. There is no need to establish a division for the Classics, and so it should be abolished."[19]

In fact, already in 1907, Sun Baoxuan 孫保瑄 (1874–1924) had suggested dividing the Classics Division into the Philosophy Category (*zhexuelei* 哲學類) and the History Category (*lishilei* 歷史類), with *Documents*, *Spring and Autumn Annals*, *Rites of Zhou*, *Yili*, and *Odes* belonging to history, and *Change*, *Analects*, and *Mencius* belonging to philosophy. He allocated *Liji* to both categories.[20] And even as late as 1920 the issue still continued to be deliberated, as evidenced by the following proposal by a librarian in Peking University, Wu Kang 吳康 (1895–1976), to reclassify the Five Classics: "The *Book of Change* should belong to the category of philosophy; the *Book of Odes* should belong to the category of literature; the *Book of Documents* and the ritual texts should belong to the categories of politics, sociology, and ethnology."[21]

One widely adopted solution to the challenge of accommodating non-Chinese bibliographic categories was to expand significantly the number of bibliographic categories, after it proved no longer feasible to follow the lead of Zhang Zhidong 張之洞 (1837–1909)—at the time a member of the Hanlin Academy and also serving as the Sichuan Minister for Schooling—who in his 1875 bibliography, *Shumu dawen* 書目答問 [Questions and answers on lists of books] classified Western books in translation holus bolus within the Masters Division of the Four Divisions and in the process "made these books a component of Chinese learning and Chinese knowledge systems."[22] For example, in his 1898 catalogue, *Riben shumu zhi* 日本書目志 [Catalogue of Japanese books], Kang Youwei 康有為 (1858–1927) moved away from the traditional Four Divisions to create fifteen bibliographic categories, mostly based on Western categories. One of these categories, however, was *lixue/rigaku* 理學, a term that had continuing resonances with the Neo-Confucian concept. Even in 1880s Japan, the term "philosophy" was sometimes still translated as *rigaku* 理學 even though *tetsugaku* 哲學 had become the standard term.[23] Kang seems to have found a way to deal with the Japanese category of *rigaku* by making it subsume without distinction titles from philosophy and the natural sciences. Under this heading Kang listed an eclectic selection of titles on the natural sciences, as well as titles on anthropology, philosophy (*zhexue*), ethics, logic, and psychology. (Titles on logic, ethics and psychology are listed in their own, separate sub-categories.)[24] A year later, Xu Weize 徐維則 in his *Dong-xi xue shumu* 東西學書目 [Bibliography of Eastern and Western learning], expanded the number of bibliographic categories to thirty. He too used the *lixue* category to subsume without distinction titles from philosophy and the natural sciences.[25]

Zhexue was finally identified as an independent bibliographic category—that is, one not subsumed under a broader category such as *lixue*—in the 1911 *Han Fen Lou xinshu fenlei mulu* 涵芬樓新書分類目錄 [Book catalogue by category of new titles from Han Fen Lou]. It was listed as the first of fourteen recognized bibliographic divisions and included the sub-categories of logic (*lunli* 論理), ethics (*lunlixue* 倫理學), psychology (*xinli* 心理), and philosophy 哲學. Chinese philosophy (中國哲學) seems not to have become a recognized bibliographic sub-category in any catalogue until the publication in 1929 of Liu Guojun's 劉國鈞 (1899–1980), *Zhongguo tushu fenleifa* 中國圖書分類法 [Rules for the classification of Chinese books],[26] one of several Chinese adaptations of the Dewey Decimal Classification.

Nevertheless, even though it was not until 1929 that a bibliographic sub-category of Chinese Philosophy was created to take its place alongside (and preceding) the sub-category of Western Philosophy (both of which were subsumed under the general category of Philosophy), by 1936, when a revised edition of *Zhongguo tushu fenleifa* was issued,[27] Chinese Philosophy was further divided into sub-categories (all numbered in the 120s) and sub-sub-categories extending from pre-Qin to modern philosophy and occupying about the same number of entries as Western philosophy (140s). To take one example, consider the sub-category of "Han Dynasty Philosophy" (122) which consists of the following sub-sub-categories: early Han masters (122.1); *Huainanzi* (122.2); Huan Kuan (122.3), Liu Xiang (122.4); other Western Han masters (122.5); early Eastern Han masters (122.6); Wang Chong (122.7); other masters (122.8); and the Jian'an masters (122.9). The application of a similar approach to bibliographic categorization for most other Chinese historical periods—often using divisions that would not have been out of place in the biography sections of traditional dynastic histories or from works such as Huang Zongxi's 黃宗羲 (1610–1695) *Song-Yuan ru xue'an* 宋元儒學案 [Case studies of Song and Yuan *ru*] and *Ming ru xue'an* 明儒學案 [Case studies of Ming *ru*]—enabled China's long history to be readily and comprehensively populated with philosophers. One consequence is that the historical parameters of "Chinese philosophy"—in this case prescribed by dint of bibliographical fiat—provided a ready pool of philosophers and texts to draw upon to define the unique contours of this new discipline.

1.3 Professionalization

Sociologist Immanuel Wallerstein describes the intellectual history of the nineteenth century as being "marked above all by [the] disciplinarization and professionalization of knowledge, that is to say, by the creation of permanent institutional structures designed both to produce new knowledge and to reproduce the producers of knowledge."[28] Wallerstein's comments refer to developments in Europe and America, although similar processes are also evident in the closing decades of the nineteenth century in Japan.

Be this as it may, sociologists remain divided on theoretical issues concerning professionalization. Intellectual historian Charlotte Furth observes that some sociologists "emphasize 'profession' as an ideal type while others prefer to think about a historical process. If the ideal type encompasses formal qualifications for practice and autonomous institutions to police membership and standards, few Chinese occupations fit this pattern before the twentieth century."[29] Indeed, if we adopt the ideal-type model, it is not until the second decade of the twentieth century in China that we witness a significant proliferation in the trend to professionalization. On reflection, however, this should not be all that surprising given that it was not until the second half of the nineteenth century that philosophy emerged as an academic discipline in Europe and America. And it was not until the twentieth century that philosophy became thoroughly professionalized. Before this, from medieval times until the beginning of the nineteenth century, Philosophy as a university academic division existed as the "lower faculty" in contrast to the "higher faculties" of Law, Medicine, and Theology. The Philosophy or Arts curriculum varied over time and in different countries, but typically it consisted of seven subjects: grammar, rhetoric, dialectic, arithmetic, geometry, music, and astronomy. From the seventeenth century, the process of the divorce of philosophy from natural science had also intensified. By the end of the eighteenth century, natural scientists had begun to regard philosophy as a substitute for theology, "equally guilty of a priori assertions of truth that were untestable."[30] Yet even as philosophy started to become institutionalized as an academic discipline in the latter half of the nineteenth century, it continued to shed much of its content as still other fields of learning—economics, sociology, political science, and psychology—gradually became independently established.

The origins of this transformation can be traced to the rise of the modern university in Germany in the second decade of the nineteenth century. This latter development is associated with Wilhelm von Humboldt's (1767–1835) "idea of the university," key to which is the combination of teaching and research. Not only was philosophy central to Humboldt's idea of the university but it remained a compulsory part of all doctoral degrees in Germany until the early years of the twentieth century.[31] This Kantian legacy, in which philosophy commands a central place within the university, was complemented by a Hegelian counterpart: the idea that the history of philosophy is part of philosophy itself such that philosophy and history become inextricably linked.[32] (The Hegelian or nineteenth-century concept of philosophy as a unified historical process had a profound impact in China.[33]) Despite these beginnings, a good deal of mid- to late-nineteenth century German philosophy was written outside the universities. In France, universities were closed after the French Revolution (1789–1799). Philosophy began to flourish as an academic discipline in universities from the early 1870s as a consequence of its place in the new university system set up by the Third Republic and of the support provided by the institutional arrangement whereby it was (and continues to be) a compulsory subject in the *baccalauréat*.

According to Jonathan Rée, "At Oxford in the first half of the nineteenth century philosophy was taught in the form of the study of a section of the arts course known as the 'science' section (to distinguish it from history and poetry).... The first signs of philosophy as a special university subject appear in England in the 1850s."[34] For most of the nineteenth century, however, philosophy was done by individuals independent of the universities: Mill, Carlyle, and Spencer being prominent examples. D. W. Hamlyn traces the beginning of what he terms "the professionalism" of philosophy in England to 1871 when the religious tests for the holding of posts at Oxford and Cambridge were abolished.[35] In the USA of the 1860s, tertiary-level instruction in philosophy principally consisted of so-called moral philosophy, a mixture of metaphysics, social science, and religion. A decade later, philosophy began to be detached from theology, and by the turn of the twentieth century the institutional features of philosophy as an academic profession had been established.

In China, professional journals were one of the earliest expressions of the trend to professionalization more generally, their numbers increasing rapidly after 1911.[36] Similarly, the post-1911 period also marked the beginning of the rise of professional associations,[37] the establishment of disciplinary-based universities,[38] and the development of regulations to mandate formal qualification requirements in professional employment.[39] In the case of Chinese philosophy as an academic discipline, professionally trained and accredited philosophers such as Hu Shi 胡適 (1891–1962), Jin Yuelin 金岳霖 (1895–1984), and Feng Youlan—all PhD graduates of Columbia University—fit this aspect of the model well.

Chinese philosophy (and indeed philosophy more generally) was, however, slower to gain some of the other formal characteristics of academic professionalization. Shigeru Nakayama argues that "If national academies and research institutes reflect a centralizing impulse, the university is decentralizing.... The university ... being a place for the teaching of students, finds the hiring of several specialists in the same field both unnecessary and extravagant. The result is a dispersal of specialists in any given field.... It creates a need for national academic associations that bring together all scholars in the same field."[40] Although the first Chinese professional association of philosophers—the Peking University Philosophy Association 北京大學哲學會—was established in 1918, its membership was confined to that of a single university. It was not until 1935 that the first national professional association of philosophers—the Chinese Philosophy Association 中國哲學會—was established.[41] If Nakayama's observations are correct, one might reasonably infer that the development of the discipline of philosophy (including the sub-discipline of Chinese philosophy) was such that there was no real need for a national association before the mid-1930s.[42] This would seem to borne out by the fact that up until 1930 only six philosophy departments had been established nationally: Peking University (1912); Dongnan University[43] (1921), Xiamen University (1922), Zhongshan

University (1924), Tsinghua University (1926), and Yanjing University (1930).

The above is in reference to what Furth calls the ideal-type model. "Nonetheless," she continues, "if the emphasis is upon a group identity based on a shared body of learning and socially recognized networks of affiliations and on specialized services provided in the context of a commercial exchange (salary or fee), it is easier to recognize that the vocational worlds of Qing medical, legal and even religious experts were moving in that direction."[44] In the case of the professionalization of medicine in China, Furth argues that this was "a process no less genuine for being expressed through lineage affiliation, discipleship, and social networks of 'scholarly currents' rather than the formal organizations of Western social theory."[45] These observations also help to shed light on some of the particularities of the formation of Chinese philosophy as an academic discipline. If we accept the emphasis on "a group identity based on a shared body of learning and socially recognized networks of affiliations" as an alternative set of characteristics contributing to the process of professionalization, this helps us to understand why even though figures such as Zhang Binglin 章炳麟 (Taiyan 太炎) (1869–1936), Xiong Shili 熊十力 (1885–1968), and Liang Shuming 梁漱溟 (1893–1988) moved in and out of employment in academic institutions,[46] their contributions to the early development of Chinese philosophy as an academic discipline were grounded in, and in turn enhanced by, their participation in "scholarly currents" which intersected with, but extended well beyond, the narrow confines of the academy. (As Thierry Meynard points out in his chapter in this volume, Xiong and Liang were able to maintain a degree of independence from academic institutions even after 1949, enabling them to "continue as independent thinkers, developing their own personal philosophy at the margins of the totalitarian regime." The same cannot be said for Feng Youlan.)

Buddhism is a key example of one such scholarly current. Zhang's early interest in Yogācāra Buddhism decisively influenced the development of his philosophical thought over the first two decades of the twentieth century. Although Liang Shuming's 1922 publication, *Dong-xi wenhua ji qi zhexue* 東西文化及其哲學 [Eastern and Western cultures and their philosophies] was published while Liang was employed in the Philosophy Department of Peking University, it had been developed on the basis of a series of public lectures given the previous year in Jinan, Shandong. In 1924 Liang retired from his academic position to engage in the practical work of rural reconstruction in Shandong. Although Xiong had developed his major philosophical writing, *Xin weishi lun* 新唯識論 [New treatise on the uniqueness of consciousness],[47] on the basis of lectures on Yogācāra Buddhism first given at Peking University, he subsequently led a peripatetic and frequently interrupted academic career. As with Liang, Xiong's networks of disciples, mentors, and intellectual adversaries extended all over China. Buddhist academic institutions also provided contexts and opportunities for social networking. As Thierry Meynard points out in his chapter in this volume: "Under the pressure of Western-style academic institutions, including Christian universities and seminaries, a number of Buddhist training centres opened. These included the Wuchang Buddhist Institute 武昌佛學院 … the Minnan Buddhist Institute 閩南佛學院 [and] the Institute of Inner Learning 支那內學院 in Nanjing…. The teaching and research of Buddhist scholars working in academic institutions developed in quite a different direction." Neo-Confucian philosophy was another significant scholarly current characterized by "a group identity based on a shared body of learning and socially recognized networks of affiliations" which decisively influenced the philosophical orientation of thinkers such as Xiong Shili, Liang Shuming, Ma Yifu 馬一浮 (1883–1967), and Zhang Junmai 張君勱 (Carsun Chang; 1887–1969).[48]

1.4 Institutions

One aspect of the social networking dimension provided by the scholarly current of Neo-Confucianism is academies (*shuyuan* 書院). A number of academies were founded even as disciplinary-based universities spread throughout China. Thus immediately after having served a three-year term as head of the Yenching University's Philosophy Department, Zhang Dongsun 張東蓀 (1886–1973) joined Zhang Junmai in establishing the Xuehai Academy 學海書院 in Guangzhou in 1934. According to Yap Key-chong:

> As a postgraduate school of philosophy and political science and named after the prestigious *Hsüeh-hai t'ang* of the Ch'ing dynasty, which was noted for the studies and publication of the classics, *Hsüeh-hai shu-yüan* recruited special kinds of research students to study the essence of the Chinese heritage (*Kuo-ku* 國故) and to compare it with Western philosophy so as to explicate and develop the precious heritage of China…. It was clear that the two Changs thought of reinvigorating the system of the academy of late-traditional China.[49]

Xiong Shili had taught at Ma Yifu's Fuxing Academy 復性書院 in 1927 and again in 1939 when it was moved to Leshan County, Sichuan, with Ma as principal. This institution is sometimes retrospectively incorporated into the history of the formation of the New Confucian school of philosophy, not only because of the involvement of Ma Yifu but also because its council included members such as Liang Shuming and Xiong Shili. Ma taught courses specifically on philosophy. Xinya Academy 新亞書院 similarly played a pivotal role in the more recent history of New Confucian philosophy's academic mainstreaming. Established in Hong Kong in 1949 by Qian Mu 錢穆 (1895–1990), Tang Junyi 唐君毅 (1909–1978), and others, in 1964 it was incorporated into the Chinese University of Hong Kong as New Asia College.

The principal institutional home of Chinese philosophy was, of course, in disciplinary-based universities. Peking University boasts China's oldest philosophy department; its early history is also reasonably well documented. According to a publication compiled by students who graduated from the Philosophy Department in 1925, although the name *zhexuexi* 哲學系 (philosophy department) was adopted in 1918,[50] the genesis of philosophy at Peking University can be traced to 1902.[51] According to a more recent publication, in 1902 the forerunner of Peking University, the Imperial University (*Jingshi daxue tang* 京師大學堂), which had been established in 1898, initiated an accelerated curriculum in which courses "related to philosophy" were taught in the teacher's college part of the university (the forerunner of *Beijing shifan daxue* 北京師範大學):[52] ethics, education, psychology, interpersonal morals, biology, and the Zhou-Qin masters.[53]

In another recent publication—commemorating the ninetieth anniversary of the Philosophy Department (哲學系) at Peking University—Wang Bo goes even further, pushing the genesis back to the curriculum that formed part of the provisional university regulations drafted by Liang Qichao and presented with a Foreign Office (*Zongli yamen* 總理衙門) memorial to the throne in 1898 on the matter of priorities to be considered when establishing the Imperial University.[54] Wang draws attention to the inclusion of Classical Studies, Principle-centered Learning (*lixue* 理學), and Masters Studies among the ten compulsory core subjects, stating that they were all connected with philosophy.[55]

In 1902 member of the newly constituted Committee of Educational Affairs (*xuewuchu* 學務處) Zhang Baixi 張百熙 (1847–1907) presented Empress Dowager Cixi 慈禧 (r. 1861–1908) a set of charters for six levels of schooling from kindergarten to university, "Qinding xuetang zhangcheng" 欽定學堂章程 [Imperially ratified charters for all levels of school], in response to Cixi's request to provide a curriculum for the country's schools and also to reorganize the Imperial University. In 1904 Zhang Baixi, Zhang Zhidong, and others prepared a revised version, the "Zouding xuetang zhangcheng" 奏定學堂章程 [Charters for new schools, as memorialized and ratified], which was promulgated nationally and served as the standard policy for running schools until 1912.[56]

In 1912 Peking University consisted of four Divisions: Letters (*wenke* 文科), Law (*fake* 法科), Science (*like* 理科), and Engineering (*gongke* 工科). The Letters Division was in turn subdivided into four departments (*men* 門):[57] Philosophy, History, Chinese Literature, and English Literature. The original intention had been to divide the Philosophy Department (*zhexue men* 哲學門) into Chinese Philosophy, Western Philosophy, and Indian Philosophy, but because this was not realized,[58] it was divided into two groups: Chinese philosophy (中國哲學) and Western philosophy (*xiyang zhexue* 西洋哲學). In 1913 sixteen subjects were prescribed for the curriculum of each. The Chinese Philosophy category lists the following subjects: Chinese philosophy; history of Chinese philosophy; religious studies; psychology; ethics; logic; epistemology; sociology; overview of Western philosophy; overview of Indian philosophy; education studies; aesthetics and its history; biology; anthropology and ethnology; psychiatry; and overview of linguistics.[59] Of particular note is the disciplinary spread of subjects nominally offered and the content of the first subject, Chinese philosophy: *Book of Change*; Mao recension of *Odes*; *Book of Ceremonial (Yili)*; *Book of Rites (Liji)*; *Spring and Autumn Annals* and the Gongyang and Guliang commentaries; *Analects*; *Mencius*; Zhou-Qin masters, and Song-Ming Principle-centered Learning. This is substantially the same content as the curriculum prescribed for Classical Studies (which included Principle-centered Learning) in the 1904 document which outlines Zhang Zhidong's blueprint for the Imperial University, "Qinding Jingshi Daxuetang zhangcheng" 欽定京師大學堂章程 [Imperially ratified charter for the Imperial University].[60]

It was not until 1914, however, that students first enrolled in the Philosophy Department, and because no one had yet been employed to teach Western philosophy, *Zhexuemen* became known as *Zhongguo zhexuemen* 中國哲學門 (Department of Chinese Philosophy).[61] Under the reforms of Cai Yuanpei, who became President of Peking University in

1917, *Zhongguo zhexuemen* changed its name to *Zhexuexi* in 1919. *Zhexuexi* included both Chinese Philosophy and Western Philosophy.

The above summary of key formal processes involved in the creation of Chinese philosophy as an academic discipline permits several observations. First, historically-informed differences between the semantic fields of "philosophy" and "*zhexue*" provided the *possibility* for the past to exercise a legitimating role in how "philosophy" was understood and practiced in China. In a sense, "*zhexue*" expanded the scope of "philosophy." The full realization of this possibility is typified by Feng Youlan, as described in the passage by Hans-Georg Moeller cited above. Second, it is evident that the trajectory followed by bibliographic categorization moved inexorably towards the displacement of Chinese categories by Western categories, even though occasional hybrid categories such as Kang Youwei's *lixue* were created in the process. The disintegration of traditional bibliographic categories provides no evidence of the past's continuing to exercise a defining influence on the present. What is apparent, however, is the application of new knowledge categories in the recovery—rather than the abandonment—of the past, as demonstrated by the 1936 revised edition of Liu Guojun's *Zhongguo tushu fenleifa*. In the case of the third formal process, professionalization, although the social networks afforded by participation in scholarly currents associated with Buddhism and Neo-Confucian philosophy provided contexts for some streams of Chinese philosophy to develop beyond the mainstream academy, this was less a function of the active continuation of the past in the present than it was an expression of conscious and concerted efforts to recover legacies bequeathed by the past. As for the fourth process, institutionalization, the list of subjects offered in the Peking University Philosophy Department between 1914 and 1923 (see Appendix) confirms that, from the outset, Chinese Philosophy, Western Philosophy, and Indian Philosophy were each regarded as legitimate philosophical traditions.

2. Chapter Synopses

The chapters are grouped thematically, showing how the discourse of *zhexue* was formed, expanded, and challenged.

Part I: From Philosophy to *Zhexue*

1   In "Nishi Amane and the Birth of 'Philosophy' and 'Chinese Philosophy' in Early Meiji Japan" Barry Steben shows how, in the 1870s and 1880s, philosophy came to be represented by positivism and utilitarianism through Nishi Amane's 西周 (1829–1897) promotion of the writings of Comte and Mill, and how Confucian concepts became the medium for the reception of this philosophy in Japan through his translations and propagation. For Nishi, the establishment of a system of precisely translated concepts was paramount because it promised that the knowledge systems of the West could be incorporated into those of East Asia. Much of this legacy lives on in Nishi's neologisms, many of which came to form the basis of the Japanese (and subsequently Chinese) philosophical and logical lexicon, including the very term for "philosophy," *tetsugaku* 哲學.

In his *Hyakugaku renkan* 百學連環 [The links among the various sciences]—modeled on Comte's *Cours de philosophie positive*—Nishi set out to show how the various fields of knowledge are related, laying the foundation for the introduction and institutionalization of all disciplines of modern Western learning—especially philosophy—and for their integration with existing systems of learning. In this work Nishi replaced Comte's sociology with philosophy as the king of all disciplines. He also strongly promoted the inductive method of Mill—a development later echoed in China by Yan Fu 嚴復 (1853–1921). This impetus to develop and impose system also keenly impacted the disciplinary formation of Chinese philosophy in China, prompted most immediately by critiques of Chinese philosophy by late Meiji scholars, a topic taken up in chapter 2.

2   In "The Role of Masters Studies in the Early Formation of Chinese Philosophy as an Academic Discipline" I begin by describing the revival of interest in Masters Studies (諸子學) in the late Qing, factors that contributed to this revival, and its consequences. In particular, I argue that the Masters Studies renaissance provided an essential impetus in the process whereby the writings of the pre-Qin masters (*zhuzi* 諸子) were re-inscribed as the foundational texts of Chinese philosophy.

After the establishment of Chinese philosophy as an academic discipline in Japan, the attitude of many Japanese scholars to Chinese philosophy and to its history was highly critical. I show how these criticisms subsequently influenced the high regard Chinese scholars such as Wang

Guowei, Liang Qichao, Liu Shipei 劉師培 (1884–1919), and Zhang Binglin came to place on logic—the hallmark of system and order—as a precondition for the development of philosophy; as indeed did the views of a minority of Japanese scholars who found evidence of the development of logic in early China, particularly in the writings of Xunzi. These developments in turn stimulated Chinese scholars to make significant efforts to identify logic in the writings of the pre-Qin masters, in particular in *Xunzi* and in *Mozi*. The chapter concludes with accounts of the connection between National Learning and Masters Studies and also of how Chinese scholars moved away from the uncritical and unreflective adoption of Japanese scholarly sources to make their own determinations about how to apply paradigms derived from Western philosophy to craft the contours of "Chinese philosophy."

3 "Zhang Taiyan, Yogācāra Buddhism, and Chinese Philosophy" is a study of philologist-philosopher-revolutionary Zhang Taiyan's efforts to use the conceptual paradigms of Yogācāra philosophy, rather than Western philosophy, to interpret the writings of pre-Qin masters as philosophy. Zhang was also one of the first Chinese intellectuals to follow the lead of Japanese scholars in maintaining that classical Chinese philosophers had developed indigenous forms of logic. He is significant for his role in preparing the groundwork for the establishment of Chinese philosophy as an academic discipline.

I show how Zhang attempted to build a philosophical edifice on the foundations of an ontology and cognitive epistemology that exclusively privileged Yogācāra Buddhist teachings. Zhang also argued that Chinese versions of Yogācāra texts on Buddhist logic and reasoning—having only recently become available again after a hiatus of many centuries—made it possible once again to gain a proper understanding of China's earliest writings on logic. I examine how Zhang applied the benchmark of Yogācāra Buddhist philosophy to assess the philosophical merit of individual pre-Qin texts such as *Xunzi, Mozi*, and *Zhuangzi*. I argue that Zhang sought to establish that early Chinese texts "bear witness" to insights into realities which transcend individual cultures but are most fully and systematically articulated in Yogācāra systems of learning; and that classical Chinese philosopher-sages had attained an awareness of the highest truths, evidence of which can be found in their writings. In short, Zhang used Yogācāra to affirm the value of "Chinese philosophy" and, in doing so, helped shape its early definition.

Part II: The Beida and Tsinghua Schools of Philosophy

4 In "Developing the Academic Discipline of Chinese Philosophy: The Departments of Philosophy at Peking, Tsinghua, and Yenching Universities (1910s–1930s)," Xiaoqing Diana Lin highlights the importance of academic institutions in shaping the development of *zhexue*. She examines how institutional influences at National Peking University, National Tsinghua University, and Yenching University affected the writings of a range of influential modern Chinese philosophers from the 1910s through to the 1930s. Lin identifies Peking University Chancellor Cai Yuanpei's vision of inclusive learning (*xiangrong bingbao* 相容並包) as having promoted a synthesis of Chinese and Western academic cultures which in turn was reflected in the curriculum and research in the Department of Philosophy at Peking University from the late 1910s to the 1930s.

At Tsinghua University, Lin finds a much greater emphasis on a "universal" philosophy built on the basis of Western logic, as evident in the writings of Jin Yuelin, Feng Youlan, Zhang Shenfu 張申府 (1893–1989), Zhang Dainian 張岱年 (1909–2004), and Shen Youding 沈有鼎 (1908–1989). Unlike the other two universities, Yenching did not mandate any external structure for the interpretation of Chinese philosophy nor did it facilitate inter-departmental dialogue to develop a systematic modern Chinese academic discipline of philosophy. Lin argues that Zhang Dongsun's 張東蓀 (1886–1973) philosophy was able to develop in this environment precisely because it was not really a China-based philosophy.

5 In "Hu Shi and the Search for System" I argue that Peking University intellectual historian Hu Shi presented pre-Qin masters (*zhuzi* 諸子) writings as the foundational texts of Chinese philosophy. I show how Hu creatively appropriated John Dewey's concept of "genetic method" and used it to give a central place to "logic" in the historical development of Chinese philosophy. I identify the connection between Hu's own "logical method" and Dewey's genetic method and Wilhelm Windelband's views on the goals of writing a history of philosophy. I also draw attention to the role that the "history of Chinese philosophy" genre played in Hu's vision of Chinese philosophy, and twentieth-century notions of "Chinese philosophy" more generally. I further argue that the genre of the "history of Chinese philosophy" enabled Hu Shi to pursue his goal of articulating the "internal threads" of Chinese philosophy. For Hu, these internal threads were revealed through discrete, isolatable chains of causes and effects that had their origins in the writings of the pre-Qin masters and subsequently shaped the parameters of the development of the Chinese philosophical tradition.

6   In "Introducing Buddhism as Philosophy: The Cases of Liang Shuming, Xiong Shili, and Tang Yongtong," Thierry Meynard examines three important scholars who taught Buddhism in the Philosophy Department at Peking University in the first half of the twentieth century. The legacies of Xiong's and Liang's respective engagements with Buddhism are still evident today in New Confucian philosophy. On the one hand, this chapter supports chapter 3 in explaining the role of Buddhism in forming *zhexue*. On the other hand, it supports chapter 4 by showing the unique style of the Beida school, which stressed textual exegesis and the uniqueness of Chinese culture.

Believing that Chinese culture was not yet developed to a stage that would enable it to enter a Buddhist cultural period (unlike India), Liang promoted Confucian moral values as a necessary preparatory stage on the path to Buddhism—a sort of convenient means or *upāya*. Meynard shows how Liang articulated his Confucian social engagement with his Buddhist faith. Xiong employed the conceptual tools of Yogācāra—after subjecting them to substantial critical modification—in his efforts to construct a Confucian ontology. Meynard provides an account of the intellectual and institutional challenges Xiong brought to Buddhism, as well as his debates with a wide range of Buddhist scholars. Unlike Liang, who had attempted to reshape the concept of philosophy inherited from the West into something more congenial to the Chinese, or Xiong Shili, who had attempted to reconstruct a Confucian metaphysics as a reaction to the pressure exerted by modern Western philosophy, Meynard argues that Tang Yong-tong's 湯用彤 (1893–1964) approach to Buddhism as an integral part of the history of Chinese philosophy was a form of resistance to the hege-monic discourse of philosophy, then dominated by Western ideas.

7   In "Daoism as Academic Philosophy: Feng Youlan's New Metaphysics (*Xin lixue*)" Hans-Georg Moeller presents an intriguing account of Feng Youlan as the twentieth-century's most successful creative transformer of traditional Daoist thought into academic philosophy. Moeller finds substantial evidence for this interpretation in the books which make up Feng's own philosophical system, developed in the 1930s and 1940s: *Xin lixue* 新理學 (New Metaphysics). Central to this New Metaphysics was

Feng's transformation or "rationalization" of key concepts drawn from the Chinese philosophical tradition, especially Neo-Confucian philosophy, with the aim of making them compatible with contemporary Western philosophical discourse.

Feng's goal was to recreate *lixue* as the "most philosophical philosophy" by transcending experience so as to describe rationally a purely formal reality, and thus ultimately transcend philosophy itself. Whereas the Vienna Circle philosophers had merely eradicated bad metaphysics, Feng was singularly inspired by the negative methodology of Wittgenstein which, according to Moeller, he regarded as having a heuristic function similar to the historical role played by Daoism within the Chinese tradition.

8 As with chapter 7, Yvonne Schulz Zinda's "Jin Yuelin's Ambivalent Status as a 'Chinese Philosopher'" is a study of the Tsinghua school of philosophy. Jin Yuelin was a pioneer in the formation of logic and philosophy as academic disciplines in China and established the Philosophy Department at Tsinghua University in 1926. As with Fu Sinian 傅斯年 (1896–1950), Jin is significant for his role in problematizing just where the boundaries of "Chinese philosophy" should lie. Indeed, he also spent much of his life sorting out the differences between "philosophy in China" and "Chinese philosophy." Schulz Zinda introduces this distinction by analyzing Jin's writings.

The problem of induction was a keystone in Jin's philosophical edifice, as represented in his two main works: the ontological *Lun Dao* 論道 [On Dao], and the epistemological *Zhishilun* 知識論 [On knowledge]. In drawing most of the key terms in his ontology and epistemology from within the Chinese tradition, Schulz Zinda suggests that Jin was attempting to rely on what she terms the "emotional attachment" of Chinese readers as he sought to indigenize philosophical thought. Likening these traditional Chinese terms to old bottles into which Jin poured the new wine of Western thought, Schulz Zinda concludes that "Jin's works may be considered an attempt to take part in the universal discourse of philosophy. He tried to add associative content drawn from Chinese tradition to this universal discourse."

Part III: The Critics' Voices

9 Carine Defoort's "Fu Sinian's Views on Philosophy, Ancient Chinese Masters, and Chinese Philosophy" is a study of an early influential figure in a counter-current which continues to refuse to accept that the academic category "philosophy" can be applied to China's indigenous intellectual traditions. This counter-current is significant because of its role in questioning the parameters of "Chinese philosophy" and in limiting its institutional presence in China over the course of the twentieth century. In Fu Sinian's case, he was particularly opposed to treating the writings of the pre-Qin masters as philosophy. As Defoort points out, Fu contributed to the rejection of Chinese philosophy as a field of study at Academia Sinica (Zhongyang yanjiuyuan 中央研究院), a legacy that has continuing ramifications even today. Moreover, he was an early and prominent spokesman for the opinion, increasingly prevalent in contemporary discourse, that ancient Chinese thought should not be lightly subjected to modern Western academic nomenclature and categories, one of the central refrains in the "legitimacy of Chinese philosophy" (*Zhongguo zhexue hefaxing* 中國哲學合法性) debate that was in vogue in the first half of the first decade of this new millennium.

10 In "Marxist Views on Traditional Chinese Philosophy Pre-1949" Yvonne Schulz Zinda presents an overview of the early roots of Marxist-oriented historiography of traditional Chinese philosophy, a topic which has received surprising little scholarly attention in English-language writings. The sources selected for the study are those that attempted to put traditional Chinese philosophy or thought as a whole into a Marxist framework. Schulz Zinda further emphasizes that because Marxist historiography on philosophy integrated social, political, and economic issues, the analysis of traditional Chinese philosophy cannot be separated from other debates. She identifies the centers as well as the major journals of Marxist scholarship in the philosophical discipline, and she argues that the Marxist scholars in war-time Chongqing formulated a series of sustained and coherent critiques of the Beida and Tsinghua schools. As such, it is pertinent to refer to them as the "Chongqing school" and to consider them as the "third path."

Appendix

List of Subjects Offered in the Peking University Philosophy Department, 1914–1923[62]

1914: Song-Ming philosophy, introduction to Western philosophy, ethics, aesthetics, linguistics, and general psychology.

1915: Song-Ming philosophy, introduction to Chinese philosophy, history of Chinese philosophy, Chinese philosophy, masters philosophy (*zhuzi zhexue*), aesthetics, linguistics, general psychology, biology, education studies, and overview of sociology.

1916: Song-Ming philosophy, introduction to Chinese philosophy, history of Chinese philosophy, masters philosophy, Gongyang learning, classical studies, Indian philosophy, ethics, biology, education studies, anthropology and ethnology, and general psychology.

1917: Chinese philosophy, history of Chinese philosophy, outline history of Chinese philosophy, outline history of Western philosophy, introduction to Indian philosophy, introduction to philosophy, ethics, logic, psychology, sociology, anthropology, biology, introduction to linguistics, principles of economics, and foreign languages.

The 2 December 1917 issue of *Beijing Daxue rikan* lists the following subjects as compulsory for undergraduates majoring in Philosophy: introduction to philosophy, outline of the history of Chinese philosophy, outline of the history of Western philosophy, psychology, ethics, and logic. It also lists the range of elective courses that could be taken: history of ancient Chinese philosophy, history of modern Chinese philosophy, history of ancient Western philosophy, history of medieval Western philosophy, history of early-modern Western philosophy, modern Western philosophy, history of Indian philosophy, psychology practical, child psychology, Indian logic, history of ethics, education theory, history of education, education pedagogy, religious studies, political philosophy, aesthetics, history of aesthetics, sociology, linguistics, Sanskrit, Greek, Latin, biology, anthropology, botany, dissection (for the section on the central nervous system), *rujia* philosophy, Daoist philosophy, Mohist philosophy, Chinese logic (*mingxue* 名學), Plato's school of philosophy,

Aristotle's philosophy, Kant's school of philosophy, and mathematical theories.

The 29 December 1917 issue of *Beijing Daxue rikan* announced a revised list of subject offerings: introduction to philosophy, Chinese philosophy (*rujia*, Daoist, Mohist, Dark Learning [*xuanxue* 玄學], Song and Ming philosophy), outline history of Chinese philosophy, outline history of Western philosophy, history of early-modern Western philosophy, modern Western philosophy, introduction to Indian philosophy, logic, psychology, psychology practical, ethics, sociology, education studies, political philosophy, social philosophy, anthropology and ethnology, biology, introduction to aesthetics, principles of economics, introduction to linguistics, history of the development of science, scientific methodology, foreign languages, and Latin. Of these, the compulsory subjects were: introduction to philosophy, Chinese philosophy, outline history of Chinese philosophy, outline history of Western philosophy, logic, psychology, psychology practical, foreign languages; or introduction to philosophy, outline history of Chinese philosophy, outline history of Western philosophy, history of early-modern Western philosophy, modern Western philosophy, logic, psychology, psychology practical, and foreign languages. It is almost certain many of these subjects were not offered in the Philosophy curriculum, and thus the above represents more of a wish list.

1918: Outline history of Chinese philosophy, Chinese philosophy, outline history of Western philosophy, Indian philosophy, history of ethics, introduction to philosophy, logic, sociology, psychology, psychological experimentation, social problems, linguistics, anthropology and ethnology, biology, biological methodology, economics, developmental history of chemistry, geological methodology, and foreign languages.

1919: Song-Ming philosophy and *Daojia* philosophy, Yogācāra (nothing but consciousness) philosophy, early-modern Western philosophy, modern Western philosophy, outline history of Western philosophy, introduction to Indian philosophy, philosophy of religion, ethics, history of ethics, education studies, history of education studies, psychology experimentation, social problems, introduction to science, and foreign languages.

1920: Song-Ming philosophy and *Daojia* philosophy, Yogācāra (nothing but consciousness) philosophy, outline history of Western philosophy, early-modern Western philosophy, modern Western philosophy, introduction to Indian philosophy, history of early modern philosophy, philosophy of religion, ethics, history of ethics, philosophical schools, intellectual movements of the past century, education studies, history of education studies, philosophy of education, psychological experimentation, social psychology, introduction to science, social problems, introduction to sociology, sociology of education, Sanskrit, and foreign languages.

1921: Song-Ming philosophy and *Daojia* philosophy, early modern Chinese philosophy, early modern Western philosophy, modern Western philosophy, outline history of Western philosophy, studies on realist schools, readings from philosophical texts in English, readings from philosophical texts in French, introduction to Indian philosophy, history of ancient Indian religions, philosophy of religion, ethics, history of ethics, Buddhist philosophy, aesthetics, biological methodology, education studies, history of education studies, education methods, teaching methods, social psychology, psychological experimentation, abnormal psychology, child psychology, advanced psychology, sociology of education, social problems, introduction to sociology, foreign languages, and scientific method.

1922: Early-modern Chinese philosophy, Cheng-Zhu philosophy, Yogācāra (nothing but consciousness) philosophy, outline history of Western philosophy, early modern Western philosophy, modern Western philosophy, the value of the theory of relativity in the history of epistemology and its criticism, introduction to Indian philosophy, history of ancient Indian religions, introduction to philosophy, philosophy of religion, aesthetics, logic, ethics, history of ethics, comparative study of religions, abnormal psychology, child psychology, social psychology, psychological experimentation, sociology, social problems, sociology of education, introduction to sociology, Comte's realist doctrines, the developmental history of social institutions, history of education studies, educational institutions of various countries, education studies, education testing, teaching methods, intermediate education, school management, history of intermediate education studies, biological methodology, introduction to science, scientific method, and foreign languages.

1923: Early-modern Chinese philosophy, Qing-dynasty intellectual history, Cheng-Zhu philosophy, the philosophy of Wang Yangming, history of *rujia* philosophy, Yogācāra (nothing but consciousness) philosophy, early-modern Western philosophy, modern Western philosophy, outline history of Western philosophy, the philosophies of Leibniz and Descartes, studies in the philosophies of Leibniz and Descartes, readings from philosophical texts in English, history of early modern epistemology, epistemology, readings from philosophical texts in French, readings from philosophical texts in German, introduction to Indian philosophy, ethics, history of ethics, history of logic, philosophy of religion, religious studies, history of religion, history of Christianity, history of ancient Indian religions, education studies, history of education studies, history of education, educational administrative organization, intellectual trends in modern education, teaching methods, educational institutions of various countries, education testing, intermediate education, abnormal psychology, child psychology, psychological experimentation, description of psychology, social psychology, sociology of education, social problems, introduction to sociology, Comte's realist doctrines, scientific method, biological methodology, and foreign languages.

In 1924 the Department of Education was established, and the Philosophy Department stopped offering education courses. In 1926 the Department of Psychology was founded, and the Philosophy Department no longer offered psychology courses. It is worth bearing in mind that up until around 1900, psychology and pedagogy were still being taught in philosophy departments in the USA.[63]

Notes

1   Feng Youlan 馮友蘭, "Beida yi jiu ji" 北大憶舊記 [Record of my memories of Beida], in *Ku le nianhua* 苦樂年華 [Bitter and sweet years], edited by Wang Zongyu 王宗昱 (Beijing: Beijing daxue chubanshe, 2004), p. 9.

2   Joseph Levenson, *Confucian China and its Modern Fate: A Trilogy* (Berkeley: University of California Press, 1968), p. 157.

3   Alisdair Macintyre, *Whose Justice? Which Rationality?* (Trowbridge: Duckworth, 1988), pp. 361–369.

4   Nishi Amane 西周 (1829–1897) began using the term *zhexue* in manuscripts dating from 1872. See Gong Ying 龔穎, " 'Zhexue,' 'zhenli,' 'quanli' zai Riben de dingyi ji qita" 「哲學」、「真理」、「權力」在日本的定義及其他 [On the definition of "philosophy," "truth," and "rights" in Japan and other matters], *Zhexue yicong* 哲學譯叢 3 (2001), p. 69. Nishi first used the term in a printed publication in 1874: *Hyakuichi shinron* 百一新論 [A new discourse on the unity of the hundred teachings], in *Nishi Amane zenshū* 西周全集 [Complete works of Nishi Amane], Vol. 1 (Tokyo: Munetaka shobō, 1960), p. 289. For a comprehensive account of the changing terms Japanese scholars used to translate "philosophy" over the period 1595–1897, see Saito Tsuyoshi 齋藤毅 "Tetsugaku gogen—Ai Rulüe kara Nishi Amane, Miyake Setsurei made" 哲學語源———艾儒略から西周、三宅雪嶺まで [The origins of the term *tetsugaku* [philosophy]—From Ai Rulüe [Giulio Aleni] to Nishi Amane and Miyake Setsurei], in his *Meiji no kotoba: Higashi kara nishi e no kakehashi* 明治のことば：東から西への架け橋 [Meiji words: The suspension bridge from East to West] (Tokyo: Kodansha, 1977), pp. 313–368.

5   See, for example, Nicolas Standaert, "The Classification of Sciences and the Jesuit Mission in Late Ming China," in *Linked Faiths: Essays on Chinese Religions and Traditional Culture in Honour of Kristofer Schipper*, edited by Jan A. M. de Meyer and Peter M. Engelfret (Leiden: Brill, 2000), passim; and more recently, Mei Qianli 梅謙立 (Thierry Meynard), "Lunli zhexue he xiucixue: Liangge bu tong duihua moshi" 論理哲學和修辭學：兩個不同對話模式 [Two different dialogic models: Ethics and rhetoric], in *Shi xin ji: Zhongguo zhexue jian'gou de dangdai fansi yu weilai qianzhan* 拾薪集：中國哲學建構的當代反思與未來前瞻 [Contemporary reflections on the formation of Chinese philosophy and its future prospects], edited by Jing Haifeng 景海峰 (Beijing: Beijing daxue chubanshe, 2007), pp. 81–105.

6   Huang Zunxian 黃遵憲, *Riben guozhi* 日本國志 [Treatises on Japan], Vol. 1 (Tianjin: Tianjin renmin chubanshe, 2005), p. 798.

7   Even in the early 1900s there were objections to the term *zhexue*. See Yan Fu 嚴復, *Mule mingxue* 穆勒名學 [John Stuart Mill's *A System of Logic*], in *Yan yi mingzhu congkan* 嚴譯名著叢刊 [Collection of famous works translated by Yan Fu], Vol. 8 (Shanghai: Shangwu yinshuguan, 1931), pp. 114–115. Yan began his translation in 1900 and the work was published in 1905.

8   Later editions were published under the titles of *Taixi xuexiao lunlüe* 泰西學校論略 or *Xiguo xuexiao* 西國學校.

9   Hua Zhi'an 花之安, *Deguo xuexiao lunlüe*, in *Taixi xuexiao, jiaohua yi he ke* 泰西學校・教化議合刻 [Western schools: Discussions on education] (1873; reprinted Shanghai: Shangwu yinshuguan, 1897), pp. 4–6.

10   Chen Qiwei 陳啟偉, "'Zhexue' yi ming kao" "哲學"譯名考 [An examination of the translations of "philosophy"], *Zhexue yicong* 哲學譯叢 3 (2001), pp. 64–66; Zhong Shaohua 鐘少華, "Qing mo Zhongguoren duiyu 'zhexue' de zhuiqiu" 清末中國人對於「哲學」的追求 [Chinese people's search for "philosophy" in the late Qing], *Zhongguo wenzhe yanjiu tongxun* 中國文哲研究所通訊 2.2 (June 1992), pp. 163–164.

11   Wang Guowei, "Zhexue bianhuo" 哲學辨惑 [Disputing confusions about philosophy] (1903), in *Wang Guowei zhexue meixue lunwen jiyi* 王國維哲學美學論文輯軼 [Edited collection of Wang Guowei's lost essays on philosophy and aesthetics], compiled by Fo Chu 佛雛 (Shanghai: Huadong shifandaxue chubanshe, 1993), pp. 5–6.

12   Saito Tsuyoshi, "Tetsugaku gogen—Ai Rulüe kara Nishi Amane, Miyake Setsurei made," pp. 342–344, shows that in lecture notes dating from 1862 Nishi Amane had already translated "philosophy" as 希哲學. He argues that Nishi's formulation may have been influenced by his contemporary Tsuda Mamichi 津田真道 (1829–1903) as early as 1861 (pp. 350–351). Nishi had studied with Tsuda at Leiden in the same period and in many of the same classes, and then was a fellow member of the intellectual society Meirokusha 明六社. Saito further notes (p. 341) that in his 1873 manuscript *Seisei hatsu'un* 生性發蘊 [On the relation of the physical and spiritual) Nishi explained that the term "philosophy" derives from the Greek *philos* "to love" and *sophos* "wise" and concluded that the learning or science of philosophy means to love the wise. Nishi further related that the meaning is compatible with Zhou Dunyi's notion of 希賢 "to emulate worthies." In the "To fix one's mind on learning" (*Zhi xue* 志學) chapter of his *Tong shu* 通書 [Penetrating the "Book of Change"] Zhou Dunyi wrote: "Sages emulate heaven, worthies emulate sages, and men of learning and social standing emulate worthies."

13   In English, the term "New Confucian" ([*dangdai* 當代/*xiandai* 现代] *xin rujia* 新儒家) is to be distinguished from "Neo-Confucian." New Confucianism is a modern neo-conservative philosophical movement, with religious overtones. Proponents claim it to be the legitimate transmitter and representative of orthodox *ru* 儒 ("Confucian") values. The movement is promoted and/or researched by prominent Chinese intellectuals based in China, Taiwan, Hong Kong, and the United States of America. Elsewhere I have argued that although most of the promoters and sympathetic interpreters of New Confucianism trace the movement to the early part of the twentieth century, in fact, there is little evidence that New Confucianism had attained a degree of integration or coalescence sufficient for it to be recognized and promoted as a distinct philosophical movement, or school of thought, before

the 1970s. "Neo-Confucian" is a category employed to describe a set of "family resemblances" discerned across clusters of philosophical ideas, technical terms, arguments, and writings associated with particular figures from the Song to Qing (960–1911) periods. See also my introduction to *Dao Companion to Neo-Confucian Philosophy*, edited by John Makeham (New York: Springer, 2010), pp. ix–xliii.

14   Standaert's comment is made in the context of discussing the Jesuit adoption of Neo-Confucian terms and concepts to discuss Aristotelian philosophy in seventeenth-century China. "The choice of the Jesuits and their collaborators to use common Chinese terms had as a result that Aristotelian philosophy was explained in (Neo-)Confucian terms, as is clear from the different branches in ethics *xiushen* [修身], *keji* [克己], etc. As such, the Chinese philosophical system prevailed over the Western system…. In the first encounter between China and the West … Westerners were predominantly compelled to talk about their own tradition in Chinese (Neo-Confucian) terms." Nicolas Standaert, "The Classification of Sciences and the Jesuit Mission in Late Ming China," p. 293.

15   For some recent ruminations on this situation, see Liu Xiaogan 劉笑敢, "'Fanxiang geyi' yu Zhongguo zhexue yanjiu de kunjing: Yi Laozi zhi dao de quanshi wei li"「返向格義」與中國哲學研究的困境——以老子之道的詮釋為例 ["Reverse analogical interpretation" and the dilemma of Chinese philosophical research: Taking the interpretation of Laozi's *dao* as an example], *Zhongguo zhexue yu wenhua* 中國哲學與文化 1 (2007), pp. 10–36; Shun Kwong-loi, "Studying Confucian and Comparative Ethics: Methodological Reflections," *Journal of Chinese Philosophy* 36.3 (2009), pp. 455–478.

16   In his discussion of the introduction and naturalization of the Western notion of logic in China, Joachim Kurtz writes:

> Modern Chinese discourses, no matter whether on social or ideological questions or on China's intellectual and cultural heritage, are articulated to a large extent in terms that were coined and normalized as translations of Western or Western-derived notions. Yet far from serving as simple equivalents of imported ways of understanding, many terms of foreign origin have unfolded a life very much of their own in modern Chinese contexts. More often than not they have acquired new meanings that creatively alter, extend or even undermine established European conceptions.

See Joachim Kurtz, "Coming to Terms with 'Logic': The Naturalization of an Occidental Notion in China," in Michael Lackner et al., *New Terms for New Ideas: Western Knowledge and Lexical Change in Late Imperial China* (Leiden: Brill, 2001), p. 147. Christoph Harbsmeier also remarks:

> I believe that the agenda of modernisation in China is set by Westernisation mainly from the 19th century onwards. But what needs careful detailed attention is the persevering constitutive interference of pre-modern traditional Chinese conceptual modes in the creative process of the Chinese appropriation of new Western conceptual content, and the way in which concepts of Western origin get

to live very much their own independent lives in the varied and evolving modern Chinese cultural contexts.

See Christoph Harbsmeier, "Concepts That Make Multiple Modernities: The Conceptual Modernisation of China in a Historical and Critical Perspective," unpublished paper at <http://www.hf.uio.no/ikos/english/research/projects/tls/publications/CONCEPTS-THAT-MAKE-HISTORY%5B1%5D.pdf >, accessed 20 January 2011.

17 Zuo Yuhe 左玉河, *Cong sibu zhi xue dao qi ke zhi xue: Xueshu fenke yu jindai Zhongguo zhishi xitong zhi chuangjian* 從四部之學到七科之學——學術分科與近代中國知識系統之創建 [From Four Divisions learning to Seven Disciplines learning: Academic disciplines and the establishment of modern Chinese knowledge systems] (Shanghai: Shanghai shudian chubanshe, 2004), pp. 358–360 for details. For some of the variations of the Dewey Decimal Classification developed in China, see Zuo Yuhe, "Dianji fenlei yu jindai Zhongguo zhishi xitong zhi yanbian" 典籍分類與近代中國知識系統之演變 [The classification of books and the transformation of modern Chinese knowledge systems], *Huadong shifan daxue xuebao*, 36.6 (2004), p. 53.

18 Wang Yunwu 王雲五, *Zhong-wai tushu tongyi fenleifa* 中外圖書統一分類法 [A unified method for classifying Chinese and foreign books] (Shanghai: Shangwu yinshuguan, 1928), p. 1; Hong Youfeng 洪有豐, *Tushguan zuzhi yu guanli* 圖書館組織與管理 [Library organization and management] (Shanghai: Shangwu yinshuguan, 1926), p. 124. For both examples, see Zuo Yuhe, "Dianji fenlei yu jindai Zhongguo zhishi xitong zhi yanbian," p. 57.

19 Cai Yuanpei, "Wo zai jiaoyujie de jingyan" 我在教育界的經驗 [My experiences in the world of education], cited in Liu Longxin 劉龍心, *Xueshu yu zhidu: Xueke tizhi yu xiandai Zhongguo shixue de jianli* 學術與制度——學科體制與現代中國史學的建立 [Scholarship and institutions: The disciplinary system and establishment of modern Chinese historiography] (Taipei: Yuanliu chuban gongsi, 2002), p. 118–119.

20 Sun Baoxuan, *Wang shan lu riji* 忘山盧日記 [Diary from the cottage on the forgotten mountain] (Shanghai: Shanghai guji chubanshe, 1983), Vol. 2, p. 1107.

21 See Wu Kang 吳康, "'Chongbian Zhongwen shumu de banfa' zhi shangque" 「重編中文書目的辦法」之商榷 [On the matter of re-classifying Chinese books], in *Beijing Daxue rikan* 北京大學日刊 [Peking University daily], 16 September 1920.

22 Zuo Yuhe, *Cong sibu zhi xue da qi ke zhi xue*, p. 336.

23 In 1886 Nakae Chōmin 中江兆民 (1847–1901) translated "philosophy" as *rigaku* in his *Rigaku enkakushi* 理學沿革史 (1886). This work is a translation of Alfred Fouillée, *Histoire de la philosophie* (1875).

24 *Riben shumu zhi*, in *Kang Nanhai xiansheng yizhu huikan* 康南海先生遺著彙刊 [Collection of Kang Youwei's surviving works], edited by Jiang Guilin 蔣貴麟 (Taipei: Hongye shuju, 1976), pp. 1–73.

25 The *lixue* category lists three books in translation: William Stanley Jevons (哲分斯; 1835–1882), *Bianxue qimeng* 辨學啟蒙 (*Primer of Logic*; London, 1876); William Muirhead (慕維廉; 1822–1900), *Gezhi xinji* 格致新機 [Novum organum], consisting of his "Gezhi lilun" 格致理論 [Principles of science] and an abridgement of his "Gezhi xinfa" 格致新法 [New methods of science]; and John Fryer (傅蘭雅; 1839–1928), *Lixue xuzhi* 理學須知 [What must be known about logic]. See Xu Weize 徐維則, "Dong-xi xue shumu" 東西學書目 [Bibliography of Eastern and Western learning) (n.p.: 1899 manuscript edition), B.31b–32a. The 1902 revised edition, *Zengban dong-xi xue shumu* 增版東西學書目 [Revised edition of the Eastern and Western learning bibliography) (Beijing: Beijing tushuguan chubanshe, 2003), 4.9a–11b, lists 31 bibliographic categories. The *lixue* 理學 category lists eleven books in translation: two works by Herbert Spencer (1820–1903), *Collected Writings* and *The Study of Sociology*; Thomas Huxley (赫胥黎; 1825–1895), *Tian yan lun* 天演論 [Evolution and ethics] (1898); Katō Hiroyuki 加藤弘之 (1836–1916), *Wu jing lun* 物競論 [Survival of the fittest], original title: *Kyōsha no kenri no kyōsō* 強者の権利の競爭 (1893)] William Stanley Jevons, *Bianxue qimeng*; William Muirhead, *Gezhi xinji*; John Fryer *Lixue xuzhi*; as well as one volume on physics and chemistry; one on the Chinese language; one on translation; and one bibliography of Japanese titles in the natural sciences. In this edition, the category of *lixue* has grown to include language studies, in addition to philosophy and the natural sciences.

26 Published in Nanjing by Jinling University 南京金陵大學.

27 Liu Guojun also published this edition with Jinling University.

28 Immanuel Wallerstein et al., *Open the Social Sciences: Report of the Gulbenkian Commission on the Restructuring of the Social Sciences* (Stanford: Stanford University Press, 1996), p. 7.

29 Charlotte Furth, "Introduction," in *Thinking with Cases: Specialist Knowledge in Chinese Cultural History*, edited by Charlotte Furth, Judith Zeitlin, and Ping-chen Hsiung (Honolulu: University of Hawai'i Press, 2007), p. 20.

30 Immanel Wallerstein et al., *Open the Social Sciences*, p. 5.

31 Jonathan Rée, "Philosophy as an Academic Discipline: The Changing Place of Philosophy in an Arts Education," *Studies in Higher Education* 3.1 (1978), pp. 12, 13.

32 Ulrich Johannes Schneider, "Teaching the History of Philosophy in 19th-Century Germany," in *Teaching New Histories of Philosophy: Proceedings of a Conference, University Center for Human Values, Princeton University, April 4–6, 2003*, edited by Jerome B. Schneewind (Princeton: University Center for Human Values, Princeton University, 2004), pp. 275–295.

33 This is, of course, most evident in Marxist accounts of the history of Chinese philosophy, as Yvonne Schulz Zinda evidences in her chapter for this volume, "Marxist Views on Chinese Traditional Philosophy Pre-1949." This influence was by no means limited to Marxists. In his chapter, Han-Georg Moeller describes Feng Youlan's *Xin yuandao* 新原道 [New history of

philosophy] as portraying the history of Chinese philosophy "as a necessary development of the Chinese 'spirit,' and as a dialectical movement oscillating between a theoretical-transcendent and a practical-moralist orientation, which ultimately attains synthesis. Feng intended the synthesis of these divergent, but not mutually exclusive, philosophical tendencies to manifest itself in his own philosophical system, which is outlined in the final chapter of the book."

34 Jonathan Rée, "Philosophy as an Academic Discipline," pp. 14, 15.

35 D. W. Hamlyn, *Being a Philosopher: The History of a Practice* (London: Routledge, 1992), pp. 97, 98.

36 Intellectual historian Wang Hui reports that between 1900 and 1919 more than 100 technical and scientific periodicals were published in China. "Such publications tripled in number in the seven years after the 1911 revolution…. The Association of Chinese Scientists (ACS) was founded in 1915 and in tandem with its monthly periodical, *Science*, constituted modern China's longest-lasting and most influential organization and publication in this sphere." Wang Hui, "Discursive Community and the Genealogy of Scientific Categories," in *Everyday Modernity in China*, edited by Madeline Yue Dong and Joshua L. Goldstein (Seattle: University of Washington Press, 2006), p. 83. In 1920 the Philosophy Society (*zhexueshe* 哲學社) was established in Beijing and published the journal *Zhexue* 哲學. The content was mostly, but not exclusively, Western philosophy. It was the first professional journal devoted to philosophy published in China. The first national professional journal was *Zhexue pinglun* 哲學評論 [Philosophical review] published from 1927. On this journal, see Azuma Jūji 吾妻重二, "Minguo shiqi de xueyuan zhexue [Academic Philosophy]: Lun *Zhexue pinglun* yu Zhongguo zhexuehui" 民國時期的學院哲學 [Academic Philosophy]——論《哲學評論》與中國哲學會 [Academic Philosophy in the Republican Period: *Philosophical Review* and the Chinese Philosophy Association], in *Xuanpu lunxue xuji: Xiong Shili yu Zhongguo chuantong wenhua guoji xueshu yantaohui lunwenji* 玄圃論學續集——熊十力與中國傳統文化國際學術研討會論文集 [Xiong Shili on learning, second collected volume: Collected essays from the Second International Academic Symposium on Xiong Shili and China's Traditional Culture], edited by Wuhan daxue Zhongguo chuantong wenhua yanjiu zhongxin 武漢大學中國傳統文化研究中心 [China's Traditional Culture Research Center, Wuhan University] (Wuhan: Hubei jiaoyu chubanshe, 2003), pp. 222–233.

37 See Xiaoqun Xu, *Chinese Professionals and the Republican State: The Rise of Professional Associations in Shanghai, 1912–1937* (Cambridge: Cambridge University Press, 2001), p. 3. This book principally focuses on professional associations in the fields of law, medicine, and journalism. Voluntary associations were already in existence before 1912. Wen-hsin Yeh, *Provincial Passages: Culture, Space, and the Origins of Chinese Communism* (Berkeley: University of California Press, 1996), p. 119 notes that the "first educational associations, created in 1906, were gentry organizations called into existence

by the state to help the government implement the reform of the national school system." Chapter 6 of Yeh's book is a detailed study of the Zhejing Provincial Educational Association which came into existence in 1912.

38   In 1912 the Ministry of Education promulgated an edict on universities stipulating that universities would be established along disciplinary divisions, with seven disciplines recognized: humanities, science, law, commerce, medicine, agriculture, and engineering. This was more or less in line with the divisions set out in the *Qinding xuetang zhangcheng* 奏定學堂章程 [Regulations for the schools as memorialized and ratified] of 1904, the major difference being that the category of classical studies was abolished. Liu Longxin, *Xueshu yu zhidu*, p. 118.

39   For example, in 1913 the Ministry of Education issued an edict stipulating that the minimum qualification required to be appointed as an academic in a non-government university was that the appointee be a graduate of a foreign university, a Chinese national university, or a private university recognized by the Ministry of Education and to have research experience; or to have high quality publications as evaluated by the Central Education Association (Zhongyang xuehui 中央學會). There is a clear emphasis on research and publications and not just the traditional role of teacher. See "Jiaoyu Bu gongbu sili daxue guicheng ling" 教育部公佈私立大學規程令 [Ministry of Education edict on the regulations for non-government universities] (1913), in *Zhonghua Minguoshi dang'an ziliao huibian* 中華民國史檔案資料彙編 [Collection of archival materials on Republican-period history], edited by Zhongguo Di'er Lishi Dang'an Guan 中國第二歷史檔案館 (Second Historical Archives of China), Third collection, education (教育) (Nanjing: Jiangsu guji chubanshe, 1991), p. 143.

40   Shigeru Nakayama, *Academic and Scientific Traditions in China, Japan and the West* (Tokyo: University of Tokyo Press, 1984), p. 130.

41   This Association grew from a series of regular meetings in the late 1920s involving the participation of philosophers from Peking, Tsinghua and Yenching universities. The Association included members who worked on non-Chinese and Chinese philosophy, as is reflected in articles published in the Association's journal, *Zhexue pinglun*, and in annual conference papers.

42   As Yvonne Schulz Zinda shows in chapter 10, it was not until the mid-1930s that academic efforts were first made to write a history of Chinese philosophy using a Marxist framework.

43   This was the precursor of Zhongyang University and subsequently Nanjing University.

44   Charlotte Furth, "Introduction," in *Thinking with Cases*, p. 21.

45   Charlotte Furth, "Producing Medical Knowledge through Cases: History, Evidence, and Action," in *Thinking with Cases*, p. 148.

46   Zhang Taiyan held an appointment in the Tsinghua National Studies Research Institute in the latter part of the 1920s, but for most of his career he was not employed as an academic. Liang was employed in the Philosophy

Department of Peking University from 1917 to 1924, while Xiong was first appointed there from 1922 to 1924.

47 This book went through several redactions and revisions, beginning in the early 1920s and culminating in the literary version of 1932 and the vernacular version of 1944.

48 Feng Youlan was also profoundly influenced by Neo-Confucian philosophy, but this did not extend to his participation in related social networks.

49 Yap Key-chong, "Western Wisdom in the Mind's Eye of a Westernized Chinese Lay Buddhist: The Thought of Chang Tung-sun (1885–1962)" (PhD Dissertation, University of Oxford, 1991), pp. 75–76.

50 Wang Bo 王博 shows that in fact the name *zhexuexi* was not put into practice until 1919. See Wang Bo, "Cong zhexue, zhexuemen dao zhexuexi: Youguan Beijing Daxue Zhexuexi zaoqi lishi de jige wenti" 從哲學、哲學門到哲學係——有關北京大學哲學係早期歷史的幾個問題 [From philosophy, philosophy "department" to philosophy department: Several issues concerning the early history of the Peking University Philosophy Department], in *Sixiang de licheng: Beijing daxue zhexuexi jiushi zhounian jinian wenji* 思想的歷程——北京大學哲學系九十周年紀念文集 [A journey of thought: Commemorative collection of essays on the occasion of the ninetieth anniversary of the establishment of the Peking University Philosophy Department], edited by Zhao Dunhua 趙敦華 and Li Silong 李四龍 (Beijing: Peking University Press, 2004), pp. 20–21. See also *Beijing Daxue zhexuexishi gao* bianweihui 北京大學哲學係史稿編委會 [Publication committee for *Peking University Philosophy Department Draft History*], *Beijing Daxue zhexuexishi gao* 北京大學哲學係史稿 [Peking University Philosophy Department draft history] (Beijing: Internal publication, Philosophy Department, Beijing University, 2004), p. 3.

51 Yang Lian 楊廉, ed., *Haitian ji* 海天集 [Collection of essays on the Peking University Philosophy Department] (Shanghai: Beixin shuju, 1926), Appendix p. 5.

52 On the teachers' college, see Timothy B. Weston, *The Power of Position: Beijing University, Intellectuals, and Chinese Political Culture, 1898–1929* (Berkeley: University of California Press, 2004), p. 46.

53 *Beijing Daxue zhexuexishi gao* bianweihui, *Beijing Daxue zhexuexishi gao*, p. 89.

54 On this document, see the discussion in Timothy B. Weston, *The Power of Position*, p. 32. According to Liu Longxin, *Xueshu yu zhidu*, pp. 29–32, in 1898 the Zongli Yamen memorialized the throne with a document entitled "Jingshi Daxuetang zhangcheng" 京師大學堂章程 [Charter for the Imperial University], the real author of which was Liang Qichao. Liang divided the courses of modern-style schools into general and specialist, modeled on the preparatory (預科) and disciplinary (分科) distinction adopted in Japan. In the general courses section, among the ten subjects (科), Liang included Classical Studies, Principle-centered Learning (*lixue*), and Masters Studies. None of these appeared in the ten subjects he proposed for the specialist

courses. In fact, Liu notes that all of the specialist subjects were based on Western disciplinary models and not on traditional Chinese models, explaining that this was because it reflected a belief on the part of the document's authors that the university should offer courses that were practical. As for the Chinese-type courses such as classics and history, they were viewed as foundation courses, reflecting a "Chinese learning as substance, Western learning as function" mentality.

55 Wang Bo, "Cong zhexue, zhexuemen dao zhexuexi," p. 13. An even earlier example and perhaps the first attempt in China to develop a philosophy curriculum—although having no connections with Peking University—is one of the four academic disciplines (*xueke* 學科) Kang Youwei developed for the school he established in Guangzhou in 1891, Changxing xueshe 長興學舍. According to Liang Qichao, "Philosophy" (*yili* 義理) studies consisted of: Confucius studies, Buddhist studies, pre-Han Masters studies, Song-Ming studies, and Western philosophy. See Liang Qichao, "Nanhai Kang xiansheng zhuan" 南海康先生傳 [Biography of Kang Youwei], in *Yin Bing Shi wenji* 飲冰室文集 [Collected essays from the Ice-drinker's Studio] (Shanghai: Zhonghua shuju, 1941), Vol. 3, p. 65. For further discussion, see Liu Longxin, *Xueshu yu zhidu*, pp. 36–37.

56 Liu Longxin, *Xueshu yu zhidu*, pp. 40–41.

57 Wang Bo, "Cong zhexue, zhexuemen dao zhexuexi," pp. 16–17; Zhang Shenfu 張申府, "Huixiang Beida dangnian" 回想北大當年 [Recalling my years at Beida], in Wang Zongyu, *Ke le nianhua*, p. 1.

58 Zhang Shenfu, "Huixiang Beida dangnian," p. 1. This account is corroborated in Feng Youlan, "Beida yi jiu ji," p. 9; *San Song Tang zi xu* 三松堂自序 [Feng Youlan's prolegomena], in Feng Youlan, *San Song Tang quanji* 三松堂全集 [Complete works of Feng Youlan] (Zhengzhou: Henan renmin chubanshe, 1985–1994), Vol. 1, p. 186.

59 Wang Bo, "Cong zhexue, zhexuemen dao zhexuexi," p. 17. Throughout most of its formative period, the Philosophy Department offered students a broad range of subjects, with training not just in Chinese, Western, and Indian philosophy but also in psychology, sociology, linguistics, education, biology, anthropology, economics, chemistry, and geology. In a history of the Philosophy Department published internally in 2004, the editors remark that between 1912 and 1929 "literature, history, and philosophy" (*wen shi zhe* 文史哲) was still treated as an undifferentiated category at Peking University and so the Philosophy Department offered many subjects cross-listed with other departments. *Beijing Daxue zhexuexishi gao* bianweihui, *Beijing Daxue zhexuexishi gao*, 13.

60 The 1902 set of documents, "Qinding xuetang zhangcheng," includes Zhang Zhidong's blueprint for the Imperial University, "Qinding Jingshi Daxuetang zhangcheng," which stipulated that eight divisions (科) be established, including a Division of Classical Learning. This Division in turn was to consist of eleven departments (門), one of which was Principle-centred

Learning. "Its main content was research methodology on Principle-centred Learning, the Cheng-Zhu school, the Lu-Wang school, and the schools of the Zhou-Qin masters." As it happens, Zhang Zhidong refused to establish a separate department for Masters Studies. This was the subject of complaint by Wang Guowei in 1906 who maintained that Zhang not only rejected foreign philosophy but was wary of Chinese philosophy, having discarded Masters Studies and relegated Song Confucian philosophy to the narrow confines of moral philosophy. See Wang Guowei, "*Zouding Jingxue ke daxue wenxue ke daxue zhangcheng* shu hou" 奏定經學科大學文學科大學章程書後 [Postface to the *Regulations for the Classics and Literature Departments at the Imperial University, as memorialized and ratified*], in *Zhongguo jindai jiaoyu shiliao huibian* 中國近代教育史料彙編 [Collection of historical materials on China's modern education], edited by Pan Maoyuan 潘懋元 and Liu Haifeng 劉海峰 (Shanghai: Shanghai jiaoyu chubanshe, 1993), pp. 7–13.

61 *Beijing Daxue zhexuexishi gao* bianweihui, *Beijing Daxue zhexuexishi gao*, p. 3.

62 The following list is based on Yang Lian, ed., *Haitian ji*, Appendix. Where I have sourced additional information from *Beijing Daxue rikan* I indicate this in the body of the text.

63 By the late 1870s in Germany, scientific methods such as experimentation and the development of physiological tools provided impetus for psychology to be differentiated from philosophy as a science. And although there were attempts after this in the USA to consolidate links between philosophy and psychology (most notably by William James), by the turn of the twentieth century, psychology had begun to be established as an independent academic discipline, even if courses were still referred to as moral or mental philosophy. The establishment of independent psychology departments was, however, a gradual process as departmentalization in American tertiary institutions only began in earnest in the 1890s.

Part I: From Philosophy to *Zhexue*

Chapter 1

Nishi Amane and the Birth of "Philosophy" and "Chinese Philosophy" in Early Meiji Japan

Barry D. Steben

This chapter examines the early stage of the establishment of Western learning in Japan in the Meiji period (1868–1912) to explore how the concepts of "philosophy" and "Chinese philosophy," both as traditions of thought and as modern fields of learning, arose through the interaction between Western and Confucian concepts. It focuses on Nishi Amane 西周 (1829–1897), a *rangaku* 蘭學 (Dutch learning) scholar who studied in Holland in the 1860s, and aims to clarify (1) the nature and discursive context of the European philosophy to which he was exposed in Holland, including its political and institutional dimensions; and (2) the way in which Confucian concepts became the medium for the reception of this philosophy in Japan through Nishi's work of translation and propagation. By means of this double clarification, I hope to reveal the basic discursive structure and educational mission of the mode of state-supported philosophical endeavour that was established in Japan through Nishi and his students to become the foundation for the academic field of philosophy (and other modern academic fields) not only in Japan, but in China as well.[1] As is well known, because of the centralization of governmental power and national purpose brought about by the Meiji Restoration, the effective reorganization of education and learning in line with European categories and disciplines occurred earlier in Japan than in China, and Japan became the model for China's modernization after 1895. Because of the huge impact in China of the thousands of Chinese students who studied in Japan after that date,[2] mediated by the common Confucian intellectual culture and Sinitic script of the two countries, as well as the widespread use of *kanbun* 漢文 in Japanese scholarly writing, the influence of Meiji thought in late-Qing and Republican China was great. The early development of Western-style intellectual disciplines in China cannot be fully understood apart from that influence.[3] Thus the present chapter, while focusing only on Japan and Holland, can be expected to contribute in important ways to our larger inquiry into the interaction between indigenous grammars of knowledge construction and Western paradigms involved in the formation of the modern discipline of "Chinese philosophy" in China.

In the Edo period (1603–1868), the pursuit of Western learning (through the Dutch language supplemented by missionary translations of Western works imported from China) had been regarded with suspicion because of its association with Christianity, contact with which was prohibited by law, so it had to be justified in terms of the more widely established schools of learning originating in China.[4] Accordingly, those Western ideas that did manage to enter Japanese intellectual discourse were evaluated and categorized in terms of familiar conceptual systems, principally the Cheng-Zhu school of Confucianism. On this basis, Edo thinkers, even late Edo scholars of Western science like Sakuma Shōzan 佐久間象山 (1811–1864), generally regarded Eastern and Western learning as qualitatively different, the former belonging to the fundamental realm of ethics and spirit and the latter merely to the practical or material realm.[5] In order for the study of Western learning beyond the realm of military technology to be fully legitimated, however, this dualism had to be overcome. In the view of translator and socio-political commentator Fukuzawa Yukichi 福澤諭吉 (1834–1901), the difference was quantitative only, a difference in the level of civilization achieved, so both could be seen on the same plane.[6] Similarly, as instructor in the Bansho shirabesho 蕃書調所 (Institute for the Study of Barbarian Books), Katō Hiroyuki 加藤弘之 (1836–1916) had already in 1861 rejected the common belief that the origin of the West's wealth and power lay in its military technology (the material realm), arguing that the real origin lay in the parliamentary system of government, giving much credit to the Christian tradition as well. Most Confucian scholars, nativist scholars, and even some Western-learning scholars continued to believe in the superiority of Eastern learning in the moral realm. But for the first ten years or so of the Meiji period, their voices tended to be drowned out by the swing toward Western learning promoted most prominently by the Meirokusha 明六社 (Meiji Six Society).

1. The Course of Nishi Amane's Education and Government Service

Nishi Amane is best known as the creator of the word *zhexue/tetsugaku* 哲學 as the translation of "philosophy," which he had first referred to as the *Western* tradition of "the study of human nature and the principles of things" (*seiri no gaku* 性理之學), that is, as the Western equivalent of Neo-Confucianism.[7] Born into the family of a physician, he was exposed from his early years to Confucian ideas, since medicine was a branch of Confucian learning. In 1848, however, he was ordered by his lord to abandon the family profession and devote himself to Neo-Confucian studies. After pursuing more advanced studies at academies in Osaka and Okayama, he returned home in 1851 and was appointed reading instructor and supervisor in the domain school.[8] Four months after he started studying Dutch, in the third month of 1854, he slipped away from the domain estate in Edo, which meant cutting his hereditary duty to his lord and relinquishing his samurai status. Nishi found some physicians who knew Dutch to teach him Dutch grammar, studied books on Dutch gunnery, and soon started attending a school of Western learning where in 1856 he began studying English. In 1857, he became an assistant instructor of Dutch at the shogunate's revamped Translation Bureau, which in 1856 had been renamed the Bansho shirabesho. With his friend Tsuda Mamichi 津田真道 (1829–1903) he soon began seeking a chance to go abroad. Finally, in 1862 both of them were sent to Holland.

Once in Holland, both men were entrusted to the care of a Leiden University professor of Chinese and Japanese, J. J. Hoffmann, who soon introduced them to Professor Simon Vissering,[9] with whom they embarked upon the study of international and domestic law, natural law, economics, and political science. Nishi also had a personal desire to study philosophy, which he had come to believe through his studies in the 1850s constituted the master key to understanding Western culture. Accordingly, both Nishi and Tsuda attended occasional lectures by C. W. Opzoomer (1821–1892), then the leading historian of philosophy in Holland, Nishi bringing a number of his books back to Japan.[10]

After two years and seven months in Holland, in December 1865 Nishi and Tsuda headed back to Japan, where—due to the turmoil precipitated by the shogunate's opening of the country through treaties signed in 1854 and 1858—the very foundations of the polity were being challenged and questioned like never before. Both were instructed to return to their teaching posts at the much expanded Translation Bureau, now called the Kaiseijo 開成所, and Nishi was soon made an assistant professor, and later full professor. He and Tsuda introduced new disciplines of instruction such as law, economics, and philosophy. In the next year Nishi was summoned to Kyoto by the new shogun, where he decided to open his own private school. He soon had almost 500 students, almost all sons of Tokugawa partisans. As a teacher and advisor in the shogunate's employ, he did not participate in the Reformation, but in 1870 he was appointed head of the translation section of the new government's Ministry of Military Affairs in Tokyo. Nishi served the Ministry with distinction for the next 17 years, which also gave him opportunities to advise the Ministry of Education and the Ministry of the Imperial Household. In 1873 he became one of the founding members of the Meirokusha, the publishing house that played the leading role in the propagation of Western Enlightenment thought in the early Meiji period. Many of his pioneering translations of Western academic concepts were introduced into public and academic discourse through the society's journal.[11] Among his many writings, Nishi translated three particularly important works into Japanese: Vissering's lectures on *International Law* (*Volkenregt* 萬國公法; 1868), Joseph Haven's *Mental Philosophy* (心理學; 1875–1876),[12] and J. S. Mill's *Utilitarianism* (利學; 1877, in *kanbun*).[13] Nishi evidently derived his translation of "international law" as *Wanguo gongfa* from the title of the Chinese translation of Henry Wheaton's *Elements of International Law* (1836), completed by W. A. P. Martin (1827–1916) and his Chinese assistants in 1864 and brought to Japan in 1865. Both works explained international law as being rooted in the philosophical concepts of natural law and natural rights, subjects that Nishi had lectured and written on in 1867.[14] Through his translations or adaptations of Comte, Mill, and other European thinkers, Nishi also introduced empiricism and positivism (實理學), strongly promoting inductive logic over the deductive logic that dominated Confucian learning. These writings constituted not only the beginnings of Western philosophy in Japan, but also of social science.

2. The Fundamental Distinctions in the Realm of Learning

Nishi's 1867 philosophical lectures, published in 1874 as *Hyakuichi shinron* 百一新論 [A new discourse on the unity of the hundred teachings], lay down two fundamental distinctions in order to clarify the boundaries of the concept of "teachings" (教) that was to be the core subject of the lectures. The first is the distinction between "government" (政) and "[moral] teachings." In Confucianism, he says, when one speaks of "the way of man" (人道), it includes the concept of the methods of ruling people, based on a misconstrual of the *Great Learning*'s linking of self-cultivation and government as indicating a *method* of governing. The idea that if the ruler's mind is sincere and rectified the land will be well-ruled is, however, totally misguided. It is unrealistic to expect rulers to be benevolent moral paragons, and self-cultivation is not a method of ruling the world. What *is* necessary for government is learning about concrete institutions; that is what Confucius meant when he spoke of rites (禮) and what Ogyū Sorai 荻生徂徠 (1666–1728)[15] meant in insisting that "the Way of the early kings is nothing other than ritual and music (禮樂)." Confucius was originally a scholar of political science (政事), that is, of the concrete methods of government of the sage-kings, and his ideas about morality were originally only a sideline (内職).[16] Thus to study Confucius and understand his ethics properly one must study the laws, rites, and institutions of different historical periods, with an eye to concrete utility.[17] In line with this distinction, Nishi divides the tradition of Confucian learning into two contrasting types of pursuit: (1) the study of historical records and decrees, institutions, laws, statutes, and precedents (典章文物律令格式) from the ancient "Three Dynasties" and the twenty-two dynasties that followed; and (2) the study of the methods of regulating the mind on the basis of moral principles.[18] As a foundation for civilization, he adds, these two sides of Confucianism together were not inferior to what Greece and Rome provided to the West, which of course can similarly be divided into teachings and institutions—Greek philosophy and Roman law.

The second essential distinction is that between the principles of physical things (物理) and the principles of the mind (心理). When people today speak of "principles" (道理), he writes, they mean both moral principles, like loyalty and filial piety, and natural principles, like the falling of rain or the shining of the sun. Both are called "principles of what ought properly to be so" (當然ノ理) or "principles of what is naturally so" (自然ノ理), and it seems there is no difference between them.[19] Because this distinction has not been clearly established in traditional Chinese and Japanese thought—that is, because of the belief that the power of the human mind can cause changes in the operation of the principles of nature—all sorts of erroneous conceptions have arisen. In China, people blame eclipses on the ruler's lack of rectitude in government, or in Japan, they believe that Nichiren's prayers moved the gods to raise the divine winds (神風) that destroyed the invading Mongol fleets.[20] Unless such mistaken ideas are eliminated, "it is impossible to talk about true morals," because moral and natural principles are different things, and, he implies, they must be investigated in different ways.[21] This passage, along with the morality vs. government distinction, has typically been cited as evidence that Nishi categorically rejected Confucianism—especially Neo-Confucianism—to pursue Western learning. Even Thomas Havens' generally sophisticated study of 1970 argues that the *Hyakuichi shinron* constitutes a "systematic refutation" of the Zhu Xi school, which Havens calls "the ideology of the *ancient régime*."[22]

These statements are not totally erroneous, but if claims of this nature are taken at face value, outside of the full context of Havens' study, they lead back to the sort of one-sided traditional interpretation of Nishi's historical significance that one still sees reproduced ubiquitously in shorter summaries of his thought. It assumes that modern Western learning and Neo-Confucianism represented fundamentally different and incompatible worlds of thought; that the latter had to be destroyed for Japan to modernize; and that Nishi's separation of ethics from the natural world represented a sharp turn away from the mainstream of Edo thought.[23] There is both discontinuity and continuity, of course, but the traditional interpretation, rooted in the rhetoric of modernism, had an ideological preference for the former. Actually, under the influence of Itō Jinsai 伊藤仁齋 (1627–1705), Ogyū Sorai, evidential learning, Dutch learning, Wang Yangming (Ō Yōmei 王陽明) learning, Ishida Baigan's 石田梅巖 (1685–1744) popular Confucianism, and the Eclectics (折衷學),[24] in the course of the eighteenth century virtually all Japanese Confucian teachers had already abandoned Confucianism's "natural philosophy" dimensions and metaphysical speculations and confined Confucian teaching to the realm of morality and self-cultivation.[25] The belief in the connectedness between morality and politics had also been progressively undermined since the eighteenth century.[26]

Particularly before post-modern critical methodologies struck the field of Japanese intellectual history, it was fashionable to find all sorts of precursors of "modern" thought within Edo intellectual history. Many argued on that basis that Japan possessed a progressive impetus toward "modernity" within its own indigenous cultural tradition that distinguished it from the supposedly "static" civilization of China (typified by

Zhu Xi learning) and entitled it to a kind of natural equality with the Western powers. It is much more apropos, however, to understand these strands of Edo Confucian thought that helped facilitate modernization as "indigenous grammars of knowledge construction." They were not necessarily "modern" in nature nor superior to parallel thought currents in China, but they provided a cornucopia of conceptions of the Way and standards of rational justification that could facilitate the naturalization of Western systems of knowledge in Japan, a naturalization that was soon to be repeated in the rest of East Asia.

Hyakuichi shinron was a compilation of a series of lectures given in 1867 at a school of Western learning in Kyoto. The series was interrupted by the defeat of the shogunate's army in the Battle of Toba-Fushima, and Nishi was not able to continue them until 1870. If the 1867 lectures had continued, they would have gone on to expound the *philosophy* that elucidates how all the *hundred teachings* are related to one another and how they all ultimately share the same import.[27] The 1870–1871 lectures in Tokyo that took up this task were published as *Hyakugaku renkan* 百學連環 [The links among the various fields of learning], a self-proclaimed "Encyclopaedia" of knowledge patterned structurally after (English translations of) the *Cours de philosophie positive* of Auguste Comte (1798–1857), its content based chiefly on the lectures Nishi heard in Leiden supplemented by various English writings, many by Mill.[28]

This work is especially relevant to our present inquiry because, by showing how the various fields of knowledge are related, it lays a foundation for the introduction and institutionalization of all disciplines of modern Western learning—especially philosophy—and for their integration with existing systems of learning.[29] As Havens writes, "His stress on the common ground between the European and East Asian intellectual heritages helped to smooth the way for a new outlook on the nature of knowledge that emphasized the ultimate social usefulness of all scholarship."[30] Nishi's introduction explains and praises the inductive method as perfected by Mill, arguing that it is the only way to truth, but that truth is useless unless applied empirically to practical problems. It then outlines Comte's three stages of social development ending in positivism, wherein speculative principles (空理) are replaced by positive principles (實理). However, in the body of the work Nishi replaces Comte's sociology with philosophy as the king of all disciplines: "As to the definition of philosophy, we may say that philosophy is the science of sciences and that it is chief among all sciences. There is a general principle governing all things, which inevitably controls all affairs. Therefore, like king and subject, philosophy controls all sciences, and they must all be controlled by it."[31] Here we find the two fundamental distinctions considered above applied to the classification of the sciences, which are first divided into "universal sciences" known to all civilizations (history, geography, literature, and mathematics) and "particular sciences," i.e., fields that have only been developed [so far] in the West. The latter are then divided into "intellectual sciences" (心理上學) and "physical sciences" (物理上學).[32] The distinction between government and "teachings," in turn, is seen in the separation of the field of philosophy, which includes ethics, from the distinct field of "political science and the science of law," which in Japan soon became institutionalized as the chief academic discipline for the training of high government officials (at the Faculty of Law of the University of Tokyo).

Although these distinctions are couched here in terms inspired chiefly by utilitarianism,[33] Nishi had first encountered both of them in Sorai's writings, which are famous for their rejection of the Neo-Confucian concept of the mutual influence between Heaven and man, i.e., the belief in the continuity between moral principles and principles of the natural world. The other core element of Sorai's critique of the Cheng-Zhu school is his teaching that the Way (道) is nothing other than the way of government of the sages and early kings, which is simply the methods of rule (禮樂, literally "rites and music")[34] that they devised—by collective human invention (作為) over and above what was given by nature— for bringing peace and contentment to human society. Here the distinction between Heaven and man reappears as the distinction between what exists naturally and what is created by man, although the civilization the sage-kings created was constructed according to the will of Heaven and in accord with human nature, and for that reason it can serve to regulate human nature and keep it within the proper bounds required for social harmony and happiness. The early kings' ceremonial forms (事) for ordering the world are described in the Six Classics, but they can only be correctly understood by recovering the original ancient meanings of the words in which the classics are written, which have often been lost due to changes in literary style that commenced during the Six Dynasties and culminated in the Song.[35] "If one [first] grasps the meaning [of the language] of the early kings, [and then] uses that to arrive at principle, then perception will have standards and principle will be achieved."[36] When one uncovers the real intent of the early kings, one sees that the concern of rulers should be the rectification of the institutions and methods of government, rather than the mind, that is, that government is a completely different thing from moral self-cultivation. Yet the early kings realized that the human community required not only external regulation by rituals, laws, and administrative structures, but also modes of culture directed at satisfying the heart, which were the concern of two of the Six Classics—*Music* and *Odes*.[37]

According to Sorai, the sage-kings understood that human nature is something *emotional* and *physical* in nature, differing with each individual and not capable of being moulded toward some ideal of sagehood by means of a system of lofty moral teachings held up as the standards for everyone to follow, though that nature can be *refined* by mastering the literary and ceremonial forms preserved in the classics. Thus followers of Sorai learning showed a much stronger interest in literature for its own sake, apart from the purpose of moral education, than the followers of the Cheng-Zhu school. So for Sorai—and Nishi—the distinction between *wuli* and *xinli* is parallel to the distinction between government and ethical teachings, the first in each pair being concerned with the external world and the second with the internal.[38] And for Sorai, in accord with his devaluation of ethical teachings, the distinction is also reproduced in his concept of the Way as the concrete forms of rites and music, for by definition the Way must deal with both the external and the internal sides of human existence. This set of distinctions in Sorai's writings was thus part of a complete indigenous epistemology for establishing true knowledge of the Way through empirical study of the literary and ceremonial forms of the classics and the application of that knowledge to the rectification of institutions. As both Confucius and Sorai taught, the rectification of institutions begins with the rectification of names—the recovery of the correct meaning of words—which in Nishi's case meant the establishment of a system of precise translated concepts whereby the knowledge systems of the West could be incorporated without losing their integrity into the language-and-thought systems of East Asia.[39]

3. Parallels between the Western and Eastern Traditions and the Need for Reform

In an 1873 article on positivism, *Seisei hatsuun* 生性發蘊 [The relation of the physical and spiritual], Nishi discusses the rise of Western philosophy, emphasizing how systematic analysis (見解) of the world began with "object contemplation" (彼觀) of the forms (象) in the heavens and the models (法) of the earth (or, alternatively, contemplation of the lord [主宰] of the universe, or of the beauty of all things), but after reaching an extreme point (極) beyond which man's power to explain (講究) could not go, it turned to "subject contemplation" (此觀) of the self (己) that was the subject (主) doing the cognizing of these things, of the mind that was the lord (主) of the self, and of the principles of human nature that were the lord (主) of the mind. Simply by explaining this transition in Confucian terms, he achieves a wonderful synthesis of Confucian and Western philosophical concepts based implicitly on the *Yijing* 易經 (Book of Change) logic of *wu ji bi fan* 物極必反 (when something reaches its limit it will turn in the other direction). Then he notes that the same thing occurred in China, with Confucius representing the turn from external observation to teachings about self-mastery, virtue, and wisdom.[40] Similarly, in an oft-quoted summary of the history of philosophy (in *kanbun*) Nishi had written, "In the Eastern lands it is called *ru* 儒; in the Western continents it is called 'philosophy' (斐鹵蘇比). Both are concerned with clarifying the Way of Heaven and establishing the fundamental norms of human life (人極). In substance they are one. This Way is coeval with the human race, and it can never be destroyed until the end of time."[41] In a letter written in 1870, after distinguishing the teachings of Confucius and Mencius from the purely speculative concepts of the five phases cosmology that got mixed in with Confucianism, he says that the former teachings are "more or less the same" (大同小異) as Western philosophy (哲學); the two traditions match without either being based on the other (未相因襲). Since both are based on the principles of human life (人理), there are no fundamental differences dividing different cultural spheres or dividing the ancient from the modern.[42]

In the *Hyakugaku renkan*, however, Nishi is more concerned with what *distinguishes* the Western and Eastern philosophical traditions:

> The root of this Confucian tradition is [the ancient states of] Zou and Lu. Since the time of these [states of] Zou and Lu, scholars have continued this school of learning of Confucius and Mencius in one continuous line without making any further changes to it. By contrast, even though the scholars of the West have received their learning in one continuous line, through the new elucidations of each succeeding scholar, the theories of previous scholars have been examined and expurgated such that only what could be shown to be immovable was retained. For that reason, [the tradition] opened up bit by

bit with the passage of time, always giving birth to new things.[43]

Here we must be careful not to take Nishi's comparison simply as an evaluative statement promoting the idea of the superiority of the Western tradition. Such assertions are almost always accompanied by statements like, "When Chinese Confucianism is reformed in the Western manner, it should be exceedingly outstanding."[44] His main intent was to call not for the destruction but for the *reform* of Confucian learning by drawing the kind of clear distinctions considered above. He wished to purge from Confucian learning those ideas and methods that make it incompatible with Western scientific learning, based on empirical evidence and clear distinctions between realms. True to the spirit of philosophy itself, what Nishi was seeking to create was not a dualistic distinction between the Eastern and Western traditions that reverses the evaluation of Edo-period Confucian scholars, but a universal foundation *drawn both from Western and Chinese philosophy* for the continuing pursuit of truth that could incorporate, develop, and synthesize what is of value in both traditions.

4. Nishi's Definitions of Civilization and Human Happiness

In *Jinsei sampō setsu* 人生三寶説 [The three treasures of human life], a serial essay of 1875 inspired by Mill's "greatest happiness" principle, Nishi put forth a utilitarian conception of social morality which was tied in with a particular conception of what constitutes "civilization." The three treasures, as one might surmise, are health, knowledge, and wealth. "The basis of human morality lies in respecting the three treasures," he wrote, and "no other rules are necessary for personal conduct or for associating with others." This is because respecting the three treasures leads to a mode of living that balances rights against obligations, legislation against morality, government responsibility against individual responsibility, and the demands of nature against the demands of society.[45] While this is a utilitarian concept of social morality intended as a replacement for feudal ethics and a foundation for a capitalist economy, it is not necessarily incompatible with the core values of Confucianism. Nishi explicitly stated that though the concepts are new, the basic values they embody are not.[46]

About two years later Nishi gave a lecture called "Happiness is something that can only be achieved when achieved on both the spiritual and physical levels."[47] In it he declared, "Even if a person has obtained affluence on the level of clothing, food, and domicile; health based on a sufficiency of money; talent and the time to develop it; as well as practical ingenuity, if that person is lacking in peace of mind and is driven around all day in an anxious state of mind because of all these things," then he cannot obtain happiness. "The supreme essential for achieving happiness is to be able to abide in a position where, from the very bottom of your heart, you feel no shame before Heaven, no shame before Earth, no shame when no one is watching you, and not a trace of guilt or worry with regard to the past or future."[48] There are several things we can say about this intriguing statement. First of all, it is Nishi's attempt to define on the basis of *experience*, not just of his learning, what true happiness really is, so it has to be totally sincere—right "from the bottom of his heart." Second, it was articulated apparently in 1877, still during the period of the Westernization discourse of which he was a leading spokesman, so it was too early to have been influenced by the resurgence of Confucian thought against Western ideas. Third, the part about the inner essential for achieving happiness—an absolutely clean conscience in a state of total stillness—is completely ethical in nature and completely constructed in terms of Confucian ideas—the idea of the "trinity" of Heaven, Earth, and man which grounds man both ethically and cosmically, as well as the idea of a person standing naked, so to speak, before the two Powers that have given rise to his existence. Fourth, this definition of happiness suggests strongly that the Confucian path of self-cultivation cannot be understood purely in terms of role ethics in which the person is seen as defined and constituted completely by the roles that he lives. This point is very relevant to our understanding of the precise ways in which Confucianism was able to provide indigenous grammars for the naturalization of Western thought in East Asia, as well as for the amalgams of Confucianism with Western philosophy that emerged in Japan and China in the late nineteenth and twentieth centuries.

Running through the Confucian tradition is a recognition of a dimension of the human self or human subjectivity that is in a real sense above all of the relationships in which a person is involved. Another hint of this can even be seen in the character compound that Nishi uses for "spiritual" in the above quotation, which combines the nature (性) with spirit (靈). Remember his statement in *Seisei hatsuun* that the principles of human nature (性理) are the "lord" of the mind. In Cheng-Zhu Confucianism the mind is part of the phenomenal world, but the "nature," where the principles inhere, is metaphysical. This resembles the distinction in Western thought between the "mental" and the "spiritual." It is precisely because "the nature" or "spirit" is beyond phenomena that Neo-Confucian self-cultivation puts great emphasis on the necessity of "vigilence in solitude" (*shen du* 慎獨). If one cannot keep oneself morally under control when alone, but only when being observed by others, one will not be able to be totally sincere, and other people will feel that one is hiding something. Vigilence in solitude, which appears in the *Great Learning* and the *Mean*, is related to the Neo-Confucian practice of "letting stillness rule over movement" (主靜). In some schools of Neo-Confucianism, *shen du* was treated as a daily meditation practice, in fact as the core of Confucian practice, making it equivalent to or an element of the quiet sitting that was enjoined in all mainstream Neo-Confucian schools.

Nishi does not use the term *shen du* here, but rather a well-known line from the *Book of Odes* that also appears in Zhang Zai's 張載 (1020–1077) *Western Inscription* 西銘: "to feel no shame before the *wu lou* (不愧 于屋漏)." *Wu lou* 屋漏 refers to the northwest corner of a house, where the god of the house is hidden behind a curtain. It is the most interior part of the house, the place that is most difficult for people to see. Accordingly, "to feel no shame before the *wulou*" means not to feel shame even where no one can see you, which is the most interior and private part of one's self. The practice of Christianity, as well, centres on a similar experience, wherein one is freed from guilt through the consumption of the flesh and blood of the Perfect Man who was sacrificed to cleanse us of our sins—a ritual re-enactment that is at once absolutely personal and absolutely communal, with each "absolutely" absolutely dependent upon the other. Here we see an apostle for Western philosophy (removed from its Christian context) who had to call on his own Neo-Confucian tradition to describe the "spiritual" dimension of human happiness, in effect drawing on the "meta-social" inner dimension of Confucianism to supplement the Comte-Mill emphasis on man's social nature. In his explorations into "happiness," Nishi in effect has followed the same path that he had laid out in *Seisei hatsuun* as characterizing the rise of Western philosophy— only he gradually became aware that this sequence from the contemplation of external phenomena to the self to the mind to the spirit represents not only the *history* of the awakening of man to self-knowledge in both East and West, but also the universal *way* to inner enlightenment, to the finding of one's true self, one's own true "nature."

5. The Convoluted Nature of the Concept of "Nature"

Nevertheless, in English and other European languages, the word used to refer to the "physical" world that is the object of the investigations of natural science is the same as the word for the forces that, embedded somehow within man's psychophysical constitution, give him his "human nature." This human nature evidently contains all kinds of tendencies derived not from man's "physical nature" but from his "social nature." And it is the "social nature" that belongs to the realm of "principles of the mind," which Nishi said are "post-Heaven" 後天 (*a posteriori*), or acquired through experience rather than inborn. We have seen how concerned Nishi was that his countrymen learn to make a clear distinction between the physical principles of nature and the moral principles of "the nature," but at least he had two different words for these two meanings of "nature." Yet obviously if in Western thought both of these things are named with the same word, there must be a very intimate genealogical connection between the two concepts. In Neo-Confucianism man's "nature" (性) is the dwelling place of "the principles of Heaven," and a major part of the meaning of "Heaven" in the Chinese language is "the natural world," that which is *tianran* 天然. So in the Confucian tradition as well there is an intimate connection between "the nature" and the "natural world," where "natural" in Chinese is usually expressed with the word *ziran* 自然: what is "so of itself," independent of any doing on the part of man. And human nature is often called *tianxing* 天性, the nature given by Heaven, i.e., the nature one is born with.

Similarly, the Western concept of "God" also subsumes a considerable portion of the "natural world," at least in pre-modern Western thought, because God is understood as the power which causes those things beyond human control to happen. Even modern legal language still refers to natural disasters as "acts of God." But philosophically speaking, the way that God is distinguished from Nature is that he is the law-giver of Nature, above and beyond all mere phenomena; thus like the laws that he "decrees," he is metaphysical. The idea of natural disasters as "acts of God"—like the stories of miracles in the Bible—conflicts with the philosophers' conception of God as the source of the *regularity* of nature. So God is not in but *behind* Nature; he is, in some sense, the source of the nature of Nature, just as in Neo-Confucianism Heaven is *behind* the principles of human nature (天理) and constitutes the lord (主宰) of Nature.

This rather convoluted nature of the concept of "nature" is also paralleled in the concept of "law," for the same word is used for the "laws of nature," the "laws of God," and the man-made "laws" that regulate the human community. Moreover, the concepts of "nature" and "law," with all their convolutions, merge together in the Western idea of "natural law," which was fundamental to both the legal philosophy and the ethico-political philosophy that Nishi was introducing to Japan.

If there is such an organic connection between the two concepts of "nature," then Nishi's (and Martin's before him) translation of "natural law" not as 自然法 but as 性法, literally "the laws of human nature," may be more logical than is at first apparent.[49] And when Nishi concludes his account of the rise of Western and Chinese philosophy in *Seisei hatsuun* with the statement that the turn from object contemplation to subject contemplation itself reflects a "natural law" (自然之理法), or when he claims that it is a "natural law" in society that those who possess the three treasures will control those without them,[50] perhaps he is not contradicting his insistence that the two realms must be clearly distinguished. But if "natural law" here means a law that exists originally (天然) in nature (or in human nature) before any human creation or human culture, then how can the development of philosophical reflection by human effort—certainly a development of "culture" and not "nature"—be an expression of that law? How would we state it? "It is a law of the natural world that human inquiry into the world will move from the object to the subject of cognition?" Or "it is a natural tendency of human nature that inquiry into the world will move from the object to the subject?" While the latter seems easier to accept, the logic of Nishi's translations suggests that the two statements may amount to the same thing. And we should remember here that he is portraying the turn from object to subject in terms of the *Yijing* principle of *wu ji bi fan*,[51] which is understood as a truly universal principle, i.e., a principle that is true simultaneously of the natural world, of the world of human action and human psychology, and of the collective unfolding of human history.

For both Nishi and his Dutch teachers there is a continuity or co-rootedness between the natural world and the social world that transcends the important distinction between physical principles and mental principles. For "natural principles," Nishi uses both the words

"Heaven-actualized" (天然) and "naturally so" (自然). Because they are "natural," as taught by Zhu Xi, they are present in all things and binding over all things. By contrast, "mental principles" are "principles that are operative only in the human world," i.e. "post-Heaven (after-birth) principles." However,

> As explained above, principles of the mind are post-Heaven, but if one thinks that that means they are completely fabricated by man, that is not the case either. In spite of the fact that they are post-Heaven, they are after all still Heaven. Even if all the greatest wise men in the world were to come together and resolve to remake these principles in a different way, it would not be possible to do so.... The principles of the mind that are followed by people today are simply impossible to destroy.

This, of course, is because the basis of these principles of the mind is the identical nature (性), which is possessed by all people in common. Here Nishi quotes the famous dictum of the *Mean*: "What is commanded by Heaven is called the nature; following this nature is called the Way." The principles of the mind are, just as much as physical principles, rooted in the principles of Heaven.[52] Nishi had recognized the "ambiguity" in the concept of Heavenly principle, but ultimately he did not change the fact that it includes both nature and human affairs.[53]

Similarly, Joseph Haven wrote that psychology "deserves in one respect to be ranked among the *natural* sciences," because "it is a science resting on experience, observation and induction—a science of facts, phenomena, and laws which regulate the same." The human mind is also a part of *nature*—in fact, the most important part.[54] And nature, we might add, is what can be studied as an object by the human mind. Thus the human mind is also an *object* of the human faculty of knowing, as paradoxical as this may sound, and the laws (principles) of the human mind are also "laws of nature." By the same token the laws that govern the human community, which as human creations are mental rather than physical principles, are also rooted in nature (and "human nature"). In his translation of Vissering's lectures on international law, Nishi wrote, "Law is founded on the natural inherent rights (天然固有之權) that are rooted in human nature (本於人之性上)."[55] But since Nishi here is using Confucian terms to translate the Western concept of "natural law," it behoves us to have a quick glance at the history of that concept.

6. "Natural Law" in Historical Perspective

The idea of "natural law" goes back to the ancient Greeks' conception of a universe governed in every particular by an eternal, immutable law and to their distinction between what is just by nature (*physis*) and what is just by law, custom, or convention (*nomos*). What the law commanded varied from place to place, but what was just "by nature" should be valid everywhere, not only in one political or cultural community. Stoicism argued that the universe is governed by reason, or rational principle, and since all humans have reason within them, they can therefore know and obey its law. Thus if human beings act in accordance with reason, they will be "following nature." For Aquinas (1225–1274), natural law is that part of the eternal law of God which is knowable by human beings through their powers of reason. Human, or positive, law, is the application of natural law to particular social circumstances. Like the Stoics, Aquinas believed that a positive law that violates natural law is not a true law. Thus it is clear that the concept of "natural law," whether or not associated with a "divine law" that is prior to any human authority, provides a higher standpoint from which one can criticize legal decisions about specific statutes, or criticize the law itself. From this it is not difficult to see how the concept could eventually evolve into the foundation for building a system of legal protections of the liberty of the individual and legal limitations on the exercise of monarchical authority.

As a matter of fact, a great deal of the earliest theorizing in Europe about the limitations of monarchical authority was carried out in Holland, as a product both of the rise of capitalism and of the "Eighty Years War" (1568–1648) against rule by the Catholic monarchy of Spain, with its belief in the divine right of kings, i.e., the doctrine that to rebel against the ruler is to rebel against God. Nishi studied in Holland because it was the only Western country with a presence in Edo Japan, but in doing so, he had gone to the land where the legal and philosophical principles of liberalism and capitalism had been first articulated, in the midst of intense commercial and naval competition among Portugal, Spain, Holland, and England.[56] The development of liberty, national autonomy, an economy based on international trade, and the international law that would further this economic development were all intertwined, and all looked to natural law theories for their legal and moral legitimization. Hugo Grotius (1583–1645), who was born two years after the creation of a Dutch republic exalting individual liberty and freedom of belief, is considered the founder of modern natural law theory, and it is to him we should look for the roots of the conception of natural law that informed Vissering's lectures on international law that Nishi was endeavouring to translate for his students.

A fundamental tenet of Grotius' thought is that moral, political, and legal norms are all based on laws derived from or supplied by nature. In his famous work *De iure praedae commentarius*, he wrote, "The Will of God is revealed, not only through oracles and portents, but above all in the very design of the Creator; for it is from this last source that the law of nature is derived." In his mature work of 1625, however, instead of emerging from or being otherwise dependent on God, the fundamental principles of ethics, politics, and law obtain in virtue of nature. As he says, "the mother of right—that is, of natural law—is human nature."[57] If an action agrees with the rational and social aspects of human nature, it is permissible; if it doesn't, it is impermissible. The law of nature "proceeds from the essential traits implanted in man."[58] Therefore, a study of nature itself—and more specifically, a study of human nature—can suffice to teach us the essentials of ethics, politics, and law. Human nature is constituted by two essential properties: the desire for self-preservation and the need for society. These two properties temper and inform each other: the desire for self-preservation is limited by the social impulse, and conversely the need for the company of other humans is limited by the self-preservation drive, for individuals must naturally strive to secure the means for their well-being. Moreover, self-preservation and sociability are each both emotive and cognitive, having the force of unreflective instinct as well as well-thought-out plans. Because we are both social and self-preserving beings, natural law obliges us to perform actions which conduce to our rationality, sociability, and need for self-preservation.[59]

7. The Discursive Context of Dutch Philosophy in the 1860s

Only by understanding the intellectual climate of Holland when Nishi was there can we understand just what sort of institutional, political, and discursive circumstances defined the field of philosophy at the time Nishi introduced it to Japan. As mentioned above, the most influential philosopher in post-1848 Holland was Cornelis Willem Opzoomer (1821–1892), who had moved from early studies in theology to the study and propagation of the positivism of Comte and Mill. Moreover, from the time he was appointed professor at Utrecht University in 1846, Opzoomer was also the leading spokesman for a new trend in Protestantism called "modernism" that sought a rapprochement between faith and modern culture, science in particular. The liberal Dutch bourgeoisie eagerly took up this philosophy in the 1850s and 1860s, proceeding to take over many positions of leadership in society and business while gaining increasing authority in the universities.[60] Hitherto the dominant theology had been that of the Groningen School, which believed in a God who intervenes in the world, in the miracles recounted in the Bible, and in a literal interpretation of the Genesis account of creation.[61] But under the influence of the successes of natural science, strongly reinforced by the publication of *The Origin of Species* in 1859, in the 1850s and 1860s modernism succeeded in displacing Groningen theology as the new "reformation" of Dutch theology.[62]

Opzoomer had started out as a staunch believer in the Reformed confessions and then became a follower of the Groningen School,[63] but by the time he was appointed professor he had abandoned the latter for a deistic position under the influence of scientific learning. His inauguration speech at the university, "Philosophy Reconciling Man with Himself," is regarded as a major manifesto of modernism.[64] Subsequently, influenced by two Darwinist friends who were science professors at the same university, he worked out what he called "the philosophy of experience," which accepted only empirical knowledge as certain and trustworthy. Everything in creation obeys the Great Law of Causality, he argued, and this and other laws were the work of the Supreme Being; thus there could be no conflict between the truth of Christianity and the truth of science. Accordingly, Opzoomer argued that miracles are impossible, Jesus was fully human, and the Bible must be fully opened to critical investigation. To quote Ilse Nina Bulhof, "Darwin confirmed the Modernists' optimism and faith in progress, for now it had been proven by science that everything obeys the law of perpetual progress. After the publication of the *Origin*, Opzoomer accepted the law of evolution as the fundamental law of the universe."[65] Particularly because he trained Protestant ministers, who were still an important intellectual force in the community, Opzoomer had great influence in society,[66] and the fact that he was also a jurist makes it even more certain that he influenced Professor Vissering's lectures on international law. Moreover, Opzoomer's chief "competitor" in propagating the philosophy of modernism, Johannes Henricus Scholten (1811–1885), endeavoured to show that the thinking of the Reformation leaders, particularly the Reformed (Calvinist) confession, found its fulfilment in idealist thought.[67] Thus in his disputes with Scholten, Opzoomer was compelled to argue forcefully for a pure empiricism as against idealist philosophy, holding that reality is determined materialistically by the laws of nature. The peremptory dismissal of idealist philosophy that we see in several of Nishi's writings is quite clearly a reflection of the influence of Opzoomer's lectures and books, reinforced by Vissering's own positions.

8. The Transition from Speculative to Reflective Philosophy

Scholten became professor at Leiden in 1843, and Opzoomer at Utrecht in 1846, when both were still young men, giving them ideal platforms to follow the tide toward liberalism and become its philosophical spokesmen. Scholten pulled theology as far as it could be pulled in the direction of scientific rationalism, which, in terms familiar to us from Nishi, meant the rejection, on the basis of the universal validity of the laws of nature, of the idea that God can intervene in the world or that man's prayers can influence what happens in the world. Then the younger Opzoomer, renouncing theology for philosophy, proceeded to mobilize the positivist ideas of Comte and Mill to the task of harmonizing science and philosophy.

In the traditional European learning system that had held sway in the universities since their founding in the Middle Ages, theology retained a higher status than philosophy per se, but under Aquinas the latter— honoured as the "handmaiden of theology"—had grown into a highly sophisticated and dynamic body of Aristotelian learning dedicated to the rational and empirical study of the natural world and the laws of human reason. Aquinas had argued forcefully for the complete compatibility of faith and rational exploration of the world, so that the pursuit of philosophy (which included natural science) was rarely felt to conflict with theology, and indeed the same basic Platonic-Aristotelian patterns of thought permeated both fields.[68] Now in the mid-nineteenth century, intellectuals were finding it necessary to separate the three fields, partly because of the need to specialize created by the rapid growth of knowledge, and partly because they recognized that the methods and aims of the three were fundamentally different.[69] But as seen above, the separation of natural science from philosophy meant that the methods used by philosophy had to attempt to move as close as possible to the methods of science. The dogmatic proclamations of the theologians were becoming less and less welcome among professors of philosophy, who had to work to cleanse themselves of the vestiges of deductive theological thinking in order to retain their intellectual prestige. This happened in universities all over Europe, with only relatively minor differences in timing. For instance, the school of theology founded by Scholten was similar to the contemporaneous Tübingen school in Germany, which initiated historical analysis of Biblical texts (usually called the "higher criticism"), and the University of Tübingen was also the first German university to establish a faculty of natural sciences—in 1863. Before this tectonic split, "science" could still refer to the same discipline as "philosophy."[70]

Modernist theology and philosophy, in turn, were based firmly in the concept of natural law, which was already the philosophical foundation of the domestic legal system, the system of international law, the movement for national independence through which the Dutch nation-state had been created, and the new political system of constitutional monarchy. Of course, when Nishi taught that the principles of the mind (and thus of morality, society, law, and the spirit) and the principles of the natural world both go back ultimately to "Heaven," he was just translating what all of his teachers and all the books he read had taught him in Holland, even if it did correspond nicely to Neo-Confucian teaching.[71] What students like Nishi brought back to Japan was not only a couple of important schools of modern European philosophy, but a direct experience of how philosophy served in Europe to tie together all the different realms of life and learning, from the relatively personal matters of religious faith and practice to social ethics, the realm of public discourse, the higher education system, the institutions of the state, the practice of government and international relations, and even the economy, for capitalist economic theory was also based on a modern version of natural law theory.

9. Forever the Twain Shall Meet

In this chapter we have seen how, in introducing the Western concept of natural law and the various philosophical and legal ideas in some way associated with it, Nishi used a wide range of well-known Confucian distinctions rooted in the traditional East Asian system of learning to introduce and explicate the concepts and distinctions which structured the world of learning in nineteenth-century Europe, fusing intellectual elements of indigenous manufacture with those of Europe to lay the conceptual foundations for the institutionalization of Western learning. This began with the distinction between ethical teachings to guide personal self-cultivation and the study of historically documented institutions and precedents to shape the practice of government—the two sides of Confucian learning. It extended to include the distinctions between normative principles (當然之理) and natural principles (自然之理；所以然之裡); between empty principles (空理) and substantial or positive principles (實理); between what is naturally so (自然) and what is created through collective human invention (作為) for ordering the world; between what is inborn (先天) and what is learned after birth (後天); between the physical, mental, and spiritual realms and their differing requirements for happiness; between the natural world and human nature; and even between Heaven itself and the principles or "edicts" of Heaven (天理). One would expect that this process of translation and explication in terms of the familiar would have led to serious distortions of Western thought, but while such misunderstandings must certainly have occurred ephemerally among Nishi's students, there is no evidence that his interpretive efforts left a significant legacy of confusion that had to be cleared away by later scholars. This is certainly because the long tradition of Confucian learning was rich enough to be able to provide all sorts of conceptual tools, and it is also because of the degree of Nishi's skill in creating new translation-concepts by making original combinations of Chinese characters or reviving ancient combinations that had fallen out of use.

Needless to say, Nishi was not the only scholar-official who relied on established indigenous concepts to introduce Western thought to Japan; it was a well-established practice. Even the name of the Kaiseijo 開成所 (Translation Bureau)[72] illustrates how Confucian concepts were used to legitimate the opening of the country to foreign ideas. The name is based on a phrase from the *Xici* 繫辭 commentary of the *Book of Change* meaning "open things up to complete our tasks" (開物成務), traditionally interpreted to mean "understand the principles of all things so as to achieve success in all our endeavours." In his teaching and publications Nishi followed the same strategy. For instance, he named his study of logic *Chichi keimō* 致知啟蒙, combining the Neo-Confucian word for "the extension of knowledge" with a word meaning "dispelling ignorance through elementary instruction," or "enlightening the masses."[73]

Indigenous grammars of knowledge construction were combined with Western concepts in the establishment of new fields of learning to serve as the foundation for building a strong united nation founded on the principle of fully utilizing the talents of the educated, regardless of their class background. Nishi's two books on logic remind us that he recognized that its study was the basis for all learning, as well as for all legal judgements, public debate, and governmental deliberations. To him, philosophy was the queen of sciences because of its concern for logical analysis and the systematization of all branches of learning, as well as its concern for finding objective grounding for knowledge. Although utilitarian empiricism later gave way to German idealism as the most popular school of *tetsugaku*, the concern for logic and system, of necessity, remained at the core of the discipline as it went on to be institutionalized and indigenized in Japan and China.

The conception of the academic field of "Chinese philosophy" was also born in an environment of the creative coming together of the Eastern and European traditions of learning, both rooted in the Axial Age and holding similar claims to universality and superiority. In its English form the name was made in Europe, and it was hardly new with the nineteenth century. In its East Asian form it was initially "made in Japan"—at a time when Japan was serving as the "middle ground" between the two civilizations and pioneering the effort to bring them into a common framework. And while modern China has at times attempted to absorb these two Others, at other times it has attempted to exclude them and define them categorically as "not us." Several chapters in this volume demonstrate that this dialectic of inclusion and exclusion has been very much reflected in the development of the field of Chinese philosophy. Yet never was this dialectic carried to the extreme of advocating the rejection of the system of philosophical and academic terminology, including the term for "philosophy" itself, that was worked out by Nishi and perfected by Inoue Tetsujirō at the University of Tokyo in the three editions of his *Dictionary of Philosophy* (*Tetsugaku jii* 哲學字彙, 1881, 1884, 1912). The law of conservation of energy dictated that, once a systematic vocabulary for Western learning written in Chinese characters had been established, along with the institutionalization of the field, one did not start again at the beginning. Alternative translations by Chinese scholars tended to fall out of use because of the wide availability of Japanese translations of Western books and translations from Japanese into Chinese. Once vocabulary has been adopted from one language into another, especially if there are no visible signs of its foreign origin, one simply forgets the foreign origin. Besides, modern academic disciplines are international in nature and transcend national boundaries. Thus it is not unreasonable at all to regard Nishi as the founder of the discipline of philosophy in East Asia, not simply Japan. This is evidenced most concretely by the quantity of his translation words that remain in daily use in modern Japanese and Chinese.[74]

Ironically, in the leading article of the first issue of the *Meiroku zasshi*, Nishi actually advocated the abandonment of Chinese characters and the *kana* syllabary for writing Japanese, in favour of the Roman alphabet. Romanization, he argued, would allow European concepts to be incorporated directly into Japanese, greatly facilitating the task of popular enlightenment.[75] If one compares the 26 letters of the Latin alphabet with the incredible complexity of the Chinese and, even more, the Japanese written languages, especially before their twentieth-century simplification, Nishi's proposal becomes quite understandable, especially as a grand opening salvo of the "civilization and enlightenment" movement, deliberately designed to shock the audience.[76] It certainly did not mean that Nishi wanted to consign his nation's rich tradition of literature and thought to oblivion by making future generations unable to read it. In 1870 he had written, "If at present one wishes to engage in Western learning, it is absolutely necessary that one first study about our own country in both ancient and recent times, then on top of that master the learning of China (漢土), and only then begin one's study of the learning of the West."[77] Fortunately, since Nishi's time it has been impossible to devote oneself to the discipline of "Chinese philosophy" without at least a basic acquaintance with the Western philosophical tradition as well. As this volume demonstrates, if we dig into the modern history of the field, we find a constant interaction of Eastern and Western ideas, each helping to reveal nuances of meaning and significance in the other that had not been visible before.

The very universalism of the discipline of "philosophy" compelled the Japanese and Chinese scholars who discovered it to seek out what corresponded to the concept in their own tradition, both to prove that they could also claim the dignity of being full-fledged "civilizations" in their own right, and to discover what it was in their own thought tradition which distinguished them from, and perhaps made them superior to, Western civilization. Subsequent Japanese thinkers, like Nishi himself, could find genuine "philosophy" in their own tradition only in the schools of thought they had imported from China, which meant that they had to either give it the name "Chinese philosophy" (*Shina tetsugaku* 支那哲學) or group the thought traditions of all three Asian civilizations together as "Oriental philosophy" (*Tōyō tetsugaku* 東洋哲學), while still working to extricate Japan's modern identity and destiny from its Asian background. Nishi stood both at the end of a long line of Edo-period *rangaku* scholars who had laboured to introduce Western learning to Japan by translation through the medium of Confucianism and at the beginning of a new line of scholar-officials who strove to transform what they had learned *directly* from the West into political, economic, military, and educational institutions that would earn their nation full membership in an international community dominated by the Euro-American powers and their concepts of international law.

The accepted interpretation that Nishi used positivism and utilitarianism to dismantle the Neo-Confucian "orthodoxy" of the Tokugawa feudal system, if not the entire tradition of Confucian learning, to clear the way for the importation of modern thought, fails to do justice to the degree to which he drew upon the *whole* system of Confucian learning—including Neo-Confucianism—to make Western philosophy comprehensible to his Confucian-educated audience. It also underestimates the degree of real co-intelligibility that pertained between Western and Eastern learning at the time; both were *evolving* traditions that were not as dissimilar in their state of development as has generally been assumed.

This is not to say, of course, that there was no tension between the new system of Western learning that Nishi was trying to translate and propagate and Confucian learning. Nor was Nishi uninfluenced by the critiques of the latter put forward by a number of Meirokusha scholars, the most famous being Fukuzawa Yukichi. The "creative tension" between the two is embodied permanently in the name *tetsugaku* itself, a compound of Chinese characters designed to name the Western field of philosophy in contradistinction to the existing East Asian traditions of learning, and yet by its very nature calling out to be applied as well to a certain portion of the East Asian intellectual heritage. The question of whether the Western concept of "philosophy" can properly be applied to East Asian intellectual traditions or to what portion of those traditions, because of the demand of "philosophy" for rigorous logic and systematization, was therefore born as soon as the word for the discipline was translated and adopted into East Asian academic vocabulary, and the debates surrounding that question run through the subsequent development of the discipline. In China especially, however, it was never really possible in practice to exclude the native thought tradition from the concept and discipline of "philosophy." Once the word and concept of *zhexue* were transmitted to China in the late nineteenth century, prominent scholars trained in Western thought such as Yan Fu 嚴復 (1853–1921), Liang Qichao 梁啟超 (1873–1929), Cai Yuanpei 蔡元培 (1868–1940), and Wang Guowei 王國維 (1877–1927) all endeavoured to draw Chinese traditional thought and Western philosophy into an interconnected system, quite aware that they were building on the foundations laid down by Nishi Amane and a few other Meiji scholars who had had direct contact with European philosophy.[78] As the discipline gradually became institutionalized, those who objected (like Jacques Derrida today[79]) that the concept of "Chinese philosophy" is actually an oxymoron were a small minority. With the large-scale revival of Confucian studies in China in the past few decades, the intermingling of concepts of Western and Chinese origin continues unabated, although this has also led to calls for the "liberation" of the study of Chinese thought from the network of concepts of Western origin that have hitherto structured the field. That cannot be done, of course, because these "concepts of Western origin" have long since become an inseparable part of the Chinese system of knowledge construction. In fact, the way the discipline of Chinese philosophy has developed and continues to develop both in China and abroad can be seen as the progressive fulfilment of the vision Nishi Amane had of an East Asian system of learning in which the Western and East Asian traditions are woven together into one integrated system of knowledge, each regarded with great respect but also with a critical eye inspired in no small part by the other tradition.

Notes

1   Other fields for which Nishi helped lay the foundations include logic, aesthetics, economics, and law.

2   The number of Chinese students surged after the abolishment of the examination system in 1905, reaching an estimated 13,000 by 1906. In the period 1902–1904, over 60% of translations done in China were of Japanese writings, and there was a marked shift from natural sciences toward the social sciences and humanities. A total of 2,204 works were translated from Japanese between 1880 and 1940, the highest proportion being in the social sciences. See Tsuen-hsiun Tsien, "Western Impact on China through Translation," *Far Eastern Quarterly* 13 (May 1954), pp. 319, 325.

3   As Jing Haifeng writes:

> In the late Qing, Western learning was gradually introduced. After the 1898 Reform it was slowly systematized, and objective writings introducing Western disciplines such as economics, political science, sociology, and philosophy began to appear, along with calls for the establishment of these disciplines. This was fundamentally different from the situation before 1898 where, to distinguish it from Chinese learning, Western learning was lumped together under the [Confucian] category of "investigating things and extending knowledge."

Zhongguo zhexue de xiandai quanshi 中國哲學的現代詮釋 [The modern interpretation of Chinese philosophy] (Beijing: Renmin chubanshe, 2004), p. 163.

4   Even as late as 1850, Takano Chōei (born 1804), a physician-scholar who had studied Western medicine and written an outline of Western philosophy, committed suicide after being discovered in hiding and getting beaten half to death by his captors. See Ellen Gardner Nakamura, *Practical Pursuits: Takano Chōei, Takahashi Keisaku, and Western Medicine in Nineteenth-Century Japan* (Harvard University Asia Center, 2006), pp. 39–40.

5   Sakuma's famous dictum, adopted after the Opium War, was "Eastern morality, Western technology" 東洋道德，西洋藝術, a distinction similar to the *zhongti xiyong* 中體西用 of late-Qing China. Sakuma, like many earlier thinkers who explored Dutch books only for their medical and scientific knowledge, was convinced that the West was incapable of discovering moral principles. On this point, see Richard Reitan, *Making a Moral Society: Ethics and the State in Meiji Japan* (University of Hawai'i Press, 2009), p. 174 note 3.

6   See Fukuzawa's *Bunmeiron no gairyaku* 文明論の概略 (1875); translated by David A. Dilworth and G. Cameron Hurst as *An Outline of a Theory of Civilization* (Tokyo: Sophia University, 1973), pp. 13–15.

7   Letter to Matsuoka Rinjirō (松岡鏻次朗), 1862, in *Nishi Amane zenshū* 西周全集 [Complete writings of Nishi Amane] (Tokyo: Munetaka shobō, 1960–1981), Vol. 1 (1960), p. 8. There is another volume 1 with different content published in 1945 by Nihon hyōronsha, which I will distinguish by the year of publication. It is interesting that as late as 1884, Nishi still refers

to European philosophers as "those who discourse upon the nature and principle" (i.e. "the principles of the nature"). Watanabe Kazuyasu 渡辺和靖, *Meiji shisōshi* 明治思想史 [History of Meiji thought], second ed. (Tokyo: Perikansha, 1985), p. 86; *Zenshū*, Vol. 1 (1960), pp. 153–156.

8   Thomas R. H. Havens, *Nishi Amane and Modern Japanese Thought* (Princeton: Princeton University Press, 1970), p. 27.

9   Vissering (1818–1888) was professor of political economy. After graduating from Leiden, he had practised law before returning to his alma mater as assistant to Professor Thorbecke, who later became prime minister. Vissering later became minister of finance.

10   Havens, *Nishi Amane and Modern Japanese Thought*, pp. 34, 43–44, 49–50, 54; *Zenshū*, Vol. 1 (1960), pp. 7–10, 514.

11   The *Meiroku zasshi* 明六雜志 published 43 issues from March 1874 to November 1875, and Nishi published 13 essays therein, some in serial form.

12   The Rev. Joseph Haven (1816–1874), whose ancestors were of English Puritan stock, was a professor of intellectual and moral philosophy at Amherst College, Massachusetts, from 1850 to 1858, and later professor of systematic theology at the Theological Seminary in Chicago. This book, published in 1857, became the most popular textbook on psychology (or the philosophy of mind) in the US before William James and the experimental method. Nishi translated it for the Ministry of Education.

13   J. S. Mill (1806–1873) was much influenced by the early ideas of Comte and agreed that knowledge must be gained by observation, although he never accepted the dogmas of philosophic positivism and, as an impassioned defender of liberty, he rejected Comte's subjection of the individual totally to society. *Utilitarianism* was published between 1861 and 1863. Its core principle for determining what is ethical behaviour is the "greatest-happiness" principle, the realization of which depends on the spread of knowledge and education.

14   Havens, *Nishi Amane and Modern Japanese Thought*, pp. 51, 94.

15   As a young man, Nishi had been deeply impressed with Sorai's teachings, and their emphasis on the concrete and the physical aroused a serious interest in medicine for the first time, which led to his first contact with Dutch learning.

16   Watanabe, *Meiji shisōshi*, p. 73; Havens, *Nishi Amane and Modern Japanese Thought*, pp. 121–123; *Zenshū*, Vol. 1 (1960), pp. 236–244.

17   Havens, *Nishi Amane and Modern Japanese Thought*, p. 123; *Zenshū*, Vol. 1 (1960), p. 242. In discussing popular enlightenment, Nishi once wrote that the study of law is a good way for people to elevate their character.

18   Watanabe, *Meiji shisōshi*, p. 76; *Zenshū*, Vol. 1 (1960), pp. 276, 288. In the Zhou dynasty, Nishi writes, *li* 禮 included ceremony, manners, and law; that is, law had not yet become separated from morality. The Qin-Han introduction of law and Legalist ideas into the Chinese system of rule as something separate from morality (when "etiquette in the sense of a tool to rule the

world changed its name" to law) was a forward step in the development of civilization, though the legal system never developed to a higher stage beyond harsh punitive law. Havens, *Nishi Amane and Modern Japanese Thought*, pp. 124–126.

19 *Zenshū*, Vol. 1 (1960), pp. 236–244.

20 *Zenshū*, Vol. 1 (1960), pp. 276–287. The Mongol invasions from Korea occurred in 1274 and 1281.

21 Havens, *Nishi Amane and Modern Japanese Thought*, p. 134.

22 *Ibid.*, p. 117. Havens' analysis is also skewed by the fact that, based on publication dates, he regarded *Hyakuichi shinron* as a later and more mature work than *Hyakugaku renkan* 百學連環, whereas Watanabe provides evidence that the former is merely a preface for the latter. If so, the fact that *tetsugaku* is uscd consistently for "philosophy" only in the former suggests pre-publication editing.

23 Reitan, *Making a Moral Society*, p. 24, states: "Although antecedent traces of such views of knowledge can be located in the eighteenth and even in the late seventeenth centuries, it was not until the mid-nineteenth century that this fact-value distinction was forcefully articulated. The positing of fact as distinct from value—an epistemological position requiring the critique of much that Neo-Confucian thought presupposed—was perhaps most clearly put forward by Nishi Amane." In spite of the bow to the rich scholarship on Edo Confucian thought since the publication of Havens' book, this account is still, in my opinion, one-sided, because it continues to assume a complete incompatibility between Neo-Confucianism and "modern" thought.

24 The "Eclectic school" (*setchūgaku*) was founded by a disciple of Kinoshita Jun'an 木下順庵 (1621–1699) named Sakakibara Kōshō 榊原篁洲 (1656–1706), who was versed in Chinese law and institutions, astronomy, divination, and martial arts as well as Confucian teachings. The school was represented in its mature form by Inoue Kinga 井上金峨 (1732–1784). Regretting the strife between different schools of Confucianism, the Eclectics attempted to harmonize them. Kinga came to condemn Sorai learning as theoretically misguided, contributing to its decline, but his teachings—which spread widely among the various domain schools—attempted to combine the best elements of Zhu Xi, Wang Yangming, Jinsai, and Sorai.

25 See Scott L. Montgomery, *Science in Translation: Movements of Knowledge through Cultures and Time* (Chicago and London: University of Chicago Press, 2000), pp. 208–212. Havens also recognizes that there were significant precedents for Nishi's ideas in the variegated world of Edo thought, although at the time he wrote, the old conception that Cheng-Zhu Neo-Confucianism was the official ideology of the Tokugawa feudal system through virtually the whole of the Edo period had still not been deconstructed. See Herman Ooms, "Neo-Confucianism and the Formation of Early Tokugawa Ideology: Contours of a Problem," in *Confucianism and Tokugawa Culture*, edited by Peter Nosco (Princeton: Princeton University Press, 1984).

26 Havens, *Nishi Amane and Modern Japanese Thought*, p. 119.

27 Watanabe, *Meiji shisōshi*, pp. 74–75.

28 The *Cours* (1830–1842) examines in turn each of the six fundamental sciences—mathematics, astronomy, physics, chemistry, biology, and sociology (a new and final science Comte was designing)—providing a way to do justice to the diversity of the sciences without losing sight of their unity. The sciences are related to one another in an encyclopaedic scale that goes from the general to the particular and from the simple to the complex. The law of classification of the sciences also has a historical aspect, giving the order in which the sciences develop. For example, astronomy requires mathematics, chemistry requires physics, and sociology needs to be based on the methods of the biological sciences.

29 The work came out right at the time when the Ministry of Education was beginning to inject huge amounts of money into the creation of a unified national school system teaching Western subjects, and also into the translation of Western books and the hiring of Western scholars.

30 Havens, *Nishi Amane and Modern Japanese Thought*, p. 96.

31 *Ibid.*, p. 107; *Zenshū* 1945, p. 146. Nishi divides philosophy into eight subfields, with logic as the first.

32 Haven similarly distinguishes "physical sciences" and "intellectual sciences," the latter including logic, ethics, politics, and ontology, plus the science of mind, for which he suggests using the new term "psychology." *Mental Philosophy*, pp. 15–16.

33 Nishi found the distinction between politics and morality emphasized not only in Mill (who said the two were not clearly differentiated in less advanced societies), but also in the *Dissertation on the Progress of Ethical Philosophy* (London, 1830) by the legal historian James Mackintosh (1765–1832), of whom Nishi wrote: "This man first discovered the fact that morals and law are of separate derivation." *Hyakuichi shinron*, p. 262; Havens, *Nishi Amane and Modern Japanese Thought*, p. 121.

34 禮樂 is Sorai's "abbreviation" for what is often more fully written out as 禮樂刑政—the totality of ancient institutions established for ordering and governing society.

35 The Ming scholars to whom Sorai credits his initial insight into the historical changes of language are the ancient-style poets Li Panlong 李攀龍 (1514–1570) and Wang Shizhen 王世貞 (1526–1590), the leaders of the "Later Seven Masters" 後七子. When Sorai came across their writings, he was shocked that he could not read them because of their cultivated classical style and frequent use of words or phrases from the classics. See Samuel Yamashita, "Nature and Artifice in the Writings of Ogyū Sorai," in *Confucianism and Tokugawa Culture*, edited by Peter Nosco, pp. 138–165, esp. 141–145.

36 *Benmei* 辨名 [Distinguishing names], in Ogyū Sorai 荻生徂來, *Nihon shisō taikei* 日本思想大系 [Compendium of Japanese thought], Vol. 36, compiled by Yoshikawa Kōjirō 吉川幸次郎, et al. (Tokyo: Iwanami shoten, 1973), p. 244,

as translated by Yamashita, "Nature and Artifice in the Writings of Ogyū Sorai," p. 156. The bracketed words in the quotation are in Yamashita's translation.

37 The "Record of Music" in the *Book of Rites* states: "Music is that emotional force that cannot be changed; ritual is that principle of order that cannot be altered. Music unites that which is the same; ritual distinguishes that which is different. The theory of ritual and music is concerned with governing human feelings." Nishi explicitly rejected the belief of "later Confucians" that 禮 and 樂 are the principal tools for transforming the world, arguing that music should be encouraged just for its intrinsic aesthetic value (*Hyakuichi shinron*, p. 240).

38 For Nishi, both items in the second pair, being based on human nature, belong to *xinli* and their divorce from *wuli* means that their application depends only on human will.

39 See John A. Tucker, *Ogyū Sorai's Philosophical Masterworks: The Bendō and Benmei* (Honolulu: University of Hawai'i Press, 2006), esp. pp. 87–92.

40 Watanabe, *Meiji shisōshi*, pp. 77–78; *Zenshū*, Vol. 1 (1960), pp. 38–40.

41 *Kaidaimon* 開題門 [Introductory Notes on a comparative philosophy], *Zenshū*, Vol. 1 (1960), p. 19.

42 Watanabe, *Meiji shisōshi*, p. 77; *Zenshū*, Vol. 1 (1960), pp. 304–305.

43 Miura Kanō 三浦叶, *Meiji no kangaku* 明治の漢學 [Han Learning in the Meiji period] (Tokyo: Kyūko shoin, 1998), pp. 87–88.

44 Havens, *Nishi Amane and Modern Japanese Thought*, p. 109; *Zenshū* (1945), p. 182.

45 Nishi Amane, *Jinsei sanpō setsu*, pp. 524, 521, 522; Havens, pp. 141–155.

46 *Ibid.*, p. 515.

47 「幸福ハ性靈上ト形骸上ト相合スル上ヘニ成ルノ論」。

48 Watanabe, *Meiji shisōshi*, p. 80; *Zenshū*, Vol. 1 (1960), pp. 558–559.

49 Douglas R. Howland, *Translating the West* (Honolulu: University of Hawai'i Press, 2002), p. 65, calls the 性法 translation a "peculiar oxymoron," meaning that the East Asian concept of "law" was not something that naturally fitted together with the concept of "human nature." Thus the roots of this translation-word clearly lie in Western thought.

50 Havens, *Nishi Amane and Modern Japanese Thought*, pp. 154–155.

51 This concept was given "canonical status" in Neo-Confucianism in works like Zhou Dunyi's *Explanation of the Diagram of the Supreme Ultimate* 太極圖説.

52 From *Hyakuichi shinron*, quoted in Watanabe, *Meiji shisōshi*, pp. 84–85; *Zenshū*, Vol. 1 (1960), pp. 277–284.

53 Reitan, *Making a Moral Society*, chapter 2 and *passim*, points out that the emphasis on the difference between value and fact, or the human realm and the realm of [an impersonalized and devalued] nature, remained the core concept of the epistemology of the academic field of ethics (*rinrigaku* 倫理學)

that was in effect founded by Nishi and systematized in the 1880s and 1890s by the University of Tokyo scholars Katō Hiroyuki 加藤弘之 (1836–1916) and Inoue Tetsujirō 井上哲次郎 (1855–1944), among others. This is an important observation, but fails to take account of the fact that in the field of philosophy that Nishi introduced from Europe, everything is ultimately connected together (by natural law).

54 Joseph Haven, *Mental Philosophy: Including the Intellect, Sensibilities, and Will* (Boston: Gould and Lincoln, 1858), p. 16.

55 Watanabe, *Meiji shisōshi*, p. 83; *Nishi Amane zenshū*, Vol. 2 (Tokyo: Munetaka shobō, 1961), p. 15.

56 The period from 1584 to 1702 is known as the Dutch Golden Age, during which Holland dominated world trade and its science and art were among the most acclaimed in the world.

57 *De iure praedae commentarius* (1604–1605; *Commentary on the Law of Prize and Booty*), translated by Gwladys L. Williams (Oxford: Clarendon Press; London: G. Cumberlege, 1950; Buffalo, NY: William S. Hein, 1995). It was written on commission from the Dutch East India Company to defend—in terms of the natural principles of justice—the company's seizure near Singapore of a Portuguese merchant ship. The ideas expounded in this work were further developed in his magnum opus, *De jure belli ac pacis* (On the law of war and peace), written in exile in Paris and published in 1625 (Published in English as *The Rights of War and Peace, Of the Rights of War and Peace*, or *The Law of War and Peace*) .

58 From this it is clear that Martin and Nishi were not confused or misguided in translating "natural law" as the "laws of human nature."

59 The summary in this paragraph is based on Jon Miller's extensive essay on Grotius in *The Stanford Encyclopedia of Philosophy*. Miller's essay gives the precise location in the work of each quotation. See http://plato.stanford.edu/entries/grotius/.

60 Ilse Nina Bulhof, "The Netherlands," in *The Comparative Reception of Darwinism*, edited by Thomas F. Glick (Chicago: University of Chicago Press, 1974), pp. 269–306 (on Opzoomer, see pp. 285–290).

61 The Groningen School, "a product of the universities," "claimed only Dutch thinkers, such as Erasmus and Arminius, as its antecedents, although in reality, the Groningen School owes its deepest debt to the German pietist thought of Friedrich Schleiermacher." Kathleen Powers Erickson, *At Eternity's Gate: The Spiritual Vision Of Vincent Van Gogh* (Grand Rapids, MI: Eerdmans Pub. Co., 1998), p. 15. On pp. 15–23 Erickson gives a cogent account of the teachings of the Groningen School in the context of the intense theological and philosophical controversies in Holland in the first half of the nineteenth century.

62 Karel Blei, *The Netherlands Reformed Church, 1571–2005*, translated by Allan J. Janssen (Grand Rapids, MI: Wm. B. Eerdmans Publishing Company, 2006), pp. 68–70.

63 Kenneth Scott Latourette, *Christianity in a Revolutionary Age* (New York: Harper, 1958), p. 244.

64 Erickson, *At Eternity's Gate*, p. 22.

65 Bulhof, "The Netherlands," pp. 285–286. Elsewhere, she expands this to say "he accepted the law of evolution not only as the fundamental law of living nature but also as that of history and of the universe as a whole." See Ilse Nina Bulhof, *The Language of Science* (Leiden: E. J. Brill, 1992), pp. 38–41.

66 *Ibid.*

67 Hans Schwarz, *Theology in a Global Context* (Grand Rapids, MI: Wm. B. Eerdmans Publishing Company, 2005), pp. 74–75.

68 "Because pure being and pure knowledge were both expressive of God (with knowledge constituting the 'being to itself' of being, the self-illumination of being), and because a finite being participates, in a partial way, in those absolutes, every act of knowing was not only an expansion of one's own being but an expanding participation in God's nature.... Thus for Aquinas, the human effort to know was endowed with profound religious significance: The way of truth was the way of the Holy Spirit." Richard Tarnas, *The Passion of the Western Mind* (New York: Ballantine Books, 1991), p. 188. For an intriguing click-to-enlarge diagram of 1180 showing Queen Philosophy seated in7 the centre of the seven liberal arts, see http://en.wikipedia.org/wiki/Medieval_philosophy (direct link: http://en.wikipedia.org/wiki/File:Septem-artes-liberales_Herrad-von-Landsberg_Hortus-deliciarum_1180.jpg).

69 The modern vision of the separation between theology, science, and philosophy, of course, was already present in Bacon (1561–1626), reinforced by Descartes (1596–1650) and Newton (1642–1727), and popularized in the Enlightenment, but its full institutional realization took over two centuries.

70 Shortly after Nishi arrived in Holland, he wrote to Hoffmann, "I should also like to investigate the field of knowledge known as philosophy or science, yet distinct from religion, which is not allowed by the law of our land—that field which in former times was represented by Descartes, Locke, Hegel, Kant and others." See Marius B. Jansen, *The Making of Modern Japan* (Cambridge, MA: Harvard University Press, 2002), p. 320, and Havens, *Nishi Amane and Modern Japanese Thought*, pp. 49–50.

71 But was "Heaven" for Nishi correspond more to the concept of "God" or the concept of "Nature"? It makes sense either way. However, in emphasizing that the "principles of Heaven" are not identical to Heaven, Nishi uses the analogy of the relationship between a king's decrees to the king himself, suggesting that the first correspondence was primary (see Nishi's serial essay published in *Meiroku zasshi*, entitled *Kyōmonron* 教門論, "On Religion," which deals with the concept of Heaven in chapter 6). None of his Dutch teachers would have taken the Spinozist position that God and nature are really the same thing. Holland was the most intellectually tolerant country

in Europe, but it was forbidden to deny the existence of God and his Providence, as that belief was regarded as the very foundation of the socio-political order.

72 This institute of Western learning where Nishi did much of his teaching became the core of the University of Tokyo, founded in 1878 (Meiji 11).

73 This work, published in 1874, was based on J. S. Mill's *A System of Logic* (1843) and constitutes the first exposition of form logic and inductive logic in Japan. Nishi's further studies of logic led to a more systematic work on the subject published in 1884 under the title *A New Theory of Logic* (論理新説).

74 The Western-pedigreed concepts that are still expressed using Nishi's translations include the words for academic 學術, technology 技術, art 藝術, science 科學, subjective 主觀, objective 客觀, instinct 本能, concept 概念, idea 觀念, deduction 演繹, induction 歸納, synthesis 綜合, analysis 分解, a priori 先天, a posteriori 後天, proposition 命題, definition 定義, attribute 屬性, entity 實體, affirmation 肯定, denial 否定, reason 理性, sensibility 感性, understanding 悟性, phenomenon 現象, reality 實在, consciousness 知覺, chemistry 化學, and psychology 心理學. Using original combinations of Chinese characters to translate Western terms was a tradition among *rangaku* scholars going back to the eighteenth century, but certainly no one had ever carried it to such an extent. See Montgomery, *Science in Translation,* pp. 228–230.

75 For comparable reasons, the same proposal was repeated in the twentieth century by revolutionary thinkers like Lu Xun and Mao Zedong, and supported by eminent foreign scholars of the Chinese language like John DeFrancis (1911–2009).

76 For an examination of the various proposals for language reform around this time and the reasoning behind them, see Annette Skovsted Hanse, "Leaders in Change: The Way to Official Language Reform," in *Leaders and Leadership in Japan*, edited by Ian Neary (Richmond, Surrey: Japan Library [Curzon Press], 1996), pp. 89–102.

77 Watanabe, *Meiji shisōshi*, p. 81; *Zenshū*, Vol. 1 (1960), p. 272.

78 In 1903 Cai Yuanpei wrote *Zhexue bianhuo* 哲學辨惑 [Dispelling confusion regarding philosophy] in which he defended the field against Zhang Zhidong's 張之洞 claim of its harmfulness, giving a systematic explanation of the relationship between philosophy and all the other fields of learning, both natural and social sciences (Jing Haifeng, *Zhongguo zhexue de xiandai quanshi*, p. 164). Jing also notes (p. 203) that it was not until about 1905 that the term *zhexue* became fixed in China as the term for "philosophy," and (p. 204) that the influence in China of the enlightenment philosophy first transmitted by Nishi was very strong, persisting long after the turn to German idealism in Japan.

79 *Shuxie yu chayi* 書寫與差異, Chinese translation of *L'Écriture et la différence* (Sanlian shudian, 2001), pp. 9–10.

Chapter 2

The Role of Masters Studies in the Early Formation of Chinese Philosophy as an Academic Discipline

John Makeham

This chapter examines the role played by one particular traditional Chinese category of knowledge in the early formation of Chinese philosophy as an academic discipline. In the translation of traditional categories of Chinese knowledge to modern categories of disciplinary knowledge, the writings of the pre-Qin masters (*zhuzi* 諸子)[1] constituted the main corpus of texts that were re-inscribed as the foundational texts of Chinese philosophy. This process culminated in the publication of Hu Shi's 胡適 (1891–1962) *Zhongguo zhexueshi dagang* 中國哲學史大綱 [An outline of the history of Chinese philosophy] in 1919, following his return to China in 1917 to take up a position in the Philosophy Department of Peking University teaching courses on the history of Chinese philosophy. I argue that the revival of interest in Masters Studies (諸子學) in the late Qing provided an essential impetus in this process. I show how the views of late-Meiji scholars strongly influenced the high regard that Chinese scholars came to place on logic—the hallmark of system and order—as a precondition for the development of philosophy; how Chinese scholars made significant efforts to identify logic in the writings of the pre-Qin masters, in particular in *Xunzi* 荀子 and in *Mozi* 墨子; and also how Chinese scholars moved away from the uncritical and unreflective adoption of Japanese scholarly sources to make their own determinations about how to apply paradigms derived from Western philosophy to craft the contours of "Chinese philosophy."

1. The Rise of Masters Studies

Before the mid-nineteenth century, Masters Studies was largely restricted to the study of "masters" texts as historical documents and as sources for historical linguistics. As Governor of Hu-Guang, Zhang Zhidong 張之洞 (1837–1909)[2] noted in 1898, however, "Beginning in the Daoguang period (1821–1850) scholars were fond of using the apocrypha and Buddhist texts in discussing Classical Studies (*jingxue* 經學); since the Guangxu period (1875–1908), there has been an even greater fondness for studying the masters of the Zhou and Qin periods."[3] At the most practical level, major contributions to collating and glossing masters texts—the fruits of a century of sustained evidential scholarship (*kaozhengxue* 考證學)— greatly facilitated the accessibility of those texts, particularly from the 1890s on.[4] A less tangible but related factor was the ongoing legacy of evidential scholarship, or Han Learning (*Hanxue* 漢學) in the broad sense. Evidential scholarship refers to the verification of sources with the purported goal of "seeking what is correct in actual matters" (*shishi qiushi* 實事求是) by employing knowledge and techniques derived from a broad range of disciplines, including philology, history, epigraphy, geography, astronomy, and palaeography. Although the terms "Han Learning" and *kaozheng* increasingly cease to overlap after about 1780, even in the late eighteenth century there is no clear and distinct demarcation between them. Evidential learning had no strict ideological commitment to Han sources. Nevertheless, for many Qing scholars, Han philological works proved to be the key to recovering the lost meaning of the pre-Han texts. This recovery was premised on the idea that Song and Ming sources were sullied with the heterodox ideas of Buddhism, Daoism, and Neo-Confucian thought and that only the Han commentaries had not been corrupted by Buddhist and Daoist notions. The great philologist, Ruan Yuan 阮元 (1764–1849), for example, related that although in his youth he began studying Song writers, he felt he was coming ever closer to the real meaning of the classical teachings as he gradually proceeded backward to Tang, Jin, Wei, and, finally, Han writers.[5]

Another hermeneutic consideration motivating Qing scholars to privilege Han interpretations seems to have been the naïve belief that because there was less historical distance separating Han scholars from the sages of antiquity, their interpretations were more valid than those of later scholars. The following comments by Ruan Yuan typify this reasoning:

> The glosses written by people in the Han period were particularly close to the time of the sages and worthies. This is analogous to people from Wu being able to understand the language of the people from Yue, whereas people from Chu are not able to do so. Or again, while my grandfather was

alive, he saw the physical form of my great-grandfather and great-great-grandfather; I, however, have not. Accordingly, the accounts provided by those who live later are never as good as those who lived earlier.[6]

In his overview of the unfolding of the history of Qing scholarship, leading intellectual, academic, and political activist Liang Qichao 梁啟超 (1873–1929) described the attitude of "Qing learning" as one of "returning to the past as liberation" which he characterizes in four phases:

> First, returning to the past of the Song was liberation from Wang [Yangming] learning; second, returning to the past of the Han-Tang was liberation from the Cheng brothers and Zhu Xi. Third, returning to the Western Han was liberation from Xu Shen and Zheng Xuan. Fourth, returning to the pre-Qin period was liberation from all types of traditions[7] and annotations. Since we have already returned to the pre-Qin period, we must liberate ourselves from Confucius and Mencius![8]

Writing in 1920, Liang's concluding comments reflect prominent developments in the years immediately before and after 1900. Not long before 1900, however, this "liberation" had not yet occurred. This is because the significance of masters and other non-canonical texts was generally seen to be limited to their role as repositories of historical, textual, and linguistic information for use in evidential scholarship, a role typically seen to be subordinate to that of the classics proper.[9] Thus even the philologist Yu Yue 俞樾 (1821–1907)—who commented on the independence of mind and creativity of the early masters—still judged their writings in terms of what they could contribute to "verifying the meaning of the classics." Writing in 1870, he remarked:

> The way of the sages is fully contained in the classics. Each of the various Zhou and Qin dynasty masters also had some insight into that way. Despite the harshness of Shen Buhai and Han Feizi or the quirkiness of Zhuangzi and Liezi, the key point is that each of them wrote books on the basis of the unique insights of their own minds. How different this is from those of later times who, despite having stolen other people's old ideas have yet others emulate them in the multitudes. Moreover, their books [that is, those of the masters] can often be used to verify the meaning of the classics. Thus without even needing to cite the passage in question from the classics, surprisingly the ancient words and ancient meanings can been seen right there [in the books of the masters].[10]

By the late 1890s, however, the swelling tide of Western learning had hastened the demise of the authority of the Thirteen Classics and in so doing had also enabled new conditions conducive to the promotion of Masters Studies. Perhaps with strategic considerations in mind, some initial responses evidence a reluctance to distance the writings of the masters from the authority of the teachings of Confucius.[11] In 1897, for example, social reformer and eclectic thinker Tan Sitong 譚嗣同 (1865–1898) argued that because traditionally the pre-Qin masters had been distinguished from the *ru* (儒) and their writings labelled as heterodox teachings, this gave the impression that the base of *ru* teachings was quite narrow. In fact, he countered, the pre-Qin masters were actually branches of Confucius' school; to disparage any one of them merely served to denigrate Confucius. He then proceeded to subject Han-dynasty historian Sima Tan's 司馬談 (ca. 180–110 B.C.) Six Schools classification to a radical makeover by identifying individual pre-Qin masters and their writings as representative of disciplines such as commerce, military studies, agriculture, engineering, philosophy (*xingli* 性理), diplomacy, law, and logic. Tan concluded: "All of the so-called new learning and new principles of recent times grew out of this."[12]

On the one hand, Tan's views could be regarded as an expression of defensiveness in the face of the sophisticated disciplinary specialization of Western learning. This sort of defensiveness is most clearly exemplified by the widespread contemporary belief in the "Chinese origins of Western learning" thesis: the belief that much of the West's scientific and technical knowledge ultimately had its roots in ancient Chinese teachings.[13] The tactic of appealing to the "Eastern origins of Western learning" (*xixue dongyuan* 西學東源) has a venerable history in China, going back at least to about A.D. 300 when the idea was used in relation to Buddhism (when India was considered to be the West). Following the introduction of Western learning by the Jesuits in late Ming times, this apologist tactic was revived and continued into the Qing period[14] when *Mozi* 墨子, in particular, was widely cited in support of this thesis. Classical scholar Zou Boqi 鄒伯奇 (1819–1869), one of the earliest figures to have revived this trend in the latter half of the nineteenth century, traced the origins of Western mathematics, geometry, mechanics, optics, and even beliefs about heaven and ghosts to *Mozi*.[15] Writing in 1887, Qing diplomat to Japan Huang Zunxian 黃遵憲 (1848–1905) asserted not only that natural science had its origins in *Mozi* but that key Western ethical and political notions were also derived from the Mohists.[16] In 1898, philologist Sun Yirang 孫詒讓 (1848–1908) maintained that the masters were the inheritors and continuers of the teachings contained in the *Zhouli* 周禮 (Book of Rites). Sun was also partial to the "Chinese origins of Western learning" thesis. Rather than dwelling on claims of cultural one-upmanship to dismiss Western learning, however, he emphasized the importance of paying renewed attention to the writings of the pre-Qin masters, in particular *Mozi*.

> Studied nowadays by Westerners, mathematical astronomy, geography, optics, mechanics, chemistry, and the science of electricity were probably generally already fully contained within [the *Zhouli*]. Hence when the Zhou declined, the schools became abandoned, yet it was the masters who could provide a summary account of its main teachings. Such examples include Zengzi's and Dan Juli's discussions of heaven [astronomy]; Guan Yiwu's [Guanzi] and Zou Yan's discussion of earth [geography]; and Lie Yuguan's [Liezi] and Mo Di's [Mozi] discussions of shadows and mirrors [optics] and balancing of weights [mechanics]. These are the most extraordinary and marvelous doctrines. As for the most technically specialist accounts, *Mozi* is the most detailed.[17]

Alternatively, Tan Sitong's views could be understood not as a form of defensiveness but as a type of rhetoric designed to further the promotion of Masters Studies precisely because Masters Studies could be presented as a field of learning in its own right, one with the potential to engage and accommodate the new systems of knowledge being introduced from the West. In 1905, for example, Deng Shi attributed the rise of Masters Studies to the fact that Chinese scholars had discovered that much of the Western learning introduced since late Ming times was compatible with the learning of the late Zhou masters (whom he compared to the schools of ancient Greek philosophy). He identified the reign of Emperor Wu 武 (r. 141–187) of the Western Han as marking the demise of this learning and the beginning of the narrowing of intellectual focus in China's native scholarship, as evidenced by the elucidation of the meaning (*yishu* 義疏) commentarial genre of the Sui and Tang, the study of the nature and principles (*xingli* 性理) in the Song and Yuan, and finally the formal style of writing cultivated by civil examination candidates (*tiegua* 帖括) in the Ming. The consequence of this trend was the final demise of ancient learning. Although the ensuing vacuum gradually led Chinese scholars to turn their attention to Western learning, the introduction of the latter also stimulated interest in Masters Studies. This was because there were normative principles (*yili* 義理) inherent in the writings of the masters that had ample parallels in Western learning, and hence the two traditions reinforced one another.

The normative principles contained within the writings of the masters embrace Western psychology, ethics, logic, sociology, history, politics, and law; acoustics, optics, chemistry and the science of electricity. No matter which one is raised as an example, in each and every case there is a profound correspondence between Western learning and masters learning. When they are compared and checked against one another, the insights to be gained are many. It is for this reason that all those who practice Western learning [in China today] also undertake the study of masters learning.[18]

Another important factor contributing to renewed interest in masters and other non-canonical texts in the late nineteenth century was the perception of their practical value. As Hao Chang observes:

As the philosophical interest in the non-canonical ancient texts spread, interest in them tended to become more practical than theoretical, inasmuch as some intellectuals turned to these texts not so much out of intellectual curiosity as out of concerns with practical problems of life and society. In this way, classical texts such as *Hsün Tzu, Mo Tzu,* and those of Legalism became intellectual resources for the growing moral and political activism of the closing decades of the nineteenth century.[19]

In 1905, for example, Liu Shipei 劉師培 (1884–1919), one of the most influential scholars of the period, wrote:

From the Eastern Zhou period onwards, although the *ru* lineages (*rujia* 儒家) boasted of "investigating things," their actual contribution to fathoming principles with reference to things has been negligible. This is not so for the Mohists, who used learning to seek for the practical. In regard to logic, mathematics, and mechanics, in each case they generally developed the early beginnings of these fields of learning. In addition to Mozi, Zhuangzi elucidated chemistry and mathematics, Guan Yizi elucidated the science of electricity, Kang Cangzi elucidated pneumatics, and Sunzi elucidated mathematics. In some cases only fragments remain or the most essential teachings have been lost, but enough remains to prove that the masters of the many schools all attached great importance to fields of practical learning.[20]

Liu's comments are also relevant for what they reveal about another dimension to the late-Qing revival of Masters Studies: its challenge to *ru* learning (*ruxue* 儒學) and *ru* moral norms. Writing at the same time as Liu, Deng Shi pointed out that Western learning fostered awareness that there were other teachings beyond *ru* teachings, such that people came to look upon masters writings as sources of new teachings and also to challenge *ru* norms directly.[21] Citing the example of Tan Sitong's use of the

Mohist ideal of ungraded concern in *Renxue*[22] to criticize Confucian ritual norms (*li* 禮),[23] contemporary scholar Zhang Yongyi describes it as having served as the forerunner for twentieth-century criticisms of the *ru* and *ruxue*.[24] The most influential early work of this genre is Zhang Taiyan's *Qiushu* 訄書 [Writings to prompt action]. Published at the turn of the twentieth century, *Qiushu* broke the traditional mould in which *ruxue* was accorded an elevated status, by treating the *ru* as just one school among many.[25] In the "Xue bian" 學變 [Transformations in learning] chapter Zhang praised Wang Chong 王充 (27–ca. 100) for his criticisms of Confucius. In the "Ding Kong" 訂孔 [Evaluating Confucius] chapter,[26] he described how the teachings of Confucius and the *ru* were based on those of Laozi; presented Confucius as a mere scribe, as having an undeserved reputation, and as being inconsistent in his doctrines; and portrayed both Mencius and Xunzi as superior to Confucius. Indeed, already in 1897 Zhang had published "Hou sheng" 後聖 [Later sage], in which he placed Xunzi on an equal footing with Confucius and claimed that for over two thousand years the meaning of Xunzi's essays such as "Zheng ming" 正名 [On the correct use of names] and "Li lun" 禮論 [Discourse on ritual] had not been properly understood.[27]

Joachim Kurtz has also drawn attention to Liu Shipei's comment in "Zhoumo xueshushi xu" 周末學術史序 [Prolegomena to an Intellectual History of the Late Zhou] (1905) that the *ru* were but one of the nine schools.[28] Commenting on the "Old Text" (*guwen* 古文) philology that connected Liu with scholars such as Zhang Taiyan, Sun Yirang, and Yu Yue, Kurtz points out that this type of scholarship "continued efforts to illustrate the diversity of China's intellectual heritage," which in turn "led to a serious erosion of the paramount position of Confucius as upheld by the unwavering guardians of orthodoxy." This erosion also encouraged Liu to "design his master plan for a new grand narrative of China's intellectual history that purposefully ignored the traditional distinction between exegetical studies of canonical works (*jingxue* 經學) and philosophical interpretations of non-canonical masters (*zixue* 子學)."[29] For others, however, this erosion of the paramount position of Confucius and the authority of the classics provided the opportunity to contrast the merits of Masters Studies with those of Classical Studies (*jingxue* 經學). Thus in his 1906 essay "Zhuzixue lüeshuo" 諸子學略說 [Brief account of the learning of the masters], Zhang Taiyan differentiated Masters Studies and Classical Studies as follows: "In Classical Studies, the only matter of concern with regard to so-called evidential commentaries (*shuzheng* 疏證)

is examination of canonical codes and institutional standards…. As for Masters [Studies], it is a type of subjective learning that is studied. The essential pursuit is normative patterns (*yili* 義理) rather than the examination of traces of similarity and difference."[30] As a consequence of this process whereby orthodoxy was deemed an anachronism, authority in texts was determined by a significantly increased number of parties. It was precisely this context that enabled Masters Studies to flourish in the first two decades of the twentieth century and gradually to be transformed into philosophy. At the same time, the notion of "subjective learning" which Zhang identifies in the writings of the masters, reveals an understanding of the philosopher as an original thinker. For Zhang and his contemporaries, the pre-Qin masters provided this model.[31]

2. Masters Studies, Logic, and Meiji Scholarship

Central to the connection between Masters Studies and the early development of Chinese philosophy as an academic discipline is the issue of logic. (The idea of philosophy as essentially a logical discipline owes much to J. S. Mill[32]). I begin with an account of the status of Chinese philosophy in late-Meiji 明治 Japan (1868–1912). By the late-nineteenth century, the Japanese had already coined the term *Shina tetsugaku* 支那哲學 to refer to Chinese philosophy as a distinct field of learning. In 1881, together with a course on modern Western philosophy, a course on Indian philosophy and Chinese philosophy was introduced into the Japanese and Chinese Literature curriculum and the Philosophy curriculum at Tokyo Imperial University.[33] In 1894 the academic journal *Tōyō tetsugaku* 東洋哲學 [Oriental Philosophy] was established, and it regularly published articles on topics in Chinese philosophy; many such articles used the term *Shina tetsugaku* in their titles and/or text. This is also the case with the journal *Tetsugaku zasshi* 哲學雜誌, launched in 1897. Between 1897 and 1903, at least five histories of Chinese philosophy—which used the term *Shina tetsugaku* in their title—were published.[34]

In the 1890s, however, the attitude of many Japanese scholars to Chinese philosophy and to the history of Chinese philosophy was highly critical. There was widespread consensus that Chinese philosophy lacked systemization; that in method and organization it was simple and naïve; and that it fell far short of the standards set by Western philosophy. In the 1894 preface to his monograph on Song learning, *Sōgaku gairon* 宋學概論,

young Sinologist Oyanagi Shigeta 小柳司氣太 (1870–1940) reported that in contemporary Japanese academic circles it was widely held that Chinese civilization was stagnant. And although Oyanagi stated that he did not personally subscribe to this opinion, he felt it was easy to understand why his colleagues did: the state of Chinese scholarship and learning "was like a mass of tangled hemp."[35] In the same year he published an article titled "What is Chinese Philosophy?" stating that Chinese philosophical thought was simplistic and naive, and that in terms of methodology and organization it just could not be compared to Western philosophy.[36] For the next several years, similar criticisms became a refrain, a trend no doubt exacerbated by China's defeat in the Sino-Japanese War of 1894–95. Consider the following examples:

> Matsumoto Bunzaburō 松本文三郎 (1898): "Chinese philosophy has always lacked a definite organizational system (組織體系). In order to describe this completely unsystematic thing such that it has some semblance of system is no easy task."[37]

> Shinsai Gakujin 心齋學人 (unidentified *nom de plume*; 1899): "Although most of the masters and the one hundred schools have writings, they can be described merely as casual jottings. They do not venture beyond matter-of-factly shedding some light on a topic. And even in those cases where each individual chapter has its own organizational structure, there is no clear connection with the chapters immediately before and after. Accordingly, because they do not constitute works in which the guiding principles and detailed contents are clearly ordered, they cannot be called systematic and ordered. And even though Chinese Studies has systematic works such as the *Commentaries to the Book of Change*, they certainly cannot be compared to the writings of Western philosophy."[38]

> Endō Ryūkichi 遠藤隆吉 (1900): "The character of the Chinese people is such that they are skilled at narration but weak on summary. That is why the writings by later generations grow more and more fragmented. Unlike Westerners, they have never described the origins of thought and its unfolding so that everything is clear at a single glance."[39]

> Uno Tetsuto 宇野哲人 (1900): "From antiquity to the present, most Chinese writings are fragmented narratives—there is not a single systematic (*keitō* [Ch. *xitong*] 系統) work among them."[40]

These same sorts of criticisms were quickly introduced into China by a growing body of scholars such as Wang Guowei 王國維 (1887–1927) who read Japanese.[41] Wang studied in Japan in 1902 but had been translating Japanese books and articles before then. Upon his return to China he continued to translate Japanese essays, selections from books, and whole books.[42] In 1903 he published an essay, "Disputing Confusions about Philosophy," in response to two memorials submitted to the throne the previous (Chinese) year by Zhang Zhidong and Zhang Baixi 張百熙 (1847–1907), both of whom served on the newly constituted Committee of Educational Affairs (*xuewuchu* 學務處). Wang objected to the critical views about philosophy that Zhang Zhidong had expressed in a memorial (31 October 1902) to Empress Cixi, "Chouding xuetang guimo cidi xingban zhe" 籌定學堂規模次第興辦摺 [Plan to ratify matters relating to the scope and sequential establishment of schools]. Zhang's fundamental position was that:

> The West's philosophy (*taixi zhexue* 泰西哲學) must not be taught [in any level of school].... If scholars admire it simply for the purpose of empty talk, then this amounts merely to its being useless. If, however, it is pursued with unfettered abandon, then its calamitous consequences will be indescribable. There is no principle (*li* 理) that the classics and traditions of China's sages and worthies do not embrace. How possibly could four thousand years of solid principles (*shili* 實理) be jettisoned so as to pursue the empty talk from several tens of thousands of miles away?[43]

Wang was also reacting to the following comments made in Zhang Baixi's memorial (probably dating from January 1903), "Guanxue dachen Zhang [Baixi] zunzhi yizou Hu-Guang Zongdu Zhang [Zhidong] deng zou cidi xingban xuetang zhe" 管學大臣張［百熙］遵旨義奏湖廣總督張［之洞］等奏次第興辦學堂摺" [At Her Majesty's command, Educational Affairs Committee member Zhang Baixi memorializes the Throne concerning the memorial by Hu-Guang Governor-General, Zhang Zhidong *et al.* on matters relating to the sequential establishment of schools], in which Zhang Baixi states:

> The "masters" category—one of the Four Divisions [of traditional bibliography]—is an old style of Chinese learning that has been transmitted for thousands of years. Its doctrines are often compatible with those of Western philosophy (*zhexue* 哲學). Masters Studies would be suitable as a reference [subject] for the Faculty of Letters in the regular university (*zhuanke* 專科), but it is not something that is a pressing requirement for the preparatory university (*yubeike* 預備科).[44] It is respectfully requested that it should not be listed in the higher education curriculum but rather be listed as a reference subject in the regular university. As for the category of

mingxue 名學 (logic), in Chinese the former translation for this was *bianxue* 辨學, what in Japan is called *ronrigaku* 論理學. *Mingxue* and *zhexue* constitute two incompatible schools (*pai* 派). The main purpose of *mingxue* principally concerns the rectification of names, and names and actualities, and clarifying what is the case and what is not the case. There is no harm in it. This is why in the Imperially Ratified Regulations for Schools [then being prepared] *mingxue* must be adopted and *zhexue* put aside and not deliberated.[45]

Wang wrote that the only way for China's philosophical legacy to be promoted and developed was by means of a thorough understanding of Western philosophy: "Philosophy is a type of learning that has always existed in China…. Our ancient books, however, are loosely organized and lacking in structure, are damaged and incomplete. Although they contain truth, it is not easy to find. When compared to the splendid systematization (*xitong* 系統) and orderly formation of Western philosophy, there is no hiding which tradition of philosophy is formally superior."[46]

What did Wang and the Japanese scholars whose views he echoed mean by "orderly," "systematic," "structured"? For some Japanese scholars this amounted to little more than adopting certain sub-categories used in contemporary Western philosophy—such as metaphysics, ethics, natural philosophy, psychology, and so forth—and applying them to one or more Chinese thinker. For example, so as to enable this "mass of tangled hemp" to be "put in proper order," Oyanagi Shigeta proposed "applying the name 'philosophy' to those elements in Chinese scholarship that can be classed according to what is called 'philosophy' (哲學) in modern times. This is in order to imitate the categories of Western learning so as to aid contemporary scholars in their research."[47] When we turn to Oyanagi's *Sōgaku gairon* to see what he had in mind by "being classed according to what is called 'philosophy' (*zhexue*) in modern times," it amounted to little other than dividing Zhu Xi's thought into "pure philosophy" (that is, metaphysics), natural philosophy, psychology, and ethics.

Other scholars emphasized diachronic narrative which highlighted schools and lineages. For example, Akimizu Iki (?) 秋水生 (unidentified *nom de plume*) wrote:

"In promoting the history of Chinese philosophy, the key thing is not simply to be satisfied with setting out the doctrines and biographies of Confucius, Mencius, Laozi, Zhuangzi, Yang Zhu, and Mozi. What really matters should be clarifying just how each school arose, tracing its tendencies and influences over time, and uncovering and elucidating the necessary and universal system [underlying] each school's transformative evolution."[48] Nakauchi Gi'ichi 中內義一 maintained that the aim in writing an ideal history of Chinese philosophy should be "to evaluate those traces transmitted from the past, differentiate points of similarity and difference between various schools (*gakuha* 學派), and systematically (*taikeiteki* 體系的) to give an account of these matters."[49]

More particularly, many late-Meiji Sinologists and intellectual historians identified logic as the hallmark of order (*soshiki* 組織) and system (系統, 體系), and the prerequisite for genuine philosophical discourse, thus throwing into question the status of Chinese philosophy as philosophy. In 1898, Matsumoto Bunzaburō bluntly asserted: "There is no study of logic in Chinese philosophy. Not only do the Chinese lack logic in their speculative thinking, we are not even able to find logical organization in Chinese philosophy."[50] A common view held by these Japanese scholars was that logic had not been a characteristic of early Chinese thought. At most, they were prepared to concede that very occasionally the seeds of logic could be discovered in the writings of early Chinese thinkers, such as in the writings attributed to pre-Qin School of Names philosopher Gongsun Long, who was often compared to Zeno.[51] For example, writing in 1895, Matsumoto Bunzaburō declared that Gongsun Long "rectified the relations between names and actualities," "elucidated concepts," and developed a useful method of argumentation; nevertheless his expositions lacked "organized" structure, so the seeds of logic in early China did not have the conditions necessary for their development.[52] In his history of Chinese philosophy, *Shina tetsugakushi* (1900), Endō Ryūkichi equated School of Names thinkers Gongsun Long and Hui Shi with the Eleatic school of classical Greek philosophy, but emphasized that unlike the Eleatic school, Gongsun Long and Hui Shi did not have a long-term influence on later philosophy. And although he analyzed Xunzi's "Zheng ming" essay, he made no comment on it as a contribution to logic, nor did he discuss the so-called "logic" chapters in the *Mozi*.[53] It is thus not surprising that a few years later, in 1906, Wang Guowei should have echoed similar sentiments:

Although Mozi raised a number of factual matters, he was unable to develop abstract principles. Compared to Aristotle's deduction his contributions pale in significance. In sum, although Mozi's logic (*mingxue* 名學) ... employed the methods of discrimination and verification just as did the Greek school of Zeno of Elea, who sought to prove that things do not change, do not move. After Zeno, however, logic in Greece … was transmitted via the Sophists to Aristotle where it became a proper science. The upshot of this is that there is effectively no place for Chinese people in the history of logic, which is a matter of great regret.[54]

As to why Chinese thought lacked organization and system, Matsumoto Bunzaburō laid the blame on Chinese syntax and grammar:

> Although we might acknowledge the existence of "the Chinese philosopher," in order for a philosopher's thinking genuinely to constitute a distinct body of thought, how could that thought be devoid of a unifying, fundamental identity? The Chinese philosopher's exposition and argumentation are disjointed as they lack a fixed organizational system that links everything together. For the past one thousand years we have been able only to guess what this thought might mean. It must be said that this malady has arisen due to the fact that Chinese philosophy itself lacks rational thought…. From antiquity to the present, China has not produced a single philosopher skilled at logical speculation…. How is it that Chinese philosophers lack logical thought? Our research reveals that the cause can be traced to the inherent character of the Chinese language. The constitution of the Chinese language is different from Western languages and Sanskrit in that it does not use an alphabet. Because of this, it does not have a grammar which reveals declension. [Moreover], the term "grammar" (*wendian* 文典) is not used with reference only to books which explain the rules of language; it can also be used to refer to books which discuss the structure of essays. This sort of book does not exist in Chinese. China never had those writings which in later times came to be referred to as "grammars."[55]

Matsumoto's essay was published in 1898. Four years later, Liang Qichao, then based in Japan,[56] expressed remarkably similar views in an essay arguing that the pre-Qin masters lacked logical thought:

> Although China had such School of Names thinkers as Deng Xi, Hui Shi, and Gongsun Long, they merely dabbled in sophistry and were unable to develop well-reasoned arguments and later had no successors…. The cause of their deficiency was first that they applied their efforts to practical matters without regard to the correctness or otherwise of the logic [of their arguments]. The second reason is that the Chinese spoken language and Chinese writing are not connected, and there have never been teachings on language grammar. As such, syntactic rules cannot be clear.[57]

A year later, in an essay on pre-Qin "logic" (*mingbian* 名辯) Liu Shipei echoed these views.

In later times, however, writing gradually became disordered, increasingly different terms were given the same glosses, and question-begging became common. As the graphic forms of characters changed, the old meanings were lost; and as many loan graphs became adopted, the original meanings were lost. The number of strokes used in characters proliferated; no distinction was made between "full" and "empty" words. Arguments were advanced without anything to refute [counter arguments], and absurd claims were made, clothed in spurious argument. Plain writing was not practiced and the glossing of old terms became inconsistent. How far we lag behind Indian logic (*yinming* 因明) and European logic (*lunli* 論理)![58]

And in his "Zhelixue shi xu" 哲理學史序 [Prolegomena to a history of philosophy] (1905) Liu maintained that the Warring States masters had achieved a level of debate and thought sufficient to be a match for that developed by "white people" (*baimin* 白民). However, this achievement occurred before logic had been developed, making it difficult to attain precision in expression. He proceeds to critique Mencius' "idealism" (*weixin zhi lun* 唯心之論) and Liezi's logic (concerning the notion of the limits of Ultimateless [*wuji* 無極]), remarking that discussions of philosophical matters by the masters are flawed: "Only the great *Book of Change* and *Doctrine of the Mean* [i.e. classics] develop and illuminate the [Aristotelian] concepts of actuality (*xiaoshi* 效實) and potentiality (*chuneng* 儲能)," which he identifies with quiescence (*xi* 翕) and activity (*pi* 闢) in the *Book of Change* and *weifa* 未發 (not yet emerged into concrete manifestation) and *zhongjie* 中節 (emerged to be in a state of due modulation) in *Zhongyong*. He concludes: "Chinese philosophy has relied exclusively on these texts for its survival."[59]

3. China Does Have Logic

Although the view that China lacked an indigenous tradition of logic was widespread in Japan in the years immediately before and after 1900 there were also a number of Japanese scholars who maintained that China originally did have its own developments in logic, even though these lacked systematic formulation. Writing in 1900, Kuwaki Genyoku 桑木嚴翼 (1874–1946) was perhaps the first Japanese scholar to apply himself to the systematization of early Chinese logic. He described Mencius' level of argument to be similar merely to that of the Chinese Sophists and stated that his use of analogy was often inappropriate. However, just as with the Greek Sophists, he maintained that Mencius' thought represents a stage in the emergence of unsystematic logical thought in early China. Compared to Confucius and Mencius, Kuwaki judged Laozi and Zhuangzi to have made a more significant contribution, in particular through their "anti-logic" (the use of paradoxes and contradiction).[60] He described the "Jing" 經 (Canons), "Da qu" 大取 (Greater Pick), and "Xiao qu" 小取 (Lesser Pick) parts of *Mozi* as making a further contribution to the development of logical thought in early China but found the "Jing" chapters extremely difficult to understand. And although *Mozi* had made many contributions to the explanations of logical method, it was extremely unorganized and far from adequately developed. Nevertheless, on balance he affirmed the value of the book's contribution to the field of logic.

He was particularly effusive in his praise of "the formal rules of pure thought" he found in Xunzi's writings, remarking that "the organized quality of Xunzi's logic is no different from that found in Aristotle's *Organon*."[61] For Kuwaki, the core element in Xunzi's logic is his "theory of conception": "Xunzi's study of logic is not concerned with the rules involved in the process of argumentation but provides an account of the main rules that must be followed when creating the 'materials' (that is, concepts) used in the construction of argument." Kuwaki further commends Xunzi for explaining the origin of concepts:

> Before concepts are discussed, it is first necessary to explain how an object represented by a concept is recognized…. This is a matter with which the logic of modern epistemology is in complete accord and may be regarded as evidencing a more profound penetration into fundamental issues than even Aristotle's logic…. Xunzi's aim in rectifying names can be favorably compared to Socrates' aim in elucidating concepts. Moreover, in setting out his abstract account of the rules for the rectification of names, Xunzi employed an organized, systematic method which in some ways may be said to resemble that of Aristotle, and his purpose in rectifying names was the same as that of Socrates [in elucidating concepts].[62]

Not surprisingly, this positive assessment was soon also widely disseminated in China. Thus in 1902 Zhang Taiyan reported that "Xunzi's 'Rectification of Names' essay has been compared with the logic of epistemology by international scholars who regard it as ranking somewhere between the achievements of Socrates and Aristotle. This is the view of Kuwaki Genyoku."[63] The following year, Liu Shipei wrote: "Alas! After the end of the Spring and Autumn period, for a long period of time names were not rectified. Xunzi's 'Rectification of Names' essay proceeds inwards from the stage where things are first named to the feelings produced in the heart. The subtle import of names and principles is dependent upon this analysis."[64] And in 1905, Wang Guowei also implicitly deferred to Kuwaki's account: "Although Xunzi's 'Rectification of Names' essay was unable to provide a theoretical [account of the] development of the doctrines outlined in *Mozi*, he did establish his theory of conception on the basis of experience in everyday life. The solid and precise quality of his doctrine is unique in the history of logic in China. Indeed, not just in China, but also in the classical period of the West, apart from Aristotle's *Organon*, who is able to match him?"[65]

The following passage from Xunzi's "Zheng ming" essay attracted comment from both Wang Guowei and Zhang Taiyan.

> [The basis upon which we judge that things are the same or different] is the awareness that the mind has of the defining characteristics which distinguish things. Only when it rests on the evidence provided by the ear is it possible for this awareness of the defining characteristics to know sound, and only when it rests on the evidence provided by the eye is it possible to know shape. This being so, the mind's awareness of defining characteristics necessarily requires that the sense organ be impressed by the type of thing to which the sense organ [is sensitive]. If the five sense organs come into contact with a thing and do not become aware of it, or if the mind notes its defining characteristics and you can offer no explanation, then everyone will agree that there is "no knowing."[66]

In his 1905 essay Wang wrote:

> What Xunzi says in this passage would have been impossible for someone who lacked a profound knowledge of epistemology. Western philosophers from ancient times until Kant regarded perception to be merely a function of sensibility and devoid of understanding. In other words, perception was taken to be a function of the five senses and not of the mind. Only Schopenhauer in his book on sufficient reason demonstrated that perception possessed an intellectual character…. This was something that Schopenhauer boasted was an unprecedented development of great import which he further verified with reference to facts taken from biology and psychology. When it comes down to it, however, the whole of section 21 of his book on sufficient reason is merely a footnote to this passage from Xunzi. Morever, Xunzi's observation that "If the five sense organs come into contact with a thing and do not become aware of it, or if the mind notes its defining characteristics and you can offer no explanation" surely makes us recall Kant's comment that "Thought devoid of content is vacuous; perceptions that are not

informed by concepts are blind"! The value of Xunzi's epistemology in the field of logic is thus self-evident.[67]

Later, Zhang Taiyan also used this *Xunzi* passage (or at least selected parts of it) to highlight Xunzi's philosophical sophistication (see chapter 3 in this volume).

The above quotations are representative of a mainstream view of Chinese logic, particularly popular amongst scholars who had studied in Japan. The quotations highlight three key points: the high regard placed on logic as a precondition for the development of philosophy; the identification of logic in the writings of pre-Qin masters; and China's failure to have developed a tradition of logic after Xunzi.

In his *Wushi nianlai Zhongguo zhi zhexue* 五十年來中國之哲學 [Chinese philosophy over the past fifty years], published in 1923, Cai Yuanpei 蔡元培 (1868–1940) noted that pioneering translator Yan Fu 嚴復 (1853–1921) also "felt that logic (*mingxue*) was the key to revitalizing Chinese scholarship." As examples of logic, Cai refers to Yan Fu's partial translations of Thomas Huxley's *Evolution and Ethics* (天演論; 1898) and John Stuart Mill's *A System of Logic* (名學; 1905); and his full translation of William Stanley Jevons' *Primer of Logic* (1909).[68] This observation is amply confirmed by Yan's 1896 preface to his translation of *Evolution and Ethics* where he argues that the value of Western learning is that it enables the recuperation of knowledge and insight developed in ancient China but which had subsequently become lost or obscured. Yan also found evidence of logic in the Chinese classical canon:

Sima Qian said "The *Book of Change* is based on the hidden and moves to the manifest and the *Spring and Autumn Annals* infers from the manifest to the hidden." Most excellent words! At first I thought that "based on the hidden and moving to the manifest" referred merely to observing the images (*xiang* 象) and appending commentaries in order to determine good and bad fortune. As for "inferring from the manifest to the hidden," I thought this referred merely to guessing the meaning of Confucius' subtle words of praise and blame. Then when I contemplated the case of Western learning, I noticed that in matters relating to extension of knowledge through the examination of things, it contained the methods of induction and deduction. Induction is to investigate the partial and so come to know the whole; to hold onto the minute so as to join together that which penetrates. Deduction is to settle a myriad of affairs on the basis of axioms; to put in place fixed regularities so as to anticipate that which is yet to be so. I put aside the book [*Shiji* 史記] and got up, exclaiming, "That's it! This certainly refers to the learning contained in our *Book of Change* and the *Spring and Autumn Annals*. What Sima Qian meant by "based on the hidden and moving to the manifest" is deduction. What he meant by "inferring from the manifest to the hidden" is induction. It was as if Sima Qian had told me himself. Both are the most important methods by which to fathom the principles in things.[69]

Yan regarded induction and deduction to be the hallmarks of logic and placed great store in particular on induction. Among the influential commentators on the issue of Chinese logic at the time, however, Yan alone seems to have dissented from the view that there was logic in pre-Qin China. Yan did not find evidence of logic in the writings of the pre-Qin masters nor did he extrapolate on his observations about early Chinese logic.[70]

4. National Learning and the Ambivalent Significance of Japanese Scholarship

Already in 1902 Liang Qichao had proposed the idea of launching a dedicated newspaper on "national learning" to be called *Guoxue bao* 國學報, although it took another four years for the proposal to be realized.[71] The motivation behind Liang's proposal was to foster an environment conducive to the free expression of thought. In an essay published in 1902, "Preserving *rujiao* is not the way to respect Confucius" (*Bao jiao fei suo yi zun Kong lun* 保教非所以尊孔論), he blamed the demise of scholarly learning since Han times on *rujiao* in which Confucius was regarded as a religious leader rather than as a philosopher. (In making these claims he was directly challenging the views of his former teacher and mentor Kang Youwei 康有為 [1858–1927].)[72] By contrast, Liang held up the Warring States period as a model of intellectual vibrancy and freedom.

As it happens, the unfolding *guoxue* movement focused inordinately on the pre-Qin masters. There were, of course, also nationalistic (and hence anti-Manchu) factors involved in this connection. As Arif Dirlik observes:

> Chinese thinkers of the late Qing located the national essence in the late Zhou period, which had witnessed the flourishing of Chinese learning (at least it was becoming Chinese, rather than Zhou, by this period). Indeed, as Kang Youwei had done with reference to Confucianism in the 1890s, *Guocui* writers viewed post-Qin thought to be a distortion of Zhou learning because of its service to imperial rule, which itself had been contaminated by

repeated foreign conquest of China. The latter was "ruler-learning" (*junxue*), not "national learning" (*guoxue*). The proper model for social and political organization was to be found in pre-Imperial texts of the Zhou Dynasty.[73]

Another leader in the *guoxue* movement was Zhang Taiyan. He was also one of the figures at the centre of the confluence of Masters Studies, logic, and Meiji scholarship on Chinese philosophy. In a 1906 lecture given in Tokyo to Chinese students he made the following claim:

> Zou Tefu 鄒特夫 [Zou Boqi] had drawn comparisons between *Mozi* and geometry and physical science, and made many truly fine points [see above]. However, *Mozi* is a work consisting of the theories of logic specialists [or more literally, experts on terms] (*mingjia* 名家)—its intended purpose was not to elucidate matters of calculation. In the past [that is, the past century or so] there was no understanding of *yinming* 因明 [Buddhist logic] and no one had any interest in *faxiang* 法相 [Yogācāra Buddhism—the Indian school associated with the development of *yinming*]; moreover, European logic had yet to be introduced into China.[74]

Accordingly, Zhang infers, it should come as no surprise that earlier generations of Chinese scholars had only a partial grasp of the true import of pre-Qin writings on logic. By *mingjia*, Zhang was not referring to the School of Names; rather he regarded the *Mohist Canons* (*Mojing* 墨經) and *Xunzi* as the core writings of pre-Qin logic:

> In any event, the correct use of terms was not a method belonging to one school. The *ru*, Daoists, Mohists, and Legalists all were certain to have included this learning [in their repertoires], for only then could arguments be established or critiqued. Thus the *ru* had the "correct use of names" and the Mohists had the two divisions of the *Mohist Canons*. Both express the true meaning of logic, which is [also] scattered in [the writings of] the other masters. As for Hui Shi and Gongsun Long, who alone are known as "the *mingjia*," … their methods are but sophistry.[75]

Zhang even appealed to the judgement of Japanese scholar Murakami Senjō 村上專精 (1851–1929) to defend China's native logic: "Some people in recent times have asserted that the three parts of the Indian syllogism are the same as the [three parts of the] European syllogism…. On the basis of this [analysis of a passage from *Mozi* using *yinming* [syllogistic reasoning] Murakami Senjō maintains that the method of *yinming* [Buddhist logic] is superior to the European [syllogistic reasoning]. For

92 · John Makeham

Mozi already [to have been so sophisticated in his account of] 'minor reason' (*xiao gu* 小故) is a wonderful achievement."[76]

It should be noted that even though Zhang here appealed to the judgment of Murakami, his real purpose was to highlight the independent and sophisticated scholarly achievements of pre-Qin philosophy, as expressed in the writings of the masters. This is made plain in the same speech:

> China's science is in a moribund state—only our philosophy will not concede inferiority to that of other peoples. Nevertheless, the philosophy of the Cheng brothers, Zhu Xi, Lu Xiangshan, and Wang Yangming is no longer particularly relevant. The most learned men are the masters of the Zhou to Qin periods, making it difficult to determine whether they or their counterparts in ancient Greece and India were superior. In comparison to [Japanese *ru* philosophers] Ogyū Sorai 荻生徂徠 [aka Mononobe Noke 物茂卿 (1666–1728)] and Dazai Shundai 太宰春台 (aka Dazai Jun 太宰純 [1680–1747]), however, Chinese philosophers are immeasurably superior. Today Japan is undergoing reform, yet Ogyū Sorai and Dazai Shundai are praised just as always. How much more pressing is it that here in China, the thought of Zhuangzi[77] and Xunzi is kept in the forefront of our minds![78]

In the essays that that make up *Qiushu*, Zhang Taiyan cited at least nine different Japanese scholars. The very opening paragraph of the "Ding Kong" chapter cites Endō Ryūkichi's *Shina tetsugakushi*. It is important, however, to determine just how Zhang was using the views attributed to these scholars. As Wang Fansen notes, Zhang actually subjected Endō's views to significant distortion and exaggeration.[79] Endō had intended to praise Confucius, but Zhang attributed opinions to Endō that were designed to diminish Confucius' authority and aura as part of his effort to revive Masters Studies.

Even when early twentieth-century Chinese scholars seem to have simply parroted the views of Japanese scholars, matters are not always so straightforward. Intellectual historian Ge Zhaoguang 葛兆光, for example, has remarked that the contemporary Japanese scholar Sueoka Hiroshi 末岡宏 has shown how Liang Qichao in his 1904 essay, "Theories of Mozi" (*Zi Mozi xueshuo* 子墨子學説), borrowed extensively from Takase Takejirō's 高瀬武次郎 (1868–1950) *Bokushi tetsugaku* 墨子哲學 [Mozi's philosophy] (1902).[80] Sueoka certainly did maintain that Liang had used *Bokushi tetsugaku* as the model to write "The Doctrines of Mozi," but Sueoka further demonstrated that his purpose in writing it was in order to promote the doctrine of altruism in China.[81] Unlike Liang, Takase was actually critical of Mozi's doctrine of "ungraded concern."[82]

Thus already by 1903 we can see that scholars such as Zhang Taiyan and Liang Qichao had begun to move away from the uncritical and unreflective adoption of Japanese scholarly sources. And although they continued to use Japanese-language materials to import paradigms from Western philosophy, they were also starting to make their own determinations about how to apply these paradigms in shaping the nascent contours of "Chinese philosophy."[83] Zhang Taiyan's understanding of "*mingjia*" and Liang Qichao's agenda to promote a doctrine of altruism bear witness to this. Zhang's defence of China's endogenous resources in logic (discussed in chapter 3 in this volume) also serves to underscore a resistance to the perceived hegemonic potential of Western philosophy to deprive Chinese philosophy of its emerging self-identity. In all of this, the writings of the pre-Qin masters continued to be central.

Notes

1   This category includes such figures as Laozi, Zhuangzi, Liezi, Han Feizi, Xunzi, Mengzi, Gongsun Longzi, Mozi, Guanzi, and so forth.

2   Zhang served as Governor of Hubei, Hunan, Guangxi, Guangdong, and surrounding areas between 1896 and 1902.

3   Zhang Zhidong, *Quanxue pian* 勸學篇 [Exhortation to learn], in *Zhang Wenxiang gong quanji* 張文襄公全集 [Complete works of Zhang Zhidong], Vol. 4 (Beijing: Zhonghua shuju, 1992), p. 556. See also the detailed statistics on the number of masters-related publications for each of the Qing reign periods provided in Kobayashi Takeshi 小林武, "Shinmatsu no shushigaku: Zahyō toshite no dentō gakujutsu" 清末の諸子学—座標としての傳統学術 [Masters Studies in the late Qing: Traditional scholarship as coordinate], *Kyōto sangyo daigaku ronshū (jimbunkagaku keiretsu)* 京都産業大学論集 (人文科学系列) 3 (1989), p. 329.

4   Important works include Yu Yue 俞樾 (1821–1907), *Zhuzi pingyi* 諸子平議 [Balanced deliberations on the masters] (1870); Sun Yirang 孫詒讓 (1848–1908), *Mozi xiangu* 墨子閒詁 [Casual glosses on Mozi] (1894) and *Zha yi* 箚迻 [Reading notes] (1894); Guo Qingfan 郭慶蕃 (1844–96), *Zhuangji jishi* 莊子集釋 [Collected explications of Zhuangzi] (1894); Wang Xianqian 王先謙 (1842–1917), *Xunzi jijie* 荀子集解 [Collected explanations on Xunzi] (1891); and Wang Xianshen 王先慎 (1859–1922), *Han Feizi jijie* 韓非子集解 [Collected explanations on Han Feizi] (1896).

5   Ruan Yuan, "Xihu gujing jingshe ji" 西湖詁經精舍記 [Notes from the refined study for glossing the classics at Xihu], in *Gujing jingshe ji* 詁經精舍記 [Notes from the refined study for glossing the classics], Congshu jicheng xinbian 叢書集成新編 [Comprehensive collection of collectanea, new series] edition (Taipei: Xinwenfeng chubanshe, 1985), p. 61.

6   *Ibid.*

7   Here *zhuan* 傳 refers to "traditions" such as the three commentaries on the *Spring and Autumn Annals*.

8   Liang Qichao, *Qingdai xueshu gailun* 清代學術概論 [Overview of Qing learning] (1921; reprinted Taipei: Taiwan shangwu yinshuguan, 1993), p. 13.

9   By "classics" Yu meant the Thirteen Classics.

10   Yu Yue, *Zhuzi pingyi* (1870; reprinted Taipei: Shijie shuju, 1962), p. 1.

11   This same willingness to accommodate Confucius is evident in Tan Sitong's *Renxue* 仁學 [A study of benevolence] (draft completed 1897). One of the basic characteristics of Tan's understanding of *ren* is interconnectedness (*tong* 通), a notion derived from Huayan Buddhism and applied in his efforts to synthesize Confucius' concept of *ren*, Mozi's notion of ungraded concern, the *ālaya* consciousness of Yogācāra Buddhism, the Christian ideal of love, and even theories of ether, centripetal force, and gravity.

12   Tan Sitong, "Lun jinri xixue yu Zhongguo guxue" 論今日西學與中國古學 [On Western learning and China's ancient learning], in *Tan Sitong quanji* 譚嗣同

全集 [Complete works of Tan Sitong], enlarged edition (Beijing: Zhonghua shuju, 1981), p. 399. Publisher, editor, and promoter of the National Essence movement, Deng Shi 鄧實 (1877–1951), also argued that the pre-Qin masters represented specialist fields of learning. Deng Shi, "Guxue fuxing lun" 古學復興論 [On the revival of ancient learning], *Guocui xuebao* 國粹學報 1.9 (1905), pp. 3a–3b.

13   See, e.g., Wang Yangzong 王揚宗, "'Xixue zhongyuan' shuo zai Ming-Qing zhi ji de youlai ji qi yanbian" 「西學中源」說在明清之際的由來及其演變 [The origins and evolution of the theory of the Chinese origins of Western learning during the Ming-Qing transition], *Dalu zazhi* 大陸雜誌 90.6 (1995), pp. 39–45. Online at <http://www.ihns.ac.cn/members/yzwang/wyz3.htm>; accessed Sept. 5, 2005; Jiang Xiaoyuan 江曉原, "Shi lun Qingdai 'Xixue zhongyuan' shuo" 試論清代「西學中原」說 [The theory of the "Chinese origins of Western learning" during the Qing dynasty], *Ziran kexueshi yanjiu* 自然科學史研究 7.2 (1988), pp. 101–108; Benjamin A. Elman, *On Their Own Terms: Science in China, 1550–1900* (Cambridge, MA: Harvard University Press, 2005), pp. 172–177; Ge Zhaoguang 葛兆光, *Zhongguo sixiangshi* 中國思想史 [A history of Chinese thought], Vol. 2 (1998; reprinted Shanghai: Fudan daxue chubanshe, 2004), pp. 504–507; and Theodore Huters, *Bringing the World Home: Appropriating the West in Late Qing and Early Republican China* (Honolulu: University of Hawai'i Press, 2005), pp. 23–42.

14   Zhang Yongyi 張永義, "Jindai Moxue de fuxing ji qi yuanyin" 近代墨學的復興及其原因 [The modern revival of Mohist studies and its cause], *Xueren* 學人 13 (1998), pp. 101–130. For examples of the variant "Mohist origins of Western learning" (*Xixue Moyuan* 西學墨源) thesis, see pp. 109–114.

15   "Lun xifa jie gu suo you" 論西法皆古所有 [Western techniques all existed in ancient China], in *Qing ru xue'an* 清儒學案 [Case studies of Qing dynasty *ru*], Vol. 5 (Taipei: Guofang yanjiuyuan and Zhonghua rendian bianyinhui, 1967), *juan* 175, pp. 3043–3044.

16   Huang Zunxian, *Riben guozhi* 日本國志 [Treatises on Japan], Vol. 2 (Tianjin: Tianjin renmin chubanshe, 2005), p. 777.

17   Sun Yirang, "Zhang Guangya Shangshu liu zhi shou xu" 張廣雅尚書六秩壽序 [Preface in celebration of Imperial Secretary Zhang Zhidong's sixtieth birthday] (1898), in *Sun Yirang yiwen jicun* 孫詒讓遺文輯存 [Edited collection of Sun Yirang's surviving writings] (Hangzhou: Zhejiang renmin chubanshe 社, 1990), p. 315.

18   Deng Shi, "Guxue fuxing lun," pp. 3a–3b.

19   Hao Chang, *Chinese Intellectuals in Crisis: Search for Order and Meaning (1890–1911)* (Berkeley: University of California Press, 1987), p. 12. For specific examples see Liu Zhonghua 劉仲華, *Qingdai zhuzixue yanjiu* 清代諸子學研究 [Research on Qing-dynasty Masters Studies] (Beijing: Zhongguo renmin daxue chubanshe, 2004), pp. 313–316.

20   Liu Shipei, "Likexue shi xu" 理科學史序 [Preface to a history of natural science], *Guocui xuebao* 國粹學報 1.3 (1905), p. 3a.

21   Deng Shi, "Guxue fuxing lun," pp. 3a–3b. Charlotte Furth has pointed to political factors motivating anti-Manchu "national essence" (*guocui* 國粹) classicists such as Liu Shipei and Zhang Taiyan 章太炎 (1868–1936), who "exploited native alternative traditions as a source of political criticism of imperial orthodoxy." Among these, "Ming loyalism, now given a sharpened racialist interpretation, the tradition of critical scholarship identified with the school of Han Learning, and the non-Confucian theories of the philosophers (*chu tzu*) of the ancient Chou" were especially important. See Charlotte Furth, "Culture and Politics in Modern Chinese Conservatism," in *The Limits of Change: Essays on Conservative Alternatives in Republican China*, edited by Charlotte Furth (Cambridge, MA.: Harvard University Press, 1976), pp. 26–27.

22   *Renxue* was published between 1898 and 1901 (draft completed in 1897) in *Qingyi bao* 清議報 in Yokohama and also simultaneously in the Shanghai-based *Yadong shibao* 亞東時報.

23   See, for example, Chan Sin-wai (trans.), *An Exposition of Benevolence* (Hong Kong: The Chinese University Press, 1984), p. 98.

24   Zhang Yongyi, "Jindai Moxue de fuxing ji qi yuanyin," p. 114.

25   This is especially evident in the following chapters: "Ru Mo" 儒墨 [Ru and Mohists], "Ru Dao" 儒道 [Ru and Daoists], "Ru Fa" 儒法 [Ru and Legalists], "Ru Xia" 儒俠 [Ru and Knights], and "Ru Bing" 儒兵 [Ru and Militarists].

26   "Ding Kong" was completed in 1902 but not included in *Qiushu* until the 1904 edition.

27   As contemporary scholar Wang Fansen 王汎森 points out, this essay was written in response to an anti-Xunzi movement in the late Qing initiated by a young Liang Qichao (who at the time still aligned himself with New Text scholarship), Tan Sitong, and other New Text partisans. Wang Fansen, *Zhang Taiyan de sixiang ji qi dui ruxue chuantong de chongji* 章太炎的思想及其對儒學傳統的衝擊 [Zhang Taiyan's thought and its assault on the *ruxue* tradition] (Taipei: Shibao wenhua chuban youxian gongsi, 1985), p. 31. See also Liang Qichao, *Qingdai xueshu gailun*, pp. 138–139.

28   Liu Shipei, *Liu Shipei quanji* 劉師培全集 [The complete works of Liu Shipei], Vol. 1 (Beijing: Zhongguo zhongyang dangxiao chubanshe, 1997), p. 500b.

29   Joachim Kurtz, *The Discovery of Chinese Logic: The Genealogy of an Invented Tradition* (Leiden: Brill, forthcoming), pre-copyedited manuscript, p. 376. Chapter 4, "Heritage Unearthed: The Discovery of Chinese Logic," provides an informative and richly detailed account of the efforts made by four scholars—Liu Shipei, Zhang Tiyan, Liang Qichao, and Wang Guowei—to recover a legacy of logic from ancient China.

30   Zhang Taiyan, "Zhuzixue lüeshuo," 諸子學略説 in *Zhang Taiyan zhenglun xuanji* 章太炎政論選集 [Selected political writings of Zhang Taiyan], 2 Vols., edited by Tang Zhijun 湯志鈞 (Beijing: Zhonghua shuju, 1977), Vol. 1, pp. 286.

31 Indeed, a similar sentiment had been expressed by Yu Yue in 1870 (already cited above): "Each of the various Zhou and Qin dynasty masters…. wrote books on the basis of the unique insights of their own minds."

32 As Barry Steben notes in the opening chapter to this volume, Nishi Amane's 1874 study of logic, *Chichi keimō* 致知啟蒙, was based on J. S. Mill's *A System of Logic* (1843).

33 Sakade Yoshinobu 阪出祥神, *Tōzai Shinoroji jijō* 東西シノロジ事情 [Matters Sinological, East and West] (Tokyo: Tōhō shoten, 1994), p. 21.

34 Kanzaki Issaku 神崎一作 (1867–1938), *Shina tetsugakusha shōten* 支那哲學者小傳 [Brief biographies of Chinese philosophers] (1897); Matsumoto Bunzaburō 松本文三郎 (1869–1944), *Shina tetsugakushi* 支那哲學史 [A history of Chinese philosophy] (between 1890 and 1902); Shimada Kin'ichi 島田鈞一 (1866–1937), *Shina tetsugaku: Shūdai shoshiryaku* 支那哲學 (周代諸子略) [A history of Chinese philosophy: An account of the Zhou-dynasty masters] (1899); Endō Ryūkichi 遠藤隆吉 (1874–1948), *Shina tetsugakushi* 支那哲學史 [A history of Chinese philosophy] (1900); and Nakauchi Gi'ichi 中內義一 (1869–?), *Shina tetsugakushi* 支那哲學史 [A history of Chinese philosophy] (1903).

35 Oyanagi Shigeta, *Sōgaku gairon* [Overview of Song learning] (Tokyo: Tetsugaku shoin, 1894), preface p. 5.

36 Oyanagi Shigeta, "Shina no tetsugaku to wa ikaga naru mono naru ka" 支那の哲學とは如何なる者なるか [What is Chinese philosophy?], *Rikugō zasshi* 六合雜誌 175 (1894), pp. 32, 34.

37 Matsumoto Bunzaburō, "Shina tetsugaku ni tsuite (tsuzuku)" 支那哲學について (續) [On Chinese philosophy (continued)], *Tōyō tetsugaku* 東洋哲學, 5.4 (1898), p. 228.

38 Shinsai Gakujin, "Shina tetsugaku no kenkyū" 支那哲學の研究 [Research on Chinese Philosophy], *Tōyō tetsugaku* 東洋哲學, 6.7 (1899), p. 327.

39 Endō Ryūkichi, *Shina tetsugashi* 支那哲學史 [A History of Chinese philosophy] (Tokyo: Kinkōdō kabushiki geisha, 1900), preface, p. 2.

40 Uno Tetsuhito, "Endō Ryūkichi gakushi cho *Shina tetsugakushi* o yomu" 遠藤隆吉學士著《支那哲學史》を讀む [On reading Endō Ryūkichi's *A History of Chinese Philosophy*], *Tetsugaku zasshi* 哲學雜誌, 164 (1900), p. 815.

41 Qian Ou 錢鷗, "Seinen jidai no Ō Kokui to Meiji gakujutsu bunka—*Kyōiku Sekai* zasshi o megutte 青年時代の王國維と明治學術文化—『教育世界』雜誌をめぐって [The young Wang Guowei and Meiji academic culture: Focusing on the journal *Education World*], *Nippon Chūgoku gakkaihō* 日本中国学会報 48 (1996), p. 259. Qian lists a number of unattributed articles published in *Jiaoyu shijie* which modern scholars claim were written by Wang; Qian shows that most were translations from Japanese sources.

42 Many of the essays and selections were published in the journal *Jiaoyu shijie* 教育世界 launched that same year by Luo Zhenyu 羅振玉 (1866–1940). This influential journal was published fortnightly and ran until 1908. Wang was

involved in editing work and translating for the journal from 1901, and he took principal responsibility for editing in 1904.

43 *Zhongguo jindai jiaoyushi ziliao huibian: xuezhi yanbian* 中國近代教育史資料彙編—學制演變 [Collection of materials on the history of education in modern China: Changes in education systems], edited by Qu Xingui 璩鑫圭 and Tang Liangyan 唐良炎 (Shanghai: Shanghai jiaoyu chubanshe, 1991), pp. 108–109.

44 Timothy Weston explains that Zhang Baixi's curriculum plan for the Imperial University was divided into four tracks: "the *daxue zhuanmen fenke* (regular university); the *yubeike* (preparatory university); the *shixue guan* (the officials' college); and the *shifan guan* (the teachers' college)." See his *The Power of Position: Beijing University, Intellectuals, and Chinese Political Culture, 1898–1929* (Berkeley: University of California Press, 2004), p. 53.

45 In *Zhongguo jindai xuezhi shiliao* 中國近代學制史料 [Historical materials on China's modern school system], second series, Vol. 1, edited by Zhu Youhuan 朱有瓛 (Shanghai: Huadong shifan daxue chubanshe, 1987), p. 66.

46 Wang Guowei, "Zhexue bianhuo" 哲學辨惑 [Disputing confusions about philosophy] (1903), in *Wang Guowei zhexue meixue lunwen jiyi* 王國維哲學美學論文輯軼 [Edited collection of Wang Guowei's lost essays on philosophy and aesthetics], compiled by Fo Chu 佛雛 (Shanghai: Huadong shifandaxue chubanshe, 1993), pp. 5–6.

47 Oyanagi Shigeta, *Sōgaku Gairon*, preface, p. 5.

48 Akimizu Iki, "Shina tetsugakushi kenkyō no hitsuyō" 支那哲學史研究の必要 [The need to study the history of Chinese philosophy], *Tōyō tetsugaku* 東洋哲學 4.1 (1897), p. 43.

49 Nakauchi Gi'ichi, *Shina tetsugakushi* 支那哲學史 [A history of Chinese philosophy] (Tokyo: Hakubunkan, 1903), p. 4.

50 Matsumoto Bunzaburō, "Shina tetsugaku ni tsuite" 支那哲學について [On Chinese philosophy], *Tōyō tetsugaku* 東洋哲學 5.4 (1898), p. 172.

51 Sakade Yoshinobu, *Tōzai Shinoroji jijō*, pp. 95–96.

52 Matsumoto Bunzaburō, "Kōson Ronshi" 公孫龍子 [Gongsun Longzi], *Tōyō tetsugaku* 東洋哲學 2.4 (1895), pp. 145–150.

53 Sakade Yoshinobu, *Tōzai Shinoroji jijō*, p. 97.

54 Wang Guowei, "Mozi zhi xueshuo" 墨子之學説 [The theories of Mozi] (1906), in *Wang Guowei zhexue meixue lunwen jiyi*, pp. 137–138.

55 Matsumoto Bunzaburō, "Shina tetsugaku ni tsuite," pp. 172, 170, 171.

56 After the failure of the reform movement in China in 1898, Liang fled to Japan and remained there for the next fourteen years.

57 Liang Qichao, "Xian-Qin xuepai yu Xila Yindu bijiao" 先秦學派與希臘印度比較 [Pre-Qin schools in comparison to Greek and Indian (schools)] (1902), later reproduced in his *Lun Zhongguo xueshu sixiang bianqian zhi dashi* 論中國學術思想變遷之大勢 [General tendencies in the development of Chinese thought] (Taibei: Taiwan guji chuban youxian gongsi, 2005), p. 55. Even though a year later Liang fundamentally changed his views about many

issues, including early Chinese logic and language, some of these ideas about the Chinese language remained pervasive for much of the twentieth century.

58 Liu Shipei, *Rangshu* 攘書 [Book of expulsion] (1903), in his *Liu Shenshu xian-sheng yishu* 劉申叔先生遺書 [Surviving works of Liu Shipei] (Wuning: Nan shi 南氏, 1936), p. 30b.

59 Liu Shipei, "Zhelixue shi xu" 哲理學史序 [Prolegomena to a history of philosophy], *Guocui xuebao* 國粹學報 3 (1905), pp. 4a, 4b.

60 Kuwaki Genyoku, "Shina kodai ronri shisō hattatsu no gaisetsu" 支那古代論理思想發達の概説 [An overview of the development of China's ancient ethical thought], *Tetsugaki zasshi* 哲學雜誌 163 (1900), pp. 742, 743.

61 Kuwaki Genyoku, "Shina kodai ronri shisō hattatsu no gaisetsu (tsuzuku)" 支那古代論理思想發達の概説 (續) [An overview of the development of China's ancient ethical thought (continued)], *Tetsugaki zasshi* 哲學雜誌 164 (1900), pp. 803, 808.

62 Kuwaki Genyoku, "Junshi no ronri setsu" 荀子の論理説 [Xunzi's logical theories] (1898), in his *Tetsugaku gairon* 哲學概論 [Overview of philosophy] (Tokyo: Waseda daigaku shuppansha, 1918 [1900]), pp. 457, 458, 459. In his "Shina kodai ronri shisō hattatsu no gaisetsu (tsuzuku), " p. 809 he provides a similar account. For an informative discussion of Kuwaki's appraisals of the development of logical thought in early China, see Kurtz, *The Discovery of Chinese Logic*, pp. 353–359.

63 Zhang Taiyan, "Ding Kong," in *Qiushu pingzhu* 訄書評註 [Critically anno-tated *Writings to Prompt Action*], edited by Liang Tao 梁濤 (Xi'an: Shaanxi renmin chubanshe, 2003), p. 39.

64 Liu Shipei, *Rangshu*, p. 12b.

65 Wang Guowei, "Zhou-Qin zhuzi zhi mingxue" 周秦諸子之名學 [The logic of the Zhou-Qin masters] (1905), in *Wang Guowei zhexue meixue lunwen jiyi*, pp. 139, 142. According to Kobayashi Takeshi 小林武, in 1904 Wang trans-lated Kuwaki Genyoku's article into Chinese and published it under the title "Xunzi zhi mingxue shuo" 荀子之名學説 [Xunzi's theories on logic], *Jiaoyu shijie* 教育世界 77 (1904). See Kobayashi, "Shoki Ō Kokui to shushigaku" 初期王國維と諸子學 [Early period Wang Guowei and Masters Studies], *Kyōto sangyo daigaku ronshū (jimbunkagaku keiretsu)* 京都産業大學論集 (人文科學系列) 29 (2002), p. 5. Joachim Kurtz, *The Discovery of Chinese Logic*, p. 420, comments that despite Wang's enthusiastic assessment, even Xunzi could not shake Wang's conviction that "Chinese logic was no more than an archival curiosity. The brief moment of logical brilliance that had produced the rudimentary theories of definition, inference and conception [Wang] had reconstructed in his articles had been stifled far too early to create more lasting effects or incite more sophisticated insights."

66 John Knoblock, *Xunzi: A Translation and Study of the Complete Works*, Vol. 3 (Stanford: Stanford University Press, 1994), pp. 129–130. NB: Knoblock transposed the final Chinese sentence to the beginning of the translated passage.

67 Wang Guowei, "Zhou-Qin zhuzi zhi mingxue," p. 145.

68 See his *Cai Yuanpei xuanji* 蔡元培選集 [Selected writings of Cai Yuanpei], Vol. 1 (n.p.: Zhejiang jiaoyu chubanshe, 1993), pp. 71, 72.

69 Yan Fu, *Yan yi mingzhu congkan* 嚴譯名著叢刊 [Collection of famous writings translated by Yan Fu] (Shanghai: Shangwu yinshuguan, 1931), preface, p. 1.

70 For a detailed study of Yan Fu's discovery of European logic and his role in raising the profile of logic in China, see Joachim Kurtz, *The Discovery of Chinese Logic*, chapter 3.

71 The Society for the Preservation of National Learning (*Guoxue baocun hui* 國學保存會), founded in 1905, published *Guocui xuebao* 國粹學報 between 1905 and 1912.

72 Liang Qichao, "Bao jiao fei suo yi zun Kong lun," in *Liang Qichao zhexue sixiang lunwen xuan* 梁啟超哲學思想論文選 [Selected essays on Liang Qichao's philosophical thought], edited by Ge Maochun 葛懋春 and Jiang Jun 蔣俊 (Beijing: Beijing daxue chubanshe, 1984), pp. 95–103. Kang's own reliance on the non-canonical texts also served to undermine his efforts to promote Confucius. Kang maintained that the Six Classics had all been written by Confucius and that the historical content of the Six Classics was merely to serve Confucius' own ideological vision by "Drawing on the [idealized] precedents of the past in order to reform the [present] political system" (*tuogu gaizhi* 托古改制). As Wang Fansen has argued, Kang had long drawn upon masters writings to support his own account of the history of ancient China, and he continued to do so when he wrote *Kongzi gaizhi kao* 孔子改制考 [A study of Confucius' institutional reforms] (1898): "It is thus apparent that when he set down his account of late Zhou history, he believed that the [writings of] the masters were more reliable than those of *ru* texts." Wang Fansen, *Gushibian yundong de xingqi* 古史辨運動的興起 [The rise of the "Disputing the history of antiquity" movement] (Taipei: Yunchen wenhua shiye gongsi, 1987), p. 271.

73 Arif Dirlik, "Guoxue/National Learning in the Age of Global Modernity," paper presented at the conference "Qinghua guoxue yanjiuyuan de jingshen" 清華國學研究院的精神 [The spirit of the Tsinghua National Studies Research Institute], 1–3 November 2009, Tsinghua University, Beijing.

74 Zhang Taiyan, "Dongjing liuxuesheng huanyinghui shuoci" 東京留學生歡迎會説辭 [Speech at the reception given by Chinese students studying in Tokyo], in *Zhang Taiyan zhenglun xuanji*, Vol. 1, pp. 272–273.

75 Zhang Taiyan, "Zhuzixue lüeshuo" 諸子學略説 [Brief account of the learning of the masters], in *Zhang Taiyan zhenglun xuanji*, Vol. 1, pp. 300–301.

76 *Ibid.*, p. 304. See also Murakami Senjō, *Inmyōgaku zensho* 因明學全書 [Complete writings on *yinming*] (Tokyo: Tetsugaku shoin, 1891), pp. 26–27.

77 For his views on Zhuangzi, see chapter 3 in this volume.

78 Zhang Taiyan, "Dongjing liuxuesheng huanyinghui shuoci," p. 279.

79 Wang Fansen, *Zhang Taiyan de sixiang ji qi dui ruxue chuantong de chongji*, p. 182.

80 Ge Zhaoguang 葛兆光, *Xichao you dongfeng* 西潮又東風 [Western tide and Eastern wind] (Shanghai: Shanghai guji chubanshe, 2006), p. 174.

81 Liang's views on altruism and benefiting others are a key element in his theory of citizenship, as set out in his *Xinmin shuo* 新民説 [Theory of a new citizenry] written mostly during 1902 and 1903. In this connection, see Hazama Naoki, "On Liang Qichao's Conceptions of *Gong* and *Si*: 'Civic Virtue' and 'Personal Virtue' in *Xinminshuo*," in *The Role of Japan in Liang Qichao's Introduction of Modern Western Civilization to China*, edited by Joshua Fogel (Berkeley: University of California Berkeley, Center for Chinese Studies, 2004), pp. 205–221.

82 Sueoka Hiroshi 末岡宏, "Ryū Keichō to Nippon no Chūgoku tetsugaku kenkyū" 梁啟超と日本の中國哲學研究, in *Kōdō Kenkyū Ryū Keichō: Seiyō Kindai Shisō Juyō to Meiji Nippon* 共同研究梁啟超：西洋近代思想受容と明治日本 [Collaborative research on Liang Qichao: Meiji Japan and the reception of modern Western thought], edited by Hazama Naoki 狹間直樹 (Tokyo: Misuzu shobō, 1999); Chinese edition, *Liang Qichao, Mingzhi Riben, Xifang* 梁啟超，明治日本，西方 [Liang Qichao, Meiji Japan, the West], edited by Hazama Naoki (Beijing: Shehuikexue chubanshe, 2001). In this connection we also note Liang Qichao's essay, "Jinshi diyi da zhe Kangde zhi xueshuo" 近世第一大哲康得之學説 [The teachings of the greatest philosopher of modern times: Kant], published seriatum between 1903 and 1904, in *Liang Qichao zhexue sixiang lunwen xuan*, pp. 151–169. Although Liang's understanding of Kant was clearly indebted to Nakae Chōmin's 中江兆民 (1847–1901) *Rigaku enkakushi* 理學沿革史 (1886), which in turn is a translation of Alfred Fouillée, *Histoire de la philosophie* (1875), as Huang K'o-wu shows, "unlike Nakae's translation, Liang's essay does not simply focus on the introduction of Western theories. Liang, influenced by the Japanese philosophical world of his time, was also attempting to engage in a dialogue between East and West." See Huang K'o-wu, "Liang Qichao and Immanuel Kant," *The Role of Japan in Liang Qichao's Introduction of Modern Western Civilization to China*, p. 145.

83 These comments apply equally to Cai Yuanpei's *Zhongguo lunlixueshi* 中國倫理學史 [A history of Chinese ethics] (*circa* 1910). Cai relates that this book was based on Kimura Takatarō (1870–1931) 木村鷹太郎, *Tōyō Seiyō rinrigakushi* 東洋西洋倫理學史 [A history of ethics East and West] (1898) and an undisclosed work by Kubo Tokuji 久保得二 (1875–1934). The difference in content and arrangement between Cai's book and Kimura's book suggests that this was less a case of using the Japanese work as a "foundation" than it was a case of major reworking. I have used the version in *Cai Yuanpei xuanji*, Vol. 2, pp. 715, 716.

Chapter 3

Zhang Taiyan, Yogācāra Buddhism, and Chinese Philosophy

John Makeham

Historians generally describe Zhang Binglin 章炳麟 (Taiyan 太炎; 1869–1936) as an anti-Manchu revolutionary and treat his Buddhism as subordinate to this larger political project. Far less commonly understood is Zhang's role in preparing the groundwork for the establishment of Chinese philosophy as an academic discipline.[1] Like a number of influential figures of the day, Zhang regarded Yogācāra as a sophisticated knowledge system which could serve as an authoritative alternative to the knowledge systems being introduced from the West. For Zhang it was an indigenized intellectual resource which could be co-opted to counter the challenges posed by the logic, philosophy (then including psychology), and science of the West, even if that did mean adopting the categories of the West for that engagement.

I begin this chapter by showing how Zhang attempted to build a philosophical edifice on the foundations of an ontology and cognitive epistemology that exclusively privileged the Yogācāra Buddhist teachings of the "three natures" (三性; *tri-svabhāva*) and the "four aspects of cognition" (四分).[2] I then turn to elucidate Zhang's belief that Buddhist logic (*yinming* 因明)[3] enables one to uncover the true meaning of certain pre-Qin writings on logic and reasoning in a way that Western philosophy cannot. Against the backdrop of an intellectual climate in Japan and China during the decades either side of 1900, in which a premium had come to be placed on logic as a precondition for the development of philosophy, Zhang was one of the first Chinese intellectuals to follow the lead of Japanese scholars such as Kuwaki Genyoku 桑木嚴翼 (1874–1946) and Murakami Senjō 村上專精 (1851–1929) in maintaining that classical Chinese philosophers had developed indigenous forms of logic. Significantly, he further argued that Chinese versions of Yogācāra texts on Buddhist logic and reasoning—having only recently become available again after a hiatus of many centuries—made it possible once again to gain a proper understanding of China's earliest writings on logic.

In the second half of the chapter I show how Zhang applied the benchmark of Yogācāra Buddhist philosophy to assess the philosophical merit of individual pre-Qin texts such as *Xunzi, Mozi,* and *Zhuangzi.* I argue that Zhang sought to establish that early Chinese texts "bear witness" to insights into realities which transcend individual cultures but are most fully and systematically articulated in Yogācāra systems of learning; and that classical Chinese philosopher-sages had attained an awareness of the highest truths, evidence of which can be found in their writings. In short, Zhang used Yogācāra to affirm the value of "Chinese philosophy" and, in doing so, helped shape its early definition.

1. Yogācāra Buddhism

Yogācāra (*Yujia xing pai* 瑜伽行派; Yogic practice) is one of the two most influential philosophical systems of Indian Buddhism, along with Madhyamaka. As the name implies, it focuses on meditative practice, as well as epistemology and logic. Competing traditions of Yogācāra thought were first introduced into China during the sixth century, with the *Weishi* 唯識 (Skt. *Vijñaptimātra;* nothing but consciousness) school rising to pre-eminence in the seventh century. By the Yuan dynasty (1206–1368), however, the major commentaries of this school had ceased being transmitted in China, and it was not until the end of the nineteenth century that a number of them were re-introduced into China from Japan where their transmission had been uninterrupted. Crucial to this revival was the friendship between Japanese scholar Nanjō Bun'yū 南條文雄 (1894–1927) and lay Chinese Buddhist scholar Yang Wenhui 楊文會 (1837–1911). Between 1891 and 1896, Nanjō sent a total of 235 Buddhist texts to Yang, including 30 Yogācāra texts that had long ceased being transmitted in China.[4]

Within the context of a broader renewal of interest in traditional philosophical writings (including other indigenous Chinese Mahāyāna texts) in the late Qing, the corpus of Yogācāra writings attracted unparalleled attention. China's Yogācāra revival—in particular the *Weishi* school—from the late 1890s to the 1930s was spearheaded by two generations of prominent intellectuals, including Yang Wenhui, Wen Tingshi 文廷式 (1856–1904), Tan Sitong 譚嗣同 (1865–1898), Ouyang Jingwu 歐陽竟無 (1871–1943), Liang Qichao 梁啟超 (1873–1929), Lin Zaiping 林宰平

(1879–1960), Han Qingjing 韓清淨 (1884–1949), Xie Wuliang 謝無量 (1884–1964), Xiong Shili 熊十力 (1885–1968), Chen Daqi 陳大齊 (1886–1983), Taixu 太虛 (1890–1947), Tang Yongtong 湯用彤 (1893–1964), Liang Shuming 梁漱溟 (1893–1988), Zhang Taiyan, and Lü Cheng 呂澂 (1896–1989). Liang Shuming and Xiong Shili were foundational figures in the early history of the Philosophy Department at Peking University[5] and, although they took issue with Zhang Taiyan's understanding of Yogācāra thought, both were influenced by him, as indeed was Hu Shi 胡適 (1891–1962) (see chapter 5 in this volume).[6]

Why was Yogācāra so attractive to Chinese intellectuals of that period? A key factor was the judgment that, just like modern scholarship derived from the West, Yogācāra learning was characterized by organized, systematized thought and concepts. Zhang Taiyan noted that he found *Weishi* easy to understand because it was essentially concerned with *mingxiang* 名相 (definitions of terms), matters in which he had been well grounded due to his rigorous training in the evidential learning techniques associated with Han Learning approaches to Classical Studies (*jingxue* 經學).[7] Moreover,

> There is a good reason for my singular respect for *faxiang* 法相 [an alternative name for *Weishi*]. Modern scholarship [in China] has gradually followed the path of "seeking verification in actual events." Of course the detailed analysis carried out by Han Learning scholars was far superior to that which scholars in the Ming were able to achieve. With the beginnings of science [introduced in China in the late-nineteenth century] scholars applied themselves with even greater precision. It is for this reason that *faxiang* learning was inappropriate to the situation in China during the Ming but most appropriate in modern times. This was brought about by the trends that have informed the development of scholarship.[8]

Zhang also approvingly cited the words of his friend Gui Bohua 桂伯華, who had also studied under Yang Wenhui: "Gui Bohua also said, 'Over the recent three hundred years the style of scholarship has become vastly different from that of the Song and Ming periods. The evidential scholarship of Han Learning was the forerunner of science, and science is the forerunner of *faxiang*. This is because that which *faxiang* discusses must be verified in reality, and its doctrines must thoroughly adhere to principle. In character it is the same as science.' These words can be said to understand the trend in scholarship."[9]

The claim that science is but a forerunner to Yogācāra is premised on the conviction that Yogācāra provides a superior means to establish verification. At the same time as views such as this were gaining currency, late-Qing promoters of Yogācāra were generally also keen to portray Yogācāra Buddhism as a philosophy and not a religion. Liang Shuming, for example, insisted that "if we seek philosophy in religion, it can be found only in *Weishi* learning."[10] This was, in part at least, motivated by the desire to avoid the charge that Yogācāra Buddhism was merely a religion and incompatible with the scientific spirit and modernity. In one essay dating from the period when he was in Japan (1906–1911), Zhang Taiyan maintained that although religion can be subsumed within philosophy, the reverse cannot apply, from which he concluded that Buddhism (佛法) can be equated with philosophy but not with religion. In support of this claim he insisted that in early India, Buddhists chose to associate with scholars of the Vaiśeṣika and Sāṃkhya schools of Indian philosophy and not with the "Brahmanists."[11] Despite this, elsewhere he also portrayed the relationship between philosophy and religion in dialectical terms.

> Those such as China's Confucius and Laozi, and Greece's Socrates and Plato, all used philosophy to replace religion. The learning of Socrates and Plato [in turn] led to the birth of Christianity just as the learning of Confucius and Laozi became Han *ru*. Thus philosophy became religion once more. To this day, these two religions are still being rapidly disseminated amongst the people in China. (The methods of the *ru* became a religion due to Dong Zhongshu. As for such doctrines as the superiority of *yang* over *yin*, this was an especially widespread popular belief.) In Europe, Bacon and Descartes, and in China, the Cheng brothers, Zhu Xi, Lu Xiangshan, and Wang Yangming once again transformed the old norms to create philosophy. The Cheng brothers, Zhu Xi, Lu Xiangshan, and Wang Yangming took the Chan school as their foundation, and more recent German masters[12] have gained insight from Buddhist texts. Thus the religion to follow next will be Buddhism without doubt.[13]

Here Zhang anticipated a new global phase for Buddhist religion that would replace Song-Ming Confucian philosophy in China and (presumably) Neo-Kantian philosophy in the West. Crucially, however, this new "religious" phase was not to be a return to conventional religion nor was it simply a further development of conventional philosophy. As he explains in the other essay cited above:

> If we carefully ponder Śākyamuni's original intention, it was simply to seek wisdom, and so he developed a most supreme [body] of wise principles (哲理). Once these principles were developed, they still needed to be personally

verified if they were to be more than empty words. It is not the case that lofty notions people speak of today such as noumenon, ego (大我), and the will fail to measure up to the Buddha's teachings (佛法); it is simply that they are not verified through the way things actually are (實證). It is for this reason that quite formal systems of learning are found to be lacking. Consider the various principles of things (物理)—in all cases they are discerned by testing the way things are; they are not discerned by relying purely on theory. Philosophy (哲學), however, relies purely on theory and lacks testing the way things are. Is not the difference considerable? The superiority of the Buddha's teachings is twofold: matters of theory are developed to the utmost and matters of sagely wisdom (聖智) are personally realized (內證). The Buddha's teachings are not only not concerned with religion nor with breaking free of the cycle of life and death—they do not promote morality either. The Buddha's teachings are concerned solely with developing interpretative accounts of thusness (真如 [*tathatā*]), and so it is necessary to verify thusness as it actually is. In order to develop accounts of thusness, it is necessary to verify the "womb of the Tathāgata" (如來藏 [*tathāgata-garbha*]). Rather than calling this a religion it would be better to refer to it as "that which provides philosophical verification based on evidence."[14]

In other words, Buddhism is a sort of scientific philosophy or philosophical science, superior not only to religion but also to both science and philosophy. This superiority is born of the fact that the object of the Buddha's teachings is the verification of the source and true nature of all existence: "thusness."[15]

> The Buddha's teachings take evidence as their touchstone and consistently value verification in actuality. Thusness cannot be verified by means of conceptualization (意想). The eight consciousnesses (八識), four marks of existent phenomena (四相), three subtle marks (三細), six course marks (六麤), five states of mind (五心), and five omnipresent mental factors (五遍行) can all be verified by observing within oneself and cross-checking with what all sentient beings share in common.[16]

> The Buddhist method of inner verification is the most incisive and profound. As for those degenerate types, they focus solely on language and the written word. Although Western philosophy is incisive in the written word, its [perspectives] still remain at the level of imagination, not yet verifiable by the mind, and quite baseless. Western philosophy is still not even able to measure up to Song learning, and the theories proposed by Western philosophers are actually quite at odds with one another. The kind of learning which is concerned with theory and not the way matters really are serves no purpose beyond talk.[17]

2. Zhang's Ontology

The ontological basis for Zhang's philosophical vision is the Yogācāra doctrine of three natures (三性; *tri-svabhāva*). The first nature is the nature of existence produced from attachment to imaginatively constructed discrimination (遍計所執性; *parikalpita-svabhāva*). The second nature is the nature of existence arising from causes and conditions (依他起性; *paratantra-svabhāva*), and hence ultimately is a false construct. He posits the third nature—the nature of existence being perfectly accomplished—(圓成實性; *pariniṣpanna-svabhāva* or 真如; *tathatā*]) as the most suitable candidate to serve as the ultimate foundation/basis for both philosophy and religion.[18] In his "Essay on establishing a religion," Zhang took the views of Plato and Kant to be representative of the first and second natures respectively:

> Without exception, even those [nowadays] who talk about philosophy or set up a religion establish something as fundamental reality (本體). Although the actual content of each may differ in detail, formally they are identical…. The various past masters of philosophy and religion who have actually established an ontological foundation have then proceeded to devise particular content for the ontological foundation and to dispute differing conceptions of its content. As for those who are ignorant of what is referred to as existence (有)—that is, those who harbor a conception of existence that is consistent with "attachment to imaginatively constructed discrimination" [the first nature (遍計所執性)]—they form a growing attachment to a view of existence from within the context of what does not have existence (非有中生增益執).[19] As such, the ontological foundation they posit does not constitute a [genuine] ontological foundation.[20]

"A growing attachment to a view of existence from within the context of what does not have existence" seems to refer to the (mistaken) belief that we can form a reliable view of existence by depending on the unsubstantiated belief that the objects of the sense organs and concepts really exist. This sort of attachment can be of two broad types: erroneous imputation (增益執) and nihilism (損減執). Erroneous imputation (*samāropa*) is the contrary to nihilism (損減). Erroneous imputation affirms what is not the case; nihilism denies what is the case. Zhang seems to be treating them as equivalents to the two extremes from which one is to seek the Middle Path, viz. eternalism and annihilationalism.[21]

Later in his essay Zhang develops a critique of Plato's concept of Forms or Ideas to illustrate the former:

Plato was indeed skilled in talking about Forms, yet he maintained that the existence (存在) of all particulars was neither together with (非即) the Forms nor separate from them. It is the case that Forms "are" (是有), and what are not Forms are not (非有). Thus in Plato's scheme, particulars both are and are not. "Are" and "are not" cannot co-exist, just as water and fire extinguish one another or just as dark colors and light colors cannot accommodate one another [without losing their characteristics]. Since Forms truly are, how is it that they do not comprehensively pervade all realms such that there still remain the "are not" in the world? Furthermore, how is it that the "are" are able to be manifest in the "are not" and combine with them, such that the "are" extend to the "are not"? If it is said that those which truly are have always been outside of the "are not," then the "are not" are also outside of those which truly are. Since the "are not" can stand in contrast to what truly are, then even though they are temporarily named as "are not," in the final analysis it must be acknowledged that they "are." Their name and actuality are contrary to one another.[22]

Zhang concluded that because Plato failed to apply the doctrine of the nature of existence arising from causes and conditions (依他起性), this led to the problem of having to reconcile the status of two ontological entities.

In the same essay Zhang used Kant to illustrate the sort of contradictions engendered by attachment to nihilism (損減執):

As for those who are resolute in rejecting empty names, some of them regard "self" as empty, while others regard the twelve categories [of understanding][23] as empty, and some regard time and space as empty. The sole exceptions are the objects of the five sense organs (五塵).[24] People of this persuasion are unwilling to insist on deeming them to be empty. They regard the objects of the five sense organs as necessarily having an ontological foundation. They refer to this ontological foundation as "noumena". Noumena are similar to what the *Vimalakīrti-nirdeśa-sātra* refers to as "as though having form" (色如) [here "form" applies to the objects of all five of the sense organs]. This is thus to treat the objects of the five sense organs as not being empty and to treat mental objects [concepts] (法塵) as empty. These same people maintain that the objects of the five sense organs have two aspects: that which is expressed in descriptions of these objects and that to which the descriptions refer. They further maintain that mental objects [concepts] can be expressed only in descriptions and [in such cases] there is definitely nothing to which these descriptions refer. Where there is something descriptions refer to, it necessarily has an ontological foundation; where there is nothing a description refers to, it is merely an empty name.

> What these people fail to be aware of is that outside of the mind the objects of the five sense organs cannot be established. As such, there is no difference between establishing the objects of the five sense organs and establishing mental objects. The existence of objects of the five sense organs is certainly illusory yet each necessarily has its ontological foundation. The existence of mental objects is also illusory—so how likely is it that mental objects [alone] lack an ontological foundation? If one develops an attachment to nihilism in the realm of illusory existence, then empty names will have no means by which to function as empty names.[25]

Kant described his twelve categories as a priori concepts and time and space as a priori particulars—these are the "empty names" referred to in the opening of this passage. Although essential to our being able to process the objects of the sense organs, they are "empty" constructs in that they are not objective, self-subsisting realities. For Kant, noumena provide the objects of sensory perception—phenomena—with an ontological foundation. Zhang objects that sensory objects are no less mental objects than are concepts such as noumena. The last sentence simply means that illusory existence applies not just to concepts but also to objects of the five senses—as such, unless we cease making mental distinctions altogether, it is wrongheaded to focus on mental objects alone as being the bearers of empty names. For Zhang, the point is that the objects of the five sense organs and concepts alike have the eighth or storehouse consciousness (阿賴耶識; *ālaya-vijñāna*)—the repository of all sensory and cognitive impressions—as their ontological foundation. Zhang's position is more subtle than the simple denial of sensory and conceptual objects. What he denies is that the referents of "sense and conceptual objects" are real as such; instead he claims they do have an ontological source, and that this is real (and, he argues, verifiable). The context of this is his refutation of the view that sense objects are real while conceptualizations are not. The first he would see as *samāropa*, the latter as nihilism.

> What gives rise to these two extreme kinds of attachment? It is due to the failure to recognize that the nature of existence arises from causes and conditions. Those who develop an attachment to negation are unaware that the objects of the five sense organs and mental objects [concepts] are each objects of perception kept within the mind [相分—that which is seen, as opposed to that which sees 見分]. These objects of perception depend on consciousness for their origination. It is just like the two horns which depend on an ox in order to arise. Hence when the mental consciousness [the sixth

consciousness]—functioning as that which cognizes—follows mental objects and deems them to be that which is cognized, these mental objects are never separate from nor lie beyond the mental consciousness. Similarly, when the five consciousnesses [visual, auditory, olfactory, gustatory, and tactile]—functioning as that which cognize—follow the objects of the five sense organs and deem them to be that which is cognized, the five consciousnesses never attempt to distinguish themselves from the objects which they cognize, to maintain that these objects of the five sense organs are separate from or lie beyond the five consciousnesses. This being the case, the mental objects are within the mental consciousness, and the objects of the five sense organs are within the five consciousnesses. If it is said that the names of the objects of the five sense organs refer to something that can be explained, then the names of mental objects also refer to something that can be explained. If it is said that the names of the objects of the five sense organs do not refer to something that can be explained, then the names of mental objects also do not refer to something that can be explained. How is this so? That which is explained [by a name] is not external: it is simply the activated object of perception kept within the mind. People nowadays reject mental consciousness, maintaining that conspicuous mental objects are deluded conceptualizations that lack [corresponding] external objects. Furthermore, they regard as external those objects made conspicuous by the five consciousnesses—things that originally were not differentiated and distinguished as external objects—premised on that which is differentiated by the mental consciousness. Thus, on the one hand, they reject mental consciousness; yet, on the other hand, they are forced to rely on mental consciousness [in order to talk about what the five consciousnesses perceive]. Succumbing thus to contradiction, how is their position tenable?[26]

In Yogācāra teachings, the sixth consciousness or *mano-vijñāna* (mental consciousness) is the thinking consciousness. It also brings together and differentiates the sensory impressions derived from the five sensory consciousnesses. That is, it can think about what the other five conscious-nesses perceive; the five consciousnesses do not have this reflective capacity. Zhang here further reiterates the untenability of deeming concepts to be illusory while claiming that the objects of the senses are not illusory. Again, the target of his criticisms is the view he attributes to Kant: that unlike the objects of the sense organs, concepts (the twelve categories, as well as space and time) are not objective, self-subsisting realities.

According to Zhang, the nature of existence arising from causes and conditions (依他起性) is a product of the false distinctions made by the eighth or *ālaya* consciousness,[27] the seventh consciousness or *manas* 末那識, and the first five consciousnesses. The Yogācāra school distinguished eight types of consciousness: "five sensory consciousnesses; an empirical organizer of sensory data (*mano-vijñāna*); a self-absorbed, appropriative consciousness (*manas*); and the eighth, a storehouse consciousness (*ālaya-vijñāna*) that retained the karmic impressions of past experiences and colored new experiences on the basis of that previous conditioning. The eighth consciousness was also the fundamental consciousness."[28] The perceptual objects of the eighth consciousness are the images or attributes (相) of all forms of differentiation. All perceptual objects are kept within the mind (相分). These objects consist of the sum total of the ever-present seeds of which the *ālaya* consciousness is itself constituted.[29] The perceptual object of the seventh consciousness is the *ālaya* consciousness, which it regards as the true self and so leads to attachment to a self (我執) and attachment to the compositional elements of existence (法執). In order to function, the first five consciousnesses require the transformed appearances (變現) of the seeds of the *ālaya* consciousness to serve as perceptual objects, but they can do this only with the involvement of the sixth consciousness (意識), which is a form of conscious awareness. Unlike the sixth consciousness, in order to be activated, the seventh and eighth consciousnesses do not need to have the transformed appearances of the *ālaya* consciousness serve as their perceptual objects.[30]

For Zhang, *zhenru* 真如 is the ontological basis of everything, but rather than being a first cause it is a logical and not an empirical entity which has existed in time before anything else. That latter role was accorded to the *ālaya* consciousness, the locus of phenomenological creation, although it did not act in a purposeful way. Zhang provides some insight into his understanding of the relationship between *zhenru* and the *ālaya* consciousness in his gloss to the following line cited in the "Jie bi" 解蔽 Dispelling blindness) chapter of *Xunzi*, 人心之危，道心之微 ("the human mind is precarious; the mind of the way is subtle"): "The human mind is the root of living things: the ten thousand things of heaven and earth are created by this mind. It is what is referred to as *ālaya* consciousness, as the nature of existence arising from causes and conditions. The mind of the way is not created; is not immediately connected to the ten thousand things of heaven and earth. It is what is referred to as *zhenru xin* 真如心, as *yuancheng shixing* 圓成實性."[31] Subscribing to the traditional Sinitic Buddhist doctrine of original enlightenment (*benjue* 本覺; the idea that sentient beings are already enlightened), Zhang held that the *ālaya* consciousness was the product of the veil of ignorance's preventing sentient beings from realizing that they are already enlightened, which for humans is a function of attachment to the notion of "self." Only by dispelling the delusion that identifies "self" with the *ālaya* consciousness—something that is a function of seventh consciousness or *manas*—can our originally enlightened state of *zhenru* be realized.[32] He also regarded the *ālaya* consciousness to be a bridge between the phenomenal world and the ontological underpinning that is *zhenru*.

3. Zhang's Cognitive Epistemology

As with ontology, Zhang also identified epistemology as crucial to a philosophical system: "From Kant onwards, metaphysicians have regarded epistemology as crucial. If one were rashly to posit the origins of a particular world without a supporting epistemology, this would be dogmatic."[33] Zhang's interests focus in particular on the cognitive dimension of epistemology—the role played by cognition in how we know the world—for which he draws substantially on the Yogācāra teaching of "the four aspects of cognition" (四分). According to Charles A. Muller, "when the cognitive mental functioning is activated, the mind itself is divided, depending upon the particular function, into four aspects, and based on this, that which we know as cognitive function is established." The four aspects are:

1. that which is seen (objective aspect; *xiangfen* 相分);
2. that which sees (subjective aspect; *jianfen* 見分);
3. the confirmation of that seeing (self-aware aspect; *zi zheng fen* 自證分);
4. the acknowledgment of that confirmation (reconfirming the self-aware aspect; *zheng zi zheng fen* 證自證分).[34]

In the account of the "four aspects of cognition" set out in *Zhuo Han wei yan*, Zhang again singles out Kant (and for good measure also Nietzsche) for criticism:

> Kant was unable to distinguish where the foundation of knowing (認識) is located. Although he knew that there are "that which is seen" (相分) and "that which sees" (見分), he was unaware of "the confirmation of that seeing" (自證分) and the "acknowledgement of that confirmation" (證自證分). Hence, later Nietzsche refuted Kant, saying that if you want to know that which does the knowing, you still need to use knowing and that this sort of proof is circular. In my view, Nietzsche was aware only of "that which is seen" and "that

which sees" and was unaware of "the confirmation of that seeing" and the "acknowledgement of that confirmation," and so he made the same mistake as Kant. In the main, what Kant and Nietzsche mean by knowing is "that which sees," whereas actually that which has a complete grasp of knowing is "the confirmation of that seeing." Not being aware of this distinction, [they] said that the knowledge of knowing still relies upon knowing.

Although "confirmation of seeing" and "that which sees" both perform knowing, their statuses differ. Take the situation of a baby being born and not yet being able to speak—who determines if the baby is human? The baby's mother and obstetrician do. It is not the case that the mother and obstetrician are not humans. Why then does getting a human to determine who is human not amount to circular proof? Because even though the three of them are humans, their statuses differ. "That which sees" is analogous to the baby; "confirmation of seeing" is analogous to the mother and the obstetrician. Thus understood, this settles the matter.[35]

(In this anecdote, presumably the obstetrician plays a dual role: both as one who provides confirmation of the seeing and acknowledgment of the mother's confirmation.) Zhang here criticizes Kant for acknowledging only that which is seen (the objective aspect) and that which sees (the subjective aspect) while failing to acknowledge the confirmation of that seeing (self-aware aspect); and the acknowledgment of that confirmation (reconfirming the self-aware aspect). From Zhang's perspective, the consequence of that failure is that Kant relegated noumena to the realm of what cannot be known. (Decades later, this same criticism came to function as a keystone in the philosophical edifice of New Confucian Mou Zongsan 牟宗三 [1909–1995]. As with Zhang, Mou also misinterpreted Kant's notion of noumena—wittingly or otherwise is a moot point—by taking the thing-in-itself to be some sort of transcendent object. For Kant, noumena are not objects at all.)

This concern about *benti* 本體 (noumena; noumenal reality) being inherently unknowable had in Zhang's time been given renewed impetus through pioneering translator Yan Fu's 嚴復 (1853–1921) introduction of positivist philosophy. Contemporary Tsinghua University philosopher Hu Weixi 胡偉希 argues that, like Huxley, Spencer, and Mill, Yan Fu was committed to the epistemological premise that human knowledge is bound by the limits of sensory experience:[36] "He concurred with Spencer's division of the world into the phenomenal and the unknowable, maintaining that all [genuine] knowledge is knowledge which relates only to the phenomenal world. Hence, [Yan said] 'there is no way we can learn about what is not of this world, and even if one should attempt to do so, it would have no bearing on human affairs.' Denying that '*benti*' can be known was not some occasional, casual remark on his part but was the core of his entire philosophical thinking."[37] There is thus some irony that Yan Fu should have cited Buddhist views in his support of Mill's claim that all we can know of the outward world is the sensations which we experience from it.[38]

As for the criticism he attributes to Nietzsche—"if you want to know that which does the knowing, you still need to use knowing, and this sort of proof leads to an endless regress"—Zhang criticized Nietzsche for similarly acknowledging only *xiangfen* and *jianfen*. Zhang emphasized that for Kant and Nietzsche "knowing" was limited to *jianfen* and that both were ignorant of the fact that that which confirms this knowing is *zi zheng fen*. Zhang proceeded to claim that the Greek Stoics had a far superior grasp of knowing and attributed the following view to the Stoics: "If [knowing] corresponds (合) with an object, then this is true [knowledge]. Yet how can one know for oneself whether it does correspond? When true concepts arise, there will necessarily be another concept that also arises and accompanies them to provide unmediated/direct verification. It is for this reason that the truth or falsity of a concept does not rely on external things to be verified." Here the reader is being asked to accept that "object" equates to *xiangfen*; that "concept" equates to *jianfen*; and that "another concept also arises and accompanies them to provide unmediated/direct verification" refers to *zi zheng fen*.

4. Yogācāra and the Writings of the Pre-Qin Masters

In the above-cited passages Zhang applies a single benchmark to determine the soundness or otherwise of the thought of Plato, Kant, Nietzsche, and the Sophists: tenets drawn from Yogācāra philosophy. How then did Chinese philosophers fare? His attitude to Song and Ming philosophers was variously lukewarm to critical; a disposition no doubt shaped by his formative training in Han Learning and evidential scholarship. The following passage succinctly states his assessment of the merits of Principle-centered learning relative to the learning of the pre-Qin masters: "If, moreover, one were to highlight [the import of] Principle-centered learning, then it would be the glossing of moral norms (that is, ethics). It falls short of dealing with issues of truth. (The problem with those associated with Principle-centered learning is their vacuousness. Incapable of giving a direct answer, they use incomprehensible language and fail to make themselves clear.) Only [study of] the [pre-Qin] masters can recover that which has been thrown away by people in recent times."[39]

From 1906 and for much of the following decade, in his writings Zhang applied the benchmark of Yogācāra Buddhist philosophy to assess the philosophical merit of individual pre-Qin thinkers (including Confucius).[40] It was in the writings of the Mohists and Xunzi that Zhang first found expressions of thinking which corresponded with key concepts and tenets of Yogācāra philosophy, as is evident in his 1906 essay "Zhuzixue lüe shuo" 諸子學略説 [A brief account of Masters Studies], where he applied the theory of the "five omnipresent mental factors" (五遍行)[41] to develop his analysis of the concepts 緣天官 and 心徵 as featured in a key passage in the "Zheng ming" 正名 [On the correct use of names] chapter in *Xunzi.* According to Zhang, the process of cognition begins with the focusing of attention (作意); this in turn leads to consciousness' coming in contact with external things (觸). Activation of this contact enables the five sense organs (五根), cognitive objects (境), and the thinking consciousness (識) to join together so that each of the five sense organs can function independently of one another to record their perceptual objects and receive sensations (受). Although the five sense organs have the capacity to perceive their objects directly, they cannot cognize these objects—that function is reserved for the mind. The process whereby the impressions of the objects of perception are transmitted to the mind is termed conceptualization (想). He refers to this process whereby the sense organs receive impressions of the cognitive objects and then transmit them to the mind as "being dependent upon" (緣). He maintains that because the concept of *yuan* is rarely touched upon in Chinese texts, Buddhist texts are needed to elucidate its meaning:

> In general terms, for a thought to arise there must be four kinds of conditions (四緣). The first is "direct internal causes that produce a result" (因緣 [*hetu-pratyaya*]):[42] the seeds in the *ālaya* consciousness (阿賴耶識). The second is "conditions for the causal support of consciousness" (所緣緣 [*ālambana-pratyaya*]):[43] perceptual objects. The third is "auxiliary conditions" (增上緣 [*adhipati-pratyaya*]): contributory factors. The fourth is "consistent and continuous conditions" (等無間緣 [*samanantara-pratyaya*]):[44] immediately prior thought. *Yuan* means "to depend upon" (攀附).

> The meaning of the phrase [in *Xunzi*] "being dependent on the sense organs" (緣天官) is as follows: the five sense organs take sense-objects as the causal support of cognition (緣境). These sense-objects are "conditions for the causal support of consciousness." The mind depends on the seeing aspect (見分) of the five senses and the seeing aspect of the five senses is an "auxiliary factor." Hence it is said [in *Xunzi*]: "By depending on the ears then it becomes possible to be aware of sound; by depending on the eyes then it becomes possible to be aware of form." Without the mind the five sense organs would not be able to sense objects of perception. Hence the thinking [*mano*—sixth] consciousness which arises with the five sense consciousnesses (五俱意識) simultaneously functions as an auxiliary condition for the five sense organs. Without the five sense organs the mind could not verify understanding (徵知), hence the mind in turn makes use of the illuminating function of the five sense organs to serve as an auxiliary function. The senses of the five sense organs are simply a direct awareness; hence it is said [in *Xunzi*]: "The five sense organs record it but do not cognize it." The mind has the capacity to cognize and possesses the capacity for both mistaken perception and inference. When the mind first began to cognize, it did not yet establish words, hence [*Xunzi*] says: "The mind verifies it but without words." Verification without words is something people deem to be ignorance, and so words and names are created by the mind.[45]

Zhang proceeds to relate that the names created as a result of the process called conceptualization (想) are only individual names (別名). General names (共名) rely upon creative volitional impulse (思), the third of the five omnipresent mental factors, which has the capacity to form concepts. Two key observations can be made in regard to Zhang's analysis. First, he deems the process of conceptualization described in *Xunzi* to be exactly congruent with the Yogācāra teaching of the "five omnipresent mental factors." Second, he implies that the correct meaning of the *Xunzi* passage had been lost but can be recovered with the application of the Yogācāra analytical framework. What he does not do is to explain why there should be this level of congruence. He is not suggesting any sort of cross-cultural transmission. Rather the implication is that the *Xunzi* text (and other early Chinese texts) "bear witness" to insights into realities which transcend individual cultures but which are most fully and systematically articulated in Yogācāra systems of learning.

4.1 *Mozi*

"Yuan ming" 原名 [Tracing the origins of (philosophers of) names] provides an equally apt example of this commitment to identifying parallels between Yogācāra philosophy and philosophically significant passages in pre-Qin texts. The following example concerns the interpretation of the terms 故 and 小故 which occur in *Mozi*, based on the application of concepts used in *yinming* logic. The text in round brackets is Zhang's auto-commentary on his primary exposition:

> The way of argumentation (辯說) is for the speaker first to confirm his tenet (旨), then to elucidate his basis (柢), and then to select an analogy to complement it and some material reason to provide an illustration. In *yinming*, this is what is referred to as the thesis (宗), the reason (因), and the example (喻). In Indian disputation, the thesis comes first, followed by the reason, and then the example. (Here "example" refers collectively to the principal statement [喻體] and the particular example [喻依]). Western disputation starts with the basis of the reason (what people today translate as major premise), which is followed by the reason (what people today translate as minor premise), and then the thesis. As three-part syllogisms, they are the same. In *Mozi*, *gu* 故 takes on the role of the reason. The sequence in which it sets out a syllogistic inference starts with the reason, is followed by the basis of the reason, and then by the thesis. This is completely different from the sequence followed in either India or the West. In the case of Indian syllogistic inference, the reason that sound is impermanent is because it possesses the character of having been created. All created things are impermanent. Sound is like pottery. (In the case of Western syllogistic inference, all created things are impermanent. Because sound is created, it is impermanent. In the case of syllogistic inference in the *Mozi*, sound is created, all created things are impermanent, hence sound is impermanent.)[46] The *Mozi* canon says: "*Gu* 故: what must obtain before something comes about." The Explanation says: "Reason (*gu*): Minor reason (*xiao gu* 小故) means having this it will not necessarily be so; lacking this it will necessarily not be so. It is a part, and is like having a starting-point. Major reason (*da gu* 大故) means that having this it will necessarily be so. (The word *wu* 無 in the original is redundant). It is like the appearing bringing about the seeing 見."

> A portion in a whole is a part. The starting-point is without a [separate] beginning and is at the front. When it is specifically identified, it is a single part (體); when it divides into a second segment, it is called seeing (*jian* 見).... Now suppose a syllogistic inference says: Sound is what is created (the cause). All created things are impermanent the basis of the reason. Hence sound is impermanent (the thesis). It begins with the reason, but because the reason is only a part [of the whole syllogism], it is called the minor reason. (It is similar to what people today translate as minor premise.) Because it is without a [separate] beginning and is at the front, it is compared to a starting-point. The principal statement (喻體) follows next. It connects with

[the reason]; hence it is called the major reason. (This is like what people today translate as major premise.) The "all things that are created" is the single part; the "sound is created" is the segment. Hence it is likened to the appearing bringing about the seeing…. Because the reason (因) and the thesis are not closely bound to one another, the Explanation says: "Having this, it will not necessarily be so."[47] Without the reason the thesis will necessarily not become established; hence the Explanation says: "Lacking this, it will necessarily not be so." The principal statement follows after the reason. Because each imposes limiting conditions on the other, the thesis will certainly be established; hence it is said "having this it will necessarily be so."[48]

Even though he finds both the Mohist and classical Western forms of the syllogism to be inferior to the *yinming* form,[49] his main point is that *yinming* enables us to recover the true meaning of the Mohist text in a way that Western philosophy cannot. This passage also brings to light another tendency in much of Zhang's use of Yogācāra terminology and doctrine to elucidate Chinese thought: concept matching (格義). Concept matching was developed by Chinese and foreign scholars and monks as a technique to translate and interpret Buddhist texts as early as the Han dynasty (206 B.C.–A.D. 220) when these texts were first transmitted to China. There is thus some irony that nearly two thousand years later Zhang resorted to this old technique when dealing with a different body of Buddhist texts and concepts.

4.2 *Zhuangzi*

From 1906 onwards Zhang's writings are replete with examples of concept matching, involving a variety of early Chinese texts. His most celebrated exercise in this regard is his 1911 *Qi wu lun shi* 齊物論釋 [Explanation of "Discourse on making all things equal"] which develops an extended, complex Yogācāra reading of the "Qi wu lun" [Discourse on making all things equal] chapter in *Zhuangzi*. At one level, his commentary attempts to bring the systematic analysis of Yogācāra philosophy to the cryptic and notoriously unsystematic *Qi wu lun*. By drawing attention to several key passages which evidence how Zhang's concept matching was applied to the interpretation of *Zhuangzi*, I will show that he attempts to do more than provide systematic analysis.

Zhang interpreted the title of the chapter to mean "Discourse on making all things equal" (rather than "Equalizing discourse on things" or "Equalizing human discourse"). By "equal" Zhang was not advocating some form of relativism or treating all things as having equal value; rather he is proposing that when images/attributes (相) and names/concepts (名) are abandoned, all that remains is the undifferentiated state of *zhenru* 真如 (*tathatā*). It is from this perspective that he understood the title to mean "making all things equal": "To equalize that which is not equal is but the base attachment of lowly persons; [to realize] the equality of inequality is the profound discourse of the most exalted wisdom. Unless one abandons names and attributes, how can this wisdom become realized?"[50]

In his opening commentary to the main texts of "Qi wu lun"—which relates the story of Ziyou's 子游 encounter with Ziqi 子綦, who had been sitting in a state of trance-like forgetfulness—Zhang explains that names and attributes are central topics of investigation in the chapter. This is because it is only by realizing their illusory nature and their grounding in the *ālaya* consciousness that the pathway to realizing *tathatā* can be cleared. "As their foundation, names and attributes rely upon the [deluded] belief that the self and the compositional elements of existence (法) have inherent existence. It is for this reason that 'forgetting the self' (喪我) is first discussed [in the text], for only then can the emptiness of names and attributes be realized…. [Ziyou] asked [Ziqi] how he had been able to abandon the self, and so Ziqi told him about the pipes of earth and the pipes of heaven so that Ziyou would understand." Historically, many different interpretations have been developed about just what the pipes of heaven and earth actually refer to. Zhang harnessed the conceptual apparatus of Yogācāra to advance his own interpretation:

> With the pipes of earth, the subjective (能) and objective (所) aspects of blowing are differentiated; with the pipes of heaven the subjective and objective aspects are not distinguished. The import of the metaphor is as follows. Wind blowing in the pipes of earth is a metaphor for being unaware that thoughts have been activated, and the angry cries of the [wind in the] myriad hollows—each one different from the other—is a metaphor for various names, attributes, and differentiations. As for the floating motes [in the *Zhuangzi* text], each has its own particular shape as it prances and soars.

With respect to the pipes of earth, Zhang is making the point that the subjective and objective arise through dependent origination. They are mutually entailing notions—one cannot exist without the other—but the distinctions they engender are not real, having no intrinsic self-nature.

> The passage about the wind blowing the myriad [things] in the pipes of heaven is a metaphor for the *ālaya* consciousness, and the myriad [things] is a metaphor for the seeds within the *ālaya* consciousness. In recent times, some have termed these seeds "archetypes." Seeds cover not only words/concepts but also the fundamental qualities of attributes; hence the text says: "Blows the myriad differences." As for "causing each to become itself," this is saying it is only by virtue of being grounded in the *ālaya* consciousness that the faculty of thought (意根) attaches itself to the *ālaya* consciousness and treats it as the "self" (我).[51]

The *ālaya* consciousness does not itself distinguish the subjective and objective; hence it does not project a notion of self-identity on itself. Rather, it is the general locus where all such differentiation occurs. The process Zhang describes in the final sentence is that whereby the seventh consciousness or *manas* forms a delusional attachment to the *ālaya* consciousness, falsely perceiving it to be the locus of self-identity. This seed of self-identity is in turn stored in the *ālaya* consciousness where it "perfumes" other concepts and so becomes entrenched.

For Zhang, Zhuangzi's solution to these problems is to "lose the self" (喪我): "The door to the way (道) of Zhuangzi and Ziqi is not to have a self (無我)."[52] This way, in turn, enables one to realize the difference between true self and illusory self; that is, between *tathatā*—the "true ruler" (真君), the "true master" (真宰)—and *ālaya* consciousness. In commenting on the well-known passage in the "Qi wu lun" chapter about whether the parts of the body all rule themselves or whether they have a "true master," Zhang extends his concept matching to appropriate the concept of the "numinous tower" (靈臺) which occurs in the "Gengsang Chu" 庚桑楚 chapter of *Zhuangzi*:

> The numinous tower holds the sensations of the five sense organs. Its name in Sanskrit is the "clinging [consciousness]" 阿陀那[識; *ādāna-vijñāna*].[53] Furthermore, because it also stores the seeds, it is called the "numinous storehouse" (靈府),[54] which in Sanskrit is *ālaya*. Because its fundamental reality (體) neither arises nor ceases, yet manifests itself as phenomena which arise and cease according to circumstances, the Buddhist canon refers to it as the womb of the *tathāgata* 如來藏. This refers precisely to its fundamental reality's neither arising nor ceasing. It is also called the *amala* consciousness (庵摩羅識 [*amala-vijñāna*]).[55] "De chong fu" says: "Use understanding/knowledge to grasp the mind; use the mind to grasp the constant mind." The mind is the "clinging consciousness"; the constant mind is the *amala* consciousness. In the "De chong fu" chapter it is referred to as the constant mind; here in "Qi wu lun" it is referred to as the true ruler.[56]

Tathāgata-garbha is a doctrine emphasized in Sinitic traditions of Buddhism. According to Dan Lusthaus, in its earliest appearances in Buddhist texts, the term "signified the inherent capacity of humans (and sometimes other sentient beings) to achieve buddhahood. Over time the concept expanded and came to signify the original pristine pure ontological Buddha-ness intrinsic in all things, a pure nature that is obscured or covered over by defilements."[57] It is this expanded sense that Zhang follows. He also equates the concept with the *amala* consciousness, a ninth consciousness free of the defilements of the *ālaya* consciousness.

Elsewhere, in commenting on the sentence, "Use understanding (*zhi* 知) to grasp the mind; use the mind to grasp the constant mind," he also equates the *amala* consciousness with "the mind of the *tathatā*" and provides a more detailed and even more intriguing commentary on the "Qi wu lun" passage just discussed:

> *Zhi* 知 is the thinking consciousness; *xin* 心 is the clinging consciousness, or what is called *ālaya* consciousness. In simple terms, it refers to "me." The constant mind is the *amala* consciousness or what is called the mind of *tathatā* (真如心), that is, the mind that neither arises nor ceases. Buddhists maintain that in order to seek the *amala* consciousness, the *ālaya* consciousness should be destroyed. It is because the *ālaya* consciousness is ever-present that humans are always beset by delusion and suffering. The mind that neither arises nor ceases can only be manifest when the phenomena of life are destroyed. In seeking for the constant mind, Zhuangzi's point is the same. He was also of the view that the constant mind is not something that can be known through ordinary means. Zhuangzi's promotion of "no self" was the same as that in Buddhism. Zhuangzi's "no self" was also the same as Confucius's "no self" [*Analects* 9.4] and Yanzi's "overcoming oneself and returning to ritual" [*Analects* 12.1]; that is, the idea that the single self and the myriad things are [part of] the same [process of] transformation (同化), is what people today mean by absorbing the small self within the large self. This lofty and profound view is absent in [the writings of] Mencius and Xunzi, and it so happens that Confucius acknowledged only Yan Hui as having realized this way. Hence, although on the surface Zhuangzi was a Daoist, he can also be said to have been a Confucian.[58]

Here Zhang not only uses Yogācāra conceptual distinctions to interpret *Zhuangzi* but also to reinforce the idea that the key insights of both Zhuangzi and Confucius were consistent with core Yogācāra teachings. In previous examples of concept matching from *Mozi* and *Xunzi*, I argued that Zhang's aim was to show that these early Chinese philosophical writings "bear witness" to insights into fundamental truths that transcend individual cultures but which are most fully and systematically articulated in Yogācāra systems of learning. In the case of Zhuangzi and Confucius, Zhang is making a slightly different point. Consider the reference to the example of *Analects* 9.4 (子絕四。毋意、無必、無固、無我。). Although this reference occurs in several of his writings, it is most developed in *Zhuo Han wei yan*:

> The Master severed four things. He did not think (意),[59] and so the appropriative consciousness (*manas*) was not given expression. He did not insist on the necessity (必) [to perceive the *ālaya* consciousness], and so the continual examination and evaluation [of external events and their relation to the self] were not given expression. He did not stubbornly adhere (固) to attachment to the notion that the compositional elements of existence are real (法執), and so attachment to the notion of the enduring self (我執) did not arise. He did not entertain a sense of self, and so the notions of the reality of an individuated self and of *dharma*s were not given expression. The appropriative consciousness (*manas*) is the foundation of the notion that the individuated self is real. The continual examination and evaluation [of external events and their relation to the self] give rise to reflection on the self. All stubborn attachments arise from attachment to the self. Accordingly, thinking (意) is dependent upon insisting on the necessity [to perceive the *ālaya* consciousness], and stubborn adherence [to attachments] and the "self" is given expression through thinking. If the four are severed, then the causes and effects that support them become dissipated.[60]

Historically, this particular *Analects* passage has consistently invited novel interpretations,[61] but Zhang's would have to rate as one of the more creative. In this example and in his comments on Zhuangzi, Zhang's concept matching served several goals: to evidence how Yogācāra teachings help elucidate early Chinese thought; to show that Confucius and Zhuangzi "bore witness" to insights that transcend individual cultures; and to portray Confucius and Zhuangzi as exceptional sages. Beyond this, however, he was making the further point that classical Chinese philosopher-sages had attained an awareness of the highest truths and that evidence of this can be found in their writings. For Zhang, the writings which record the teachings of Confucius, Mozi, Xunzi and Zhuangzi are repositories of philosophical meditations and reflections on those truths.[62] For better or worse, a commitment to this inspiration has continued to sustain the development of Chinese philosophy in China.

Notes

1   Even though Zhang certainly did not see himself as playing such a role.

2   In this chapter my understanding of Zhang Taiyan's Yogācāra thought has benefited from reading Guo Yingchuan 郭應傳, *Zhen su zhi jing: Zhang Taiyan Foxue sixiang yanjiu* 真俗之境—章太炎佛學思想研究 [The realm of the true and the realm of the mundane: Studies on Zhang Taiyan's Buddhist thought] (Hefei: Anhui jiaoyu chubanshe, 2006); and Ma Tianxiang 麻天祥, "Zhang Taiyan de faxiang weishi zhexue" 章太炎的法相唯識哲學 [Zhang Taiyan's Yogācāra philosophy], in his *Wan Qing Foxue yu jindai shehui sixiang* 晚清佛學與近代社會思想 [Late-Qing Buddhism and modern social thought] (Kaifeng: Henan daxue chubanshe, 2005), pp. 460–487. I am grateful to Dan Lusthaus and Viren Murthy for reading a draft of this chapter and offering valuable critical feedback.

3   *Yinming* 因明 (knowledge of reasons) is the Chinese interpretation of Buddhist reasoning and logic: *hetuvidyā*. See Christoph Harbsmeier, *Language and Logic in Traditional China*, in *Science and Civilisation in China*, Vol. 7, pt. 1 (Cambridge: Cambridge University Press, 1998), pp. 358–408.

4   Chen Jidong 陳繼東, "Shinmatsu ni okeru yuishiki hōsō tenseki no kankō ni tsuite" 清末における唯識法相典籍の刊行について [On the publication of Yogācāra texts at the end of the Qing dynasty], *Indogaku Bukkyūgaku kenkyū* 印度學佛教學研究 44.2 (1996), p. 811.

5   Appointed in 1917, Liang taught Indian philosophy (principally Buddhism) from 1918 to 1924, after which he retired from his position to engage in the practical work of rural reconstruction. Xiong taught *Weishi* philosophy when first appointed in 1922 and later taught his own *Xin weishi lun* 新唯識論 [New treatise on the uniqueness of consciousness].

6   In his 1920 preface to *Weishi shuyi* 唯識述義 [The meaning of nothing but consciouness Buddhism], Liang noted that Ma Xulun's 馬敍倫 *Zhuangzi zhaji* 莊子劄記 [Notes on *Zhuangzi*] (1919) used *Weishi* philosophy to interpret *Zhuangzi*. See Liang Shuming, *Liang Shuming quanji* 梁漱溟全集 [The complete works of Liang Shuming], Vol. 1 (Ji'nan: Shandong renmin chubanshe, 1994), p. 253. Ma was at the time teaching Lao-Zhuang philosophy in the Philosophy Department of Peking University. This example also evidences the influence of Zhang Taiyan.

7   Zhang Taiyan, *Zhuo Han wei yan* 菿漢微言 [Zhang Taiyan's subtle words] (Hangzhou: Zhejiang tushuguan, postface dated 1917), p. 72b. Zhuo Han is one of Zhang's styles and literally means "making the Han great." 菿 is a loan graph for *zhuo* 倬.

8   Zhang Taiyan, "Da Tiezheng" 答鐵錚 [Reply to Tiezheng], in *Zhang Taiyan ji* 章太炎集 [Collected writings of Zhang Taiyan], edited by Huang Xia'nian 黃夏年 (Beijing: Zhongguo shehuikexue chubanshe, 1995), p. 19.

9   Zhang Taiyan, *Zi shu xueshu cidi* 自述學術次第 [My sequence in learning], in his *Zhuo Han san yan* 菿漢三言 [Three books by Zhang Taiyan] (Shenyang: Liaoning jiaoyu chubanshe, 2000), p. 166.

10 Liang Shuming, *Weishi shuyi*, p. 269. Liang criticized Theravada teachings on the grounds that they ignore metaphysical problems and that their epistemology is poorly developed.

11 Zhang Taiyan, "Lun Fofa yu zongjiao, zhexue yi ji xianshi zhi guanxi" 論佛法與宗教、哲學以及現實之關係 [The relationship between Buddhism, religion, philosophy, and the real world], *Zhongguo zhexue* 中國哲學 6 (1981), p. 300.

12 Here he probably has Schopenhauer in mind.

13 Zhang Taiyan, "Jianli zongjiao lun" 建立宗教論 [Establishing a religion] (1906), in *Zhang Taiyan quanji* 章太炎全集 [Complete Works of Zhang Taiyan], Vol. 4 (Shanghai: Shanghai renmin chubanshe, 1985), p. 418.

14 Zhang Taiyan, "Lun Fofa yu zongjiao, zhexue yi ji xianshi zhi guanxi," p. 300.

15 It should be pointed out that Zhang used the concepts *zhenru* 真如 (*tathatā*), *rulaizang* 如來藏 (*tathāgata-garbha*), *anmoluoshi* 庵摩羅識 (*amala-vijñāna*), and *zhenxin* 真心 interchangeably.

16 Zhang Taiyan, *Zhuo Han wei yan*, 11b.

17 Zhang Taiyan, *Guoxue gailun* 國學概論 [Overview of National Studies] (Shanghai: Shanghai guji chubanshe, 2006), p. 69.

18 As Dan Lusthaus observes, "since the notion of 'self-nature' is itself a parikalpic idea that presumes self-hood, it too must be eliminated. Thus the three self-natures are actually three non-self-natures." See his entry, "Yogācāra School," in *Encyclopedia of Buddhism*, edited by Robert E. Buswell, Jr., Vol. 2, (New York: Thomson Gale, 2004), p. 918.

19 As a technical term, *zengyi* 增益 can also mean *samāropa*: superimposition; reification; positing something to be the case which it is not, and then insisting that it is. It is likely that Zhang here is using 增益 in a double sense so that it also implies attachment to baseless *samāropa* views.

20 Zhang Taiyan, "Jianli zongjiao lun," p. 404.

21 Eternalism usually refers to the view that the self exists in life and persists after death; and nihilism or annihilationalism to the view that sentient beings are annihilated when they die. In turn, the Middle Path—the doctrine of conditioned or dependent arising—avoids these extreme views by claiming there is no independently existing entity with self-nature to exist eternally or to be annihilated in the first place.

22 Zhang Taiyan, "Jianli zongjiao lun," 407.

23 That is, the twelve categories of understanding identified by Kant.

24 Colour, sound, odor, taste, and tactile quality.

25 Zhang Taiyan, "Jianli zongjiao lun," p. 404.

26 *Ibid.*, pp. 404–405.

27 This is a doctrinally unusual claim, since usually the *ālaya-vijñāna* is said not to make distinctions, its *ālambana* 所緣 (one of the six sense objects taken up, apprehended by a consciousness [*vijñāna* 識]) and *ākāra* 相 ([mental] image) being *aparicchinna* (indistinct).

28 Dan Lusthaus, "Buddhist Philosophy, Chinese," in *Routledge Encyclopedia of Philosophy*, edited by E. Craig (London: Routledge, 1998), electronic version

retrieved 20 April 2008, from http://www.rep.routledge.com/article/ G002SECT4.

29 Dan Lusthaus, "Yogācāra School," p. 919. "These seeds, embodying wholesome or unwholesome implications, regenerate new seeds each moment. These causal seed chains remain latent until a new conscious experience causes the seed to sprout, infusing a new cognition."

30 Zhang Taiyan, "Jianli zongjiao lun," pp. 403–404.

31 Zhang Taiyan, *Zhuo Han chang yan* 菿漢昌言 [Zhang Taiyan's frank words], in *Zhuo Han san yan,* p. 71.

32 Zhang Taiyan, "Bian xing, A" 辨性 (上) [Argumentation on the nature, A], in his *Guogu lunheng* 國故論衡 [Discourses on the national heritage weighed in the balance] (Shanghai: Shanghai guji chubanshe, 2004), p. 134; *Zhuo Han wei yan*, 17b.

33 Zhang Taiyan, *Zhuo Han wei yan*, 8a.

34 Charles A. Muller, "四分" in *Digital Dictionary of Buddhism*, edited by Charles A. Muller, <http://buddhism-dict.net.virtual.anu.edu.au/ddb>. Edition of 26 March, 2009.

35 Zhang Taiyan, *Zhuo Han wei yan*, pp. 8a–8b.

36 See also Wang Hui, "The Fate of 'Mr. Science' in China: The Concept of Science and its Application in Modern Chinese Thought," in *Formations of Colonial Modernity in East Asia*, edited by Tani E. Barlow (Durham: Duke University Press, 1997), p. 40.

37 Hu Weixi, *Zhuan shi cheng zhi: Qinghua xuepai yu ershi shiji Zhongguo zhexue* 轉識成智：清華學派與20世紀中國哲學 [Transforming consciousness into wisdom: The Qinghua School and twentieth-century Chinese philosophy] (Shanghai: Huadong shifan daxue chubanshe, 2005), pp. 124–125.

38 Yan Fu, *Mule Mingxue* 穆勒名學 [Mill's *A System of Logic*], in his *Yan yi mingzhu congkan* 嚴譯名著叢刊 [Collection of famous writings translated by Yan Fu], Vol. 8 (Shanghai: Shangwu yinshuguan, 1931), p. 58.

39 Zhang Taiyan, "Zhi *Guocui xuebao* She shu" 致國粹學報社書 [Letter to the *National Essence Journal* Society] (1909), in *Zhang Taiyan zhenglun xuanji* 章太炎政論選集 [Selected political writings of Zhang Taiyan], Vol. 1, edited by Tang Zhijun 湯志鈞 (Beijing: Zhonghua shuju, 1977), p. 498.

40 By 1922 he had long revised his earlier critical assessments of Confucius. In *Guoxue gailun*, pp. 47–48, he cites a number of passages—many already featured in earlier writings—to illustrate his claim that each of the "nine schools" of pre-Qin masters had touched upon aspects of the profound teachings that were consistent with Buddhist teachings.

41 Contact 觸 (*sparāa*); focusing of attention 作意 (*manaskāra*); receiving sensations 受 (*vedanā*); conceptualization 想 (*saājñā*); and volitional impulse 思 (*cetanā*).

42 According to Charles A. Muller: "This refers to a directly produced effect within a person—seeds 種子 and their manifestations 現行. [This refers to]

the production by the seeds in the *ālaya* consciousness 阿賴耶識 of the world cognized through the seven consciousnesses." See under "四緣" in *Digital Dictionary of Buddhism*, edited by Charles A. Muller, <http://buddhism-dict.net.virtual.anu.edu.au/ddb>. Edition of 26 March 2009.

43   *Ibid.*: "For the mind to arise, its object must be present, so every object becomes a cause for the mind."

44   *Ibid.*: "Since the prior instant of mind/mental functioning gives rise directly to the succeeding instant of mind, there is no gap in their leading into one another."

45   Zhang Taiyan, "Zhuzixue lüeshuo" 諸子學略説 [Brief account of the learning of the Masters], originally published in 1906 and included in *Zhang Taiyan zhenglun xuanji*, Vol. 1, pp. 301–304.

46   There are several problems here. First of all, the third statement, "Sound is impermanent" is a conclusion in this format, not a thesis. Second, since the *hetu* (reason) has to be a property of the thing to be proven (the *sādhya*, which for Buddhists is the *pakṣa*/thesis), this order of statements would be unacceptable to Indians. Zhang does not have a clear sense of how Indian syllogisms work; he is treating them like Aristotelian syllogisms, which they are not. He does seem to be aware that in the full version of the three-part syllogism, the "example" statement includes the axiomatic relation between the *sādhya* and the *hetu* ("whatever is produced is impermanent"), which is something distinct from the actual examples.

47   That is, the reason by itself does not entail the thesis.

48   Zhang Taiyan, "Yuan ming," (1909) in *Guogu lunheng*, p. 121.

49   *Ibid.*, 122. The full form of the standard *yinming* three-part inference or syllogism is as follows. "Sound is impermanent (thesis 立宗) / because it is produced (reason 因) / Example (*yu* 喻): [a] Whatever is produced, that is known to be impermanent, like a pot, etc; [b] Whatever is permanent, that is known to be unproduced, like *ākāśa* (unlimited expansiveness; 虛空), etc." See under "能立" in *Digital Dictionary of Buddhism*, edited by Charles A. Muller, <http://buddhismdict.net.virtual.anu.edu.au/ddb>. Edition of 14 October 2009. Zhang's criticism is that the Mohist and Western versions have no place for the example (*yu*) and hence are more limited in their application.

50   Zhang Taiyan, *Qi Wu Lun shi ding ben* 齊物論釋定本 [Definitive edition of "Explanation of 'Discourse on making all things equal'"] (circa 1914), in *Zhang Taiyan quanji* 章太炎全集 [Complete works of Zhang Taiyan], Vol. 6 (Shanghai: Shanghai renmin chubanshe, 1986), p. 61.

51   *Ibid.*, p. 65.

52   *Ibid.*, 70.

53   According to Charles A. Muller and Dan Lusthaus, 阿陀那識 (*ādāna-vijñāna*) is a "Yogācāra term, basically synonymous with *ālaya-vijñāna* 阿賴耶識 (store consciousness), which expresses the special connotation of 'that which holds the body and the sense organs together.' It is also understood to be the

consciousness that contains all seeds, and which is responsible for the linking of rebirths." See under "阿陀那識" in *Digital Dictionary of Buddhism*, edited by Charles A. Muller, <http://buddhismdict.net.virtual.anu.edu.au/ddb>. Edition of 26 March 2009.

54   This term occurs in the "De chong fu" 德充符 [Tally of complete virtue] chapter of *Zhuangzi*.

55   This is a variation of 阿摩羅識 (*amala-vijñāna*). According to Charles A. Muller, "An additional layer of consciousness ('ninth' consciousness 第九識) originally posited in the Shelun School 攝論宗 by Paramārtha 眞諦 and his colleagues … based on explanations of a pure consciousness beginning to appear in *tathāgatagarbha*-influenced texts such as the *Awakening of Mahāyāna Faith* and *Laṅkāvatāra-sūtra*. The *amala-vijñāna* was seen by its advocates as a way of supplementing the eight consciousness scheme developed in the Yogācāra school, since they felt that the system of the Yogācāra, based on their understanding of the *ālayavijñāna* 阿賴耶識, being defiled, or at best, neutral, was inadequate for explaining enlightenment as the clear birthright of all sentient beings." See under the entry "阿摩羅識" in *Digital Dictionary of Buddhism*, edited by Charles A. Muller, <http://buddhismdict.net.virtual.anu.edu.au/ddb>. Edition of 26 March 2009.

56   Zhang Taiyan, *Qi wu lun shi ding ben*, p. 71.

57   Dan Lusthaus, "Buddhist Philosophy, Chinese." Retrieved 20 April 2008.

58   Zhang Taiyan, *Guoxue gailun*, p. 35.

59   Here this refers to a special type of thinking: thinking with constant reference to the eighth consciousness as the self.

60   Zhang Taiyan, *Zhuo Han wei yan*, 32a.

61   See, for example, John Makeham, *Transmitters and Creators: Chinese Commentators and Commentaries on the Analects* (Cambridge MA: Harvard University Asia Center, 2003), pp. 50–51, 114, 128–129, 219, 224.

62   Zhang Taiyan, *Zhuo Han wei yan*, 73a–73b.

Part II: The Beida and Tsinghua Schools of Philosophy

Developing the Academic Discipline of Chinese Philosophy: The Departments of Philosophy at Peking, Tsinghua, and Yenching Universities (1910s–1930s)

Xiaoqing Diana Lin

This chapter examines how institutional influences affected the writings of modern philosophers such as Hu Shi 胡適 (1891–1962) and Feng Youlan 馮友蘭 (1895–1990), as well as their colleagues Jin Yuelin 金岳霖 (1895–1984), He Lin 賀麟 (1902–1992), Xiong Shili 熊十力 (1885–1968), and Zhang Dongsun 張東蓀 (1886–1973), among others. These were all prominent figures in early twentieth-century China whose work and efforts helped establish the parameters of Chinese philosophy as an academic discipline in China. Their approaches varied, but they all shared a common reliance on Western philosophical concepts and frameworks for the new Chinese discipline they constructed. Institutional differences also had a salient impact on the styles and approaches they pursued in their scholarship. The institutions where they taught were three of the six universities where a Department of Philosophy existed in China by 1930. My institutional study focuses on the philosophy departments in these three universities.

1. Peking University: Academic Liberalism and Resistance to a Unified Approach to Philosophy

The institutional goals and policies of National Peking University corresponded to a great extent with the research and curriculum output on its campus. The interactions between institutional policies and individual faculty members also helped shape the pattern of the development of the discipline of philosophy in early twentieth-century China. As Peking

University Chancellor from 1917 to 1927, Cai Yuanpei 蔡元培 (1868–1940) promoted a vision of *jianrong bingbao* 兼容並包 (all subjects of learning to be tolerated and included). His aim was to create a new Chinese culture that would be conducive to a new national identity, just as Wilhelm von Humboldt of Prussia in the early nineteenth century had wanted to create a new German culture that would be conducive to a new German national identity. Chancellor Cai Yuanpei's goal of educational autonomy needs to be understood in the context of Chinese politics at his time, when political instability and regime change were the norm. For three months, Cai himself was Minister of Education under the Yuan Shikai regime, before going on to study in Germany as he could not agree with Yuan's policies. For Cai, the university had to be independent of corrupt political regimes and take sole responsibility for creating a new Chinese culture.

Although, like many Chinese scholars, Cai Yuanpei was motivated to transform China through science, he had no intention of promoting the wholesale introduction of science into China. Cai scorned the material forces that science unleashed, which to him stunted any emotional cultivation that religion used to give. Cai rejected Confucian learning because it had been associated with Chinese politics for too long. On the other hand, he also appreciated the emphasis on humaneness and emotional cultivation in Confucian learning.[1] Therefore Cai's policy of inclusion was a way to have the forces of science and Confucian learning balance one another, and the synthesis thus created would avoid the pitfalls of a lopsided emphasis on science or a sustained Confucian dominance of Chinese culture, including political culture, a synthesis that would transcend the East-West divide and provide a modern and viable identity for the new China.

This plan was reflected in his selection of faculty members in the Arts and Sciences, from the more conservative Cui Shi 崔適 (1852–1924) and Huang Kan 黃侃 (1886–1935); to the conservative innovators such as Liang Shuming 梁漱溟 (1893–1988), Xiong Shili 熊十力 (1885–1968), and Liu Shipei 劉師培 (1884–1919), who utilized Western/Indian values and goals in their discussion of Chinese society; to innovators such as Tang Yongtong 湯用彤 (1893–1964) and Chen Yinke 陳寅恪 (1890–1969) who utilized more Western methodologies in their teaching and research; and to the trend-setters such as Hu Shi and Xu Zhimo 徐誌摩 (1897–1931). Through newspapers and journals, the classroom podium, clubs, and public lectures, different ideas of culture and approaches to scholarship were bounced back and forth and debated. Cai's resistance to the wholesale introduction of Western science led to the proliferation of different approaches to Chinese and Western learning on campus. In that sense, Peking University served as a microcosm of the divergent intellectual and cultural forces at work in China.

This was reflected in the Department of Philosophy, which had just been transformed from a component of the Division of the Humanities (*wenke zhexuemen* 文科哲學門) (where the first students were enrolled in 1914) to an independent department in 1919. Courses also took on a distinct nature that reflected the campus culture and policies. A major motivation was the development of a new epistemology: from Liang Shuming's division of cultures and civilizations, to Xiong Shili's reinterpretation of Confucian learning and Buddhism, to the courses in Western philosophy taught by the likes of Tang Yongtong 湯用彤 in the 1920s and 1930s. These epistemological approaches often varied greatly from one another, but their authors all seemed to realize there was an urgent need to develop a new approach to the understanding of Chinese and Western cultures. Courses in classical Western epistemology, such as the thought of Descartes, Locke, Spinoza, and Kant, far outnumbered the courses on more contemporary philosophers, such as August Comte or even John Dewey. The focus of teaching was on eighteenth- and nineteenth-century European epistemology which dealt with the European transition from a religious to a more secular society, as reflected in the treatment of the authority of God and humans in the writings of all the classical philosophers mentioned above. Related to this preoccupation was an emphasis on the histories of both Chinese and Western philosophies, the extent of which distinguished the Philosophy Department at Peking University from that at Tsinghua and Yenching Universities.[2] History enabled a search for broad frameworks behind complex ideas and concepts. Tang Yongtong, for instance, taught both Western epistemology, history of Western philosophy, and the history of Chinese philosophy (especially the Wei and Jin dynasties). Both Western approaches to deal with conflicting sources of authority and broad frameworks connecting varied ideas and concepts helped facilitate Peking University philosophers' search for new ways to connect Chinese and Western cultures and create a modernized version of Chinese culture. And if epistemology was a common approach many Chinese scholars employed to link Chinese thought to a framework of Western philosophy, a historical approach linked many different aspects of Chinese thinking that could not be readily incorporated into Western philosophical frameworks. It allowed more components of Chinese thought to be treated as philosophy because of their interconnectedness.[3]

History, especially as reflected in the style of textual exegesis (combining philological and evidential scholarship), permeated the humanities at Peking University. Tang Yongtong, Meng Sen (1868–1937), Yao Congwu (姚從吾 1894–1970), Chen Yinke, Chen Yuan 陳垣 (1880–1971), and many others, often employed a philological approach combined with a critical cross-examination of various classical texts inspired by Western values in their research in Chinese history and philosophy. Textual exegesis became characterized by detailed analysis combined with an eclectic blend of various approaches, such as a combination of a scientific hypothesis, Western humanism and progressivism, and Confucian moral concerns.[4] This testifies not only to the self-assertive approach to philosophy at Peking University in the 1920s and 1930s,[5] but also to how Chinese thought was incorporated into the modern disciplinary framework of philosophy through the methods of textual exegesis. Tang Yongtong, for example, typically wrote in the style of textual exegesis, allowing him simultaneously to apply a functionalist approach to Chinese philosophy of the Wei and Jin Dynasties, which inducted Chinese thought into a pro-Western style philosophical inquiry, and to include many details that could not be easily summarized or categorized by ready-made concepts.[6] Textual exegesis became the response to a call for the fashioning of a new Chinese culture, based on a synthesis of Chinese and Western cultures. It satisfied the need to be inclusive of Chinese culture and to be flexible in adopting Western approaches which facilitated incorporating Chinese learning into some form of Western cultural or academic framework. It alleviated the anxiety over not including the "crucial" elements in Chinese culture, as the detail-oriented style of textual exegesis enabled the inclusion of an open-ended amount of knowledge, and forestalled a "misfit" between Chinese culture and Western frameworks.

A historical approach combined with textual exegesis also proved to be a very useful way for Hu Shi to inject an element of logical analysis into his construction of Chinese philosophy. In his path-breaking *Zhongguo zhexueshi dagang* 中國哲學史大綱 [An outline of the history of Chinese philosophy], Hu Shi—the champion of American pragmatism and logical approaches to Chinese philosophy—favored textual exegesis, believing that it was scientific and would reveal significant messages hitherto hidden.[7] Inspired by John Dewey's historical/genetic method, "Hu

Shi assumed not only that history is a matter of evolutionary progression, or historical development, but also that there is a logical sequence, a causal relationship, between one historic event and another. Importantly, he applied this thinking to his understanding of the history (and internal dynamics) of Chinese philosophy." The result was Hu's conception of "historical change as involving isolatable chains of causes and effects," and it greatly facilitated his project to "re-organize the national heritage" (整理國故).[8]

Parallel to a predominantly text-based exegetical approach to the study of the history of Chinese philosophy was one based on a Lu Xiangshan 陸象山 / Wang Yangming 王陽明 focus on intuition, in the construction of Chinese philosophy by the likes of Liang Shuming, Xiong Shili, and He Lin. Especially as developed by Xiong Shili, this arguably became the foundation for twentieth-century New Confucians such as Mou Zongsan 牟宗三 (1909–1995) and Tang Junyi 唐君毅 (1909–1978). This reliance on the Lu/Wang intuitive style to learning was also fostered by the macro-atmosphere at Peking University, more specifically by Cai Yuanpei's concern that the material forces science unleashed would stunt emotional development and by what Cai perceived to be the positive emphasis of Confucian learning on self-cultivation.[9] To address this issue, Cai himself offered ten lectures on aesthetics on the campus of Peking University between 1919 and 1920.

Xiong Shili started teaching Buddhism at Peking University at Cai Yuanpei's invitation in 1922. His tenure was sporadic, from 1922 to 1924, then 1925 to 1926, and 1932 to 1937. It was interspersed by an early attempt to follow Liang Shuming to a middle school in Shandong Province and trips to Nanjing and Hangzhou. Xiong Shili's background in Buddhist studies and his frequent "enlightenment" through intuition in his early life[10] combined with his knowledge of modern philosophy, especially of Henri Bergson, to help him reconstruct Chinese philosophy through a synthesis of Chinese, Buddhist, and Western ideas. Xiong made Liang Shuming's acquaintance in Beijing in 1919, beginning a half century of friendship. In 1920, upon Liang's recommendation, Xiong went to study at the Chinese Institute of Inner Learning in Nanjing (Zhina neixueyuan 支那內學院), under Ouyang Jingwu 歐陽竟無 (1871–1943). And in 1922, also upon Liang's recommendation, Cai Yuanpei invited Xiong to teach Buddhism at Peking University.[11]

One of Liang Shuming's influences on Xiong was an interest in Bergsonian philosophy, especially Bergson's argument for a universe in constant flux due to the movement of the vital impulse and the insepara-bility of the (spiritual) vital impulse and the material. Xiong's *New Trea-tise on Unique Consciousness* was a self-conscious effort to create an ontology where knowledge of the world, a world outlook, and an outlook on life, were integrated. It reinterpreted a dynamic connection between the individual and the universe. Based on his extensive knowledge of Buddhism, Bergsonian philosophy, and Confucian learning, Xiong created a universe in constant flux. Xiong rejected the Buddhist renuncia-tion of this world but absorbed much of the Buddhist *descriptive style* of the universe which had also influenced Bergson: amorphousness and constant change. On the other hand, through the philosophy of Henri Bergson and Confucian writings by Wang Yangming, Xiong gave a greater affirmation to material life while still keeping it subordinate to the spiritual realm.[12] His ontology was a reinterpreted Lu/Wang world of the heart/mind, infused with Bergsonian philosophy and Buddhism. Chung-ying Cheng interprets this ontology as consisting of two layers: a self-reflection of the world, and a world view based on this self-reflection integrated with one's sense of self. In other words, Xiong saw the human being as self-aware and constantly seeking to understand his/her interac-tion with the outside world through self-reflection.[13] His writings opened the door for a modern reinterpretation of Confucian concepts.[14]

A Lu/Wang intuitive approach to Chinese learning was also champi-oned by He Lin, who, on the surface, appears quite different from Xiong Shili in background and field of study. A specialist in Hegel, he had studied at Tsinghua College from 1919 to 1926, before a series of sojourns in the US and Germany. From 1926 to 1928, He studied at Oberlin College, where he was awarded a B.A. From March to September 1928, He Lin was at the University of Chicago, where he audited courses on phenomenology, Bergson, and the ethics of T. H. Green (1836–1882), Henry Sidgwick (1838–1900), and G. E. Moore (1873–1958). He was espe-cially attracted to the philosophy of T. H. Green, whose criticism of English empiricism and attempt to provide a metaphysical basis for ethics eventually led He Lin to Josiah Royce (1855–1916) and Hegel. From 1928 to 1930, He attended graduate school at Harvard, where he took classes from W. E. Hocking (1873–1966) and Alfred North Whitehead (1861–1947), and read Royce extensively. The Hegelian influence on Royce made He determined to study Hegel as well as Kant in their homeland. From 1930 to 1931, He Lin studied at the University of Berlin, focusing on Hegel and gradually branching out to Spinoza and Kant. Upon returning to

China, He was hired to teach Western philosophy at Peking University in 1931.[15]

He Lin said that he was first influenced by an intuitive approach to Chinese learning through Liang Shuming in 1921[16] when He Lin was 19 years old, two years after he was admitted to Tsinghua College as a preparatory student to embark on studies in the US Unlike Liang, who contrasted the rational and the intuitive, He tried to reconcile the two. In doing so, he built a continuum between what would be usually classified as "rational," (Zhu Xi), and "intuitive," (Lu Xiangshan and Wang Yangming). He classified both as different types of intuitions: that of Lu and Wang, pre-rational intuition, and that of Zhu, post-rational intuition.[17] Pre-rational intuition was the beginning of human thinking and based on an inchoate (*hundun de* 混沌的) experience. It was not knowledge itself but rather an experiential approach to knowledge. Post-rational intuition, on the other hand, was built on the basis of extensive scholarship and a "fermentation (*chunshu* 醇熟)" of knowledge and skills acquired over time.[18] Intuition, therefore, was not contrary to rationality, but something which could deepen and flourish after extensive studies of knowledge and rationalization. It was He Lin's goal to "update the philosophy of the Lu-Wang School in the light of modern idealism in general and Hegel in particular."[19] In an assessment of traditional Chinese ethical principles and practices published in *Eastern Miscellany* (*Dongfang zazhi* 東方雜誌) in 1936, He cautioned against an overly eager overthrow of Confucian practices simply because they did not fit with contemporary practices and expectations. Instead, He asked for an intuitive examination of the true spirit of these practices and a separation of the spirit from praxis. This way, many Confucian ideas would still prove to be beneficial to present life. On the other hand, many Western ideas would also be found compatible with the spirit of Confucian ideas. For example, He even suggested that absorbing Christian sentiments, with their persistence of belief, love, kindness, and service to humanity, as well as transcendental spirit, would greatly strengthen Confucian learning, which to He already resembled a religion in ritual and spirit.[20] The "Chinese learning as essence, and Western learning as application" formula, for He, was definitely impracticable. An intuitive approach would continue to bring together the universe and human experience, a central notion in Confucian learning, while bypassing structural and social differences between Chinese and Western cultures and integrating the latter two at an experiential level.

In general, there was a close correlation between Cai Yuanpei's "all inclusive" (*jianrong bingbao*) policy and the curriculum and research in the Department of Philosophy at Peking University from the late 1910s to the 1930s. From textual exegesis to a reinterpretation of Lu/Wang idealism, there was an attempt to find a balance and synthesis between Chinese thought and Western philosophy in both content and methodology.

2. Tsinghua University: Synthesis of Western Logic and Chinese Humanism through New Realism

This conscious effort to be "all-inclusive" of Chinese and Western thinking—especially Chinese thinking—at Peking University was less obvious in the Department of Philosophy at Tsinghua University. Here instead there seems to have been a more overt emphasis on a "universal" philosophy built on the basis of Western logic. Tsinghua University had a very different founding from that of Peking University. Whereas the latter was the flagship university set up to rebuild Chinese culture, Tsinghua, financed by the Boxer Indemnity Fund, was from the very beginning meant to serve as a conduit for American-style liberal education. Tsinghua changed from a two-year college which prepared students to go to the US to a four-year university only in 1928. According to Bertrand Russell, who visited in 1920, Tsinghua

> had an atmosphere exactly like that of a small American university, and a (Chinese) President who is almost a perfect reproduction of the American college president.... As one enters the gates, one becomes aware of the presence of every virtue usually absent in China: cleanliness, punctuality, exactitude, efficiency.... One great merit, that belongs to American institutions generally, is that the students are made to learn English.[21]

For many visitors, the two universities formed a sharp contrast: a structured life with a relatively low level of interest in politics, and a robust, youthful student body fluent in English at Tsinghua versus the generally older student body at Peking University, often less bound by a strict academic curriculum and more radical politically.[22] More faculty and administrators at Tsinghua University had studied in Europe and especially in the US, and they had a better understanding of American society and culture. As a preparatory college, Tsinghua had also emphasized training and education in Western culture, which provided the background for an open exchange of Chinese and Western cultures. Thus the cultural radicalism of Peking University became moderated once it reached Tsinghua.[23] The influence of Western, especially American, culture on the Tsinghua campus was apparent in the uniforms Tsinghua students wore in physical education; their Peking University counterparts often wore gowns to such classes. Tsinghua, in the words of Hu Weixi, had a multi-centered approach to culture. Tsinghua, like Peking University, practiced faculty self-rule (*jiaoshou zhixiao* 教授治校). Administrative committees consisting of professors discussed matters from the school budget to the establishment of particular academic disciplines or subfields, from faculty appointments to the selection of students to go to the US. These committees were actively supported by President Mei Yiqi 梅貽琦 of Tsinghua University (1931–1949).[24]

This openness to administration and diverse cultural developments at Tsinghua was translated into curricula, fields of study, and new appointments that furthered such trends. In the Department of Philosophy, for instance, the appointment in 1926 of Jin Yuelin 金岳霖, a student deeply influenced by early champions of analytical philosophy such as Bertrand Russell and G. E. Moore, led to the appointment of Feng Youlan 馮友蘭, Zhang Shenfu 張申府 (1893–1986), Zhang Dainian 張岱年 (1909–2004), Shen Youding 沈有鼎 (1908–1989), and a few others who had similar interests in a logical approach to philosophy, even though they varied from one another in their specific approaches. The focus on analytical philosophy at Tsinghua was aimed at building a true understanding of Chinese thought through universal science.[25] Yet, compared with Peking University, where the focus was to explore the Chinese past through history and epistemology, and to capture its nuances through textual exegesis or the intuitive approach, a logical, analytical conceptualization of Chinese thought in history risked missing out on some aspects that did not fit the definition of philosophy by Western standards. In this respect, the Tsinghua philosophy faculty were aided by a legacy of humanism which encouraged them to pursue a more metaphysical synthesis between Chinese and Western learning.

The logical orientation of the philosophers at Tsinghua University was tempered by the scholarly influence of the National Studies Research Institute (國學研究院),[26] where renowned scholars Wang Guowei 王國維 (1877–1927), Liang Qichao 梁啓超 (1873–1929), Zhao Yuanren 趙元任 (1892–1982) and Chen Yinke—the "four giant mentors" (四大導師)— created an atmosphere of communication between Chinese and Western learning. These four scholars had very different backgrounds and temperaments, but all were erudite in Chinese and Western learning and able to weave both traditions into a discursive framework. They left an indelible impact. Even though the Research Institute of Chinese Studies only lasted for four years (1925–1929), it imparted to Tsinghua's humanities departments the importance of literary and historical studies and of parallelism between Chinese and Western learning, especially the introduction of Western methodology. By the early 1930s, this humanistic approach led to a quest for closer integration. As Feng Youlan commented: "Our comparisons between Chinese and Western thought are not meant to judge which is right or wrong, but rather to clarify one with the other. We hope that in the not so distant future, European philosophy will be supplemented by Chinese philosophy on intuition and experience, and Chinese philosophy by Western logic and clear arguments."[27]

In practice, the Tsinghua philosophy faculty members relied heavily on New Realism, an early twentieth-century Euro-American school of thought that linked the objective and experiential realms in logical relationships decipherable through language. The New Realists believed they could do away with cognition, minimize epistemology almost to insignificance, and build a direct and reliable means of access for human consciousness to things in the external world through a modification of sensory data via critical reflection through logic and language. The ultimate terms of knowledge are those that survive an analysis which has been carried as far as possible. Thus if a circle is defined as the "class of points equidistant from a given point," this means that a circle is a complex object whose components are specified by the words in the given phrase. The single word is virtually an abbreviation of the phrase. Whether a word was used to denote one simple fact, or to compress several facts, as in the example above, the result is the same: to give an exact description to things.[28]

In historical perspective, New Realism could be considered the last stance of metaphysics against the onslaught of science. New Realism developed in the United States in the early 1900s on several campuses, including but not confined to Columbia, Princeton, and Harvard. Some New Realists, the neutral monists, followed a strict adherence to a balance between inner human experience and the external world; ideas and specific phenomenon or experience were equally important. Prominent adherents of neutral monism included Ralph Barton Perry (1876–1957) and Edwin Holt (1873–1946), both professors at Harvard University

(1900s–1930s and 1920s respectively). In his early years, Bertrand Russell also took this stance. An example is the argument that Russell argued that behind every human sense experience there was an idea that the experience captured, such as the idea of whiteness, or the idea of direction as in the sentence, "Edinburgh is north [of] London." These ideas did not just exist as particular examples of color or direction, or of abstract ideas, but were also manifested in innumerable other places and experiences. Both "whiteness" and "north of" were objects of one's thought, not of thought itself,[29] because they denoted objective universal existences. Similarly, resemblances and similarities as well as relationships in space and time were all universal objective existences in the sense that they had actual correlates in reality, and therefore they were not merely linguistic and mental, even though they were characterized by concepts.[30] Another branch of New Realism leaned toward a neo-Platonic recognition of a higher level of truth in these logical relationships *prior to* experience and acknowledged these logical relationships as independent concepts subsisting in reality before they materialize in real life. Such a view was championed by William Pepperell Montague (1873–1953), who taught at Columbia University from 1903 to 1947. Either way, however, experience and thinking were validated to different extents in light of science and mathematical logic. The New Realists differed markedly from a later school of philosophy, the Vienna Circle, the representative thinkers of which wanted to rest logic solely on empirical experience. The latter was a group of philosophers centered on Moritz Schlick of Vienna University in the 1920s who denounced metaphysics as an unreliable source of truth, an art rather than a science, and believed all knowledge came from experience or logical statements that could be reduced to empirical statements. The New Realists, on the other hand, tried to use logic to save metaphysics.

New Realism proved useful to Tsinghua faculty members who wanted to find a set of universal criteria for philosophical studies, while linking them to a more traditional Chinese humanistic emphasis, in order to attain a level of universal thinking higher than a superficial matching of Western and Chinese philosophical concepts and content. In his introduction to the Department of Philosophy at Tsinghua University, Zhang Shenfu, after describing the various logic classes the department offered, such as mathematical logic, symbolic logic, history of logic, and so forth, commented that the majority of the faculty members specialized in logical analysis and leaned toward New Realism. The goal of the department was to become the Cambridge of China. Zhang did not forget to add that, besides logic, knowledge of China was also important, and survey courses in that area would meet social needs and should not be ignored.[31]

By New Realism Zhang meant primarily G. E. Moore and Bertrand Russell. Both were founders of the analytic school of philosophy and taught at Cambridge University at various points in the early twentieth century. Tsinghua University philosophy professors Zhang Shenfu and his younger brother Zhang Dainian (Zhang Shenfu from 1930 to 1935, and Zhang Dainian from 1933 to 1943, then from 1946 to 52) were both greatly influenced by Russell. Zhang Shenfu first read Russell in 1915 as a sophomore in mathematics at Peking University. This led Zhang to switch from mathematics to philosophy and, in particular, to understand the world through logic.[32] As one of the editors of the *New Youth* magazine, Zhang Shenfu translated and introduced Russell to the Chinese reader. He also met with Russell when the latter visited China in 1920 and maintained a lifelong correspondence with him until the Communist takeover in 1949.

One example of closer integration between Chinese thought and Western philosophy is the coining of logical concepts such as *shi* 式, *neng* 能, *dao* 道, and *daquan* 大全 by Tsinghua philosophers Jin Yuelin and Feng Youlan. These were traditional Chinese terms that were imbued with new meaning. They would often go beyond the parameters of Western philosophy, including some terms originally meant to be grasped through intuition. They enabled these philosophers to create a system of philosophy that suited certain trends in Chinese learning, such as the emphasis on the universe in continuous movement and the dynamic connection between the material and the spiritual/ethical. The trend was led by Jin Yuelin, who did his PhD in political science at Columbia University before switching to philosophy. Jin's doctoral dissertation was on T. H. Green, whose neo-Hegelian thinking had a profound impact on him. Subsequent study at the University of London in 1921 enabled Jin to read David Hume and especially Bertrand Russell. This marked a turning point in his academic interests, from political science to philosophy and logic. Russell's *Principles of Mathematics* laid the foundation for Jin's analytical logic. Although Jin's sojourn at the University of London lasted only eight months, it transformed him from an idealist to a believer in the truth of an external reality, defined by logic.[33] Since Jin was the first chairman of the Department of Philosophy at Tsinghua University—he was hired in 1926 to establish the department and taught there until 1952—his impact cannot be overestimated.

Inspired by David Hume and Bertrand Russell, Jin went beyond them. He wanted to build a more abstract system of the world and knowledge than Hume and provide a more systematic explanation of the world than Russell. Drawing on, but not confined to, traditional Chinese concepts, Jin used a series of logical concepts to delineate a world where abstract rules manifested in various material forms that constituted the phenomenal world. The various rules governing the world, or *li* 理, were divided into *keneng* 可能 (possibility or possible forms of specific things) and *shi* 式 (all possible forms of concrete things). *Shi* roughly corresponds to Zhu Xi's Supreme Ultimate (*taiji* 太極): the ultimate development of all rules in the universe. The world of possibilities would become reality with the injection of *neng* 能 (energy) into the possible forms, *keneng* 可能. A synthesis of Aristotle's concept of matter and the Chinese concept of *qi* 氣, for Jin, *neng* was the pure matter which all other relationships or characteristics modified and which would remain after all its modifications were taken away. *Neng*, or what constituted the fundamental materiality of the world, once it filled the framework of *keneng*, would transform *keneng* from possibility into reality. Through a delineation of the specific steps from *keneng* as possibility to full-blown reality, Jin tried to build an ontology based on a scientific and logical description.[34] For Jin, logic constituted the essence of the world, but this logic was based on concepts coined to reflect Chinese thought, although now situated in a larger, universal framework. The new world of philosophy Jin created was neither purely Chinese nor purely Western.

In his pre-publication review of the first volume of Feng Youlan's *Zhongguo zhexueshi* 中國哲學史 [A history of Chinese philosophy] (1931), Jin questioned whether Feng was "acknowledging Chinese philosophy as philosophy developed in China," or simply writing a history of philosophy by applying Western philosophical methods to Chinese thought.[35] Despite Jin's objections, Feng firmly believed in the existence of a philosophical tradition in China. Similar to Jin, Feng Youlan, who taught at Tsinghua University from 1928 to 1952, pursued a logical discussion of ontology so as to incorporate Chinese philosophy into a Western academic framework of philosophy.

Much more than Jin, however, Feng believed in the compatibility between Western and certain aspects of Chinese philosophies. Feng Youlan followed his Columbia University adviser, William Pepperell

Montague, who classified philosophy into three parts: universe, life, and methodology. According to Feng, correspondence between traditional Chinese thought and the first two categories could be identified, but not the third category. Whereas the Chinese concept of *tiandao* 天道 (the way of heaven) corresponded roughly to the Western notion of cosmology (*yuzhoulun* 宇宙論), the discussion of philosophical methods, while still in evidence at the establishment of orthodox Confucian learning in China (roughly 100 B.C.), disappeared after the Song Dynasty (A.D. 960–1279). On the other hand, the methodology used in connection with norm-ative principles (*yili zhi xue* 義理之學) flourished. It was, however, not about knowledge, but rather ethical cultivation.[36] Although certain writings bore evidence of the beginnings of metaphysical reasoning, such as the works of Gongsun Long or Zhu Xi, the attempt to build a purely logical argument was sacrificed to the ultimate moral goal to which such reasoning was directed. Zhu Xi, for Feng Youlan, reached the epitome of metaphysical reasoning in Chinese history, but Zhu, like all other Chinese thinkers, failed to transcend the moral framework of his reasoning. Therefore, in Feng's eyes, the lack of compatibility between Chinese thought and Western philosophical methodology—especially the separation between Western logical and Chinese ethical reasoning—was something which could be overcome only if the metaphysical reasoning of Chinese thinkers could be directed towards a logical rather than an ethical end.

Feng Youlan synthesized the Vienna Circle's concern for experience and New Realism's emphasis on logic in his writings. Contrary to the New Realists, he acknowledged the truthfulness of empirical knowledge. But contrary to the Vienna Circle, this empirical knowledge, instead of being the end of knowledge, was to Feng only the beginning—a knowledge that would be furthered through analytic logic. Here he drew on the New Realist attempt to bridge the dichotomy of subjective human experience and external reality through logical relationships. On the other hand, Feng leaned more toward Montague's neo-Platonic approach. This combined human experience and the external world in a logical relationship, while prioritizing the importance of ideas. It enabled Feng Youlan to incorporate ethical concerns and traditional Chinese outlook on life including concepts that reflected such outlook into his discussion of Chinese philosophy.

This multi-stranded framework allowed Feng to rebuild Chinese philosophy along logical lines and to go beyond a natural or ethical cosmology to a study of ontology. His new Chinese philosophy was characterized by concepts such as *qi* 氣 or *dao* 道—the latter, for Lao Zi, was a material force—but these concepts were now metaphysical and meant to be universal in their application. These ideas or concepts, in Feng's view, preceded reality. This was a far cry from Lao Zi's *dao*, which was self-generating into myriads of things in the universe. The new Chinese philosophy was founded on the premises of the Vienna Circle and legitimated with the continuum between human experience and the external world as championed by the New Realists. It was not a simple matching of Chinese content and Western concepts. For Feng, *li* 理 (principle), *qi* 氣 (vital energy), *daoti* 道體 (processual emergence),[37] and *daquan* 大全 (the great whole) were both logical concepts and the most fundamental components of the universe. They were meant to capture those elements of Chinese learning that Feng deemed most pertinent to his vision of a reconstructed Chinese philosophy: a universe infused with material forces and in eternal flux. The most notable change was the metaphysical nature of what these concepts represented. Unlike Zhu Xi, who believed *qi* and *li* were metaphysical but had tangible existences, Feng saw them as logical concepts that were subsistent in reality, realizable only through concrete matter.

Thus Jin and Feng tried to reorient metaphysics along the path of logic. Not everyone agreed with their goal. Hong Qian 洪謙 (1909–1992), a PhD in philosophy at the University of Vienna and a student of Moritz Schlick of the Vienna Circle, was hired by the Department of Philosophy at Tsinghua University in 1934. When he expressed strong opposition to the rebuilding of metaphysics as a path to truth, his relationship with Jin and Feng deteriorated, and Hong became distanced from the department.[38] Jin and Feng both tried to navigate a path that would classify metaphysics as compatible with science and especially with logic. They tried to transcend any logical obstacles that would prevent their metaphysical systems from explaining the whole world. For instance, they disagreed with the "silence" that Ludwig Wittgenstein (1889–1951) exercised over the subjective experiences of the meaning of life, or disciplines based on the value of human beings such as ethics, aesthetics, and religion. For Wittgenstein, who believed real metaphysical issues could not be expressed through words, the mystery of the world that existed as an integral whole was inaccessible to human explanation. In general, Wittgenstein advocated linguistic explanations for matters of scientific inquiry, and silence for metaphysical issues.[39] His intention was to defend metaphysics against empiricism, a position which Jin and Feng embraced. But instead of opting for silence, both Jin and Feng believed that higher levels of metaphysical explanation, removed from direct empirical experience, were still possible.

Feng and Jin took different paths to a metaphysical explanation of matters of life. Feng drew on Chinese and Western traditions eclectically in defining his concepts and his approach to these concepts. To transcend the limitations of metaphysics, Feng used Daoism[40] and Chan Buddhism to empower his concepts with the capacity of explanation by relying not on words but on intuition. Feng did agree with Wittgenstein that certain concepts characterizing the nature and movement of the universe, such as *daoti* (processual emergence), *daquan* (great whole), and *qi* (vital energy) defied logical explanation. Together with *li* (principles), they stood for absolute categories beyond language. Accessing the world of *li*, Feng explained, was like reading a wordless book from heaven (無字天書), and it was only for people who were able to ascend to a certain realm (境界). The concept of *daquan* was unspeakable, unthinkable, and beyond human understanding; it represented a stage of being in which one had transcended all distinctions in the universe.[41] Rationalizations of *li* or *daquan* would invariably delimit their content, making them finite rather than infinite.[42] Yet Feng believed that this did not mean one had to refrain from thinking about these concepts. If logical thinking was not feasible, alternative forms of thinking, such as meditation or intuition, would work. Therefore the highest stage of understanding of the universe and ultimate reality was not through logic, but through some kind of intuition, or even some form of mystical experience.

Jin Yuelin tried first of all to deal with Wittgenstein's conundrum from a linguistic qua logical standpoint: a logical explanation might not be in place for the kind of metaphysical questions about which Wittgenstein kept silent, but, nonetheless, some form of verbal explanation would still be practicable, which Jin termed "describing it as it has always been" (本然陳述). One might answer such questions with non-logical or simple narrative means, such as "*neng* (existence/energy) is potentiality," even though *neng*, as a logical concept, could not quite be defined or logically described. Jin contrasted the different forms of narrative which could be applied to logical concepts, such as "description" (描述), "expression" (表達), and "prescription" (規定). A prescription, or simple definition, as in "*neng* is substantiality and activity," showed a pursuit of the rich meanings that *neng* embodied as a philosophical concept.[43]

Jin also attempted to solve the potential conflict between metaphysics and empiricism by finding universality in concrete objects and not in abstract logical commonalities. Here, Jin again drew on a traditional Chinese form of empiricism, by emphasizing the materiality of universal truth, such as in the concept of *qi*. In his eyes, Bertrand Russell's biggest problem was to have failed to connect logical necessity and the material that constituted concrete things in life; that Russell only had mathematical logic, but no logic constituted by concrete materiality. Even though the latter was random and inconstant, it was the most basic material of everyday life. The former should be derived from the latter.[44] Also, like Confucian/Daoist thinkers, Jin believed the world was not just material but also in flux. Although his concept of *neng* was partly derived from Aristotle's matter, it fundamentally differed from matter in its active movement, which was derived from the notion of *qi*. For Aristotle, the ultimate source of movement was form, not matter, whereas for Jin it was *neng*. Thus Jin continued a Chinese explanation of the movement of the world from within, instead of the Aristotelian explanation of an external force.[45] Also, Jin sought a concrete, not an abstract, approach to universal truth (*gongxiang* 共相). The world of logical possibilities (*keneng* 可能) was not truth. Truth was constituted by logical relationships realized in life, when the energy (*neng*) entered into the logical possibilities of *keneng*.[46] Therefore for Jin universal truth was concrete and not the product of human minds. Universal truth (*gongxiang*) contrasted with concepts. The latter are the products of the mind, while the former have external existences.[47] Jin not only claimed that universal truth derived from specific existences, but also from the logical transition from the objective world of specifics to the world of truth and universals, creating ample room for human experiences.

Although not as directly as Feng, Jin did draw on the Chinese tradition of the interconnectedness of external reality and subjective experience.[48] This dynamic conception describes the infinite temporal and spatial character of the universe and links the empirical and metaphysical worlds into an interactive whole.[49] Jin utilized traditional terms more for their connotations than their direct meanings. His definition of *neng* as a self-moving material force in both humans and nature implied interaction between the universe and human experience, the empirical and the metaphysical. Jin also had emotional motives:

> Even though the *dao* I discuss I may not completely comprehend or explain clearly, from the point of view of a human being, I cannot help being involved in those concepts, and my mind cannot help but setting these as my own goals…. When doing scholarship I may forget I am human, but I cannot forget that I am one with the universe and everything in it. I am not just trying to achieve an intellectual understanding of *dao*, but also an emotional gratification. If I used concepts other than those with which I am familiar, I may not derive the same kind of gratification…. I know I am pouring a lot of new wine into old bottles, but the concepts I am using, especially *wuji* 無極, *taiji* 太極, *ji* 幾, *shu* 數, *li* 理, *shi* 勢, *xing* 性, *qing* 情, *ti* 體, and *yong* 用 are my way to shift my feelings for these terms to the logical concepts in this book.[50]

Jin defined and used most of these concepts in new ways, but potentially they could connote more traditional meanings, if needed. Just as Feng Youlan's *li* 理 and *qi* 氣 in some ways overlapped with those of Zhu Xi, Jin's *wuji, taiji, li, qing, xing,* and so on could easily evoke more traditional interpretations as physical forces. If anything, their meanings were easier to grasp for the Chinese reader than Western borrowings such as absolute freedom; they also capture the traditional world of Chinese thought better than concepts such as rationality.

In general, the Tsinghua philosophers upheld a more logical approach to building a discipline of philosophy in China. But their logical focus was primarily on the reconstruction of metaphysics, and the formal analysis they championed, with logical justification, allowed for the continuation of some form of integration between the experiential/emotive and the universe they developed through logical concepts.

3. Philosophy at Yenching University: The Absence of Disciplinary Parameters

In comparison with Peking and Tsinghua Universities, the intellectual milieu at Yenching University was very different. For one thing, it was a Christian university, based on the merger of four Christian schools in north China between 1915 and 1920, the largest of them being the Methodist-run Peking University. In 1919, John Leighton Stuart (1876–1962), a Presbyterian missionary who had grown up with his missionary parents in Hangzhou, was appointed president by the university board of trustees, which was based in New York.[51] From the very start, Yenching University was imbued with a heavy religious atmosphere and was meant to "train Chinese leaders for the missionary enterprise, which by the twentieth century was as much devoted to the 'good works' of teaching, healing, and social service, as it was to make converts to Christianity."[52] In the 1920s, the anti-Christian movement and government regulations—especially the Nationalist government's regulations after 1927—motivated President Stuart to help make the university "more Chinese" by revising the content of non-religious courses and by employing more Chinese administrators. In 1923, along with other missionary colleges and universities, it was required to register with the government as a private university and offer a more secular curriculum. Several departments developed rapidly in the 1920s, such as sociology/anthropology, journalism, and Chinese language and culture. Prominent appointments included leading Chinese scholars, such as Chen Yuan, who specialized in textual exegesis. The teaching of Chinese language and classics was Yenching's way to make the university more effectively bicultural.[53]

Greater sinicization, however, did not spread to the Department of Philosophy. Because of the steady decline of enrollment in the School of Religion after 1923, its faculty members often adjuncted in other departments,[54] especially philosophy. Feng Youlan was appointed to the Department of Philosophy of Yenching University in 1926, but he left in 1928 for Tsinghua, saying that the atmosphere at Yenching made him uncomfortable and that he did not think it was the right place to conduct work on Chinese philosophy. In 1928–1929, the department was headed by Xu Baoqian 徐寶謙 (1892–1944), a Chinese Christian, and consisted of Lucius C. Porter (1880–1958), a Divinity PhD and pastor; Zhao Zichen 趙紫宸 (1888–1979), a prominent Chinese Christian theologian and priest; two associate professors from the School of Religion; and Feng. One quarter of the courses were on Christianity.[55] In 1930, full-time faculty members in the Department of Philosophy dropped to three, with only one regular faculty member—a newly appointed Zhang Dongsun 張東蓀, a graduate of Tokyo Imperial University—and two visiting professors from abroad, I. A. Richards (1893–1979), a philosopher and literary critic from Cambridge University, and John Martyn Warbeke (1879–1950), a philosophy professor from Mount Holyoke College.[56] By 1936, the department was headed by Lucius Porter.[57] Despite the strongly Christian atmosphere of the department, Zhang Dongsun emerged as a prominent philosopher who rivaled Hu Shi and Feng Youlan. Arguably Zhang was the first Chinese philosopher to develop his own school of epistemology.[58] If Feng Youlan felt uncomfortable working out a Chinese philosophy at Yenching

University, Zhang Dongsun's philosophy took off precisely because his philosophy was not China-based.

Zhang Dongsun's philosophical system was the result of his personality and his environment. Zhang pursued a "third path" in philosophy, so to speak, distinct from the focus on epistemology and textual exegesis at Peking University and preference for a logical approach to ontology/epistemology at Tsinghua. The same could be said of his politics, in which he was always very active. Zhang leaned first toward socialism and then toward democracy, moving between Karl Marx and Bertrand Russell. Ultimately, he settled for a middle path between socialism which advocated social classes, class struggle, and democracy. He founded the National Socialist Party with New Confucian Zhang Junmai 張君勱 (1886–1969) in 1932, advocating the welfare of all, not just the proletariat, and the strong hand of a benevolent government, not the limited role of a democratic one. He finally split with Zhang Junmai in their reorganized party, the Democratic Socialist Party, because he could no longer trust in a democratic alliance under the leadership of Chiang Kai-shek. Because of his persistent criticism of the Communist Party, he was fired from his professorship and finally imprisoned in 1968; he died in prison.[59]

Zhang's philosophical "third path" was more successful than his political one, and arguably may gain more influence as time goes on. Eclectically drawing on various schools of Western philosophy, including Kant, Bergson, F. H. Bradley (1846–1924), and Russell, Zhang Dongsun tried to forge a middle path between theories of internal and external relations. The former, championed by F. H. Bradley, argues that relations between things could change the nature of the things in question. In other words, relationships determined nature. For Zhang Dongsun, knowledge was a relationship between the knower and the outside world. Anything from the outside entering the knowledge relationship would invariably be altered by it. Zhang did accept that external relations, advocated by Russell, existed, such as the relationship between books and desks, bow and arrow, but he felt such external relationships could not serve to explain the nature of knowledge.[60] Zhang's argument was a rebuttal to those influenced by the New Realist approach such as Feng Youlan and Jin Yuelin. Zhang complained that Jin and Feng put an inordinate emphasis on the external nature of truth. Both Jin and Feng tried to incorporate Chinese philosophy into a logical system based on the structures of Western philosophy, including epistemology and ontology. For Zhang Dongsun, ontology and substance did not exist in Chinese philosophy, and he gave examples from the Chinese language to illustrate his contention. Unlike Western languages, the Chinese language did not distinguish between the subject and the predicate; thus it failed to distinguish either. For these and other reasons, Chinese thought did not develop the concepts of subject and substance.[61]

Zhang was certainly not the first to argue that a separate ontology did not exist. As argued above, Feng Youlan himself made accommodations for an interactive relationship between humans and the universe, instead of creating an independent ontology separate from human experience. Zhang Dongsun tried to prevent an overly systematic logical rendition of Chinese philosophy. For example, he criticized Feng Youlan for relying too much on a New Realist approach and so infusing Chinese philosophy with too many concepts and rules (*li* 理), which, for Zhang, failed to render the integral world unified by one thread of *li* as seen in Song Confucian learning. Instead of multiple *li* that separated things in the world, Zhang proposed one unifying *tiaoli* 條理, or order that would govern human relations, relations in nature, and heavenly order, and subdivide into more specific rules governing the myriads of things in the world. Zhang believed that in this way he could maintain the integral relationship between humans and the universe through the unifying *li* of Chinese tradition.[62]

To build an epistemology of the Chinese system of thought, Zhang also introduced the "non-apprehensional theory" (*fei xie zhi shuo* 非寫真說), a term he borrowed from critics of New Realism. He used this theory to combine what are usually considered external and internal knowledge: feeling/experience/external stimuli and sensation/knowledge. Zhang argued that these elements were never completely separate in human perception of the outside world, that feelings/experience of the outside were not an objective reflection of the outside world on which an explanationof the world could be based, but the explanation itself. Sensations did not just pattern after feelings/stimuli but put meaning into these feelings; therefore sensations helped shape feelings. Concepts came from sensations but went beyond sensations. The existence of an external world, for Zhang, depended completely on a physical or metaphysical explanation of it.[63] This account of knowledge certainly provided ample room for the internal experience cherished by generations of Confucians. On the other hand, it also represented an attempt to go beyond the conventional internal/external approach to knowledge by rendering the distinction irrelevant because the two were indistinguishable from each other. Even though Zhang did try to avoid a mystical or metaphysical approach to knowledge, his dismissal of ontology because humans could never go beyond an explanation of the world did make him appear more metaphysical than he would have liked to.

Would this have been the case if Zhang had not taught in a department where he was, more often than not, one of a very few, if not the only, full-time faculty members? Had Zhang worked with more like-minded colleagues, would he have been under more pressure to build a systematic approach to Chinese philosophy? One thing that seems certain, however, was that a combination of personality and the absence of institutional pressure for a systematized Chinese philosophy enabled Zhang to adopt a more eclectic approach and perhaps be more innovative in building his epistemology than peers in institutions where developing a systematic new philosophy was a more pressing goal. But that might also have been why Zhang's philosophy never developed into an influential school of thought compatible with those developed at Peking and Tsinghua Universities.

The nature of scholarly exchanges at Yenching University and Tsinghua University differed starkly. At Yenching, although Zhang Dongsun was a sworn brother of his colleague, the theologian Zhao Zichen,[64] and even though his brother Zhang Ertian taught in the Department of History, Zhang Dongsun does not seem to have had a very close relationship with other members of the Department of Philosophy. Zhang Dongsun and Feng Youlan did have occasional exchanges. Zhang was Feng's replacement at Yenching University after Feng left Yenching for Tsinghua University. Their acquaintance and occasional scholarly exchanges also led to Zhang Dongsun's appointment as an adjunct faculty member at Tsinghua, as a lecturer. But intellectually they developed in different directions. There were some opportunities that Zhang might have been able to seize on for good intellectual gain at his own institution. I.A. Richards, his colleague for at least one semester, was a founder of the New Criticism school in poetry, and became interested in Chinese philosophy after his first trip to China in 1927, on a stopover during his honeymoon from Japan to the Himalayas. He returned for a one-year visiting professorship in English literature at Tsinghua University from autumn 1929 to December 1930.[65] During this period he also served as a visiting professor in the Department of Philosophy at Yenching University. Richards's interest in intercultural communications and the Chinese language led to his book, *Mencius on the Mind*, which he started before he left China in 1930, and completed with the help of colleagues L. T. Hwang, Li An-che, and Lucius Porter from Yenching University,[66] none of whom was a philosopher by training. *Mencius on the Mind* is a book concerning language as a medium of expression, concepts, and their translatability from one culture to another. Revealingly, Richards probed into cultural territories in which Zhang Dongsun was also interested. Take the following passage from *Mencius on the Mind*: "Can we, in attempting to understand and translate a work which belongs to a very different tradition from our own, do more than read our own conceptions into it? Can we make it more than a mirror of our minds, or are we inevitably in this undertaking trying to be on both sides of the looking-glass at once?"[67] Richards probably overlapped with Zhang Dongsun for several months at Yenching University, from August/September 1930 to December 1930, yet there is no record that they ever met or exchanged ideas.

In contrast, at Tsinghua University lively teacher-student round-tables occurred as often as once a week, or once every two weeks.[68] The small size of the department, about eight or nine philosophy majors and three to four full-time faculty members in the late 1920s and early 1930s, made the round-table discussion format a viable form. Almost all professors, if not all majors, attended those forums. There were often very lively exchanges among the participants. Feng Youlan was often the most vocal, championing New Realism and bringing Plato in as a member of the New Realist camp, while Jin Yuelin, who almost always spoke at the end, would disagree with Feng's version of New Realism when Feng, like Plato, recognized the existence, or subsistence of an essential reality. The *li* 理 or rules that Feng championed, to Jin, were still phenomena, like blueprints for airplanes.[69] By stating this, Jin was adhering to an interpretation of the ultimate reality where ideas did not constitute reality. Universal truth would rely not on subsistence, but existence.[70] Here Jin went beyond Feng's equating of the reality of ideas and external reality, or Russell's argument that ideas were reality. Jin recognized ideas more as logical concepts and potential reality.

In conclusion, institutions seemed to have had a distinct influence on the development of modern Chinese philosophy. The open-ended, laissez-faire structure of Peking University, combined with an intense preoccupation with China's future among its faculty members, appears to have promoted a type of philosophical construction that allowed both the introduction of Western concepts and rules as well as traditional Chinese modes such as textual exegesis or the Lu-Wang approach to learning. The individual interpretations of Chinese philosophy that emerged from this environment brought many nuances of the Chinese intellectual past into the newly constructed discipline of Chinese philosophy. In this way, they unified Chinese and Western learning at the experiential level to create a new Chinese philosophy while continuing a Confucian emphasis on experience as a central component of knowledge. The open, American-influenced National Tsinghua University, free of the baggage of being *the* university to reconstruct Chinese culture, facilitated a more direct incorporation of Chinese learning into Western modes of philosophy, through the adoption of mathematical logic (Jin Yuelin) and creating what they perceived as logical and universal concepts that could objectively reveal the world as it is, although this logical approach was tempered by humanist qua metaphysical approaches drawn from both Chinese and Western traditions. Private Yenching University, on the other hand, as a Christian university undergoing secularization in the 1920s to 1940s, did not mandate any external structure for the interpretation of Chinese philosophy. This provided more opportunities for innovative approaches yet at the same time did not facilitate inter-depart-mental dialogue to develop a systematic modern Chinese academic disci-pline of philosophy. Thus, unlike Peking and Tsinghua Universities, Yenching University never brought forth its own distinct schools of philosophy.

In the process, personalities, as well as individual and institutional selections, also played an important role. Feng Youlan, who was initially appointed at Yenching University in 1926, decided to leave for Tsinghua in 1928 because the Yenching environment was not conducive to his goal of constructing Chinese philosophy. At Tsinghua, Feng's colleague Jin Yuelin, with more training in logic than Feng, enabled a rather historically-oriented Feng to develop a more logical and conceptual approach to Chinese philosophy, as seen in Feng's *New Philosophy of Principle* (*Xin lixue* 新理學). Zhang Dongsun, on the other hand, did not mind working in the atmosphere of the Department of Philosophy at Yenching University, perhaps because his personality equipped him to explore his own path, as he did in both philosophy and politics. Xiong Shili, who had a penchant for the Lu-Wang style of Confucian learning, was hired to work at Peking University because his predecessor, Liang Shuming, had similar interests, even though their official duties were to teach Buddhism and

Indian philosophy respectively. He Lin, who was hired at Peking University in 1931, had first been started on his philosophical investigations by Liang Shuming's Lu/Wang style intuitive approach to Chinese learning.

On the one hand, one does see common trends in the development of Departments of Philosophy at all three universities, such as the incorporation of Western epistemology into Chinese philosophy to "overcome" the lack of it historically. On the other hand, one observes different forms of defense of the traditional Chinese integration of the subjective and the objective, the universal and individual human experience, in the various interpretations of ontology as it was introduced to explain Chinese philosophy, or even in its outright rejection, as in the case of Zhang Dongsun.

Notes

1   See chapter 4 of Xiaoqing Diana Lin, *Peking University, Chinese Intellectuals and Scholarship, 1898–1937* (New York: SUNY Press, 2005).

2   *Beijing daxue zhexuexi jianshi 1914–1994* 北京大學哲學系簡史1914–1994年 [A short history of the Department of Philosophy at Peking University, 1914–1994] (Beijing: Beijing daxue zhexuexi, 1994), p. 31.

3   See Jing Haifeng 景海峰, "Yi zhiduhua wei Beijing de Zhongguo zhexue jian'gou" 以制度化為背景的中國哲學建構 [A reconstruction of Chinese philosophy against the background of institutionalization], *Xueshu yuekan* 學術月刊, no. 3 (2000), pp. 59–61.

4   See chapters 5 and 6 in Lin, *Peking University*.

5   Jiang Menglin 蔣夢麟 (1886–1964), the most important president of Peking University after Cai Yuanpei, continued Cai's policies to a great extent. Jiang was deputy president of Peking University during Cai's long absences in the 1920s and official president of the university from 1930 to 1937.

6   Lin, *Peking University*, chapter 6.

7   Chen Pingyuan 陳平原, *Zhongguo xiandai xueshu zhi jianli* 中國現代學術之建立 [The establishment of academic disciplines in modern China] (Beijing: Beijing daxue chubanshe, 1998), pp. 161–179, 191–193.

8   John Makeham, "Hu Shi and the Search for System," in this volume.

9   Cai Yuanpei, "Yu *Shidai huabao* jizhe de tanhua" 與《時代畫報》記者的談話 [A discussion with a journalist from *Times Pictorial*], in *Cai Yuanpei meiyu lunji* 蔡元培美育論集 [Cai Yuanpei's writings on aesthetics and education], edited by Gao Pingshu 高平舒 (Changsha: Hunan renmin chubanshe, 1987), p. 214.

10   Li Xiangjun 李祥俊, "Shengming tiyan yu zhexue jiangou: Xiong Shili zhexue tixi jidian tanmi" 生命體驗與哲學建構：熊十力哲學體系基點探秘 [Life experience and philosophical construction: An investigation of the basic structure of Xiong Shili's philosophy], *Beijing shifan daxue xuebao* 北京師範大學學報 (social sciences edition 社會科學版), no. 5 (2008), pp. 96–101.

11   Besides Liang Shuming, another source of philosophical influence on Xiong Shili was Zhang Dongsun. Their friendship started in the 1930s after Zhang was appointed to the Department of Philosophy at Yenching University in 1930 and Xiong returned to Peking University in 1932. Qian Mu 錢穆 (1895–1990), a colleague of Xiong's at Peking University, said that because of the proximity of their homes, he, Zhang Dongsun, Zhang's brother Zhang Ertian 張爾田 (1874–1945) and Xiong Shili often got together, and usually Qian talked with Zhang Ertian, who taught Chinese history at Yenching University, while Zhang Dongsun talked with Xiong Shili about philosophy and politics. However, Xiong Shili's first major work, *New Treatise on Unique Consciousness* (*Xin weishi lun* 新唯識論), published in 1932 (literary language edition), was apparently not influenced by Zhang's knowledge of Western philosophy, as Xiong had only returned to Beiping that year after a

five-year absence and had just made Zhang's acquaintance. Their scholarly exchanges about Chinese philosophy—by then Zhang Dongsun had developed a liking for the subject—were eventually published in *Chen bao* 晨報. See "Shili nianpu" 十力年譜 [Chronology of Xiong Shili] at http://bbs. guoxue.com/viewthread.php?tid=508543, accessed 25 January 2009; Qian Mu, *Bashi yi shuangqin, shiyou zayi* 八十憶雙親，師友雜憶 [At eighty, remembering my parents, teachers and friends] (Beijing: Sanlian, 1998), p. 181, cited in Zuo Yuhe 左玉河, *Zhang Dongsun xueshu sixiang pingzhuan* 張東蓀學術思想評傳 [A critical biography of Zhang Dongsun's scholarship and thinking] (Beijing: Beijing tushuguan chubanshe, 1999), pp. 86–94. On Liang and Xiong's friendship, see Thierry Meynard's chapter in this volume.

12   See chapter 4 of Lin, *Peking University*.

13   Cited in Jing Haifeng 景海峰, "Jieshixue yu Zhongguo zhexue" 解釋學與中國哲學 [Hermeneutics and Chinese philosophy], *Zhexue dongtai* 哲學動態 7 (2001), pp. 13–18.

14   Jing Haifeng 景海峰, "Qingmo jingxue de jieti he Ruxue xingtai de xiandai zhuanhuan" 清末經學的解體和儒學形態的現代轉換 [The disintegration of Classical Studies and the modern transformation of the modality of Confucian learning in the late Qing], *Kongzi yanjiu* 孔子研究, no. 3 (2000), pp. 85–97.

15   Zhang Xuezhi 張學智, "Qianyan" 前言 [Foreword] to *He Lin xuanji* 賀麟選集 [Selected writings of He Lin], edited by Zhang Xuezhi (Changchun: Jilin renmin chubanshe, 2005), pp. 1–4.

16   He Lin, "Song Ru de sixiang fangfa" 宋儒的思想方法 [The intellectual methods of Song Confucians], *Helin xuanji,* pp. 60–79.

17   *Ibid.*

18   *Ibid.*; Chen Yongjie 陳永傑, "He Lin de zhijueguan kaocha" 賀麟的直覺觀考察 [He Lin's study of intuition], *Shehui kexuejia* 社會科學家, no. 5 (General no. 127) (Sept. 2007), pp. 187–189, 203.

19   Ci Jiwei, "He Lin's Sinification of Idealism," in *Contemporary Chinese Philosophy*, edited by Chung-ying Cheng and Nicholas Bunnin (Oxford: Blackwell, 2002), p. 188.

20   He Lin, "Wenhua de ti yu yong" 文化的體與用 [The substance and function of culture], *Helin xuanji*, pp. 116–124; He Lin, "Xin daode de dongxiang" 新道德的動向 [The trajectory of new ethics], *Helin xuanji*, pp. 125–129.

21   Bertrand Russell, cited in Rodney Koeneke, *Empires of the Mind: I. A. Richards and Basic English in China, 1929–1979* (Stanford, CA: Stanford University Press, 2004), p. 53.

22   See, for instance, Fabio Lanza's quoted sources in his "Politics of the Unbound: 'Students' and the Everyday of Beijing University," *Positions* 16.3 (Winter 2008), p. 573. See also Wen-hsin Yeh's interesting presentation of life at Tsinghua University in her chapter on college life in *The Alienated Academy: Culture and Politics in Republican China, 1919–1937* (Cambridge, MA: Harvard University Press, 2000), especially pp. 208–210, 213–222.

23 Hu Weixi 胡偉希, *Zhuan shi cheng zhi: Qinghua xuepai yu ershi shiji Zhongguo zhexue* 轉識成智：清華學派與二十世紀中國哲學 [Transforming knowledge into wisdom: The Tsinghua school and twentieth-century Chinese philosophy] (Shanghai: Huadong shifandaxue chubanshe, 2005), p. 15.

24 *Ibid.*, p. 19.

25 Jing Haifeng, "Zhexueshi leixing yu Zhongguo sixiang de xushu fangshi" 哲學史類型與中國思想的敘述方式 [Types of histories of philosophy and narrative modes of Chinese thought], *Zhongguo renmin daxue xuebao* 中國人民大學學報, no. 3 (2004), pp. 12–18.

26 This institute has recently been re-established at Tsinghua, with Chen Lai 陳來 (long-time luminary of the Peking University Philosophy Department) serving as the inaugural director.

27 Feng Youlan, "Zhongguo xiandai zhexue" 中國現代哲學 [Contemporary Chinese philosophy] (1934), in Feng Youlan, *Sansongtang xueshu wenji* 三松堂學術文集 [Collected scholarly essays from the Hall of Three Pines] (Beijing: Peking University Press, 1984), p. 289. This quotation and the arguments from the preceding paragraph about the influence of the Institute of China Studies on later Tsinghua scholars are cited in Hu Weixi, *Zhuanshi chengzhi*, pp. 30–32.

28 Edwin Holt, Walter Marvin, William Pepperrell Montague, Ralph Barton Perry, Walter B. Pitkin, and Edward Gleason Spaulding, *The New Realism: Cooperative Studies in Philosophy* (New York: The MacMillan Company, 1912), pp. 23, 24, 32, 40–41.

29 Bertrand Russell, *The Problems of Philosophy* (1912; reprinted New York: Cosimo, 2007), pp. 68–70.

30 Bertrand Russell, *The Problems of Philosophy*, chapter 10, and John Perry's Introduction, pp. vii–xxvi.

31 Zhang Shenfu 張申府, "Zhexuexi gaikuang" 哲學系概況 [Introduction to the Department of Philosophy], *Qinghua zhoukan* 清華週刊, no. 13–14 (1934), pp. 20–22.

32 Vera Schwarcz, *Time for Telling Truth Is Running Out: Conversations with Zhang Shenfu* (New Haven, CT: Yale University Press, 1992), pp. 40–41.

33 Hu Jun 胡軍, "Dao lun" 道論 [On the Dao], in *Jin Yuelin sixiang yanjiu* 金岳霖思想研究 [A study of the intellectual thought of Jin Yuelin], edited by Hu Jun 胡軍 and Liu Peiyu 劉培育 (Beijing: Zhongguo shehui kexue chubanshe, 2004), p. 5.

34 Qiao Qingju 喬清舉, "Lun Jin Yuelin lixue liqiguan de fazhan" 論金岳霖理學理氣觀的發展 [On the development of the concepts of *li* and *qi* in Jin Yuelin's metaphysics], *Zhongguo zhexue* 中國哲學, no. 5 (2007), pp. 87–94; Yvonne Schulz Zinda, "Jin Yuelin's Ambivalent Status as a 'Chinese Philosopher,'" in this volume; Liu Junzhe 劉俊哲 and Cheng Jin'gang 程晉剛, "Jin Yuelin zhishi lun tixi de goujian ji qi xiandaixing kaocha" 金岳霖知識論體系的構建及其現

代性考察 [An examination of the structure of Jin Yuelin's system of episte-mology and its modernity] *Xihua shifandaxue xuebao* 西華師範大學學報 (哲學社會科學版 Philosophy and social sciences edition), no. 6 (2008), pp. 22–26.

35 Jin Yuelin, "Shencha baogao" 審查報告, in Feng Youlan, *Zhongguo zhexueshi* 中國哲學史 [A history of Chinese philosophy] (Shanghai: Shangwu yinshuguan, 1934), appendix to first volume, p. 5.

36 Feng Youlan, *Zhongguo zhexueshi*, Vol. 1 of *Sansongtang quanji* 三松堂全集 [Complete works from the Hall of Three Pines], Vol. 2 (Zhengzhou: Henan renmin chubanshe, 1988), p. 9.

37 Here the definition follows Hans-Georg Moeller, "Daoism as Academic Philosophy: Feng Youlan's New Metaphysics (*Xin Lixue*)," in this volume. Moeller describes *daoti* as "the 'processual emergence' of everything: the materialization of the world as a whole, the continuous actualization of 'whatnesses,' the process of existence, the coming into being of all there is."

38 Hu Jun, "Dao lun," p. 7.

39 Yu Zhenhua 鬱振華, "Shuobude de dongxi ruhe neng shuo: Weitegensitan de chenmo he Feng Youlan, Jin Yuelin de huiying" 說不得的東西如何能説：維特根斯坦的「沈默」和馮友蘭，金岳霖的回應 [How to say things that are unspeakable: Wittgenstein's silence and the responses of Feng Youlan and Jin Yuelin], *Zhexue yanjiu* 哲學研究, no. 6 (1996), pp. 71–77.

40 Hans-Georg Moeller gives an elaborate discussion of how Feng employed a transformed Daoist approach in dealing with this issue; see his essay in this volume.

41 Chen Lai 陳來, "Lun Feng Youlan zhexue zhong de shenmizhuyi" 論馮友蘭哲學中的神秘主義 [Mysticism in Feng Youlan's philosophy], in *Jiexi Feng Youlan* 解析馮友蘭 [Analyzing Feng Youlan], edited by Zheng Jiadong 鄭家棟 and Chen Peng 陳鵬 (Beijing: Shehui kexue wenxian chubanshe, 2002), pp. 317–318.

42 Chen Lai, "Lun Feng Youlan zhexue zhong de shenmizhuyi," pp. 307–326.

43 Yu Zhenhua, "Shuobude de dongxi," pp. 71–77.

44 Jin Yuelin, "Luosu zhexue" 羅素哲學 [Russell's philosophy], cited in Hu Jun, "Dao lun," p. 37.

45 Hu Jun, "Dao lun," pp. 56–57.

46 *Ibid.*, pp. 80–81.

47 *Ibid.*, p. 84.

48 Jing Haifeng 景海峰, "Zhongguo zhexue tizhi de yiyi cong xifang quanshixue de guandian kan" 中國哲學體知的意義，從西方詮釋學的觀點看 [Understanding the experiential approach to knowledge in Chinese philosophy from the perspective of Western hermeneutics], *Xueshu yuekan* 學術月刊, no. 5 (2007), pp. 64–72.

49 Shan Chun 單純, *Jiuxue xintong: Feng Youlan sixiang tonglun* 舊學新統：馮友蘭哲學思想通論 [Old learning and new order: A survey of Feng Youlan's philosophy] (Chengdu: Sichuan daxue chubanshe, 2005), p. 225.

50 In Jin Yuelin, *Lun Dao* 論道 [On Dao], cited in Qiao Qingju, "Lun Jin Yuelin lixue liqiguan de fazhan," p. 93. Yvonne Schulz Zinda discusses the emotive element in Jin's choice of logical concepts in chapter 8 of this volume.

51 Philip West, *Yenching University and Sino-Western Relations, 1916–1952* (Cambridge, MA: Harvard University Press, 1976), pp. 34–35.

52 Philip West, "Reframing the Yenching Story," *The Journal of American-East Asian Relations* 14 (2007), p. 174.

53 *Ibid.*, pp. 177, 179.

54 *Ibid.*, p. 176.

55 *Yanjing daxue benke kecheng yilan (bugao di 21 hao), 1928–1929* 燕京大學本科課程一覽 (佈告第21號), 1928–1929 [Announcement #21 of undergraduate course offerings at Yenching University, 1928–1929] (Beida wenku 北大文庫), pp. 64–69.

56 *Yanjing daxue xiaokan* 燕京大學校刊 (Yenching University news), 26 September 1930.

57 *Sili Yanjing daxue benke ge xueyuan kecheng gaiyao* 私立燕京大學本科各學院課程概要 [An overview of the curriculum of the undergraduate colleges at private Yenching University] (April 1936), p. 4.

58 Xinyan Jiang, "Zhang Dongsun, Pluralist Epistemology and Chinese Philosophy," in *Contemporary Chinese Philosophy*, pp. 57–81.

59 Edmund Fung, "Socialism, Capitalism, and Democracy in Republican China: The Political Thought of Zhang Dongsun," *Modern China* 28.4 (October 2002), pp. 399–431.

60 Zhang Yaonan 張耀南, *Zhang Dongsun zhishilun yanjiu* 張東蓀知識論研究 [Zhang Dongsun's epistemology] (Taipei: Hongye wenhua shiye youxian gongsi and Zhonghua fazhan jijin guanli weiyuanhui, 1995), pp. 296–297.

61 Xinyan Jiang, "Zhang Dongsun, Pluralist Epistemology and Chinese Philosophy," pp. 72–73. Zhang Yaonan, *Zhang Dongsun*, pp. 271–295.

62 Zhang Yaonan, *Zhang Dongsun*, pp. 58–77.

63 *Ibid.*, pp. 300–301.

64 Yap Key-chong, "Culture-bound Identity: The Interactionist Epistemology of Chang Tung-sun," *East Asian History* 3 (June 1992), p. 82.

65 Ming Xie, "Trying to Be on Both Sides of the Mirror at Once: I. A. Richards, Multiple Definition, and Comparative Method," *Comparative Literature Studies* 44.3 (2007), pp. 279–297; John Paul Russo, *I. A. Richards, His Life and Work* (Baltimore, MD: Johns Hopkins University Press, 1989), pp. 419–420.

66 Rodney Koeneke, *Empires of the Mind, I. A. Richards and Basic English in China, 1929–1979* (Stanford, CA: Stanford University Press, 2004), pp. 78–79. Also, I. A. Richards, *Mencius on the Mind; Experiments in Multiple Definition* (1932; reprinted Routledge, 1997), p. xi.

67 Ming Xie, "Trying to Be on Both Sides of the Mirror at Once," p. 280.

68 According to Zhou Fucheng 周輔成, who was a philosophy major at Tsinghua between 1929 to 1933, the discussions took place at least several times as

arranged by the Department of Philosophy. See Zhou Fucheng, "Yi Jin Yuelin xiansheng" 憶金岳霖先生 [In memory of Mr. Jin Yuelin], in *Jin Yuelin de huiyi yu huiyi Jin Yuelin* 金岳霖的回憶與回憶金岳霖 [Jin Yuelin's memories and memories of Jin Yuelin], edited by Liu Peiyu 劉培育 (expanded edition; Chengdu: Sichuan jiaoyu chubanshe, 2000), p. 141. According to Zhang Dainian, the research forum was held bi-weekly; see Zhang Dainian, "Huiyi Qinghua zhexuexi" 回憶清華哲學系 [Reminiscences of the Philosophy Department at Tsinghua University] *Xueshu yuekan* 學術月刊, no. 8 (1994), cited in Hu Jun, "Dao lun," p. 7.

69   Zhou Fucheng, "Yi Jin Yuelin xiansheng," p. 141.

70   Hu Jun, "Dao lun," p. 81.

Chapter 5

Hu Shi and the Search for System

John Makeham

Where can we find a congenial stock with which we may organically link the thought-systems of Modern Europe and America, so that we may further build up our own science and philosophy on the new foundation of an internal assimilation of the old and the new?

—Hu Shi (1922)[1]

This chapter argues that intellectual historian Hu Shi 胡適 (1891–1962) presented pre-Qin masters (*zi* 子) writings as the foundational texts of Chinese philosophy in his *The Development of the Logical Method in Ancient China* and *Zhongguo zhexueshi dagang* [An outline of the history of Chinese philosophy]. I show how Hu creatively appropriated John Dewey's concept of "genetic method" and used it to give a central place to "logic" in the historical development of Chinese philosophy. By placing philosophers and schools of thought in an historical narrative, Hu sought to use "historical method" to reveal the unfolding course of this inner logic over time: the system of Chinese philosophy. I identify the connection between Hu's own "logical method" and Dewey's genetic method and Wilhelm Windelband's views on the goals of writing a history of philosophy; and draw attention to the role that the "history of Chinese philosophy" genre played in articulating Hu's vision of Chinese philosophy, and twentieth-century notions of "Chinese philosophy" more generally.

In chapters 2 and 3 I argued that over the course of the first decade of the twentieth century, the confluence of three factors—the revival of interest in Masters Studies (諸子學), the impact of Meiji scholarship on the evaluation of Chinese philosophy, and the re-introduction of Yogācāra philosophy in China—contributed to logic's (論理學, 名學, 名辯學) being regarded as a necessary precondition for the existence of "Chinese philosophy."[2] Intriguingly, regardless of whether scholars at the time (Chinese and Japanese) acknowledged or denied the existence of China's own early traditions of logic, the ensuing discourse played a vital role in shaping the nascent form of Chinese philosophy as an academic discipline. It is little wonder Hu Shi's watershed 1919 publication *Zhongguo zhexueshi dagang* 中國哲學史大綱 [An outline of the history of Chinese philosophy]—based on his 1917 Columbia University PhD dissertation, *The Development of the Logical Method in Ancient China*—devoted large sections to topics such as Confucius' rectification of names, Mohist disputation, Hui Shi, and Gongsun Long, as well as Xunzi's theories about names, *mingxue* 名學 (or logic as Hu regarded it).[3]

Hu Shi's intellectual development was, of course, profoundly influenced by his dissertation supervisor and teacher, pragmatist philosopher John Dewey (1859–1952), on the matter of logic. He relates, for example, that when he took Dewey's class on "Schools of Logic," "it inspired me to decide upon 'The Evolutionary History of Chinese Philosophical Method' as my dissertation topic." Moreover, even before taking Dewey's class, "I had already read his writings, one of which was called 'The Various Stages of Logical Thought.' … In the essay Dewey maintained that the process of thinking for both humankind and individuals has to proceed through four stages." The second stage "has to be founded upon a fondness for disputation and the practice of open discussion, and then this will lead to thinking consistent with logic. This point greatly stimulated my interest because in Chinese we refer to logical thinking as *bian* 辯 (disputation)."[4] The young Hu Shi also had a special fondness for the pre-Qin masters because "it seems as if the future of Chinese philosophy will depend greatly on the revival of those early philosophical schools…. The sort of soil suited to the transplantation of the most outstanding results from Western philosophy and science can be found among these schools."[5]

Particularly noteworthy is that Hu also specifically praised Zhang Binglin 章炳麟 (Taiyan 太炎) (1869–1936) for his contributions to the revival of Masters Studies:

> In modern times, scholars such as Sun Yirang 孫詒讓 (1848–1908) and Zhang Binglin poured all of their energies into developing Masters Studies. Hence, nowadays, Masters Studies—which formerly was an appendage to classical studies—has actually become a specialist field of learning…. Only with Zhang Taiyan did Masters Studies develop in a systematic fashion, quite independent of the Masters Studies used merely for textual collation

and the glossing of old terms and phrases [in Qing evidential and textual scholarship].[6]

Clearly, Hu had been inspired by Zhang in regard to Masters Studies. One obvious example is that just as Zhang Taiyan did not use the term *mingjia* to refer to the School of Names represented by Gongsun Long and Hui Shi, but used it more generally to refer to works on logic such as *Mozi* and *Xunzi*, Hu Shi made the following comments in his 1918 essay "Hui Shi, Gongsun Long de zhexue" 惠施、公孫龍的哲學 [The philosophy of Hui Shi and Gongsun Long]:

> In ancient times there never was a School of Names (名家). Irrespective of to which school of philosophy one might refer, they all had a basic scholarly method. This method is the "science of names" (*mingxue* 名學 [*luoji* 邏輯] [JM: this is Hu's own gloss]) of that particular school.... Because each school had a science of names (名學), there was no "School of Names." Nevertheless, research on the science of names produced by the later Mohists was a little more profound than that produced by other schools, that is all.[7]

It follows that Hu would similarly have been well aware of the new field of early Chinese logic that had been opened up by Zhang and other late-Qing scholars. The major innovation taken by Hu was to draw upon this newfound interest in logic and its connection with Masters Studies as the basis for writing a history of Chinese philosophy.

1. Histories of Chinese Philosophy before Hu Shi

For much of the twentieth century the writing of histories of Chinese philosophy and the ongoing elaboration, refinement, and re-telling of those histories were instrumental in defining and sustaining the development of the discipline of Chinese philosophy. Crucially, particular aspects of traditional thought and scholarship became identified as exemplifying Chinese philosophy. There was a precedent for this in nineteenth-century Germany, where, it has been argued, "the history of philosophy was indeed part of philosophy—philosophy understood as an academic discipline.... To know the history of philosophy in detail was seen as a prerequisite for philosophizing. This was a widespread belief in the 19th century."[8] The significance of this is suggestive, given Hu's debt to German philosopher Wilhelm Windelband's (1848–1915) *A History of Philosophy with Especial Reference to the Formation and Development of its Problems and Conceptions* (discussed below).

Hu Shi made a seminal contribution to the writing of histories of Chinese philosophy in China. He was not, however, the first scholar to do so. As already noted, quite a few histories of Chinese philosophy written by Japanese scholars at the turn of the nineteenth century provided models for Chinese scholars. In addition, two Chinese scholars had already produced the first Chinese histories of Chinese philosophy: Xie Wuliang's 謝無量 (1884–1964) *Zhongguo zhexueshi* 中國哲學史 [History of Chinese philosophy]; and Chen Fuchen's 陳黻宸 (1859–1917) *Zhuzi zhexue* 諸子哲學 [Philosophy of the [pre-Qin] Masters] (1914, manuscript) and *Zhongguo zhexueshi* 中國哲學史 [History of Chinese philosophy] (1916, manuscript).

Xie Wuliang, who had studied in Japan in 1903 and 1904, was working as an editor with the publishing house Zhonghua shuju 中華書局 when he published *Zhongguo zhexueshi*, the first general history of Chinese philosophy written by a Chinese scholar in 1916. In the preface, Xie acknowledged the achievements earlier scholars had made to the genre of the history of Chinese philosophy: "When it comes to writing a book describing the origin and development of a single school of thought (學派), none is more precise than Zhu Xi's *Yi-Luo yuanyuan lu* 伊洛淵源錄 [Records of the Yi-Luo school]. When it comes to writing a book that draws together the schools of thought in a single dynasty, none is more detailed than Huang Zongxi's 黃宗羲 (1610–1695) *Song-Yuan ru xue'an* 宋元儒學案 [Case studies of Song and Yuan *ru*] and *Ming ru xue'an* 明儒學案 [Case studies of Ming *ru*]. The stylistic layout of each is also close to what today we call histories of philosophy."

Unlike these compilations, however, Xie set himself the goal of writing the first general history (that is, one not restricted to a single dynasty or a single period such as the pre-Qin period or the Han period) of Chinese philosophy, spanning individual thinkers and schools from Confucius until the Qing dynasty.[9] The next such general history, Zhong Tai's 鍾泰 (1888–1979) *Zhongguo zhexueshi* 中國哲學史, was not published until 1929. (Hu Shi's *Zhongguo zhexueshi* is not a general history, despite the title.) Japanese scholars had already produced a number of general histories of Chinese philosophy. Their model for the writing of general histories was provided by nineteenth-century publications by German scholars such as Wilhelm Gottlieb Tennemann (1761–1819), Georg Wilhelm Friedrich Hegel (1770–1831), Heinrich Ritter (1791–1869), Albert Schwegler (1819–1857), Albert Stöckl (1823–1895), and Wilhelm Windelband, among others. Xie also included a discussion of the genesis of

Chinese philosophy in the high antiquity of the sage kings and cultural heroes. In these respects the book resembles some of the Japanese histories of Chinese philosophy already published, as does the periodization scheme adopted as the broad framework: Ancient (上古), Medieval (中古), and Early Modern (近世). From the 1880s Meiji historians had begun to write national histories for both China and Japan, many of which were translated and adopted for use in China as textbooks. In this process the model of the general history came to displace that of the dynastic history.[10] Zhang Taiyan's early views (1900) on revising the way national histories were compiled rejected the dynastic approach in favor of a four-part periodization: Age of Uncultivated Simplicity (樸略時代), Age of Humanism (人文時代), Age of Full Development (發達時代), and Age of Decline (衰微時代). Similarly in his 1901 "Zhongguoshi xulun" 中國史敍論 [Prolegomena to a history of China], Liang Qichao 梁啟超 (1873–1929) adopted a tripartite division: Age of Antiquity (上世), Medieval Age (中世), and Modern Age (近世).[11] Hu Shi's *Zhongguo zhexueshi dagang* also subscribed to a tripartite periodization for the history of Chinese philosophy: Ancient, Medieval, and Modern. The ancient period extended from the time of Laozi to that of Han Fei. He also referred to this period as the Age of Masters' Philosophy.[12]

Xie outlined the task of writing a history of philosophy as follows: "to describe the broad trend of changes in philosophy since its beginning; to discuss individuals in the context of their times; to select key doctrines; to examine differences and similarities in thought; and to adopt the genre of historical biography." This approach combines the narrative form of intellectual history, historical biography, and analysis of concepts. Although Xie stated that he selected the key doctrines of the individuals and schools included in the volume and described those doctrines using the methods of classification employed in modern philosophy—metaphysics, epistemology and ethics—his lack of familiarity with Western philosophy quite possibly contributed to the book's failure to generate much interest among his contemporaries. This lack of familiarity with the content and scope of Western philosophy is evident in the following comments: "In ancient times, it was *daoshu* 道術 (methods of the way) that always constituted the learning of men of education and the gentleman. [So long as] one was up to the task of learning, then the way would be found therein. When ancient officials lost [responsibility for learning], then learning became scattered [amongst the people] and came to be called *ruxue, daoxue* and *lixue*. The Buddhists call it *yixue* 義學; in the West it is called *zhexue*. The actual referent in each case is the same."[13]

Chen Fuchen was appointed professor of history at Peking University in 1913, and in the following year he started teaching a course called "Masters Philosophy" (*zhuzi zhexue* 諸子哲學). In 1915 he began offering "The History of Chinese Philosophy" (*Zhongguo zhexueshi* 中國哲學史). (As continued to be the practice, students in the Division of Letters could take a range of courses offered by other departments.) Lecture notes based on each course are preserved in Chen's collected writings. The course on Masters Philosophy is significant because it confirms that the writings of the pre-Qin masters were classed as philosophy at Peking University no later than 1913, two years after the establishment of the University and one year before the establishment of the Philosophy Department (*Zhexue men* 哲學門). In fact, Masters Studies courses had been taught at the Imperial University (*Jingshi daxuetang* 京師大學堂), the forerunner of Peking University, since at least 1902. According to a publication compiled by students who graduated from the Philosophy Department of Peking University in 1925, courses "related to philosophy" were taught in the teacher's college part of the university (the forerunner of Peking Normal University): ethics, education, psychology, interpersonal morals, biology, and Zhou-Qin masters.[14]

The first point to note about Chen's *Zhongguo zhexueshi* is that its coverage barely steps out of the prehistoric era: it starts with cultural hero Fuxi 伏羲 and finishes with the legendary Jiang Taigong 姜太公.[15] The second point is that Chen clearly privileged *ru* teachings over Masters texts. In the preface, after having also commented on the importance of *daoshu* in early Chinese philosophy, he concluded: "The methods of the *ru* provide the ultimate model. When Zhuangzi discussed the learning of the eleven lineages beginning with Mo Di and Qin Huali, he did not list Confucius and Mencius. This is because the *daoshu* proceeded from the *rujia*."[16] After he died in 1916, the History of Chinese Philosophy course at Peking University was taken over by historian Chen Hanzhang 陳漢章 (1863–1938), and then by intellectual historian Ma Xulun 馬敍倫 (1885–1970). When Hu Shi took up his position in the Philosophy Department in 1917, he joined Chen and Ma in teaching the course.[17]

2. *Zhongguo zhexueshi dagang*

In the preface to Hu's *Zhongguo zhexueshi dagang*, President of Peking

University Cai Yuanpei 蔡元培 (1868–1940) identified four distinguishing features of the book:

1. It gave extensive attention to verifying authorship and textual authenticity.
2. It began the history of early Chinese philosophical thought with Laozi and Confucius rather than with the sage kings of antiquity.
3. It placed the various masters on an equal footing rather than giving preferential treatment to one group or sub-group.
4. It provided systematic accounts of the schools and their development over an extended period.[18]

According to intellectual historian Yu Yingshi 余英時: "In regard to these four points, of course Hu had been influenced by Western history of philosophy, but at the same time [Hu's approach] was compatible with the inner development (內在發展) of evidential learning. If there are only external influences and no internal basis [for a change in intellectual orientation or paradigm], then it can only be called a 'conquest' and not a 'revolution.'"[19] Yu proceeds to draw particular attention to the second and third points, identifying them as bearing the hallmarks of a truly revolutionary approach to historiography. He identifies them as the inevitable products of the unfolding of the "inner logic" and "inner development" of Qing-dynasty evidential learning.[20]

Hu's own recollection suggests a more complex situation:

Dewey's analysis of systematic thought helped me to understand the basic steps of ordinary scientific research. He also helped me [to understand] Chinese classical learning (古典學術) of the past several thousand years—in particular of the past three hundred years—as well as the methods of Chinese historians, such as *kaojuxue* 考據學 and *kaozhengxue* 考證學. In English, I translate these traditional methods of research as "evidential investigation" (the investigation of evidence), that is, evidence-based investigation. Something should not be believed if it lacks verification. At that time very few people (indeed, no-one) had thought of the methodological points in common shared by modern scientific methods and China's ancient evidential investigation. I was the first person to talk about this. I was able to do this because of what I had learned from the theory in the relevant parts of Dewey's thought.[21]

This does not, of course, mean that Hu was not influenced by developments closer to home, particularly the revival of Masters Studies.[22] As with his predecessors in China, Hu also identified logic as a distinguishing feature of classical Chinese philosophy, arguing that Chinese philosophy had developed various logical methods that had been over-looked. He also emphasized the role of ordered structure and system. Thus in the preface to his 1917 dissertation, *The Development of the Logical Method in Ancient China* (Chinese translation 1919), he wrote: "The most important … task in a work of this kind is, of course, the interpretation and construction or re-construction of the philosophical systems."[23] As discussed in chapter 2 of this volume, this dual emphasis on logic and on providing ordered, systematic accounts of thought and schools of thought had its origins in Japanese scholarship of the late Meiji period.

3. Genetic Method

The model for Hu's system came via Dewey's pragmatism, which Hu regarded as a method and not a theory, the spirit of which was "experimentalism" (實驗主義). According to Hu, experimentalism consists of two methods: the laboratory method and the genetic method. The laboratory method eschews certainties and absolute truths and is character-ized by the ongoing replacement of old hypotheses with new ones. The genetic method studies how and why something came about, in order to understand what it is. I believe that Hu's "revolutionary" contribution actually lies in his idiosyncratic interpretation of Dewey's "genetic method" (or as applied to history, "historical method"). Dewey had cred-ited Darwin's theory of the origin of the species as freeing-up a new logic—one no longer constrained by a teleology or by immutable or abso-lute truths—that could be applied to morality and values. In particular, he understood this "new logic" to refer to "process" and "enabling condi-tions" *rather than cause and effect*. He referred to this new logic as the "genetic method": "The genetic method, whether used in experimental or historical science, does not 'derive' or 'deduce' a consequent from an antecedent, in the sense of resolving it or dissolving it, into what has gone before.… The antecedent is of worth because it defines one term of the process of becoming; the consequent because it defines the other term. Both are strictly subordinated to the process to which they gave terms, limits."[24]

Hu Shi maintained that "the consequence of applying the evolu-tionary perspective to philosophy is the production of a type of 'historical method.'" He glossed historical method as *zusun de fangfa* 祖孫的方法 (the method of grandfather-grandson; presumably a rendering of Dewey's "genetic method"), stating that "Dewey never regarded an institution or a doctrine as something autonomous; he always regarded it as a segment, one end of which is its enabling cause and the other end of which is the effect that it brought about. At one end is its grandfather; at the other end is its grandson. Once both ends have been grasped, then it will never run away again!"[25] The opening sentence of the first substantive paragraph in Hu's *Zhongguo zhexueshi dagang* states:

> Generally, a particular theory does not just fall out of the sky. If we are able to study it carefully, we will certainly be able to find that the theory has had many antecedent causes and many subsequent effects. For example, in an essay, the theory is simply one part of the essay. That part certainly does not arise and depart without leaving traces. For sure there will be a relationship of receiving and opening up, of inheriting what has preceded and ushering in what is to follow. If the causes of the theory are not understood, then its true import cannot be understood. If the effects of the theory are not understood, then its place in history cannot be understood.[26]

Later he stated: "I have always sought to find the cause and effect of every single thing and institution rather than regard them as autonomous things lacking any trace of where they have come from or where they go to. This attitude is the historical attitude.... The historical attitude is an important element in pragmatism."[27]

Whereas for Dewey, the genetic or historical method was concerned with identifying "process" and the conditions/circumstances under which something comes into existence, Hu's (mis-)understanding of Dewey's notion of genetic method[28] led him to conceive of historical change as involving isolatable chains of causes and effects. The following remarks are from Hu's 1919 clarion call to "re-organize the national heritage" (整理國故):

> In regard to old learning and thought, I have only one positive proposal and that is to "reorganize the nation's past." Re-organizing consists of finding an ordered sequence within disarray; of finding causes and effects within complete disorder; of finding real meanings within rubbish and nonsense; of finding true values within arbitrariness and superstition…. Therefore, the first step is to organize a logical sequence. Because very few of the former scholars who studied the ancient books had held the outlook of historical evolution [the genetic theory of history], they were not particular about origins and learning and the causal relations of thought. Therefore, the second step is to find out how all learning and thought arose, and after arising, what influences and results it had.[29]

In other words, Hu Shi assumed not only that history is a matter of evolutionary progression, or historical development, but also that there is a logical sequence, a causal relationship, between one historical event and another. Importantly, he applied this thinking to his understanding of the history (and internal dynamics) of Chinese philosophy, distinguishing two threads (*xiansuo* 線索): external (外的) and internal (內的). "External threads" refers to social, political and other contextual factors; "internal threads" refers to "a kind of method, a philosophical method, the foreign name of which is logic." He maintained that "logic" here refers to something broader in compass than *mingxue* 名學 or *lunlixue* 論理學. "External threads simply undergo change, whereas no matter how many changes an internal thread experiences, it can never move from a definite path [of development]."[30] Elsewhere he explains: "The particular perspective adopted in this book seeks to grasp the logical method (名學方法) (logical method [邏輯方法], that is, the method of thought) of each philosopher or each school of thought. I take this to be the central topic of the history of philosophy."[31]

What was this fixed path of development, this inner logic, which Hu identified with the application of his logical method to Chinese philosophy? His most succinct account is provided in his 1921 essay on the topic of the "threads" in Chinese philosophy where he presents Laozi and Confucius as marking the beginnings of Chinese philosophy. Whereas Laozi was strongly opposed to all forms of social institutions, Confucius maintained that social institutions could and should be improved. "After Chinese philosophy experienced the appearance of these two systems (系統), its inner thread (內在)—its method—continued to change but not move beyond [the parameters delineated by] these two types."[32] Hu does not deny that context also has a bearing on this inner thread, but this inner thread has its own integrity:

> Thought necessarily develops according to context: as context changes, so too must thought change. In all cases, if a particular method cannot adapt to new demands, then new methods will develop. Some of these methods will adjust to the various former methods in order to adapt to the new demands. If one is able to identify the changes in method, then one will be able to grasp the thread of thought. Thought "inherits what has gone before and opens up what is to come"—it has a definite thread and does not fluctuate erratically, in a completely undisciplined fashion.[33]

Central to the inner thread of traditional Chinese philosophy is the concept of names (名), with one parameter being marked by Laozi's method of "no names" (無名), the other by Confucius' rectification of names (正名). The Mohists' attention to names and actualities (名實) occupied a position in between. Hu proceeded to apply his method to identify Ji Kang 嵇康 (223–262), Lu Jiuyuan 陸九淵 (1139–1192), Wang Yangming 王陽明 (1472–1529), and Tan Sitong 譚嗣同 (1865–1898) as all inclining to the "no names" persuasion, and Mencius, Xunzi, and Dong Zhongshu 董仲舒 (179–104 B.C.) as inclining to the pro-names persuasion. "The internal thread consisted of these two great systems (系統)…. The two schools of Cheng-Zhu and Lu-Wang controlled thought for over nine hundred years, and during this period there were seventy or eighty different interpretations of *ge wu* 格物. In reality, however, this was still in the orthodox tradition of the 'name and actuality' [internal thread of discourse. The two positions] differed only in a change of their direction: should *ge wu* be inwardly focused or outwardly focused?"[34] In other words, the thread of traditional Chinese philosophical thought was bound by the parameters of name and actuality discourse which was animated by a dialectical tension between philosophers who argued that names had a social role to play and those who disagreed.

The genetic method inspired Hu to trace Chinese philosophy to its origins, to find a "congenial stock" to match Chinese and Western thought systems. In *The Development of the Logical Method in Ancient China* he claims that the *ge wu* 格物 (reaching out to things; extending knowledge; rectification of thoughts) and *zhi liangzhi* 至良知 (extension of pure knowing; extension of innate knowledge of the good) methods of the *Great Learning* functioned as the de facto logical method for the past one thousand years and that as a consequence early material had been overlooked or misunderstood, resulting in "modern" (since the tenth century) Chinese philosophy's having become narrowly focused on issues surrounding conflicting interpretations of *ge wu* in the *Great Learning*: the approach associated with Zhu Xi 朱熹 (1130–1200) concerning the steady and sequential accumulation of knowledge through the investigation of things versus the approach associated with Wang Yangming concerning the intuitive grasp of knowledge through inner reflection:

> The new schools of the Sung and Ming rejuvenated the long-dead Confucianism by reading into it two logical methods that never belonged to it…. [viz.] the theory of investigating into the reason in everything

for the purpose of extending one's knowledge to the utmost, which is the method of the Sung School; and the theory of intuitive knowledge, which is the method of the School of Wang Yang-ming.... I believe that the revival of the non-Confucian schools is absolutely necessary because it is in these schools that we may hope to find the congenial soil in which to transplant the best products of occidental philosophy and science.... The emphasis on experience as against dogmatism and rationalism, the highly developed scientific method in all its phases of operation, and the historical or evolutionary view of truth and morality—these which I consider as the most important contributions of modern philosophy in the Western world—can all find their remote but highly developed precursors in those great non-Confucian schools of the fifth, fourth, and third centuries B.C.[35]

Hu devoted particular attention to the period he refers to as the age of logic, featuring Confucius' rectification of names: "The problem of Confucianism ... was one of establishing an ideal world, a world of universals, of ideal relations, for the real world to imitate and approximate"; the *Book of Change* (in which he identifies the 64 hexagrams as early words/names and links them with Confucius' rectification of names); Mozi who emphasized actualities (實) and not just names; the Neo-Mohists (including Gongsun Long and Hui Shi) and inductive logic (something that did not develop in the West until Bacon) and paradoxes; Zhuangzi and Hui Shi: "Chuang-tzu's philosophy of evolution ... resulted in a fatalistic conception of progress and in a logical theory which denies all distinctions and thereby all reality of knowledge"; and Xunzi: "It was against this philosophy [of Zhuangzi] that Hsun Tze [Xunzi] seems to have directed his attack in his attempt to rescue philosophy from skepticism."[36]

Thus rather than privileging a small, select group of masters or one or two schools (家) of thought as representative of early Chinese philosophy, Hu's "logical method" enabled him to incorporate a broad spectrum of pre-Qin masters as foundational in the early flourishing of Chinese philosophy. With Hu Shi, the transformation from masters to philosophers was complete. The key for Hu was being able to identify the "inner logic" revealed by the "logical method" of each philosopher or school of thought, central to which was the concept of *ming* 名 (names/terms). And by placing these philosophers and schools of thought in an historical narrative, the "historical method" (genetic method) was able to reveal the unfolding course of this inner logic over time: the system of

Chinese philosophy. That is why Hu made the task of writing a history of Chinese philosophy his most pressing goal.

> No matter what we study we must set about by attending to its historical aspects. If we study philosophy or literature, we must first study the history of philosophy and the history of literature. Politics is the same. If we study social institutions, we must first study the history of changes in those institutions, looking for the relationship between cause and effect, for what is crucial in regards to what comes first and what comes after. It requires us to find system (系統) in literature, philosophy, and politics where there is no system.[37]

The mantra of system and systematization also dominates a 1920 proposal to establish a National Studies Institute at Peking University. Although the author of the proposal is not attributed, Hu Shi seems a highly likely candidate. Having made the argument that the key rationale for putting traditional scholarship in order was to avoid the disdain of Westerners, who found China's traditional scholarship to be chaotic and disordered, the author writes:

> Only after the various venerable gentlemen of the Qianlong [1736–1795] and Jiaqing [1796–1820] periods appeared did the old form of scholarship begin somewhat to gain order and system (條理系統).... These gentlemen were able to apply themselves to matters of nomenclature and glossing old terms, yet even so, a great many paths to normative principles remained overgrown and uncleared. Thus today if we want to expound and propagate our country's own scholarship, it is even more crucial that the paths to it be first put in order.... Putting this scholarship in order consists in using scientific method to analyze the doctrines of people in former times so that the boundaries separating them from one another are clearly distinguished, and their systems (系統) [of thought] are not compromised.[38]

In his preface to Hu Shi's *Zhongguo zhexue dagang*, Cai Yuanpei identified two difficulties in preparing a history of ancient Chinese philosophy:

> The first is the problem of materials. With books from the Zhou period, authentic and forged texts are mixed together. Even with authentic texts, incorrect or simplified characters are common. If it were not for the efforts of Qing "Han Learning," then the materials that we have would have many mistakes. The second is a problem of form (形式). Ancient Chinese scholarly works were never compiled as systematic records. If we want to compile them systematically, there is nothing we can rely on to do so in the writings of the

ancients, so we have to rely on the histories of philosophy by Westerners. Hence, without having studied the history of Western philosophy, an appropriate form cannot be constructed.[39]

For Hu, system is not only an object of research but is also central to the methodology informing that research. In the Reading Guide (導言) prefacing *Zhongguo zhexueshi dagang*, Hu outlines the steps involved in writing a reliable (可靠) history of Chinese philosophy. Having emphasized the fundamental importance of textual criticism and acknowledging the advances made in Qing-dynasty evidential scholarship, he explains that the historian's task is to interconnect (貫串) the philosophical doctrines and theories of individual schools such that those doctrines and theories become ordered and have system (有條理有系統). Only when this has been achieved can the following three sequential goals be achieved: clarifying change (明變), seeking causes (求因), and setting forth an evaluation (評判). Clarifying change is concerned with tracing the historical transmission of theories and the influences between schools, so as to identify the "thread of intellectual change" over time.[40] Seeking causes aims to uncover the causes leading to the rise, decline, and transformation of individual schools. Finally, in setting forth an evaluation, the aim is to make a judgement about the theories of a particular school on the basis of the outcomes and influences generated by its doctrines and theories.[41]

Hu's "historical method" was, however, not inspired solely by Dewey's "genetic method." The very first title listed in the bibliography of Hu's Reading Guide to *Zhongguo zhexueshi dagang*—German philosopher Wilhelm Windelband's *A History of Philosophy with Especial Reference to the Formation and Development of its Problems and Conceptions*—provides an important clue to this. In the Introduction to his *History*, Windelband identified three tasks for the history of philosophy:

(1) To establish with precision what may be derived from the available sources as to the circumstances in life, the mental development, and the doctrines of individual philosophers; (2) from these facts to reconstruct the genetic process in such a way that in the case of every philosopher we may understand how his doctrines depend in part upon those of his predecessors, in part upon the general ideas of his time, and in part upon his own nature and the course of his education; (3) from the consideration of the whole to estimate what value for the total result of the history of philosophy belongs to the theories thus established and explained as regards their origin.

Windelband further stipulated that "To establish its facts the history of philosophy must proceed to a careful and comprehensive examination of the sources."[42] The similarities with Hu's approach are unmistakable.

4. Philosophy and Genre

Chinese scholars continued to write new histories of Chinese philosophy during the 1920s and 1930s.[43] Indeed, the writing of histories of "Chinese philosophy" and the continued elaboration and re-telling of those histories has sustained the discipline known as *"Zhongguo zhexue."* The modern Chinese concept of *zhexue* has been defined through an ongoing process of selective historical recovery and discovery in which various aspects of traditional scholarship have been identified as exemplifying Chinese philosophy. Now while this can often be seen as having led to the disciplinary conflation of Chinese philosophy and the history of Chinese philosophy, we should also bear in mind the important role that genre plays in philosophical discourse.

As an illustration, consider the impact of genre in Neo-Confucian philosophy. Hilde De Weerdt has pointed out that the recorded conversation (語錄) genre enabled Neo-Confucian teachers in the twelfth and thirteenth centuries to draw together "passages and ideas from the entire classical corpus in order to explain Neo-Confucian concepts and beliefs," enabling themselves to become the locus of authority. This contrasts with the genre of the traditional interlinear commentary where "authority is primarily vested in the classical text as it is." When the recorded conversations genre reached its apogee in the thirteenth century with the publication of various versions of Zhu Xi's recorded conversations, this confronted Zhu's first- and second-generation disciples with two basic questions: "how to transmit Neo-Confucian philosophy after the passing of the core masters, and, how to preserve the personal voice and interaction that had become emblematic of Learning of the Way philosophizing." This situation led to the development of new genres of texts: lexicons of Neo-Confucian terms and the notebook. The exemplar of the lexicon, Chen Chun's 陳淳 (1159–1223) *Beixi ziyi* 北溪字義 [The correct meaning of terms], is characterized by an arrangement in which the entries were designed to be read "as connected elements in a coherent moral philosophy and as steps in a program of learning that joined understanding and moral action."[44]

Zhen Dexiu's 真德秀 (1178–1235) *Xishan xiansheng Zhen Wenzhong gong dushuji* 西山先生真文忠公讀書記 [Reading notes], in which cases (*an* 案) were used to construct argument, may also have influenced the subsequent development of the case genre. In her introduction to a recent collection of studies of the case genre as developed in China, Charlotte Furth maintains that in the late Ming, when the Cheng-Zhu Learning of the Way (道學) tradition was splintering into factions "the very idea of a single doctrinal line of transmission from antiquity via the Song to the present Ming-era masters was increasingly hard to maintain…. The genre of the case (*an*, *xue'an*) encouraged a different way of doing philosophy. It accommodated debate among partisans who had to back their positions with evidence and who could rely on no transcendent or unquestioned authority of sagely transmission to fall back on."[45]

The subject of Hung-lam Chu's chapter in the same volume on case studies is the sub-genre of *xue'an* 學案—which Chu translates as "Confucian case learning." Drawing upon the tradition of recording a master's words and deeds, late-Ming *xue'an* presented this material not as canon or history but as evidence, "and the body of the text on him called for the reader's evaluative judgment (verdict) of the case put together by the author-compiler."[46] Focusing in particular on Huang Zongxi's *Ming ru xue'an* 明儒學案 [Case studies of Ming Ru], Chu argues that rather than promoting a particular notion of orthodoxy or a hierarchy of competing doctrines and schools, the aim of the work was to provide students with a set of dossiers on the many different modes of learning practiced by Ming *ru*, leaving it up to the student to contemplate these cases for their own edification and guidance just as the Chan Buddhist contemplated "public cases." This may be so, but we should not underestimate the role that Huang (and his fellow compilers) had in determining who should be represented in the collection—as Chu himself notes, Li Zhi 李贄 (1527–1602) is conspicuously absent—and which selections from their writings should be included. Julia Ching, for example, argues in the introduction to her translation of *Ming ru xue'an* (1987), that Huang organized his work around two central figures—Liu Zongzhou 劉宗周 (1578–1645) and Wang Yangming—allowing Huang to advance his own views indirectly.[47]

So too, the genre of the "the history of Chinese philosophy" was an innovation with its own philosophical import. In China, the mature exemplar of this genre is Feng Youlan's 馮友蘭 celebrated and hugely popular *Zhongguo zhexueshi* 中國哲學史 [A History of Chinese Philosophy; 1934 (English translation, 1937)]. (Hu's *Zhongguo zhexueshi dagang* was only the first part of an anticipated general history which was never realized. It covers only the period of the masters.) Feng's *Zhongguo zhexueshi*, and its later iterations, decisively shaped subsequent understanding of Chinese philosophy. Like Hu, Feng wrote his histories of Chinese philosophy to introduce system where none was apparent. Writing at the very end of his life, Feng opined that the single most important contribution of Hu's *Zhongguo zhexueshi dagang* was to have provided Chinese philosophy with a "formal system." "At that time, the method of conducting academic research on the history of Chinese philosophy followed that of Huang Zongxi's *Song-Yuan ru xue'an*. Because Chinese philosophy does not have a formal system, the first task of the historian of Chinese philosophy is to re-organize (整理) the actual system of the thought of individual philosophers."[48] Feng was also impressed with another "formal" aspect of Hu's presentation, one which, like the "history of Chinese philosophy" genre, greatly facilitated the locus of authority to shift to the narrator. Brian Moloughney provides the following account of Feng Youlan's reaction to the publication of Hu Shi's *Zhongguo zhexueshi dagang*:

> Whereas in the past writers had expressed their thoughts through commentaries on the classics, and it was those classical texts that featured prominently while the author's own words were presented in smaller characters, with Hu Shi's book his own words dominated: "They were printed in large characters going all the way up to the top of the page, while his quotations of ancient authors were indented and in smaller characters". In other words, this reversed what Feng Youlan believed to be the normal order of things.... [He saw] it as a significant departure from past practice.[49]

Nevertheless, as with Hu, Feng did not believe that Chinese philosophy was in fact devoid of its own inherent system. To this end, he had long distinguished "formal" (形式) system and "real" (實質) system. Identifying this real system, however, requires a particular sort of perspicacity:

> The fact is that Chinese philosophers were accustomed to express themselves in the form of aphorisms, apothegms, or allusions, and illustrations.... Aphorisms, allusions, and illustrations are thus not articulate enough. Their insufficiency in articulateness is compensated for, however, by their suggestiveness. Articulateness and suggestiveness are, of course, incompatible.... These sayings and writings of the Chinese philosophers are so inarticulate that their suggestiveness is almost boundless.... According

to Taoism, the Tao (the Way) cannot be told, but only suggested. So when words are used, it is the suggestiveness of the words, and not their fixed denotations or connotations, that reveals the Tao.[50]

It was precisely their ability to articulate the suggestiveness of those sayings and writings in the systematic format of a "history" that allowed intellectual historians like Feng Youlan and Hu Shi to promote their particular visions of the "inner logic" of "Chinese philosophy." And in doing so, they helped secure a fundamental role for the "history of Chinese philosophy" genre in prescribing "Chinese philosophy's" lineaments and trajectories.

Notes

1   Hu Shih (Hu Shi), *The Development of the Logical Method in Ancient China*, second edition (1922; New York: Paragon Book Reprint Corporation, 1968), p. 7.

2   For the role played by the educational curriculum and school textbooks in securing for logic a place on China's intellectual map in the early years of the twentieth century, see Joachim Kurtz, *The Discovery of Chinese Logic: The Genealogy of an Invented Tradition* (Leiden: Brill, forthcoming), pre-copy-edited manuscript, chapter 5.

3   *Zhongguo zhexueshi dagang* was completed in 1918 and published in 1919. Within two months it was republished. By 1922 it had been republished 8 times and by 1930, fifteen times.

4   Hu Shi, *Hu Shi koushu zizhuan* 胡適口述自傳 [Hu Shi's oral autobiography], in *Hu Shi wenji* 胡適文集 [Collected writings of Hu Shi], Vol. 1, edited by Ouyang Zhesheng 歐陽哲生 (Beijing: Beijing daxue chubanshe, 1998), pp. 263, 264, 265.

5   Hu Shi, "Xian-Qin zhexueshi daolun" 先秦哲學史導論 [An introduction to Pre-Qin philosophy], in *Hu Shi quanji* 胡適全集 [Complete works of Hu Shi], Vol. 5 (Hefei: Anhui jiaoyu chubanshe, 2003), p. 12.

6   Hu Shi, *Zhongguo zhexueshi dagang*, in *Hu Shi xueshu wenji: Zhongguo zhexueshi* 胡適學術文集：中國哲學史 [Collected essays of Hu Shi's scholarship: History of Chinese philosophy], edited by Jiang Yihua 姜義華, Vol. 1 (Beijing: Zhonghua shuju, 1998), pp. 13, 27.

7   In *Hu Shi quanji*, Vol. 5, pp. 324, 325. This same view is repeated in *Zhongguo zhexueshi dagang*, p. 130.

8   Ulrich Johannes Schneider, "Teaching the History of Philosophy in 19th-Century Germany," in *Teaching New Histories of Philosophy: Proceedings of a Conference*, edited by J. B. Schneewind, pp. 279, 283. Philosophy Documentation Center, <http://www.pdcnet.org/tnhp.html>, accessed 4 February 2009. Schneider further notes (p. 281): "The canon of subjects regularly taught within the discipline of philosophy would have been incomplete without lecture courses on the history of philosophy and seminar courses on individual philosophers or single philosophical texts. These two 'historical' courses taken together accounted for 10 percent of all of the philosophy courses of all 19 German universities at about 1810. At the end of the 19th century, they accounted for 50 percent of all courses."

9   Ge Zhaoguang 葛兆光, "Daotong, xipu yu lishi: Guanyu Zhongguo si-xiangshi mailuo de laiyuan yu queli" 道統、系譜與歷史—關於中國思想史脈絡的來源與確立 [Succession of the way, genealogy, and history: The origins and establishment of the thread of Chinese intellectual history], *Wenshizhe* 文史哲 294.2 (2006), p. 50 has commented on what he terms a "succession of the way" (道統) narrative model's informing the basic structure of Xie's *History*. First, Xie's account of the pre-Qin period adheres to the orthodox portrayal

of a Confucius-Zisi-Mencius lineage, in which Ziyou, Zixia 子夏, and Zizhang 子長 are effectively ignored. Second, his coverage of the Tang period focuses principally on Han Yu 韓愈 (768–824) and Li Ao 李翱 (722–841) as forerunners of Neo-Confucianism. Third, Xie's treatment of Song developments uncritically replicates traditional works such as Zhu Xi's *Yi-Luo yuanyuan lu* and *Song-Yuan Ru xue'an* in portraying Zhou Dunyi 周敦頤 (1017–1073), Zhang Zai 張載 (1020–1077), the two Chengs [Cheng Yi 程頤 (1033–1107) and Cheng Hao 程顥 (1032–1085)], Zhu Xi 朱熹 (1130–1200), and Lu Jiuyuan 陸九淵 (1139–1193) as the representative protagonists of Song philosophy.

10   See for example, Li Xiaoqian 李孝遷, "Qingji Zhinashi, Dongyangshi jiaokeshu jieyi chutan" 清季支那史、東洋史教科書介譯初探 [An initial exploration into the translation of history textbooks of China and Asia from Japan], *Shixue yuekan* 史學月刊 9 (2003), pp. 101–110.

11   See Liu Longxin 劉龍心, *Xueshu yu zhidu: Xueke tizhi yu xiandai Zhongguo shixue de jianli* 學術與制度—學科體制與現代中國史學的建立 [Scholarship and institutions: The disciplinary system and establishment of modern Chinese historiography] (Taipei: Yuanliu chubanshe, 2002), pp. 107, 108. She further notes that textbooks used in schools (學堂) of the day mostly adopted similar periodization schemes.

12   Hu Shi, *Zhongguo zhexueshi dagang*, preface, p. 12.

13   Xie Wuliang, *Zhongguo zhexueshi* (Taipei: Taiwan Zhonghua shuju, 1967), pp. 2, 1. In his *Zhuzixue lüeshuo* 諸子學略説 [A brief account of Masters Studies] (1906), Zhang Taiyan relates that each of the various pre-Qin schools had some insight into the whole that is the *dao*. In *Zhang Taiyan zhenglun xuanji* 章太炎政論選集 [Selection of Zhang Taiyan's essays on politics], Vol. 1, edited by Tang Zhijun 湯治鈞 (Beijing: Zhonghua shuju, 1977), pp. 285–306. This view had already been expressed in the writings of Zhang Xuecheng 章學誠 (1738–1801), where he said that the masters each grasped one aspect of the *daoti* which they then developed into their school's doctrine. See his *Wenshi tongyi jiaozhu* 文史通義校注 [Comprehensive studies in literature and history, collated and annotated] (Beijing: Zhonghua shuju, 1985), pp. 60, 166. The classic statement of this sentiment is in the "Tian xia" 天下 chapter of *Zhuangzi*. See Wang Shumin 王叔岷, *Zhuangzi jiaoquan* 莊子校詮 [Collated and annotated edition of *Zhuangzi*], Vol. 3 (Taipei: Zhongyang yanjiuyuan lishi yuyan yanjiusuo, 1988), p. 1298.

14   *Haitian ji* 海天集, edited by Yang Lian 楊廉 (Shanghai: Beixin shuju, 1926), p. 5. The same year, an Advanced College (高等學堂) was also established. It functioned as a preparatory college for entry into tertiary education. Among its courses were ethics, classical studies, Masters Studies, and logic (名學). See *Beijing daxue zhexuexi shigao* 北京大學哲學系史稿 [Draft history of the Philosophy Department of Beijing University], edited by Yang Lihua 楊立華 (Beijing: Philosophy Department of Beijing University internal publication, 2004), p. 89.

15 Historian Gu Jiegang 顧頡剛 (1893–1980) recalled that when he was a student in Chen's class, Chen began the course with Fuxi and got no further than the "Hong Fan" 洪範 [Great Plan] chapter of *Shangshu*. See *Gushi bian* 古史辨 [Disputing ancient history], Vol. 1 (Shanghai: Shanghai guji chubanshe, 1982), preface, p. 36.

16 *Chen Fuchen ji* 陳黻宸集 [Collected writings of Chen Fuchen], edited by Chen Depu 陳德溥 (Beijing: Zhonghua shuju, 1995), p. 415.

17 *Beijing daxue zhexuexi shigao*, 5.

18 Cai Yuanpei, "*Zhongguo zhexueshi dagang* xu" 中國哲學史大綱序, in Hu Shi, *Zhongguo zhexueshi dagang*, 2.

19 Yu Yingshi, *Chongxun Hu Shi licheng: Hu Shi shengping yu sixiang zai renshi* 重尋胡適歷程—胡適生平與思想再認識 [Retracing Hu Shi's path: Hu Shi's life and thought examined anew] (Taipei: Lianjing, 2004), p. 241.

20 The urge to provide Hu with a ready-made, native intellectual lineage is not new. In his 1918 preface (p. 1) to *Zhongguo zhexueshi dagang*, Cai Yuanpei claimed: "Hu was born into the Hu clan of Jixi 績溪 which has been transmitting Han Learning for several generations, and so he is endowed with the genetic character of that tradition." These remarks, coming from the then President of Peking University and a leading scholar in his own right, no doubt enhanced the native scholarly credentials of the young returnee, but they are in fact incorrect. Curiously, at the time Hu did not point out that Cai's claim about his provenance was mistaken.

21 Hu Shi, "Hu Shi de zizhuan" 胡適的自傳 [Hu Shi's autobiography] in *Hu Shi zhexue sixiang ziliao xuan* 胡適哲學思想資料選 [Selected materials on Hu Shi's philosophical thought], edited by Ge Maochun 葛懋春 and Li Xingzhi 李興芝, Vol. 2 (Shanghai: Huadong shifan daxue chubanshe, 1981), p. 109.

22 See for example the comments in his preface to *Zhongguo zhexueshi dagang*, pp. 13–14.

23 Hu Shih, *The Development of the Logical Method in Ancient China*, p. 2.

24 John Dewey, "The Evolutionary Method As Applied to Morality: 1. Its Scientific Necessity," *Philosophical Review* 11 (1902), pp. 115–116.

25 Hu Shi, "Duwei xiansheng yu Zhongguo" 杜威先生與中國 [Mr. Dewey and China] (1921), in *Hu Shi wenji*, Vol. 2, p. 280.

26 Hu Shi, *Zhongguo zhexueshi dagang*, p. 30.

27 Hu Shi "Wenti yu zhuyi" 問題與主義 [Problems and ideology], in *Hu Shi wencun* 胡適文存 [Hu Shi's extant writings], *Minguo congshu, di yi bian* 民國叢書, 第一編 edition, Vol. 93 (Shanghai: Shanghai shudian, 1989), *juan* 2, pp. 196–197.

28 In an insightful discussion of Hu Shi's appropriation of Dewey's genetic method—from which I have benefited—intellectual historian Nakajima Takahiro 中島隆博 points out that Dewey's use of the terms "antecedents" and "consequents" in the context of his "genetic method" is not as unequivocal as it might be, as the former concept can be construed as giving rise to the latter, hence implying a causal relationship. See Nakajima Takahiro,

"'Chūgoku tetsugakushi' no keifugaku: John Dewey no hasseiteki hōhō to Ko Teki" '中国哲学史'の系譜学—ジョン・デューイの發生的方法と胡適 [The genealogy of "The History of Chinese Philosophy": John Dewey's genetic method and Hu Shi], *Chūgoku tetsugaku kenkyū* 中学哲学研究 19 (June 2003), p. 58. An English version of this essay, "Pragmatism and Modern Chinese Philosophy: The 'Genetic Method' of John Dewey and Hu Shi" is included in Nakajima's *The Chinese Turn in Philosophy* (Tokyo: The University of Tokyo Center for Philosophy, 2007). The content of the English version is substantially different in places from that of the Japanese version.

29 Hu Shi, "Xin sichao de yiyi" 新思潮的意義 [The significance of the new intellectual tide], in *Hu Shi wencun, juan* 4, p. 162.

30 Hu Shi, "Zhongguo zhexue de xiansuo" 中國哲學的線索 [The thread of Chinese philosophy] (1921), in *Hu Shi xueshu wenji: Zhongguo zhexueshi*, Vol. 1, p. 522.

31 Hu Shi, preface to the Taipei edition of *Zhongguo zhexueshi dagang* (renamed *Zhongguo gudai zhexueshi* 中國古代哲學史 [History of ancient Chinese philosophy]), *Hu Shi xueshu wenji: Zhongguo zhexueshi*, Vol. 1, p. 5.

32 *Ibid.*, p. 523.

33 *Ibid.*, p. 526.

34 *Ibid.*, pp. 524–525, 526.

35 Hu Shih, *The Development of the Logical Method in Ancient China*, pp. 7, 8, 9.

36 *Ibid.*, pp. 150–151.

37 Hu Shi, "Yanjiu guogu de fangfa" 研究國故的方法 [The method to research the national heritage," in *Hu Shi yanjiang lu* 胡適演講錄 [A record of Hu Shi's speeches and lectures], Vol. 3 (Taipei: Yuanliu chuban gongsi, 1988), p. 13.

38 "Guoli Beijing daxue yanjiusuo zhengli guoxue jihuashu" 國立北京大學研究所整理國學計劃書 [Plan by the National Peking University Graduate Institute to re-organize national learning), in *Beijing daxue rikan* 北京大學日刊 [Peking university daily], 9 October 1920, pp. 2, 3.

39 Cai Yuanpei, *Zhongguo zhexueshi dagang*, preface, p. 1.

40 As Brian Moloughney and Peter Zarrow note:

… in the early 1920s Hu Shi initiated a program to "put in order the nation's past" (*zhengli guogu* 整理國故), a proposal that was taken up with enthusiasm by many younger historians. This involved organising the vast body of historical material handed down from the past into logical sequences so that the causal relationships that led to the production of these materials were made evident.

See their introductory essay, "Making History Modern: The Transformation of Chinese Historiography, 1895–1937," in *Transforming History: The Making of a Modern Academic Discipline in Twentieth-Century China*, edited by Brian Moloughney and Peter Zarrow (Hong Kong: Chinese University Press, 2011).

41 Hu Shi, *Zhongguo zhexue dagang*, pp. 10, 27–29.

42 Wilhelm Windelband, *A History of Philosophy with Especial Reference to the*

Formation and Development of its Problems and Conceptions, translated by James Hayden Tufts, second revised edition (New York: Macmillan, 1901), Introduction p. 15. It might be noted that James Hayden Tufts (1862–1942) had been a colleague of John Dewey at the University of Michigan in the 1880s and again at the University of Chicago in the 1890s; in 1908 they co-authored *Ethics*.

43　Lu Maode 陸懋德, *Zhou-Qin zhexueshi* 周秦哲學史 [History of philosophy from the Zhou to Qin periods] (1923); Zhong Tai 鍾泰, *Zhongguo zhexueshi* 中國哲學史 [History of Chinese philosophy] (1929); Feng Youlan 馮友蘭, *Zhongguo zhexueshi* 中國哲學史 [A history of Chinese philosophy] (1934); Yao Shunqin 姚舜欽, *Qin-Han zhexueshi* 秦漢哲學史 [History of philosophy during the Qin and Han periods] (1936); and Jiang Weiqiao 蔣維喬 and Yang Daying 楊大膺, eds., *Zhongguo zhexueshi gangyao* 中國哲學史綱要 [Outline of the history of Chinese philosophy] (1934); and Fan Shoukang 范壽康, *Zhongguo zhexueshi tonglun* 中國哲學史通論 [Comprehensive account of the history of Chinese philosophy] (1936).

44　Hilde De Weerdt, "Neo-Confucian Philosophy and Genre: The Philosophical Writings of Chen Chun and Zhen Dexiu," in *Dao Companion to Neo-Confucian Philosophy*, edited by John Makeham (New York: Springer, 2010), pp. 224, 226, 228–229.

45　Charlotte Furth, "Introduction" to *Thinking with Cases: Specialist Knowledge in Chinese Cultural History*, edited by Charlotte Furth, Judith Zeitlin, and Ping-chen Hsiung (Honolulu: University of Hawai'i Press, 2007), p. 16.

46　Chu Hung-lam, "Confucian 'Case Learning': The Genre of *Xue'an* Writings," in *Thinking with Cases*, pp. 255–256.

47　Julia Ching, "Introduction," in Huang Tsung-hsi (Huang Zongxi), *The Records of Ming Scholars*, translated by Julia Ching in collaboration with Zhaoying Fang (Honolulu: University of Hawai'i Press, 1987), p. 9.

48　Feng Youlan, *Zhongguo xiandai zhexueshi* 中國現代哲學史 [A history of modern Chinese philosophy] (Guangzhou: Guangdong renmin chubanshe, 1999/1992), p. 4.

49　See his "Derivations, Intertextuality and Authority: Narrative and the Problem of Historical Coherence," *East Asian History* 23 (2002), p. 138.

50　Feng Youlan, *Zhongguo xiandai zhexueshi*, p. 12.

Chapter 6

Introducing Buddhism as Philosophy: The Cases of Liang Shuming, Xiong Shili, and Tang Yongtong

Thierry Meynard

The early-twentieth century saw the introduction of Buddhist studies into the Chinese academic world. For the most part, this occurred in the philosophy departments of the newly established universities. The subsequent academic discourse on Buddhism was a great challenge to the traditional teachings of the monasteries. Some Buddhist monks, such as Taixu 太虛 (1890–1947), and Buddhist laymen, such as Ouyang Jingwu 歐陽竟無 (1871–1943), responded by developing a modern approach to their intellectual tradition.[1] Under the pressure of Western-style academic institutions, including Christian universities and seminaries, a number of Buddhist training centres opened. These included the Wuchang Buddhist Institute 武昌佛學院 and the Minnan Buddhist Institute 閩南佛學院, established in 1922 and 1925 respectively by Taixu, and the Institute of Inner Learning 支那內學院 in Nanjing, which was established (and subsequently directed) by Ouyang in 1922.[2] The teaching and research of Buddhist scholars working in academic institutions developed in quite a different direction, but they maintained close contact with the Buddhist institutes throughout the Republican period.

This chapter examines three important scholars who contributed to Buddhist studies in the first half of the twentieth century. All three taught Buddhism in the Philosophy Department at Peking University. Broadly speaking, they were representative of three different academic approaches: the cultural, the metaphysical, and the historical. Liang Shuming 梁漱溟 (1893–1988) developed a cultural philosophy in which Buddhism represented the future religion for all humanity. Xiong Shili 熊十力 (1885–1968) used Buddhism as a conceptual tool in his own metaphysical system. Finally, Tang Yongtong 湯用彤 (1893–1964) was an historian of Buddhism.

Through an analysis of these three figures, I clarify how, and why, Buddhism came to be classified as "philosophy." In particular, I investigate how their understanding of Buddhism was transformed by their use of this label. More specifically, I focus on three questions concerning the relation between philosophical discourse and Buddhism. First, could Buddhism be completely comprehended within the limits of philosophy? Second, what was the status and relevance of a Buddhist philosophy detached from practice? Third, was the academic discourse on Buddhism neutral, or did it ultimately serve other purposes?

1. Liang Shuming: Buddhist Philosophy in the Service of an Existential Commitment

1.1 The Discovery of a "Philosopher"

It was by chance that Liang joined philosophical circles. Between 1914 and 1915, he was dealing with existential issues. These included the meaning of life after a friend's death; and following the outbreak of the First World War, the future of civilization itself. During a kind of quasi-retreat, Liang intensively read both Buddhist sutras and Western philosophy. In his first philosophical essay, "Treatise on Finding the Foundation and Resolving Doubt" (1916), Liang proposed overcoming the existential and intellectual crisis of the age by exploring the foundation of human existence and the universe; a foundation which he expressed using the Buddhist term "suchness" (*zhenru* 真如).[3] In writing this article, Liang was most probably unaware that he was "doing philosophy" as such. He was motivated not by a love of knowledge or speculation, but rather by his need to solve an existential crisis. In his preface to *Essentials of Chinese Culture* (1949), Liang confessed that he did not engage in academic work for its own sake but because he was forced to do so in order to solve personal issues.[4]

The chancellor of Peking University, Cai Yuanpei 蔡元培 (1868–1940), discovered Liang's article and recognized it as a work of philosophy. Cai also realized that Liang could teach philosophy and invited him to lecture on Indian philosophy. Liang was very much aware of his lack of credentials: "Concerning my qualifications, first, I did not go to university; second, I did not study abroad. Concerning my specialization, I had only diligently studied some disciplines by myself and acquired a smattering of knowledge."[5] He was given the label of "philosopher" by an academic institution eager to attract bright minds. Without Cai's invervention, Liang would most probably never have started his career as a "philosopher" and would likely have become a Buddhist monk.[6]

Here, we face an important historical issue: after the abolition of the imperial examination system in 1905, what careers were available to young intellectuals? With the split between intellectual and political elites, could intellectuals be satisfied with a prestigious position in teaching and research, albeit one that was cut off from their traditional involvement in public life? Going beyond the historical period under consideration, we can ask what the role of a philosopher is in society, whether a philosopher can exist outside of philosophy departments or research institutes, and what price a philosopher should be willing to pay for the support he or she receives from an academic institution.

1.2 A Buddhist "Science"

Once Liang had joined an institution devoted to the professional pursuit of philosophy, he embraced the neologism of "philosophy." He followed the Anglo-Saxon pragmatism that was so prevalent at the time, after the lectures given at Peking University by John Dewey and Bertrand Russell. Liang was clearly influenced by Hu Shi's experimental method and advocated building a "scientific" philosophy. He attempted, in all of his works, to tie his own philosophical discourse to the world of science, including particle physics, the social sciences and biology. Like Hu Shi (1891–1962), Liang did not consider science limited just to particular objects. Rather, he believed it referred mostly to a spirit and method of rigorous analysis. Liang also held that theory was not, as such, sufficient for something to be scientific. What ultimately mattered was an agreement with facts, or, as Liang said: "A credible theory has to be proven in practice."[7] Philosophical rationality implied a continuous dialectic between theory and its confirmation by practice. It was in this very sense that Liang recognized Western philosophy as truly a "scientific philosophy" (*kexue de zhexue* 科學的哲學), as he stated in his *Eastern and Western Cultures and Their Philosophies* (1921).[8]

Liang applied this definition of philosophy to Eastern thought but arrived at a very different conclusion from that of either Hu Shi or Feng Youlan (1895–1990), both of whom sought to unearth a logical method in ancient Chinese thought. Liang instead held that Eastern thought was mostly "unscientific." Although Confucianism could provide some interesting insights into human life, because it lacked a rigorous method, it failed to reach the ultimate truth. Liang also rejected Pure Land Buddhism as superstitious, and Chan Buddhism as inarticulate and inconclusive.[9] He thus came to consider the Buddhist school of Yogācāra to be the only Asian theory of knowledge able to match its Western rivals.[10] Yogācāra was at that time experiencing an astounding revival, appearing as an Asian alternative to Western scientific discourse. Furthermore, it was considered typically Asian by virtue of its focus on the mind rather than matter. Liang's interest in Yogācāra was spurred by the reprints of Buddhist texts and by the works of Zhang Taiyan 章太炎 (1868–1936), who is also discussed in this volume. Liang Shuming inherited many of Zhang's ideas and methods, including the idea that Yogācāra could compete with Western epistemology.[11] Liang was also influenced by Zhang's notion that Buddhism could have a positive role as a religion for modern times.[12] However, Liang expressed his disapproval of Zhang's *Qi wu lun shi* 齊物論釋 [Explanation of "Discourse on making all things equal"] (1914), in which Zhang used Yogācāra to interpret Chinese philosophy.[13] Later on, Liang came to consider Zhang to be an amateur outsider (*waihang* 外行) to Buddhism, and he distanced himself from Zhang's thinking.

In his *Outline of Yogācāra* (1920), Liang considered Yogācāra's theory of knowledge to be scientifically sound and as forming the necessary philosophical basis upon which a metaphysics could be built.[14] He even held that "Yogācāra represents the entirety of Buddhist doctrine."[15] As we can see, Liang's conception of Buddhism and philosophy was very much shaped by Western empiricism. At the same time, Liang strongly criticized Western science for its limited use of the human mind and, therefore, for its inability to reach ultimate reality. The instrumental reason (*lizhi* 理智) of Western science, he pointed out, was only able to grasp appearances. Liang praised Henri Bergson for the role he gave to intuition, but he held that Yogācāra alone had developed a thorough method. This enabled it to reach the highest degree of reality through direct perception (*xianliang* 現量). Therefore, Liang strove to establish Buddhism as a philosophical science—a science that met the criteria of the West, yet went even further, in the direction of a complete science encompassing both matter and mind.

1.3 Buddhism as Anti-Philosophy

While Buddhism was, for Liang, true philosophy, he also made philosophy relative by stressing that religious experiences were central to the human experience overall: "What we call philosophy is thought systematized into a doctrine. What we call religion is thought, with a special attitude, leading to a certain behaviour."[16] Although religion aimed at a transcendental reality, religion as a practice was more anchored in the present world than philosophy was.

As with philosophy, Liang adopted the Western concept of religion but radically transformed it. Instead of building upon the notion of God's existence or the experience of the divine, Liang defined religion from a Buddhist perspective: as a radical negation of the present world. This meant two things. First, Buddhism, as a religion, went further than philosophy. It reached a non-conceptual reality, beyond the dichotomy of the thinking subject and the object of thought. Second, in its method, Buddhism used a thorough-going dialectic: reason was systematically used to deny ultimate reality to any element of experience. In the end, even reason itself was negated, leading Liang to state that "Buddhist philosophy is the exhaustion of philosophy."[17] In another very concise formulation, he described the Buddhist method as "canceling understanding through understanding" (*yi lijie quxiao lijie* 以理解取消理解).[18] Whereas ordinary philosophy developed positive knowledge about reality, Buddhism was an anti-philosophy. It destroyed philosophy itself and sought after a wisdom that was beyond both Western rationality and Confucian moral intuition.[19] The mind could access ultimate reality only when reason had systematically eliminated all the conceptual attachments it had created in the first place. The mind could then fuse with the ultimate reality, without any distinction between the inner and outer worlds. Within the mind, there would no longer be any self-reflection, nor would there be space for self-awareness. Instead, there would be only pure, spontaneous activity.

Therefore, Liang saw Buddhist philosophy as the death of philosophy: "By making Buddhism an object of study and research, it loses its meaning. The original intention of Buddhism was not to practice philosophy; [it] in fact meant the death of philosophy."[20] Indeed, Indians had adopted the necessary attitude for understanding ontological reality,[21] but their understanding did not remain at the intellectual level. By destroying the conceptual constructions of the mind regarding the absolute, Indians were finally able to succeed in uniting with it.

1.4 Philosophy and Practice

Liang's culturalist approach to philosophy allowed him to give an important role to different methods of self-cultivation: religion in the West, practical morality and self-cultivation in China, and meditation in India. In the case of India, Liang affirmed the importance of religion: "India has no individual philosophers, but only religious schools." [22] Indeed, a philosophy reflected only the thinking of one individual, sometimes with a limited influence. Only religion could transform individuals and society in concrete ways. Liang started from questions encountered in the cultural realm, clarified them through the mediation of philosophical enquiry, and then, in the third stage, returned to the issues of culture and practice, discussing their general orientation and concrete expressions. In this scheme, philosophy worked mostly as a tool.

Liang's cultural philosophy could be very fruitful. Not only did he integrate praxis into the philosophical field, but he also attempted to understand the philosophies of each tradition at their roots. Liang thus judged particular philosophies in terms of their degree of connection to culture. This approach led him to consider Western philosophy to be mostly an intellectual activity which could produce efficient results in the empirical world but which was alienated from the question of meaning. Liang's judgment was severe:

> Philosophies of life in the West do not deserve the name philosophy. From ancient times up to now, almost all of them have the same style. What style? In short, the emphasis is on the intellect. Either the focus is on efficiency, and then it is a matter of intellectual computing; or the focus is on knowledge, and then it is a matter of intellectual enterprise; or else the focus is on the absolute, and even then, it is a problem of rationality. [23]

Here, Liang departed from his own definition of philosophy as science, given above. He attempted to expand philosophy's scope, holding that Indian philosophy was not only an intellectual activity but a true mode of life. In regards to Confucianism, Liang also understood it not as a theory but as grounded in concrete methods of self-cultivation. He always refused to consider his thinking a purely theoretical activity that was limited to the academic arena. For him, ultimate reality could not be grasped by philosophical reason. The mistake of modern scholars was to try to solve, through philosophy, questions that were outside its scope. Therefore, Liang invited them to look in the direction of a practice that was necessary, individual, and communitarian. [24]

As suggested above, Liang understood very clearly that real competition did not occur between philosophical systems. Among philosophers, there was no real need to oppose one another in order to establish oneself. In fact, the real conflict occurred between groups competing for members.[25] This was one of the reasons Liang left Peking University and became involved in rural reconstruction in the twenties and thirties. His experience with academia had allowed him to clarify his ideas, but he realized that institutions of higher learning were limited when it came to changing people and society. His shift to more direct forms of engagement reveals that Liang felt quite constrained within the narrow limits of academia, and that he considered educating the peasant masses to be more important, and effective, than the education of elites.

1.5   Liang's Crypto-Buddhism

Throughout his life, Liang advocated the revival of Confucianism for our present age. Indeed, he has been considered the forerunner of New Confucianism and has famously been called the "last Confucian."[26] However, Liang maintained a conviction that Confucianism could not address the ultimate questions of meaning for either the individual or for the world. The complex relationship Liang had with Buddhism has been understood only recently by the academic community, primarily after the publication of the interviews Liang gave in his later years, in which he revealed he had remained a Buddhist throughout his life.[27] The academic community's misperception of Liang's true identity is understandable. Believing that humanity was not yet ready to enter into the Buddhist cultural period, Liang promoted Confucian morality as a necessary step, since in fostering self-reflection and personal cultivation it prepared the ground for eventual Buddhist enlightenment. Considering his philosophical approach to solving problems, we may surmise that Liang's silence concerning his Buddhist faith was due to his hope that people would concentrate on the issues they were presently facing, without being distracted by issues with which they were not yet ready to deal.

From this perspective, the intellectual itinerary of this crypto-Buddhist becomes quite clear. During his twenties, Liang turned to Buddhism as a way of resolving existential issues, such as the question of suffering and death. At that time, he adopted the conviction that he should engage in cultivation and aim eventually "to leave this world" (*chushi* 出世). Later on, he felt the need to find a more rational foundation for his Buddhist faith. He proceeded to adopt Yogācāra, which provided him with a rational discourse that, pushed to its extreme conclusions, was self-negating and opened into the extra-rational realm of Buddhahood. Liang articulated his Confucian social engagement with his Buddhist faith. Confucianism and Buddhism constituted two complementary poles for Liang: Buddhism reminded Confucianism that its worldly engagement should lead to transcendence, and Confucianism reminded Buddhism that true transcendence could only be obtained through an active engagement with the world.

Although Liang himself believed in Buddhism, he opposed reviving it in the culture and society of China, since he did not consider the time ripe for addressing ultimate questions. He rejected the concept of "Buddhism for human life" with which Taixu had attempted to establish a modern form of Buddhism.[28] Taixu and his followers took issue with Liang on this precise question—Buddhism's relevance as a social and cultural force. In doing so, they represented and defended the interests of the *sangha*. But they also displayed a sectarianism that was contrary to the spirit of Buddhism. Indeed, from the perspective of Buddhist teachings, anything that helped people alleviate their suffering could be called "Buddhist." Liang's promotion of Confucianism was a departure from Buddhist orthopraxis, but Buddhists could still consider it a legitimate form of "skilful means" (*upāya*; *fangbian* 方便).

In concluding this section on Liang, I should say that he held an ambiguous position regarding Buddhism as philosophy. He understood Yogācāra as the highest form of rationality, and yet he pointed to the limitations of philosophical discourse. Liang's stance can be seen as both a cultural and an intellectual form of resistance. It was cultural resistance in the sense that he attempted to reshape the concept of philosophy, inherited from the West, into something more congenial to the Chinese. This cultural resistance was itself supported by an intellectual resistance. First, he employed reason practically, making it serve the Buddhist liberation project. Second, he claimed that rational discourse could not encompass the supra-mundane reality envisioned by Buddhism. These two characteristics of Buddhism—its practicality and its extra-rationality (or even anti-rationality)—show the *aporia* of a "Buddhist philosophy." By understanding Buddhism as *the* true religion, Liang displaced philosophy from the central position it was supposed to occupy. Whereas Hu Shi and Feng Youlan contributed to the establishment of philosophy as the centre of human experience, Liang was critical of this notion of philosophy, as was Fu Sinian (shown by Carine Defoort in this volume). Let us now turn to Xiong Shili, who followed Liang's lead in developing an academic discourse on Buddhism, but in a very different way.

2. Xiong Shili: Buddhist Philosophy in the Service of Confucian Metaphysics

2.1 The Life of an Independent Thinker

Early in their careers, Xiong Shili and Liang Shuming were both politically active. However, by the time they met in the summer of 1919, both were distressed by the ongoing political chaos and had already turned to Buddhism.[29] It was at that time that Liang introduced Xiong to Ouyang Jingwu, for the purpose of studying Yogācāra at the Institute of Inner Learning in Nanjing. Xiong stayed there for two years. In 1922, Liang invited Xiong to join him at Peking University. There, Liang regularly met with a group of teachers and students to read and discuss Chinese Classics. After *Eastern and Western Cultures and Their Philosophies* became a bestseller, Liang gained quite a number of followers who were reacting against the radicalism of the New Culture Movement. Xiong was one of them. He was probably deeply influenced by Liang's shift from Buddhism to Confucianism, although he may not have fully understood that this did not represent the complete denial of Buddhism. Also, through the influence of Liang, Xiong started to read works by Western philosophers, such as Bergson, in Chinese translation. At some point, Liang and Xiong lodged together in the same house. The university setting played an important role for Xiong, as it had for Liang. Constantly exposed to new ideas, Xiong could gain intellectual independence from Buddhism and develop his own ways of thinking.

In 1924, when Liang decided to undertake a rural reconstruction project in Shandong, he invited Xiong to accompany him. After a few months, however, Xiong gave up and returned to his teaching position. From there, the two followed different paths: whereas Liang became a cultural and social activist engaged in rural reconstruction, Xiong was engaged in a metaphysical construction project at Peking University. After the Japanese invasion and until 1949, Xiong and Liang were both in Sichuan, but they had substantial contact with each other only between 1950 and 1954. At that time, both were staying in Beijing, and they had many discussions. Xiong always made sure that Liang was the first to read his manuscripts.[30] After 1954, Xiong moved to Shanghai and stayed in his son's house. When the Cultural Revolution broke out in 1966, he wrote letters to political leaders denouncing it.[31] He died in 1968. In the words of Ng Yu-kwan, "not only did Xiong have an existential understanding of the truth, but also he was able to put into practice the Confucian moral principles and values of neither fearing nor submitting to political power."[32] Because of this, Mou Zongsan 牟宗三 called Xiong a "true man" (*zhenren* 真人).[33]

2.2   *The Use of Buddhism for Confucian Metaphysics*

Xiong Shili was foremost a metaphysician, searching for the "fundamental state" (*benti* 本體) of cosmic reality.[34] Only when this state had been secured would it be possible to know the foundation of human, moral, social, and political life, and finally the foundation of human knowledge. Xiong therefore aimed at constructing a philosophical system. He used the conceptual tools of Yogācāra for this project, specifically its analysis of the mind and the concept of instantaneous transformation. Yet, as with Liang, his analysis depended more on a Chinese interpretation of Yogācāra than on genuine Indian Yogācāra. Deeply influenced by the *Awakening of Faith* (*Dasheng qixinlun* 大乘起信論) and the Flower Garland school (*Huayan zong* 華嚴宗), Xiong moved in the direction of ontology. He stood with Chinese Buddhism on the side of the "emptiness school" (*Kong zong* 空宗; Madhyamaka) and its fundamental ontology, against the "*dharma*-character school" (*Faxiang zong* 法相宗), which deconstructs reality and resists building an ontology. Xiong constantly referred to the Buddhist metaphor of the sea water and waves, expressing the underlying ontological relationship between mental acts and the original mind.

Whereas Yogācāra posits the mind to be an illusion that must be transcended, Xiong held that the mind was the ultimate reality. Indeed, for Yogācāra, consciousness was the only way to liberation. At the same time, however, it was also the final obstacle and illusion to be overcome, since consciousness tended to strengthen belief in both the existence of the world and the subject. Xiong completely overturned Yogācāra's analysis: the subject and the mind, as flows of consciousness, were no longer problems. They instead became invested with the highest level of reality. Therefore, while Yogācāra understood the mind to be "nothing but consciousness," Xiong reinterpreted it as a "special consciousness." For the Buddhist dialectic of transcendence and immanence, Xiong substituted a monistic trans-consciousness.

Xiong fully embraced the Neo-Confucian concept of an original mind present in the cosmos, as developed by the Lu-Wang school of the mind. He maintained the unity of fundamental state (*ti* 體) and function (*yong* 用), which he clearly identifies with principle (*li* 理) and material force (*qi* 氣). Xiong also borrowed the ideas of "unceasing creativity" (*shengsheng buxi* 生生不息) and "closing and opening" (*xi pi* 翕闢) from the *Yijing* 易經. These ideas gave his Neo-Confucian thought a very dynamic dimension.[35]

In opposition to the scientific and materialist thought of the West, Xiong felt that philosophy should be based not on the investigation of the external world, but rather on the inner knowledge of the "fundamental state." Like Liang, Xiong thought that Buddhism had in place the appropriate elements of an epistemology that led to ontology. But unlike him, Xiong held Buddhist ontology to be very partial and flawed. For Xiong, the "fundamental state" could not be empty since it permeated the whole universe. Therefore, while Buddhism had a workable epistemology, it fell short of "seeing the fundamental state" (*jianti* 見體). In his masterwork, *New Yogācāra* (*Xin weishi lun,* 1932), Xiong affirmed his ontological premise:

> The purpose of epistemological enquiry is to help us bear witness to the fundamental state. If we are determined to not recognize that there is a fundamental state, and spend all of our energy working through epistemology, this kind of enquiry can [yield] no result. How can this not be said to have departed from the philosophical position?[36]

Thus, for Xiong, philosophy corresponded to the inner quest of the mind for a fundamental ontology. Philosophy was ontology, but, as Xiaoqing Diana Lin rightly points out in her contribution to this volume, Xiong's ontology was very different from classical Western philosophy, since it was not based on the notion of a static essence. In the first edition of *New Yogācāra*, Xiong contrasted scientific rationality with the intuition gained from cultivation, but he later recognized that both were in fact needed: "As a rule, philosophy is a discipline in which reason and cultivation are intimately connected."[37] Yet, Xiong would still maintain that intuition alone allowed for "seeing the fundamental state."

2.3 From Traditional Buddhism to Buddhist Philosophy

When Cai Yuanpei wrote the preface for Xiong's *New Yogācāra*, he under-lined the novelty of an approach emancipated from the Buddhist institution:

> When the gentlemen at the China Institute for Inner Learning edit and expound the texts, they do not dare to do so with a critical approach. In his *New Yogācāra*, Xiong Shili has now entirely discarded the set pattern of religious followers and, as a philosopher, he has brought new explanations. Xiong is not a Buddhist but proclaims himself a Confucian. To rely entirely on Buddhist commentaries amounts to a pure religious attitude. In fact, although the religious dimension of the sutras is quite strong, their philosophical dimension is not insignificant. All religions rely on the philosophical thinking of their founder. Judaism, Christianity, and other religions have philosophical principles. Only Buddhism considers itself more profound. What one sees depends on one's viewpoint, the reader examining from his standpoint. For two thousand years, Buddhism has been separated from education. It does not use a philosophical method of analysis and investigation, but it deals with its questions, attempting to resolve them by itself. The philosophical investigation of Buddhism starts now, with Xiong Shili's *New Yogācāra*.[38]

Cai Yuanpei here announced the birth of Buddhist philosophy in China; a rational discourse on Buddhism which critically evaluated the Buddhist teachings and even corrected them. He noted that Judaism and Christianity were able to submit their teachings to philosophical enquiry, but Buddhism lagged behind. Cai considered philosophy to have presented Buddhism with a chance to develop a rational discourse that was adapted to the modern age. Much later, Wing-tsit Chan evaluated Xiong's contribution along the same lines: "He [Xiong] has subjected Buddhism to lengthy, careful, and profound criticism. In fact, he is the first one in Chinese philosophy to do so."[39] More recently, the Taiwanese philosopher Lin Anwu 林安梧 considered Xiong to have pushed forward, more than anyone before him, the systematization and deepening of Chinese philosophy.[40]

The challenge Xiong brought to Buddhism was intellectual but it was also institutional. Buddhist discourse in the university setting was subjected to academic procedures quite different from the ones in Buddhist monasteries or Buddhist theological institutes. In the pluralistic milieu of the university, Buddhist discourse became autonomous from religious orthodoxy and was used as a resource for constructing philosophical discourses completely detached from Buddhism's initial aim.

We thus see two discourses begin to compete with each other. I am referring here to the lengthy dispute, which lasted more than twenty years, between Xiong and Buddhist believers. In *New Yogācāra*, Xiong launched a frontal attack on Buddhist dualisms: the belief in reincarnation and *nirvāna*, and the attitudes of detachment and escapism from the world. Fundamentally, Xiong's rejection of Buddhism was grounded at the intellectual level, since he considered Buddhist philosophy to be conceptually flawed. However, during the controversy with his former Buddhist master and fellows, Xiong's critiques came to be more and more virulent. He eventually considered reincarnation to be a superstition that had deceived ignorant people.[41]

On the other side, Buddhist intellectuals such as Ouyang Jingwu, Taixu, Lü Cheng 呂澂 (1896–1989), and Yinshun 印順 (1906–2005) could easily claim that Xiong had distorted Buddhism's original meaning and had committed gross mistakes from the point of view of Buddhist orthodoxy.[42] For example, Xiong misunderstood Yogācāra along the lines of a fundamental ontology.[43] His ontological thinking also led him to misunderstand Madhyamaka. In addition, Xiong wrongly believed that Mādhyamika advocated "eliminating phenomena in order to reach the ontological substance of emptiness" (*poxiang xianxing* 破相顯性), while this school, in fact, rejects separating ontological reality from phenomena.[44] Clearly, Xiong came to believe that the monistic conception of the "unity of the fundamental state with the function" (*tiyongbuer* 體用不二) was an idea exclusive to Confucianism. He thus came to judge Western philosophy and Buddhism as crude dualisms.

It is important to recognize that the two Buddhist discourses were not on the same level. Both Xiong and the Buddhist intellectuals failed to notice this, which may explain the virulence and bitterness of the dispute. In fact, Xiong's discourse should be recognized as a philosophical hermeneutic of Buddhism. Such a stance is perfectly legitimate. His *New Yogācāra* was a philosophical elaboration which used elements of Buddhist epistemology and served the larger project of developing a Confucian ontology. Buddhist intellectuals could perhaps have accepted and welcomed this as a chance to discuss critically their traditional teachings. Xiong's philosophical system had important implications for Buddhism—it provided intellectual stimulus, an opportunity for a rational cleansing of their discourse, and an open hermeneutics beyond strict religious boundaries. Unfortunately, as was the case with Liang, Buddhist intellectuals did not make a sufficient effort to engage with Xiong's philosophical insight. Institutional Buddhism was too sectarian to value his philosophy positively, as a form of *upāya*.

A dogmatic attitude also prevailed on Xiong's side. He considered his own philosophy to be the only correct one, and dismissed some Buddhist tenets as erroneous. Although he was a creative thinker with penetrating insights, Xiong had a superficial understanding of the history of Buddhism. While he was still critical of Buddhism after 1949, by then it was mostly for political reasons.[45] Indeed, Xiong's dogmatism was later inherited by his disciple, Mou Zongsan. On both sides, a lack of recognition of the specificity of different discourses prevented a mutual enrichment.

2.4   A Road from Ontology to Existence?

Due to his long acquaintance with Xiong, Liang Shuming was quite familiar with his work. In the early sixties, Liang made a special effort to read systematically Xiong's works, and then wrote a lengthy report.[46] Liang basically accused Xiong of westernizing Chinese philosophy. This accusation may come as a surprise, since Xiong carefully avoided using Western concepts and mostly drew from Buddhist or Chinese traditions. For example, he used the term "profound studies" (*xuanxue* 玄學) instead of "philosophy" (*zhexue* 哲學). In fact, Liang meant that Xiong's project was similar to Western philosophy because it established an ontology out of a theoretical discourse. However, for Liang, the true foundation could only be known from practical experience; it was revealed in human experience in an intuitive way, rather than an intellectual one.[47]

Indeed, Xiong may have recognized the fact that Yogācāra was not an epistemological construction in the service of an ontology. Like Liang, Xiong would have agreed that Yogācāra epistemology was intimately connected to the concrete project of liberation. Also, Xiong clearly expressed that his ultimate aim was not intellectual in the narrow sense of the word; as Xiong himself said: "My learning begins with conceptual speculation and ends with existential identification. If learning does not ascend towards existential identification, it is in the end completely isolated from the truth."[48] Accordingly, in the words of Du Weiming, only an enlightened mind could return to its original state, but then had to go back to "authentic existence."[49]

Therefore, the divergence between Xiong and Liang was not so much about the existential dimension of this authentic existence. The cutting edge of Liang's critique was that Xiong committed the mistake of detaching intellectual enquiry from practice. His excessive intellectualization was cut off from personal practice. For Liang, the intellectual stage and the practical stage were never to be separated, as was the case in Xiong's philosophy. This was how Liang understood Yogācāra: as rooted in the meditative practice of yoga.[50] In other words, for Liang, there could be no path from a theoretical ontology to authentic practice. On the contrary, theoretical analysis should never leave the milieu of concrete engagement with society: one should start with questions arising out of practice and use theoretical tools to deepen one's understanding of existence. From this perspective, Liang considered Xiong's metaphysical system to be merely "empty talk."[51]

Liang's critique of Xiong helps us to understand better the pitfall into which many philosophers have stumbled: they completely detach Yogācāra from its overall project of individual, and social, liberation. Although philosophical research may require, to a certain degree, the abstraction of oneself from direct, worldly action and the mobilization of one's intellectual resources, the real place for intellectual elaboration could not be the university setting, which was cut off from social and political life. Liang criticized Xiong for situating the transcendental mind in a very rationalistic system, far away from practical life and the social structure (community and rituals) that could support it.

In this second section, we have considered Xiong's attempt to reconstruct a Confucian metaphysics as a reaction to the pressure exerted by modern Western philosophy. Like many intellectuals in the twentieth century, Xiong first went back and forth between different traditions, including Buddhism, Confucianism, Daoism, and Western thought. Then, he creatively built a new Confucian system, drawing from other intellectual traditions. He built a philosophical monism, an encompassing and exclusive system, around the concept of a "fundamental state," not unlike Hegel's absolute spirit. However, Xiong's discourse fell into the same traps as many other metaphysical discourses in the West and in China, which often resulted in solipsism and an inability to enter into a true dialogue with the human sciences, as Liang suggested. Having considered the culturalist approach of Liang Shuming and the metaphysical approach of Xiong, we shall now discuss a representative of the historical approach: Tang Yongtong.

3. Tang Yongtong: A History of Buddhist Philosophy in the Service of Academic Life

3.1 A Professional Academic

As we saw above, Liang Shuming developed an academic discourse in which Buddhism played a fundamental role. Although Liang made an unconventional use of Buddhism, he always remained within the bounds of the basic project of Buddhist liberation. For Xiong Shili, in contrast, Buddhism was a philosophical tool that could be detached from its original purpose and incorporated into his Confucian metaphysics. In the case of Tang Yongtong—the third Chinese intellectual to be considered here, Buddhism was for the most part approached as an historical artefact. Tang studied Buddhism using methods of historical and textual criticism that he had learned mostly from the West. While Liang was a crypto-Buddhist and Xiong an opponent of Buddhism, Tang attempted to maintain (with some difficulty, as we will see) the neutral attitude of a scholar.

Tang Yongtong attended high school in Beijing with Liang Shuming, and together they read about Indian philosophy and the Buddhist sutras. After graduating from Tsinghua University in 1917, Tang went to America. Besides knowing Chinese, Japanese, and English, once in the United States he learned Sanskrit and Pali. In 1922, Tang received his master's degree in philosophy from Harvard University. On his return to China, he began an academic career that lasted four decades. He was appointed to the Philosophy Department of South-East University (Dongnan daxue 東南大學), in Nanjing. It was then that he attended classes with Xiong Shili at the newly opened Institute of Inner Learning, where Ouyang Jingwu was lecturing on Yogācāra. The next year, Ouyang invited Tang to give classes on Pali and on the *Commentary on the Sāṃkhya Verses* (*Jin qishi lun* 金七十論). In the first issue of the Institute of Inner Learning's journal, Tang published an article entitled "Heterodox Teachings at the Time of the Buddha" (*Shijia shidai zhi waidao* 釋迦時代之外道). Tang also collaborated with friends in launching the culturally conservative journal *Critical Review* (*Xueheng* 學衡). In 1932, the year in which Xiong Shili published his *New Yogācāra*, Tang became a professor in the Philosophy Department at Peking University. Following Liang Shuming and Xiong Shili, Tang Yongtong took his turn at teaching Yogācāra and also lectured on Western rationalism and empiricism.

In April 1938, following the Japanese invasion, Tang was appointed chair of the Philosophy, Psychology, and Education Department of the National South-western Associated University in Sichuan. In 1947, he was named as a researcher at the Academia Sinica and went to the United States to give a series of lectures at the University of California. After his return to Beijing in 1948, confronted with the imminent takeover of the capital by the communists, he refused to leave and go to Taiwan, as Hu Shi invited him to do. Tang witnessed the establishment of the People's Republic in 1949. He later became involved in administration, serving as vice-president of Peking University. In addition, Tang was a member of the Standing Committee of the first, second, and third National People's Congresses.

His main work was *A History of Buddhism from the Han and Wei Dynasties to the Northern and Southern Dynasties* (*Han-Wei Liang-Jin Nanbeichao Fojiaoshi* 漢魏兩晉南北朝佛教史), a book he finished in 1930 but revised four times before its publication in 1938. His other works include *A Draft History of Buddhism in the Sui and Tang Dynasties* (*Sui-Tang Fojiaoshi gao* 隋唐佛教史稿, 1929) and *A Short History of Indian Philosophy* (*Yindu zhexueshi lue* 印度哲學史略, 1945).

3.2 *Buddhist Studies from the Perspective of Religious Faith and Philosophical Enquiry*

Tang was primarily an historian of Chinese Buddhism. He approached his research in a scientific way, through historical and textual criticism. His well-rounded training in the humanities, including literature, philosophy, and languages, allowed him to avoid narrow specialization and superficial understanding. In the postscript to *A History of Buddhism from the Han and Wei Dynasties to the Northern and Southern Dynasties*, he wrote: "Buddhism is both a religion and a philosophy."[52] Regarding religion, Tang held that:

> The religious feeling lies deep inside the human heart. Something groundless historically often becomes a symbol, unleashing powerful influences. [One] cannot reach the truth only by searching for historical evidence, without a silent sympathy.[53]

Tang reacted here against the tendency of modern historians to put aside religious symbols and legends. These historians limited their research to proven historical facts and were therefore unable to grasp the inner spirit of the object of their study. They considered faith to be irrational and irrelevant. Such a purely external approach was not conducive to gaining a thorough understanding, since religious beliefs were indeed capable of transforming and making history. Tang sought to gain a deeper understanding of Buddhism by taking a broad perspective, regarding religion as a cultural movement that involved social practices and was grounded in faith. In order to achieve this, Tang used a wide range of documents in his Buddhist studies.

Besides understanding the faith of Buddhists, Tang attempted to approach his studies from a more universal position based in philosophy. In the same postscript, he continued to remark that:

> Philosophical subtlety allows one to penetrate reality. Ancient wisdom brings simplicity. Very often, words seem remote, but an example, even a contemporary one, allows one to see a profound and far-reaching meaning. Therefore, only using textual criticism, without the experience of the heart and mind, leads to inadequate results.[54]

For Tang, historical research could not only be concerned with facts and figures. It instead had to address questions of meaning and significance that lay beyond Buddhism's concrete cultural and historical expressions. Like Liang Shuming, Tang advocated the use of comparative philosophy. But whereas Liang mostly expounded on the differences between cultures, Tang was more interested in showing the commonalities Buddhism shared with both Chinese and Western thought. Xiaoqing Lin states: "These comparisons led Tang to conclude that there was a universal human quest to reconcile the finite self and the infinite universe, a tendency that governed all human societies across history."[55] While Tang's postscript had been included in the first edition of the book in 1938, it had disappeared by the 1955 edition. Such a sympathetic attitude toward religion was not encouraged at that time. We shall return below to the question of politics.[56]

3.3   *The Indian Roots of Buddhism*

Like Liang Shuming, but unlike Xiong Shili, Tang Yongtong attempted to understand the historical roots of Buddhism. It was thus necessary for him to go beyond Chinese Buddhism and understand how Buddhism in general had evolved from its roots as an unorthodox Indian school. Previously, the only Chinese-language information on the Indian schools could be found in the Tripitaka. This knowledge was very partial and sectarian. Only in the twentieth century, stimulated by Western and Japanese scholarship, did Chinese Buddhist scholars start to do academic research on the Indian origins of Buddhism.

Liang Shuming offered a class on Indian philosophy at Peking University in 1917. The corresponding book was published in 1919 as *An Outline of Indian Philosophy*. A corrected and augmented version appeared in 1922.[57] The book is structured according to the categories of modern Western philosophy; for example, the second chapter discusses ontology (*bentilun* 本體論) and the third chapter epistemology (*renshilun* 認識論). Tang Yongtong taught the same class again in 1929, but his notes were published only in 1945 as *A Short History of Indian Philosophy*. Tang had an advantage over Liang since he knew Sanskrit and Pali. In contrast to Liang, Tang avoided using philosophical concepts from the West. In the preface, he stated that "every time a Western category is used, it is a wrong comparison, which makes things more confused and the truth more distorted."[58] As we have seen, Tang was in favour of comparative philosophy but not of analyzing Buddhism through Western concepts.

Like Liang, Tang considered Indian thought to be a true philosophical tradition. For Tang, while this had initially been dominated by a polytheistic religion, it did not evolve into monotheism as in Egypt or Israel. Instead, it gave rise to a philosophical enquiry about the origin of the cosmos.[59] Tang found in the *Vedas* a philosophical questioning of traditional religion. Yet this philosophical enquiry was in service of another aim: religious liberation from the mundane world.

3.4 *Buddhism and Chinese Culture*

At a time when Chinese culture was being subjected to foreign influences, Tang Yongtong reflected on the link between it and Buddhism. He recognized that this foreign religion had transformed Chinese culture, "but not yet to the point of a total and radical change."[60] Tang adopted Hu Shi's basic position concerning the indigenization of Buddhism in China.[61] Through different examples, Tang showed that Buddhist teachings had been influenced by the Chinese cultural environment and had thus been modified, becoming something that was genuinely Chinese.

Tang's interest in Chinese culture led him to focus on the history of Chinese Buddhism. Later on, he became interested in the cultural interaction between Chinese Buddhism and the "dark learning" (*xuanxue* 玄學),

a metaphysical school of the Wei and Jin dynasties. According to Tang, dark learning developed its metaphysics mostly through Taoist concepts, independent of Buddhist influence. The two systems of thought were not connected at the theoretical level. However, Tang saw mutual influences at work in a later stage. On one hand, the metaphysics of dark learning prepared the ground for Buddhism, so the latter became acceptable to the Chinese. On the other, Chinese Buddhism pushed the questions addressed by dark learning further. Tang concluded that Buddhism could be considered a part of dark learning: "At that time, Buddhist terminology mostly consisted of words that had been borrowed from the *Laozi* and *Zhuangzi*. Buddhism was therefore simply homologous with dark learning."[62]

This conclusion gave the higher ground to the Chinese tradition, articulating a process in which Chinese culture had selected a foreign intellectual resource, here Buddhism, to advance its own intellectual agenda. Unlike the cultural conservatives who affirmed the superiority of Chinese culture, however, Tang can be considered a "cultural liberal" who recognized the positive contribution foreign cultures had made, while stressing the specificity of Chinese tradition.[63] Yet, as we shall see, his position was not completely devoid of nationalistic tendencies.

3.5   *The Chinese and Japanese Rivalry in Buddhist Studies*

When Chinese scholars started their academic investigations of Buddhism at the beginning of the twentieth century, they lagged far behind their Japanese, European, and American counterparts. Chinese scholars who could read studies in Western and Japanese languages had a great advantage over colleagues who could read only Chinese. At the same time, Buddhist studies became the site of a fierce rivalry between China, the West, and Japan. Here, it will suffice to mention the competition between English, French, Japanese, and Chinese researchers to secure, translate, and interpret the Dunhuang 敦煌 materials. The repercussions of this battle can be felt even today.[64]

Buddhist studies became a question of national pride for Chinese scholars. This was especially true with regard to Japan. Yet many Chinese Buddhist scholars had to deal with Japanese Buddhist research. In 1959, during the Anti-Rightist Movement (*fanyoupai yundong* 反右派運動) and some fifteen years after the publication of *A Short History of Indian Philosophy*, Tang Yongtong made an embarrassing confession: his book was, in fact, a mere compilation of the "books of Western and Oriental bourgeois scholars."[65] Tang gave a list of his sources in English: Surendranath Dasgupta (1887–1952), Sarvepalli Radhakrishnan (1888–1975), Augustus Hoernle (1841–1918), the *Sacred Books of the East* edited by Max Müller (1823–1900), and the English translations of the *Dīgha Nikāya*. However, who were the "Oriental bourgeois scholars"? Although not explicitly named, they would almost certainly have included Japanese academics. However, Tang did not feel comfortable writing the names of these Japanese researchers, whose scholarship he had previously used without providing any explicit references.

In fact, we find in Tang, as in other Buddhist scholars, a double strategy toward Japanese scholarship. When Tang found something sound in Japanese Buddhist studies, he used it, but without necessarily mentioning its source. However, whenever he found mistakes, he would criticize his Japanese counterparts. In the thirties, Tang wrote an article criticizing and rejecting a number of leading Japanese scholars.[66] We have the testimony of Tang Yijie 湯一介, Tang's son, concerning the motivation behind Tang's Buddhist studies:

> Tang Yongtong spent so much energy researching this question while he was ill. One reason was that he wanted to write off the widespread academic influence of some incorrect conceptions held by Japanese scholars, to reform [things] thoroughly, and to return to the original historical truth.[67]

It is therefore apparent that Tang did not pursue his Buddhist studies from a purely academic standpoint, in which he sought solely after the "original historical truth." In part, his research became a way for him to oppose Japanese aggression and demonstrate his patriotism to others, even after the end of the war. This nationalistic agenda cannot be completely ignored when reading Tang's Buddhist studies.

3.6 *Academic Freedom Endangered and the End of Academic Life*

It seems that Tang's decision to remain in Beijing in 1949 was due to his attachment to Peking University. In 1945, he had organized the return of the school from Kunming to Beijing. In 1949, he probably thought that academic freedom would continue under the new regime. Tang also felt that the Party had presented the country with a unique opportunity, and his patriotism therefore led him to stay. After the onset of Communist rule, there was a short period of collaboration and trust between intellectuals and the Party. Many intellectuals were impressed with the Party's early results and enthusiastic about the prospect of building a new country. From the Party's perspective, there was the need to gain intellectual legitimacy after the military victory.

However, Tang Yongtong soon became entangled in the Party's efforts to gain ideological control of the university. After Hu Shi resigned from his position as chancellor in December 1948, Tang's fellow professors elected him, through a democratic process, Chairman of the Administrative Committee (*Xiaowu weiyuanhui zhuxi* 校務委員會主席) in May 1949. In the absence of a formal chancellor, Tang therefore became the acting president of the university. In 1951, in order to strengthen its ideological control, the new regime installed Ma Yinchu 馬寅初 (1882–1982) as the new president. When Ma came to Peking University, Tang refused to meet with him. Nevertheless, he was later forced to work with him and to accept the position of vice-president.[68] Tang's position was a pure façade. He had no real power and could not express his own views. Starting with the "thought reform" (*sixiang gaizao* 思想改造) campaign of 1951, Peking University, like other universities, was progressively turned into an institute of ideology. This was a great departure from the academic freedom Tang had enjoyed previously while studying at Tsinghua and Harvard, or while teaching at Peking University in the thirties.

As we have seen above, Tang had, at times, placed his scholarship in the service of his nationalist interests, such as when he opposed the dominance of Japanese scholarship. With the party requesting proof of intellectual allegiance, Tang, like many intellectuals in the university, lost his independence of thought. When the campaign against Hu Shi started in 1954, Tang wrote some speeches against his former chancellor. He could not resist the mental pressure and had a cerebral haemorrhage. In 1957, Tang gave speeches criticizing Xiang Da 向達 (1900–1966), a fellow professor from the history department.[69] Tang also wrote a postscript to the 1959 reprint of *A Short History of Indian Philosophy*, in which he admitted that his previous research had been completely flawed by "bourgeois idealism." He stated that he should rewrite all of his past research from the perspective of Marxist-Leninist historical materialism.[70] By this point, the life had gone out of Tang, both physically and intellectually.

The ideological control that was exerted over Tang Yongtong can be contrasted with the situations of Liang Shuming and Xiong Shili. Because they succeeded in maintaining some independence from academic institutions and from the state machine, they could continue as independent thinkers, developing their own personal philosophy at the margins of the totalitarian regime. Both Liang and Xiong produced creative and independent works, such as Xiong's *Yuanru* 原儒 [An enquiry on Confucianism] (1956) and Liang's *Renxin yu rensheng* 人心與人生 [Human mind and human life] (1984). In contrast, Tang's career was linked with the academic institution. When this was annexed by national ideology, as had also occurred in Japan, Germany, and the Soviet Union, the result was the death of any true research or scholarship. Reflecting on this kind of extreme situation, one can ponder the cost of serving at academic institutions that bow to state ideology. The illusion that one could both pursue pure academic knowledge and neglect the independent political engagement that could guarantee true intellectual freedom, came to be an illusion for which many academics, including Tang, would pay a very high price.

Tang's intellectual collapse was also a personal one. There is nothing more telling that the short dialogue he had with Mao during the 1963 May Day celebrations at Tian'anmen Square. Mao apparently told him: "Your health is getting better. I have read your articles. But if you do not feel well, you can write short essays; this is all right." According to Ren Jiyu 任繼愈 (1916–2009), then a student of Xiong, Tang was very excited that day, saying that he should dedicate his knowledge to the people even further.[71] If Ren Jiyu's description is accurate, this story tells us a lot about the loss of Tang's ability to think independently.

4. Conclusion

Above, we have considered three representatives of academic Buddhism from the first half of the twentieth century. Liang, Xiong, and Tang taught Buddhist philosophy at universities, yet they spoke from different perspectives. At that time, Buddhist philosophy was recognized as a branch of Indian philosophy and was distinguished from both Western and Chinese philosophy. These terms define Buddhism as a foreign tradition. This was quite a departure from the traditional studies of Chinese Buddhism that had been practised in monasteries and had focused on Chinese texts. When Buddhist studies started in the philosophy departments of China, scholars attempted to go back to the Indian roots of Buddhism. However, because resources were scarce and because of a patriotic focus on national studies, Buddhist studies came to be dominated by the patterns of thought, and by the schools, of Chinese Buddhism.

Liang Shuming was representative of this initial effort to distinguish Buddhist philosophy from Chinese philosophy. From the perspective of his cultural philosophy, he established a clear division between Chinese, Indian, and Western philosophies. Yet, Liang was not interested in academic life for its own sake, but rather in building a cultural and existential philosophy that could help societies and individuals to free themselves. He became, quite by chance, a Buddhist scholar for the relatively short period of eight years. He developed a conceptualization of philosophy that was based on concrete forms of cultural life, as an alternative to rationalistic and abstract forms of philosophy. Buddhism was a practical answer to the contingencies imposed by life and human reason. Logically, Liang decided to leave the academic institution, and engage himself in education and social reconstruction.

Xiong Shili used Buddhism as a conceptual tool with which to build a Confucian system—one that could become the theoretical framework for a reconstruction of Chinese culture, and of the country. Because Xiong was pursuing his own intellectual project, he was quite independent, both from the academic institution and from state ideology. He was not searching for the prestigious social position offered by universities but for the satisfaction which comes from leading an authentic life. However, this intellectual endeavour became isolated from society and, finally, disconnected from concrete issues.

Tang Yongtong developed a humanistic approach to Buddhism, making use of history, religion, and philosophy. Early in his career, he focused on Buddhism's Indian roots, but later shifted to Chinese Buddhism. He made pioneering efforts in understanding the indigenization of Buddhism in China. Unlike Liang, who saw Buddhism as a foreign culture and philosophy, and Xiong, who saw it as an analytical tool transcending cultures, Tang came to conceive of Buddhism as an intrinsic part of the history of Chinese philosophy. His historical approach may be understood as a form of resistance to the hegemonic discourse of philosophy, then dominated by Western ideas. This led him to focus on the intellectual history of China. Yet, lacking the philosophical depth of Liang Shuming or Xiong Shili, he put his Buddhist scholarship in the service of his own career, of the academic institution, and of his country.

Indeed, Tang's intellectual and personal failures at the end of his life illustrate the loss of freedom that occurs in academic discourses under state dictatorship.

Quite importantly, Buddhism was not fully treated as a religion. Since the universities were dominated by the liberal intellectuals of the New Culture Movement, who largely opposed religion as such, there were only a few religious schools or departments. Buddhism therefore found its place within philosophy departments. Even though Liang insisted on the practical dimension of Buddhism as a religion, his understanding was very individualistic and disconnected from society. Xiong similarly regarded Buddhism in quite a narrow sense, as metaphysics. Tang probably had the broadest perspective on Buddhism, considering it from the angle of comparative religious studies, as well as cultural, social, and intellectual history.

Finally, the three figures discussed here may remind us of three dimensions essential to any intellectual work: practical engagement and commitment, as in the case of Liang; intellectual depth, as in the case of Xiong; and historical research, as in the case of Tang. At a time when Buddhist studies had been emancipated from religious affiliations and schools, these three scholars contributed a great deal to the development, for the first time in China, of an academic discourse on Buddhism within a pluralistic environment, at least up until 1949.

Notes

1   Jing Haifeng further distinguishes five different kinds of Buddhist studies: traditional studies by the Buddhist community, modern Buddhist studies by monks, modern Buddhist studies by lay Buddhists, academic Buddhism by historians, and creative Buddhism by philosophers. Jing Haifeng 景海峰, *Xin ruxue yu ershishiji Zhongguo sixiang* 新儒學與二十世紀中國思想 [New Confucianism and Chinese thought in the twentieth century] (Zhengzhou: Zhongguo guji chubanshe, 2005), pp. 125–128.

2   Cf. Chen Bing 陳兵 and Deng Zimei 鄧子美, *Ershishiji Zhongguo Fojiao* 二十世紀中國佛教 [Chinese Buddhism in the twentieth century] (Beijing: Minzu chubanshe, 2000), pp. 101–102.

3   Liang Shuming, "Jiuyuan jueyi lun" 究元決疑論 [Treatise on finding the foundation and resolving doubt], *Dongfang zazhi* 東方雜誌 XX (1916), p. x. For an alternate source, see *Liang Shuming quanji* 梁漱溟全集 [Complete works of Liang Shuming], Vol. 1 (Ji'nan: Shandong renmin chubanshe, 1989–1993), pp. 3–22.

4   Liang Shuming, *Zhongguo wenhua yaoyi* 中國文化要義 [Essentials of Chinese culture], in *Liang Shuming quanji*, Vol. 3, p. 5.

5   Li Yuanting 李淵庭 and Yan Binghua 閻秉華, eds., *Liang Shuming xiansheng nianpu* 梁漱溟先生年譜 [Chronicles of Mr. Liang Shuming] (Guilin: Guangxi shifan daxue chubanshe, 1991), p. 31.

6   See Liang Shuming, *Wo de guoqu* 我的過去 [My past], in *Liang Shuming quanji*, Vol. 6, p. 71.

7   Liang Shuming, *Dongxi wenhua ji qi zhexue* 東西文化及其哲學 [Eastern and Western cultures and their philosophies], in *Liang Shuming quanji*, Vol. 1, p. 363.

8   *Ibid.*, p. 350.

9   Like many intellectuals of his generation, Liang was especially harsh in his condemnation of popular forms of Buddhism, such as the prayers and rituals for the soul kept in hell during the Chinese Buddhist Festival of Yulanpan 盂蘭盆節. However, Liang maintained a kind of faith in "supernatural power," or *shentong* 神通, throughout his life. See Thierry Meynard, "Intellectuels chinois contemporains en débat avec les esprits," in *Le Sacré en Chine*, edited by Michel Masson (Brussels: Brépols, 2008), pp. 163–190.

10 Yogācāra had disappeared in China as an independent school in the Tang dynasty and had usually been held in low regard because of its failure to grasp Buddhahood. However, it influenced other Chinese Buddhist schools such as Tiantai, Huayan, and even Chan, as well as some Confucian thinkers during the Qing dynasty, such as Wang Fuzhi 王夫之 (1619–1692).

11 Liang Shuming, "Jiuyuan jueyi lun," p. 16.

12 See Zhang Taiyan 章太炎, "Jianli zongjiao lun" 建立宗教論 [On founding a religion], *Min bao* 民報, 1906.9, pp. 1–26. See Liang Shuming, "Ru Fo yi yong

lun" 儒佛異同論 [Treatise on the differences and similarities between Confucianism and Buddhism], in *Liang Shuming quanji*, Vol. 7, p. 159.

13   Liang Shuming, *Weishi shuyi* 唯識述義 [Outline of Yogācāra], in *Liang Shuming quanji*, Vol. 1, p. 253.

14   *Ibid.*, p. 271. In this chapter, I do not distinguish between the Indian term "Yogācāra" and the Chinese term "*Weishi*" (or *Vijñānavāda* in Sanskrit) for the theory of consciousness-only. *Weishi* was the core teaching of Yogācāra and became an alternative name for it in China.

15   *Ibid.*, p. 269.

16   Liang Shuming, *Dongxi wenhua ji qi zhexue*, p. 395.

17   Liang Shuming, *Yindu zhexue gailun* 印度哲學概論 [An outline of Indian philosophy], in *Liang Shuming quanji*, Vol. 1, p. 73.

18   *Ibid.*, p. 158.

19   Here, I do not detail Liang's anti-intellectualism in his understanding of Confucianism. He contrasted Confucianism's moral intuition with the abstract and utilitarian rationality of the West. See Fang Keli 方克立 and Cao Yaoming 曹耀明, "Liang Shuming feilixingzhuyi zhexue sixiang pingshu (shang)" 梁漱溟非理性主義哲學思想評述 (上) [The anti-intellectualism of Liang Shuming (part one)], *Zhongguo luntan* 中國論壇 (Taipei) 26.7, 307 (1988), pp. 54–63; "Liang Shuming feilixingzhuyi zhexue sixiang pingshu (xia)" 梁漱溟非理性主義哲學思想評述 (下) [The anti-intellectualism of Liang Shuming (part two)], *Zhongguo luntan* 中國論壇 (Taipei) 26.8, 308 (1988), pp. 60–68.

20   Liang Shuming, *Yindu zhexue gailun*, p. 72.

21   Liang Shuming, *Dongxi wenhua ji qi zhexue*, pp. 415–416.

22   Liang Shuming, *Yindu zhexue gailun*, p. 58.

23   Liang Shuming, *Dongxi wenhua ji qi zhexue*, p. 482.

24   See my paper, "Is Liang Shuming Ultimately a Confucian or Buddhist?" *DAO: A Journal of Comparative Philosophy* 6.2 (2007), p. 145.

25   Liang Shuming, *Yindu zhexue gailun*, p. 61.

26   This is in reference to Guy Alitto, *The Last Confucian* (Berkeley: University of California Press, 1979).

27   See Liang Shuming, "Meiguo xuezhe Ai Kai xiansheng fangtan jilu tiyao" 美國學者艾愷先生訪談記錄摘要 [Excerpts from the recorded interview with the American scholar Guy Alitto], in *Liang Shuming quanji*, Vol. 8 [1980], pp. 1137–1178.

28   See Liang's critique of Taixu in *Dongxi wenhua ji qi zhexue*, p. 536. For Taixu's response, published in 1920, see: "Lun Liang Shuming *Dongxi wenhua ji qi zhexue*" 論梁漱溟東西文化及其哲學 [A discussion of Liang Shuming's *Eastern and Western Cultures and Their Philosophies*], *Haichao yin* 海潮音 1.11 (1921); reproduced in *Taixu dashi quanshu* 太虛大師全書 [Complete works of Master Taixu], 35 vols. (Taipei: Shandaosi, 1946), vol. 25, pp. 302–304. For a more systematic answer to Liang, see Taixu, *Renshengguan de kexue* 人生觀的科學 [The science of the philosophy of life] (Shanghai: Taidong tushuju, 1929).

29　Xiong's despair was related to the atmosphere of political chaos following the 1911 Revolution. Liang's pessimism was deeper, and it explains his profound commitment to Buddhism.

30　Jing Haifeng, *Xin ruxue yu ershishiji Zhongguo sixiang*, pp. 159–166.

31　Umberto Bresciani, *Reinventing Confucianism* (Taipei: Ricci Institute, 2001), p. 120.

32　Ng Yu-kwan, "Xiong Shili's Metaphysical Theory," in *New Confucianism*, edited by John Makeham (New York: Palgrave Macmillan, 2003), p. 240.

33　Mou Zongsan 牟宗三, *Wushi zishu* 五十自述 [My autobiography at 50 years old], in Mou Zongsan, *Shengmingdexuewen* 生命的學問 (Guilin: Guilin shifan daxue chubanshe 廣西師範大學出版社, 2005), p. 106.

34　I translate *benti* as "fundamental state" in order to signify that Xiong built not a substance ontology but a process ontology.

35　Cf. Wing-tsit Chan, *A Source Book in Chinese Philosophy* (Princeton: Princeton University Press, 1963), pp. 763–765.

36　*Xin weishi lun*, edited by Yudi, vol. 1, pp. 3b–4a, quoted in *Sources of Chinese Tradition*, edited by Wm. Theodore de Bary and Irene Bloom (New York: Columbia University Press, 1999, vol. 2, p. 547; translation modified.

37　Xiong Shili 熊十力, *Shili yuyao chuxu* 十力語要初續 (Shanghai: Shanghai shudian chubanshe, 1949), p. 180.

38　Cai Yuanpei, "Preface," *New Yogācāra*; quoted in Jing Haifeng, *Xin ruxue yu ershishiji Zhongguo sixiang*, p. 91.

39　Wing-tsit Chan, *A Source Book in Chinese Philosophy*, p. 687.

40　Lin Anwu 林安梧, *Dangdai xin rujia zhexueshi lun* 當代新儒家哲學史論 [Essays on the philosophical history of contemporary New Confucians] (Taipei: Mingwen shuju, 1996), pp. 55–56.

41　Xiong Shili, quoted in Jing Haifeng, *Xin ruxue yu ershishiji Zhongguo sixiang*, p. 92.

42　In 1932, Liu Dingquan wrote *Po Xin weishi lun* 破新唯識論 [Defeating *New Yogācāra*] (Nanjing: Zhina nei xue yuan, 1932). Xiong answered in 1933 with *Po Po Xin weishi lun* 破破新唯識論 [Defeating "Defeating *New Yogācāra*"] (Beiping: Beijing daxue chubanbu, 1933; reprinted Wuhan: Hubei jiaoyu chubanshe, 2001). On the occasion of Ouyang Jingwu's death in 1943, a dispute erupted between Xiong Shili and Lü Cheng. See "Bian Foxue genben wenti: Lü Cheng, Xiong Shili wangfu han'gao" 辯佛學根本問題——呂澂、熊十力往覆函稿 [Basic issues in distinguishing [true] Buddhism: Letters exchanged between Lü Cheng and Xiong Shili], *Zhongguo zhexue* 中國哲學 11 (1984), p. 171.

43　Xiong's interpretation was probably pushed in this direction under the influence of Neo-Confucian and Western philosophy. In the twentieth century, Western scholars like Louis de la Vallée Poussin (1869–1938) and Etienne Lamotte (1903–1983) considered Yogācāra to be subjective idealism. However, recent scholarship on Indian Yogācāra has explained it as a form of phenomenology, radically opposed to any ontologization. See Dan Lusthaus, *Buddhist Phenomenology* (New York: Routledge, 2002).

44 Cf. Ng Yu-kwan, "Xiong Shili's Metaphysical Theory," p. 242.

45 In the 1953 edition of his *New Yogācāra*, many parts that dealt with Buddhism were deleted. See Bresciani, *Reinventing Confucianism*, p. 136.

46 Liang Shuming, "Du Xiong zhu ge shu shuhou" 讀熊著各書書後 [Remarks after reading the works of Xiong], in *Liang Shuming quanji*, Vol. 7 [1961], pp. 734–786.

47 *Ibid.*, p. 764.

48 Cited in Ng Yu-kwan, "Xiong Shili's Metaphysical Theory," p. 240.

49 Du Weiming 杜維明, *Jindai sixiang renwu* 近代思想人物 [Contemporary thinkers] (Taipei: Shibao chubanshe, 1982), cited in Lin Anwu, *Dangdai xin rujia zhexueshi lun,* p. 59.

50 Liang Shuming, *Yindu zhexue gailun*, pp. 66–73.

51 Liang Shuming, "Du Xiong zhu ge shu shuhou," p.764.

52 Tang Yongtong, *Han-Wei Liang-Jin Nanbeichao Fojiaoshi*, in *Tang Yongtong quanji* 湯用彤全集 [Complete works of Tang Yongtong], Vol. 1 (Shijiazhuang: Hebei renmin daxue chubanshe, 2000), p. 655.

53 *Ibid.*, p. 655.

54 *Ibid.*, p. 655.

55 Xiaoqing Lin, "Historicizing Subjective Reality: Rewriting History in Early Republican China," *Modern China* 25.1 (1999), p. 15.

56 The postscript was inserted again in *Tang Yongtong quanji*.

57 Liang Shuming, "Yindu zhexue gailun," p. 26. As Liang mentioned in the preface to the 1922 edition, he inherited notes from Xu Jishang 許季上 (1891–1953), who had taught the class before him at Peking University. According to Liang, these notes were themselves derived from "three or four Japanese books, and two or three English books." Liang completed his manual by adding further material from other Japanese books on Indian Buddhism that he obtained through a colleague, Wu Chengshi 吳承仕 (1884–1939).

58 Tang Yongtong, preface to *Yindu zhexueshi lüe* 印度哲學史略 [A short history of Indian philosophy] (Chongqing: Duli chubanshe, 1945; reprinted Beijing: Zhonghua shuju, 1988), p. 5.

59 Tang Yongtong, "Yindu zhexue zhi qiyuan" 印度哲學之起源 [The origins of Indian philosophy], in *Tang Yongtong xueshu wenhua suibi* 湯用彤學術文化隨筆 [Essays on learning and culture by Tang Yongtong], edited by Sun Shangyang 孫尚揚 (Beijing: Zhongguo qingnian chubanshe, 2000), p. 38.

60 Tang Yongtong, "Wenhua sixiang zhi chongtu yu tiaohe" 文化思想之衝突與調和 [Conflict and conciliation of cultures and thought], in *Xueshu jikan* 學術季刊 1.2 (1943); reprinted in *Tang Yongtong xueshu wenhua suibi*, p. 11.

61 Hu Shi, *Zhongguo zhexueshi dagang* 中國哲學史大綱 [Outline of the history of Chinese philosophy] (1919; reprinted Beijing: Dongfang chubanshe, 1996), p. 6.

62   Tang Yongtong, "Wei-Jin sixiang de fazhan" 魏晉思想的發展 [The develop-
     ment of thought during the Wei and Jin dynasties], in *Tang Yongtong xueshu
     wenhua suibi*, p. 259.

63   See Chen Bin and Deng Zimei, *Ershishiji Zhongguo Fojiao*, p. 136.

64   The Dunhuang manuscripts were sealed in a cave in Gansu province in the
     twelfth century, and discovered only at the beginning of the twentieth
     century. Many of the documents are now kept in England, France, Russia,
     and Japan.

65   Tang Yongtong, postscript to the reprinted edition of *Yindu zhexueshi lüe*, p.
     165.

66   Tang Yongtong, "Dalin shuping" 大林書評 [A critique of many scholars], in
     Tang Yongtong xueshu wenhua suibi, pp. 290–295.

67   Tang Yijie 湯一介, "Preface," in Ma Tianxiang 麻天祥, *Tang Yongtong ping-
     zhuan* 湯用彤評傳 [Biography of Tang Yongtong] (Nanchang: Baihua zhou
     wenyi chubanshe, 1993), p. 9.

68   I rely here on a personal communication with Sun Shangyang 孫尚揚—a
     professor in the philosophy department of Peking University and a student
     of Tang Yijie.

69   See Tang Yijie, "Tang Yongtong yu Hu Shi" 湯用彤與胡適 [Tang Yongtong
     and Hu Shi], in *Zhongguo zhexueshi* 中國哲學史 4 (2002), pp. 104–105.

70   See Tang Yongtong, postscript to the reprinted edition of *Yindu zhexueshi
     lüe*, pp. 165–171.

71   Tang Yijie, preface to *Tang Yongtong pingzhuan*, p. 48.

Chapter 7

Daoism as Academic Philosophy: Feng Youlan's New Metaphysics (*Xin lixue*)

Hans-Georg Moeller

In this chapter, "academic philosophy" is understood in a sociological sense. In other words, it is considered to be institutionalized philosophical communication within a specific social organization, namely modern academia, or, to use a more common term, the modern *university*. The latter, if applying the terminology of social systems theory,[1] can be understood as a hybrid organization functioning within a number of separate social systems. These include, most importantly, science and education, although other systems could also be mentioned, such as the economy, the legal system, or, particularly in North America, sports. Concretely speaking, *academic* philosophy means, for instance, philosophy classes taught at universities, faculty meetings in philosophy departments, the grades assigned to philosophy students, or academic books and papers on philosophical subjects. I will focus on the last here.

From the perspective of social systems theory, academic philosophy is a product of the transformation that took place in Europe between the sixteenth and the eighteenth centuries, from a society based on stratified differentiation into one based on functional differentiation. This shift has taken on global proportions; one can therefore now speak of a world society in which "academic philosophy" has become "world philosophy." Functionally speaking, academic philosophy is now essentially the same type of communication, irrespective of its location. In this sense, it does not matter if an "academy" is located in Europe, America, Asia, or Africa. The emergence of academic philosophy is thus a social phenomenon that has to be understood in the context of the globalization of functional differentiation.

With respect to China (and many other non-Western regions), the transition to functional differentiation has usually been described, both within and without China, as a process of Westernization. However, I doubt that such a geographical concept is sociologically accurate. China (like so many other regions around the world) was facing a dilemma: it could become an integral part of world society only if it started to take part in the types of communication that had evolved into truly globally functional systems. If China was to be a place where academic communication could take place, it would have to establish this type of communication within itself. In concrete terms, this meant, for example, the establishment of organizations such as the modern university. In turn, as outlined above, this could function only if corresponding systems, such as an education system and a system of scientific research, each with their specific codes, functions, media, and so on, were developed. In other words, there is no academic philosophy without an academy (i.e. a university), and there is no (modern) university without social systems, such as those related to science and education.

In the decades before and after the turn of the twentieth century modern functional systems, such as the political system, the legal system, the modern world economy, as well as modern science and education, were implanted in East Asia—first in Japan, and then, often via Japan, in China. To become part of a global society, non-Western regions had not only to change their social structures but also their semantics. Traditional vocabularies had to be recoded as "politics," "science," "religion," "sport," and so on. To establish academic philosophy, it was therefore not only necessary to institutionalize philosophy at universities but also to create a new philosophical language. Newly emergent terminology typically first developed in Japan and then, shortly after, was also adopted in China. Academic philosophy was thus named *zhexue* 哲學, which was a Chinese neologism borrowed from Japanese.[2]

In the Introduction to this volume, John Makeham refers to Joseph Levenson's remark that the intellectual and cultural exchange between China and the West changed China's language, but only changed the West's vocabulary. Levenson's thesis, that the intellectual history of China in the twentieth century was fundamentally shaped by Western influences has, as Makeham shows in the Introduction, been challenged by other scholars who have argued that endogenous developments were of much larger importance than Levenson admitted. This historical argument is in line with philosophical arguments made by Feng Youlan, and, among others, Hu Shi 胡適 (1891–1962), who tried to identify an internal logic, an inner thread, or an internal system uniting Chinese philosophy from ancient times up to, and including, the twentieth century. Ironically, one may say in Levenson's defence that such attempts are in themselves just one more aspect of the Chinese adaptation of Western models, in this case the Hegelian concept of philosophy as a unified historical process. It is noteworthy, in this context, that Hegel's idea had a profound impact on Feng Youlan's writings on the history of Chinese philosophy in the 1920s and 1930s. It could thus be argued that Feng's attempt to identify the "spirit" of Chinese philosophy, and to see his own philosophy as its very culmination, follows very closely in the footsteps of Hegel—and is thus not very endogenous. I return to this issue in section five (below).

What has taken place in academic philosophy over the past century in China, and what is still going on, is a twofold semantic effort. This has involved reinterpreting certain traditional Chinese texts (in the broad sense of the term "texts") in a specifically philosophical way, i.e. communicating them philosophically; and integrating them into a global philosophical discourse by way of both comparison and contrast with Western philosophical communication. Here I will discuss this effort with respect to one particular group of texts, namely those that are conceived of as constituting Daoist philosophy. In particular, I will focus on Feng Youlan 馮友蘭 (1895–1990), who between 1890 and 1949 was arguably the most prolific contributor to the transformation of traditional Daoist texts into academic philosophy.

Within a group of thinkers who are often called, by scholars of modern and contemporary Chinese philosophy, New Confucians (*xin ruxue* 新儒學), Feng Youlan was a sort of maverick. This was not only because he did not consider himself to be a part of this group as such, or because of his "conversion" to Marxism after 1949, but also, I would say, because in the course of constructing and publishing his own philosophical system, *xin lixue* 新理學 (which I translate as New Metaphysics),[3] he developed what has been called (though not explicitly by Feng himself) a "New Daoism" (*xin daojia* 新道家).[4] Whereas other philosophers who have been called New Confucians, such as Xiong Shili 熊十力 (1885–1968) and Mou Zongsan 牟宗三 (1909–1995), could also be fairly classified as "New Buddhists,"[5] Feng's philosophy of the 1930s and 1940s clearly culminates in a recoding of traditional Daoist texts and notions. Thus, I would claim that Feng Youlan's philosophy was the most significant (and, relatively speaking, the most successful) attempt to transform Daoism into academic philosophy in China in the first half of the twentieth century. Below, I will outline how he did this within his New

Metaphysics. Since I focus here solely on Feng's work on Daoism within academic *philosophy* in the strict sense of the term, I will largely ignore three other significant aspects of his Daoist studies, namely a) his *philological* research on the *Laozi* 老子 and the *Zhuangzi* 莊子 (which, in particular in the 1920s and 1930s, was quite extensive[6]); b) the treatment of Daoism in his works on the *history* of ideas; and c) the various Marxist, and thus *politically* oriented, views on Daoism that he expressed after 1949. This is not meant to deny the very close relation that all of these different types of Daoist studies have to Feng's attempt to create a new Daoist philosophical system.

1. New Metaphysics[7]

The New Metaphysics represents both the summation, as well as the conclusion, of Feng Youlan's creative philosophical work before 1949. It is a work that, on the one hand, conceives of itself as a continuation of the entire history of Chinese philosophy, and, on the other hand, attempts to contribute to a new world philosophy that gives equal consideration to the entirety of Western philosophy.

The increasingly important methodological role taken on by logical and linguistic analysis in academic philosophy in the first part of the twentieth century, as represented, for instance, by American Neo-Realism, the Vienna School, and philosophers such as Whitehead and Russell, exerted a strong influence on Chinese academic philosophy.[8] As early as 1920, Feng studied at Columbia University in New York.[9] Here, although he was originally a student of John Dewey (1859–1952), he became strongly influenced by W. P. Montague's (1873–1953) version of Neo-Realism.[10] Feng was fascinated by the notion of reality as an onto-logical realm that was completely open to rational understanding, which could be achieved through logical analysis, formal reasoning, and stringent linguistic conceptualization. Following these ideas, he revised traditional Neo-Confucian philosophy not, like most of his contemporaries, by connecting with its intuitive *xinxue* 心學 wing, but with the more rationalistically inclined *lixue* 理學. This is also reflected in Feng's analysis of the modern Chinese word for thought: *sixiang* 思想. Feng interprets the first syllable (*si* 思) as denoting the "pure" kind of thought that he aims at, whereas the second syllable (*xiang* 想) is said to denote a kind of thinking that still clings to the empirical.[11] In this vein, he criticized, for instance, Wang Yangming 王陽明 (1472–1529), one of the most important representatives of *xinxue,* for being too concerned with (empirical) actuality.[12] His "new system"[13] of *lixue* was intended to be nothing less than the elevation of Song and Ming Confucian thought to the level of the "most philosophical philosophy" (*zui zhexue de zhexue* 最哲學的哲學).[14]

What makes one particular philosophy the "most philosophical"? For Feng, this was an issue of methodology. The most philosophical philosophy is the most abstract one—in other words, the one that moves furthest beyond the empirical and is able to operate in a conceptual sense. The initial methodology of the New Metaphysics consists of a transformation of the Chinese philosophical—and, in particular, the Neo-Confucian—vocabulary into concepts, and thus its "rationalization," so that it becomes compatible with contemporary Western philosophical discourse.

Given the background of traditional Chinese thought, the articulation of a philosophy that openly attempted to make abstractions based on experience required quite a radical effort. It produced a foundational distinction, namely the division of the world into two categorically different ontological realms, which was scandalous to some.[15] Feng distinguished between a realm of existence (*cunzai* 存在), which he called "actuality" (*shiji* 實際) and which was accessible through experience, and a realm of subsistence (*qianyou* 潛有), which he termed "reality" (*zhenji* 真際) and which was accessible only through pure thought. The New Metaphysics thus begins with the distinction between actuality and reality. Philosophy must, according to Feng, begin with "actuality," on which it must reflect; but this intellectual reflection consists of a purely rational interpretation of the actual in order to grasp the formal "reality" on which it is founded. Just as geometry begins with a rational interpretation of actual objects in order to arrive at the purely formal concept of the square, philosophy has to interpret actual objects rationally in order to expose the ontological realm—their reality—which "subsists" (logically) prior to their actual existence.[16]

Unlike the natural sciences, the most philosophical philosophy is not interested in returning from "reality" to actuality in order to describe and predict existing objects or events. Once children have learned to calculate, they no longer need to use their fingers to add two and three.[17] Independent from actual experience, they can operate with numbers in a purely formal manner. Likewise, the most philosophical philosophy will be able to go beyond actualities and transcend experience so as to describe rationally a purely formal reality.

The construction of a purely formal and conceptual interpretation of reality is quite removed from the often rather practical and pragmatic orientation of the Neo-Confucian tradition. It is thus not surprising that for Feng, the most philosophical philosophy does not end with conceptual analysis. Its final goal is to transcend philosophy itself. One engages in rational analysis not merely to understand reality, but, more importantly, to transform oneself into a *sheng ren* 聖人: the ideal of the wise human being that has figured so prominently throughout the history of Chinese philosophy. Philosophy is thus conceived of as a discipline that, in the end, shapes a person and opens one up to the possibility of not only knowing the world but also of integrating oneself within it, and thus becoming epistemologically and ethically wise. Feng explicitly reiterates the traditional definition of a perfect human being: *nei sheng wai wang* 內聖外王, or "inwardly wise and outwardly kingly." [18]

The rational and formal methodology of the New Metaphysics dialectically turns into the opposite of itself: a "positive" (*zheng* 正) method evolves into a "negative" (*fu* 負) one. That which can be said, and that to which the positive concepts relate, is transcended, and another dimension is opened up: that which cannot be said. The positive method of philosophy is supposed eventually to contradict itself, thereby transforming into a negative philosophy that not only allows for the attainment of superior knowledge, but also for becoming a better person. In the following section, I will outline how Feng used Daoist philosophy to develop the positive methodology of his "most philosophical philosophy" into its final negative shape by examining *New Metaphysics (Xin lixue)*, *New Practical Philosophy (Xin yuanren)*, *New History of Philosophy (Xin yuandao)*, and *New Methodology (Xin zhiyan)*.

2. Daoism in *New Metaphysics*

New Metaphysics was published in 1939, and the negative method does not yet have a role. It presents only what Feng later called the positive method. In sum, it lists and explains the most essential concepts of a "rationalized" and "formalized" Confucianism. The Daoist tradition is not often referred to, and when it is, it is most often simply in the form of a criticism of its terminology. [19]

Since *New Metaphysics* operates (at least implicitly) strictly within the confines of a positive methodology, it has a hard time with concepts of negativity. Thus, it is only natural that Feng does not yet embrace Daoist "negative" ideas. The use of the term *wu* 無 (nothing, non-being, or emptiness) in *New Metaphysics* is very different from its use in most Daoist philosophical texts. In the latter, *wu* is often identified with *dao* 道. In *New Metaphysics*, however, it simply means "not being" or "there is no (…)"; it is simply a, or the, negation of being. It is an ontological negation that is entirely dependent on positive ontological propositions. There *are* squares—they exist—and the *li* 理 (the "whatness") of a square subsists. Non-square is a mere negation that has no existence or subsistence. This term does not denote anything that "is." It is simply a linguistic statement that denies something. There is no "nothing." Or, put differently, there is no specific *li* ("whatness"), which things that are *not square* have, as opposed to everything that is square. That which is not also does not have a *li*.[20]

There is no negativity in reality. Still, *New Metaphysics* applies one central aspect of the Daoist *wu* or *dao*, namely its negative quality of being *wu ming* 無名 or "nameless."

Insofar as the Daoists identify *wu* or *dao* with *wu ming*, such as in chapters 1, 32, and 41 of the *Daodejing* 道德經, the usage of this term denoting namelessness is similar to that of *qi* 氣 ("thatness" or "materiality") in *New Metaphysics*.[21] According to Feng, the Daoists contributed to the construction of a formal, logical, and philosophical terminology capable of reaching beyond actuality through their conceptions of *dao* and *wu ming*. This is what he praises them for. Feng acknowledges a certain convergence of the *dao* of the Daoists and his own usage of *qi*, since both are conceived of as something that has no qualities at all, and therefore as the foundation of the qualities of existing things and events. In his eyes, both are conceptual conditions for the actual existence of what is, but they themselves are external to being.

Feng Youlan insists, however, that the Daoists' own usage of the term *qi*, as it occurs in parts of the *Zhuangzi* and the *Huainanzi* 淮南子, has nothing to do with its usage in *New Metaphysics*.[22] In particular, works such as the *Huainanzi* are accused of not having reached the abstract and formal heights of earlier Daoist texts, and of being merely a proto-scientific discourse concerned only with actuality. These later Daoist texts cannot be considered relevant to the construction of the most philosophical philosophy.

New Metaphysics also makes use of the term *dao*, but, once more, not in a Daoist fashion. As stated above, in the language of *New Metaphysics* the term *qi* comes closest to the Daoist *dao*. When the term *dao* is used in *New Metaphysics*, it is meant to denote more than *qi*, or "whatness." Here, *dao*, or *dao ti* 道體, is the "processual emergence" of everything: the materialization of the world as a whole, the continuous actualization of "whatnesses," the process of existence, and the coming into being of all that there is.[23] *Dao* is change; it is the process of flux of which all actually existing things and events are a part. The coming in and out of existence is what the Daoists called *hua* 化, or *da hua* 大化 ("great transformation").[24] The notion of "returning" (*fan* 反) in the *Daodejing* is also quite important in this context. Feng thus acknowledges in *New Metaphysics* that the Daoists did come up with a philosophical conceptualization of processual change in the realm of what actually exists.[25]

3. Daoism in *New Practical Philosophy*

In *New Practical Philosophy*, Feng presents a four-stage model of human development towards perfection. The four stages, or "spheres," are, in Feng's own words, moments of a "Hegelian dialectic development." They are to be understood as different stages in the development of the idea of the self within consciousness.[26] The first stage is called the "natural realm" (*ziran jingjie* 自然境界); it is characterized by a lack of the consciousness of the "self." In the second stage, the "utilitarian realm" (*gongli jingjie* 功利境界), the self becomes the central aspect to which all conscious activity and action relates. In the next level, the "moral realm" (*daode jingjie* 道德境界), the self is sacrificed for the sake of the social group; it is transcended for the sake of the non-self. Finally, once the "universal realm" (*tiandi jingjie* 天地境界) is reached, the "great non-self" is realized, and the individual integrates himself or herself not just into the larger social community but into the world, the cosmos or the "universal" in general. The final two realms of the non-self are, however, not stages in which the self is merely negated; they are also the realms in which the "true self" attains fruition and completion. The "great non-self" is the sublated self that is no longer merely an individual among the objects and events of the world, but is rather self-identical with the universal. Thus, the great non-self is in fact the highest possible form of the self.

Feng believed that the Daoists had not distinguished clearly enough between the first and fourth stages. The natural realm is characterized by the absence of a self and of knowledge. In the highest realm, both self and knowledge are sublated. *Not yet* possessing self and knowledge, however, is something entirely different from *no longer* possessing self and knowledge. The Daoist insistence on "non-self" and "not knowing," Feng claimed, blurred the essential difference between these two levels.[27]

The Daoists did not contribute much to the moral realm. This remained more or less dominated by Confucians who, in turn, according to Feng, committed a similar error to the Daoists: they did not sufficiently distinguish the third and fourth stages.[28]

There is a Daoist idea that Feng associates with the utilitarian sphere.[29] If at every moment in an organic, holistic system, every person within a community functioned in accordance with their nature and acted "naturally" (*ziran* 自然)—but also in their own interests—thereby performing their respective roles perfectly, this would be beneficial not only to the individual, but, more importantly, to the community as a whole Feng here sees some similarities, or at least compatibilities, with Adam Smith's (1723–1790) social theory.

4. Daoism in *New History of Philosophy*

New History of Philosophy is an original account of the development of Chinese philosophy. It is portrayed, in a rather Hegelian fashion, as a necessary development of the Chinese "spirit" and as a dialectical movement oscillating between a theoretical-transcendent and a practical-moralist orientation, which ultimately attains synthesis. Feng intended the synthesis of these divergent, but not mutually exclusive, philosophical tendencies to manifest itself in his own philosophical system, which is outlined in the final chapter of the book.

While the structure of *New History of Philosophy* is largely chronological, it is not meant to be a strict historical-temporal study. What is attempted is instead a demonstration of the inner logic within the development of Chinese thought. Feng formulates the most basic ideal of the Chinese "spirit" in terms from the *Zhongyong* 中庸; that is, as "attaining the sublime and yet performing the common task" (*ji gaoming er dao zhongyong* 極高明而道中庸).[30] A similar ideal can, according to Feng, already be found in the "Tianxia" 天下 chapter of the *Zhuangzi*, which he obviously regards as a predecessor to his own *New History of Philosophy*.[31] The "attainment of the sublime" consists in entering the "universal realm," taking on the viewpoint of the philosophical sage, and cultivating one's inner wisdom. The "performance of the common task" correspondingly refers to the development of one's "outer kingliness," which is manifested in the perfect performance of one's social tasks and a life lived perfectly in the "ordinary" world of one's community. Feng believes that the degree to which the various philosophical schools contribute to the realization of this ideal constitutes the measurement of their success.

New History of Philosophy locates Daoism (which for Feng basically means the *Daodejing* and the *Zhuangzi*) as being close to the end of pre-Han philosophy. This is therefore after Confucius 孔子 and Mencius 孟子, after Yang Zhu 楊朱 and Mozi 墨子, and after the "school of names" (*mingjia*). However, it is prior to the "Great Commentary" (*da zhuan* 大傳) on the *Yijing* 易經, and the *Zhongyong*. While Feng praises the "school of names" for attempting a transcendence of the world of "forms" by instead reflecting on "names," he considers the Daoists even more advanced, as he had already hinted in *New Metaphysics*. Unlike the "school of names," they did not focus only on the "names" that transcended actual things and events but also on the unnameable, thus opening up an essential new avenue in metaphysics.[32] The philosophical "destruction of the bridge after crossing the river"[33] enabled the Daoists, for the first time in the history of Chinese philosophy, to use their concepts in a purely formal way, without concrete reference to existing actuality. From the perspective of *New History of Philosophy*, the concept of the *dao* as the origin of the world and as synonymous with "nothingness" or "emptiness" (*wu*), the nameless (*wu ming*), and "oneness" (*yi* 一), should not be understood as a designation for an actually existing power of creation within temporality, but as a purely analytic and logical concept.

Feng treats these Daoist concepts as formal expressions of the unnameable. They are beyond the differentiated world of experience and point to the non-differentiated. They are thus indeterminable. With these concepts, the Daoists manage to transcend the world of "forms." The actual world retains its differentiated shape, whereas the Daoists reach the undifferentiated at the centre of all differences. Feng asserts that from the position of the "axis" or the "hub" of the wheel, the Daoist philosopher looks at the world from "the perspective of heaven."[34]

The Daoists thus attain what Feng calls "a posteriori non-knowledge" (*hou de de wu zhi* 後得的無知),[35] which is beyond actual knowledge. They forget about distinctions and reach a form of non-knowledge that is higher than knowledge. Feng concludes that, although their transcendent point of view is still reached *in the midst* of the differentiated actual world, the Daoists manifest a certain preference for being "inwardly wise" over "outwardly kingly." In this way, the Daoists have failed to understand fully that the two paths they tried to walk simultaneously, namely the path of transcendence and the path of the ordinary, were, in the final analysis, one and the same.[36] The Confucian tradition attempted to resolve this contradiction with the *Zhongyong*. For Feng, as we will see in the next section, the preoccupation with this discrepancy also constitutes one of the main similarities between Daoism and Chan Buddhism (禪宗).

5. Daoism in *New Methodology*

New Methodology discusses in detail the connection between the two methods of the New Metaphysics, namely the "positive" and the "negative." According to Feng, both Daoism and Chan Buddhism should be credited with the invention and practical application of the negative method.[37] This is the necessary complement of the positive and may very well be conceived of as the climax of metaphysics. The positive method marks the beginning of the most philosophical philosophy. However, when this rational method reaches its limits, or when the limits of that which can be spoken of are attained, rather than simply stop, metaphysics has to face the unnameable. The negative method must replace the positive one. But just as the positive method on its own cannot bring metaphysics to its conclusion, the negative method cannot be established without the prior use of its positive counterpart. The mystical non-knowledge of the Daoists is, in Feng's definition, a posteriori, and thus it is essentially dependent on the completion of positive knowledge.

Feng Youlan states that "the negative method represents the non-representability of metaphysics."[38] He compares this method with the famous painting technique that "brings the moon to the fore by contrasting it with the clouds" (*hong yun tuo yue* 烘雲托月).[39] This means that the artist only paints the clouds; the part of the scroll not painted is then perceived as the moon. Similarly, the negative method of metaphysics applies a technique of conceptualization that exposes that which escapes conceptualization.

In *New Methodology*[40] and in an article from the late 1940s,[41] Feng compares the negative metaphysical method of the Daoists (and Chan

Buddhists) with Kant's critique of reason. Both, he states, drew a line between that which can be cognized and that which cannot, and between that which can be spoken of, and that which cannot. For Kant, this line is the one between the phenomenal appearance and the thing-in-itself. The Daoists, on the other hand, distinguish between that which is within the realm of linguistic differentiability, and that which transcends it. Kant's boundary could not be crossed using reason, but this was not the case for the Daoists. The negation of the rationality of distinctions, as Feng stresses, is itself a rational act. This rational act is a negation of rationality itself, which also negates the distinction between the differentiated and the undifferentiated. Once beyond the differentiated, even this difference disappears. The crossing of this boundary leads to the realm of *silence*. Feng states: "The combination of Taoism and Buddhism resulted in Ch'anism, which I should like to call a philosophy of silence. If one understands and realizes the meaning and significance of silence, then one has apprehended something about the object of metaphysics."[42] The crossing of the boundary is preceded by the concepts of negative metaphysics. But once the boundary is crossed, the concepts of the negative method—and even the concept of negativity itself—disappear.[43]

Feng calls the negative method of the Daoists and Chan Buddhists the "mystical method," and he thinks that it also has its representatives in Western philosophy. But he critically remarks that, when seen from a Daoist perspective, Western mystical philosophers are not mystical enough. Feng believes that so long as mysticism still clings to the concept of God, and so long as there are still concepts of intellectual insight, one will remain on this side of the boundary.[44] Still, the positive method cannot simply be dismissed. Feng demands that a future philosophy should follow the example of his *New Methodology* and not only be more mystical than traditional Western philosophy, but also more rational than traditional Chinese thought.[45] Daoist mysticism is therefore to be enriched with the Western philosophy of reason—and vice versa.

In *New Methodology*, Feng discusses the philosophy of the Vienna Circle and Wittgenstein's *Tractatus logico-philosophicus* in more detail than he does Kant's *Critique of Pure Reason*.[46] In addition to his exposure to American Neo-Realism during his time at Columbia University, Feng was quite familiar with European Neo-Positivism, and in 1934 he participated in the 8th International Philosophy Congress in Prague, where this philosophical school played an important role. For Feng, Neo-Positivism and Wittgenstein must have appeared to be the most advanced version of

Western philosophy at the time. He was particularly interested in the Vienna Circle's radical criticism of traditional Western metaphysics. The Vienna Circle aimed to show that traditional metaphysical propositions, such as "God exists," "the soul is immortal," or "the will is free," were meaningless since they were synthetic but not empirically verifiable. That is to say, they were neither analytically deduced from propositions based on experience, nor could they be verified through induction from experience. Propositions that could not be methodologically verified were deemed by the Vienna Circle to be meaningless propositions.[47]

Feng supports this criticism but claims that it applies only to "bad metaphysics" and not to the "good" New Metaphysics. Since the propositions of the latter do not refer to anything empirical, are formal, and are empty of actual content, they fulfil the criteria of meaningfulness set by the Vienna Circle. Feng accepted the philosophy of the Vienna Circle as a methodology for the foundation of a new metaphysics.[48] In their philosophy, he detects the seed of the negative methodology—which was developed much further by Wittgenstein—and this is why its heuristic function is similar to the historical role played by Daoism within the Chinese tradition.

According to Feng, the Vienna Circle criticized the propositions of (bad) metaphysics because while they pretend to say something about actuality, they cannot be formally or empirically proven. All metaphysical propositions may thus seem to be meaningless. Feng believes that Daoist philosophy did, in a similar fashion, "deconstruct" previous attempts at expressing the truth in Chinese philosophy. From the perspective of the Daoist sage in the *Zhuangzi*, the conflicting propositions of the Confucians and the Mohists cancel each other out. From the perspective of the wheel's axis, the contradictory positions appear as particular views on actuality, which are incapable of transcending the realm of the differentiated. Feng thinks that both the Vienna Circle and the Daoists take aim at the ultimate meaninglessness of philosophical propositions that claim to make valid statements about actuality.[49]

Feng does not believe, however, that the philosophers of the Vienna circle managed to come up with something in addition to these criticisms. They eradicated bad metaphysics, but they did not touch upon good metaphysics. Their logical argumentation was formal and without content (which, for Feng, was obviously a good thing), but it was unfortunately also meaningless in another sense, since it avoided genuine philosophical problems, which therefore remained unanswered.[50] But Feng stressed that there *was* someone associated with this philosophy who in fact applied the negative method of metaphysics, although perhaps unknowingly: Ludwig Wittgenstein.[51]

At the end of the chapter on the negative method of metaphysics in *New Methodology*, Feng writes:

> One of the modern Western philosophers, Ludwig Wittgenstein, despite being a prominent representative of the Vienna Circle, nevertheless distinguishes himself to a large degree from the other members of this school. Although he also intended to eliminate metaphysics, he in fact, in our view, practised metaphysics, and he did so by applying what we call the "negative method of metaphysics." Even if his teaching was not supposed to be called metaphysics, it still seems able to convey non-knowing knowledge.[52]

In this context, Feng also refers to the famous final sentence of the *Tractatus*: "What we cannot speak about we must pass over in silence."[53] Here he sees, so to speak, a deep "family resemblance" with the Daoist (and Chan Buddhist) negative method of metaphysics.[54] Feng believed that, like Laozi and Zhuangzi, Wittgenstein used language at the end of the *Tractatus* as metaphysical poetry;[55] in other words, he used language in accordance with the negative method.[56] This kind of language expresses that which cannot be experienced and only thought of, as well as that which neither can be experienced nor thought of, in a poetical fashion. It shows it by not showing it, once rational analysis comes to its conclusion.[57]

6. Final Remark

I do not intend here to evaluate the success of Feng Youlan's attempt to come up with a new Daoist philosophy as a truly global world philosophy. Certainly, his New Metaphysics is not often studied in philosophy departments, particularly in the West. Be that as it may, in the first half of the twentieth century, he was one of the few philosophers (if not the only one) to have made a serious attempt to recreate the Daoist textual tradition in the form of a thoroughly "academic philosophy"—in the sense of the term that I tried to outline at the beginning of this essay. Even if people like myself do not adopt Feng's system and do not apply his methodology, we still continue to work in the *spirit* of his pioneering effort.

Notes

1   By "social systems theory," I mainly mean the version appearing in the works of Niklas Luhmann (1927–1998). For my understanding of Luhmann and a synopsis of his thought, see Hans-Georg Moeller, *Luhmann Explained: From Souls to Systems* (Chicago: Open Court, 2006).

2   See the Introduction and chapter 1 in this volume on the history of this term.

3   In this chapter, *New Metaphysics* refers to the book entitled *Xin lixue*. New Metaphysics refers to the philosophical system as such. This translation is not literal but interpretative. The term *li* 理 in the context of Neo-Confucian philosophy has often been translated as "principle"; in Feng's philosophy it is used in the sense of "whatness." By reinterpreting this and other terms, Feng hoped, as he repeatedly states, to establish a new "metaphysics" (*xing er shang xue* 形而上學). For Feng, his "new *lixue*" was a New Metaphysics. The six books expressing this philosophy are: *Xin lixue* 新理學 [New metaphysics] (Changsha: Shangwu yinshuguan, 1939)—references here cite the Hong Kong edition of 1961 published by Zhongguo zhexue yanjiuhui); *Xin shilun* 新事論 [New social philosophy] (Shanghai: Shangwu yinshuguan, 1940); *Xin shixun* 新世訓 [New moral philosophy] (Shanghai: Kaiming shudian, 1940); *Xin yuanren* 新原人 [New practical philosophy] (Chongqing: Shangwu yinshuguan, 1943)—this chapter cites the edition in *Sansongtang quanji* 三松堂全集, Vol. 4, Henan: Henan renmin chubanshe, 1985 ff.; *Xin yuandao* 新原道 [New history of philosophy] (Chongqing: Shangwu yinshuguan, 1945)—references here cite the Hong Kong edition of 1961, also by Zhongguo zhexue yanjiuhui, which has been translated into English by E.R. Hughes as *The Spirit of Chinese Philosophy* (London: Kegan Paul, Trench, Trubner, 1947); and *Xin zhiyan* 新知言 [New methodology] (Shanghai: Shangwu yinshuguan, 1948), which has been translated into English by Chester C. I. Wang as *A New Treatise on the Methodology of Metaphysics* (Beijing: Foreign Language Press, 1997). The translations of these book titles are not literal, but reflect the respective topics of those works. See Hans-Georg Moeller, *Die philosophischste Philosophie. Feng Youlans Neue Metaphysik* (Wiesbaden: Harrassowitz, 2000). This book contains a translation of *New Methodology* into German.

4   At an International Conference on Daoist Studies held in Beijing in August 1996, a number of younger scholars argued precisely this, namely that Feng's New Metaphysics should be classified as New Daoism rather than as New Confucianism. Among these scholars were Chen Xiaoping 陳小苹 and Zhang Binfeng 張斌峰. Their claims initiated some rather lively discussions.

5   See Thierry Meynard's chapter in this volume on the problems connected with assigning such labels as "(New or Neo-) Confucian" or "(New or Neo-) Buddhist" to Chinese philosophers in the first half of the twentieth century. Also see John Makeham's chapter on Zhang Taiyan 章太炎 (1869–1936) in this volume on the same issue.

6   Feng offered a number of (conflicting) theories about the respective dates and authenticity of the *Laozi* and the *Zhuangzi*. When he wrote his PhD thesis in 1923, entitled *A Comparative Study of Life Ideals*, he obviously still believed that the *Laozi* predated the *Analects* (論語), since he stated that "most probably Confucius was influenced by it [Laozi's philosophy]" (p. 121). For a later republishing of this thesis, see Feng Youlan, *Selected Philosophical Writings of Feng Youlan* (Beijing: Foreign Language Press, 1991). Later, in a dispute with Hu Shi, he vigorously defended the idea that the *Laozi* was of a much later date and that one should distinguish between Laozi the person and the work under this title. See Feng's articles "Laozi niandai wenti" 老子年代問題 [Problems regarding the age of Laozi], in *Gushi bian* 古史辨, Vol. 4, edited by Gu Jiegang 顧頡剛 (1933; reprinted Hong Kong: Taiping, 1962–1963), pp. 420–422 and "Du 'Pinglun jindai ren kaoju Laozi niandai fangfa' huida Hu Shi zhi Xiansheng" 讀評論近代人考據老子年代方法答胡適之先生 [Reading 'Comments on the methods of textual research by modern people on the age of Laozi'—in Response to Mr. Hu Shi], *Gushi bian*, Vol. 6, pp. 410–417, originally published in *Da gongbao* 大公報 on 15 November 1934. On this subject, see also Michel C. Masson, *Philosophy and Tradition: The Interpretation of China's Philosophical Past: Fung Yu-lan 1939–1949* (Taipei, Paris, Hong Kong: Institut Ricci, 1985), pp. 26–27. Finally, Feng proposed that the *Laozi* was historically even later than the "school of names" (*mingjia* 名家), and that it had not been composed before the late third century B.C. See Feng Youlan, A *Short History of Chinese Philosophy*, edited by Derek Bodde (New York: Macmillan, 1948) as reprinted in *Selected Philosophical Writings of Feng Youlan*, pp. 294–295. With respect to the *Zhuangzi*, Feng stressed that the work was of a heterogenic nature and could not possibly have been written by a single author. See *Selected Philosophical Writings of Feng Youlan*, pp. 397–398; and "Zhuangzi nei wai pian fenbie zhi biaozhun" 莊子內外篇分別之標準 [The criteria for division in the inner and outer chapters of *Zhuangzi*] in *Yanjing xuebao* 燕京學報 20 (Dec. 1936), pp. 155–158. Feng was also among the first philosophers in the twentieth century to have highlighted the philosophical importance and innovativeness of the *Zhuangzi* commentator Guo Xiang 郭象 (252–312), looking at him not merely as an "editor" but as a philosopher in his own right. See Feng Youlan, "Guo Xiang de zhexue" 郭象的哲學 [The philosophy of Guo Xiang], in *Zhexue pinglun* 哲學評論 1.1 (Apr. 1927), pp. 103–124; and Feng Youlan, trans., *Chuang Tzu: A New Selected Translation with an Exposition of the Philosophy of Kuo Hsiang* (1931; reprinted New York: Paragon, 1964).

7   The sections below follow parts of Hans-Georg Moeller, "Der philosophische Daoismus in der *Neuen Metaphysik* (*Xin Lixue*) Feng Youlans," *Monumenta Serica* 45 (1997), pp. 381–398.

8   This is not only the case for Feng Youlan, but also, for instance, for Jin Yuelin 金岳霖 (1895–1984) as documented by Yvonne Schulz in this volume. See also Carine Defoort's chapter, as well as Xiaoqing Diana Lin's remarks

9　on Feng Youlan and Jin Yuelin's logical approach in her contribution to this volume. See section six (below).

9　After returning from the USA, Feng took up various positions at leading Chinese universities. See Xiaoqing Diana Lin's chapter in this volume on Feng's professional career in China prior to 1949.

10　Cf. Azuma Jūji, "The Formation of New *Lixue*: Feng Youlan and New Realism," *Journal of Chinese Philosophy* 21 (1994), pp. 303–335; Yin Lujun, "From Montague to Neo-Confucianism: Feng Youlan's New *Lixue* and Logical Analysis," *Journal of Chinese Philosophy* 21 (1994), pp. 337–361.

11　Feng, *Xin lixue*, p. 5 ff.

12　Feng, *Xin yuandao*, pp. 187–188, and *The Spirit of Chinese Philosophy*, pp. 202–203.

13　The last chapter in *Xin yuandao*, which introduces Feng's own philosophy, is entitled "A New System" (*xin tong* 新統).

14　See the section on "The Most Philosophical Philosophy" in Feng, *Xin lixue*, pp. 8–12.

15　See, for instance, the quite polemical criticism of Feng Youlan in Zhang Junmai 張君勱, "Yi feng bu ji xin—Ze Feng Zhisheng" 一封不寄信——責馮芝生 [An unposted letter—a rebuke of Feng Youlan], *Zaisheng zazhi* 再生雜誌 23 (1950), reproduced in *Dangdai Zhongguo shi wei zheren ji qi wenzhang* 當代中國十位哲人及其文章 [Ten wise people in contemporary China and their writings], edited by Lan Jifu 藍吉富 (Taipei: Zhengwen chubanshe, 1969), pp. 66–70.

16　Feng, *Xin lixue*, pp. 6–7.

17　*Ibid.*, p. 13.

18　Feng, *Xin yuandao*, pp. 206–207; and Feng, *The Spirit of Chinese Philosophy*, pp. 219–220.

19　There are a number of "Daoist" terms that do come up with respect to their usage in Neo-Confucianism, the most important example being *taiji* 太極 (Feng, *Xin lixue*, pp. 51–58). Feng also criticizes some more "practical" Daoist ideas, such as political "non-action" (*wu wei* 無為) (pp. 205–208), and the idea of a socially detached sage (pp. 299–303).

20　Feng, *Xin lixue*, p. 33.

21　*Ibid.*, pp. 67–70.

22　*Ibid.*, p. 70.

23　*Ibid.*, p. 95ff.

24　*Ibid.*, p. 98.

25　*Ibid.*, p. 106ff.

26　Feng, *Xin yuanren*, p. 558ff.

27　*Ibid.*, pp. 570, 636.

28　*Ibid.*, chapter 6. See also Feng, *Xin yuandao*, p. 30, and Feng, *The Spirit of Chinese Philosophy*, p. 28.

29　See Feng, *Xin Yuanren*, pp. 590–591.

30 This is how Feng interprets this quote from the *Zhongyong* (section 26). See Feng, *Xin yuandao*, pp. 3–5; and Feng, *The Spirit of Chinese Philosophy*, pp. 3–5.

31 Feng, *Xin yuandao*, p. 6; Feng, *The Spirit of Chinese Philosophy*, p. 5.

32 Feng, *Xin yuandao*, p. 63; Feng, *The Spirit of Chinese Philosophy*, p. 60.

33 Feng, *Xin yuandao*, p. 61; Feng, *The Spirit of Chinese Philosophy*, p. 58.

34 Feng, *Xin yuandao*, p. 71, p. 74; Feng, *The Spirit of Chinese Philosophy*, p. 67, p. 70. The images of the "axis" and the "hub" are used with reference to the *Zhuangzi* (chapter 2) and the *Daodejing* (chapter 11).

35 Feng, *Xin yuandao*, pp. 80–81; Feng, *The Spirit of Chinese Philosophy*, p. 78.

36 Feng, *Xin yuandao*, p. 83; Feng, *The Spirit of Chinese Philosophy*, p. 80.

37 Feng, *Xin zhiyan*, chapter 9.

38 *Ibid.*, p. 9.

39 *Ibid.*, p. 9.

40 *Ibid.*, pp. 45–46.

41 Fung Yu-Lan, "Chinese Philosophy and a Future World Philosophy," *The Philosophical Review* 57 (1948), pp. 539–549.

42 Feng, *A Short History of Chinese Philosophy*, p. 341.

43 Fung, "Chinese Philosophy and a Future World Philosophy," pp. 542–544.

44 *Ibid.*, p. 544.

45 *Ibid.*, p. 545.

46 Wittgenstein's *Tractatus logico-philosophicus* was published in English in 1922 and translated by F. P. Ramsey and C. K. Ogden (London: Kegan Paul). Soon afterwards, Zhang Shenfu 張申府 translated it into Chinese under the title *Mingli lun* 名理論, in *Zhexue pinglun* 1.5 (1927) and 1.6 (1927). In his autobiography, Feng briefly discusses a meeting he had with Wittgenstein in London in early 1934. See Feng Youlan, *Sansongtang zixu* 三松堂自序 (Beijing: Xinhua, 1984), p. 272.

47 See Feng, *Xin zhiyan*, p. 51ff. Feng may be referring here to a remark by Friedrich Waismann in his preface to Moritz Schlick's (1882–1936) *Gesammelte Aufsätze 1926–1936* (Vienna: Gerold, 1938), p. xxiii. See note 51 in my article "Der philosophische Daoismus in der *Neuen Metaphysik (Xin Lixue)* Feng Youlans" for a more detailed discussion.

48 Feng, *Xin zhiyan*, chapter 5.

49 Feng, *Xin yuandao*, p. 68 ff; Feng, *The Spirit of Chinese Philosophy*, p. 65 ff.

50 Feng, *Xin zhiyan*, p. 85.

51 *Ibid.*, pp. 55, 87.

52 *Ibid.*, pp. 96–97. Wittgenstein is usually no longer seen as a "representative" of the Vienna Circle, but as someone who, for a certain period, was close to it.

53 Ludwig Wittgenstein, *Tractatus Logico-Philosophicus*, translated by D. F. Pears and B. F. McGuiness (London: Routledge and Kegan Paul, 1961).

54 Similar ideas about "family resemblances" between Wittgenstein and Daoism (and Chan Buddhism) were also expressed, much later, by several Western

scholars—but without reference to Feng. See Paul C. L. Tang and Robert David Schwarz, "The Limits of Language: Wittgenstein's *Tractatus Logico-Philosophicus* and Lao Tzu's *Tao Te Ching*," *Journal of Chinese Philosophy* 15 (1988), pp. 9–33; and Thomas T. Tominga, "Ch'an, Taoism, and Wittgenstein," *Journal of Chinese Philosophy* 10 (1983), pp. 127–145.

55   See Feng, *Xin zhiyan*, p. 103.

56   In an obvious allusion to Wittgenstein, the last sentence in Feng's *A Short History of Chinese Philosophy* is: "One must speak very much before one keeps silent."

57   See Feng, *Xin zhiyan*, p. 98. See note 61 in my article "Der philosophische Daoismus in der *Neuen Metaphysik (Xin Lixue)* Feng Youlans" for a more detailed discussion of how Feng refers to the Vienna Circle in this context.

Chapter 8

Jin Yuelin's Ambivalent Status as a "Chinese Philosopher"

Yvonne Schulz Zinda

Jin Yuelin 金岳霖 (1895–1984) was a leading Republican-era philosopher.[1] Belonging to the first wave of scholars returning from the United States, he was a pioneer in the formation of logic and philosophy as academic disciplines in China. He established the Philosophy Department at Tsinghua (Qinghua) University in 1926 and headed it until 1929, when he asked Feng Youlan to succeed him. Jin taught not only Western philosophy but also a course in logic that was compulsory for students—such as Hu Qiaomu 胡喬木—who were pursuing other majors.[2] He also introduced logical analysis based on Moore and Russell to China. According to Zhang Dainian 張岱年, this then became the main theoretical and analytical tool used by, and a defining feature of, the so-called "Tsinghua School."[3] After 1949, many of his students joined the Faculty of Philosophy at Peking University or the Chinese Academy of Sciences. These included Shen Youding 沈有鼎 and Wang Xianjun 王憲鈞, both of whom specialized in Western philosophy; as well as Ren Hua 任華 and Zhou Liquan 周禮全, who specialized in logic. In 1935, Jin was one of the twelve founders of the Chinese Philosophy Association (Zhongguo zhexuehui 中國哲學會). He was also a member of the editorial board for the society's journal, *Zhexue pinglun* 哲學評論. In 1928, Jin was elected to be among the first group of eighty-one academicians at the Academia Sinica.

Like many other Chinese intellectuals of his time, he was greatly influenced by Western ideas and terms. Jin wrote many articles in Chinese, and some in English, on the problems of reality, theory, and logic.[4] Early on, he discovered the problem of induction, which became the central thread in his thought. Jin approached this problem from both ontological and epistemological standpoints. These approaches are reflected in his two main works: the ontological *Lun Dao* 論道 [On Dao], and the epistemological *Zhishilun* 知識論 [On knowledge].[5]

To date, substantial research on Jin Yuelin's philosophy has not been undertaken in the West.[6] However, a number of monographs on his work have been published by Chinese authors. These consist of introductions to his three books. Due to the abundance of material, the interpretations offered in these studies often manage only to scratch its surface.[7] In the PRC, research on Jin Yuelin increased during the 1980s and 1990s. Those studies interpreted his works either within an ideological or a nationalistic framework. The first type of study approached Jin's philosophy from the perspective of dialectical materialism, which conflicted with Jin's own views. In 1926, Jin published an article in which he rejected both materialism and idealism as scientific methods.[8] Other scholars have tried to categorize his thought as a particular kind of "ism."[9] Although neo-positivist methods might be discernable in Jin's works, it seems that he was far from a "neo-positivist." He neither shared a belief in the end of metaphysics, nor, like Wittgenstein in the final proposition of his *Tractatus*, did he refuse to talk about it. In fact, when writing his ontology, he is reported to have said that he intended to create a universal *Weltanschauung*.[10]

In works on the history of modern Chinese philosophy, along with Xiong Shili 熊十力 (1885–1968), He Lin 賀麟 (1902–1992), and others, Jin is classified as one of the "non-Marxist" (*fei Makesizhuyi* 非馬克思主義) philosophers, who were subjected to less criticism than those who were "anti-Marxist" (*fan Makesizhuyi* 反馬克思主義).[11] Jin's contribution to the progress of Chinese philosophy has been seen in the broader context of the synthesis of Chinese and Western philosophy.[12] Recently, doubts have arisen as to whether Jin's *Lun Dao*, described as consisting of "90% Western philosophy and 10% Chinese tradition," still belongs to the realm of Chinese philosophy. However, these doubts have not been expressed in detail.[13]

Jin Yuelin's thought is closely connected to the terminology he employed in his three main works, including his textbook, *Logic* (*Luoji* 邏輯).[14] He believed that although the content of thought, and its structure, relied on language or other forms of expression, it was independent from any specific language.[15] However, in spite of the already existing standardized neologisms for Western terms, which Jin also employed, he seems to have specifically chosen traditional Chinese terms to signify the key metaphysical concepts he used to address the problem of induction. The inductive problem arose because inductive generalizations relied on the outside world and thus could not be considered necessary for future cases. This led to Hume famously expressing doubt as to whether the sun would rise tomorrow.[16] Jin situated traditional Chinese terms in a Western context, with hardly any reference to Chinese schools of thought. This points to the ambivalent status of Jin Yuelin as "Chinese philosopher." In his epistemology, he defined the problem of induction as a problem of "*zhixu* 秩序" (order), thereby resorting to a standard neologism.[17] In his introduction to *Lun Dao*, however, he employed traditional Chinese terms and portrayed the problem of induction as one of "disharmony between *li* (理) and *shi* (勢)." He mixed styles of Western and Chinese traditional scholarship not only in content, but also in form. In seeking to arrange Chinese and Western thought so they both served the needs of his time, Jin was representative of another feature of the "Tsinghua School."[18]

The following analysis is based on the assumption that Jin should primarily be considered a philosopher from China, rather than a philosopher who tried to preserve or develop a particular Chinese philosophy. A short outline of Jin's intellectual background will be provided; then his philosophical style, his expositions on language, and his play on the terms that were crucial to his thought will be introduced. The epistemological and ontological answers he provided will then be analyzed in light of his understanding of the problem of induction. The following questions will be explored: what form of philosophical reasoning did Jin choose, and why did he resolve not to employ standardized neologisms such as *zhixu* in his answer to the problem of induction? The conclusion will discuss the extent to which the traditional terms Jin did employ might be considered neologisms in his newly constructed game of language (in Wittgenstein's sense), or if they should merely be understood as part of a process of indigenization.

1. Intellectual Background

Jin came into close contact with Western culture while attending a middle school run by missionaries.[19] He later studied political science at the University of Pennsylvania, graduating in 1918.[20] In 1920, he wrote his PhD thesis on "The Political Theory of Thomas Hill Green" at Columbia University.[21] His studies in political theory exposed him to different branches of contemporary philosophy and philosophical problems.[22] In 1921 he went to London, which proved crucial for his work. It was then that Hume's *A Treatise of Human Nature* and Russell's *Principles of Mathematics* sparked his intellectual interest. Jin later proclaimed that these two works had exerted the most influence on his thought. Through Russell, he became acquainted with the analytical school, which led him to distance himself from the Neo-Hegelian Green. Jin was attracted to Russell's approach, in which he discussed philosophy in the framework of everyday life rather than taking an idealistic approach to the great philosophical questions.[23] Hume's *Treatise* further alerted Jin to the problem of induction. Upon returning to China, he first lectured on the English language and on history, before entering Tsinghua University.

Despite receiving a Western education, Jin kept in touch with traditional Chinese thought, mainly through his friend Feng Youlan (1895–1990). Jin did not intend to take part in the nationalistic discourse on the preservation and transformation of traditional Chinese thought. In his appraisal of Feng's work, he stated that philosophy should not be confined to national boundaries but discussed in a broader, more general context.[24] He seemed to cherish hopes for progress towards a universal philosophy. Jin also repeatedly argued, based on Peirce's "type-token" theory, in favour of a universal logic. Accordingly, he stated that there was *one* metaphysical logic or "type"; this could not be expressed, and thus all existing logical systems were particular "tokens" of it.[25]

2. Jin's Philosophical Style

The philosophical style considered here is the form in which Jin chose to compose his works.[26] Four distinct features are to be found, most notably in *Zhishilun* and *Lun Dao*: the numerical structure of the texts; his dualistic approach to the treatment of philosophical questions; his extensive employment of suffixes; and his creation of idioms.

Jin Yuelin structured his texts according to contemporary analytical school conventions, and in a fashion reminiscent of works on mathematical logic such as Whitehead and Russell's *Principia Mathematica* (1903) and Wittgenstein's *Tractatus logico-philosophicus* (1921).[27] These are divided into chapters, with each chapter organized according to theorems. These, in turn, are treated in subsections with numeric or alphabetic headings (such as 1.1, 1.2; 2.1, 2.2; 1, 2; A, B; or 1., 2.), in which each theorem is explained in short paragraphs.

Secondly, the most prominent feature of Jin's work was his dualistic approach to dealing with philosophical questions. In his epistemology, dichotomies featured in great abundance. These were derived from Western, as well as Chinese, traditional contexts:

Epistemology refers to knowledge, or *li* 理 (regularity) of the knowledge of objects. Two [meanings] of the word *li* will be employed. On the one hand, there is the *li* of the object; on the other hand, there is the *li* of the content.... We can make use of the differences between universal qualities (*gongxiang* 共相) and concepts (*gainian* 概念) to distinguish the two different kinds of *li*. Drawing on the sense of inner and outer, the universal qualities are outside (*wai* 外) and the concepts are inside (*nei* 內).[28]

In Jin's epistemology, we mainly find dichotomies of attributive character, such as the inside/outside distinction mentioned above. In his ontology, Jin introduced a framework of dichotomies of traditional Chinese terms of nominal character, such as *li—shi* 理—勢, *ti—yong* 體—用, or *wuji—taiji* 無極—太極.

The third characteristic of Jin's philosophical style in *Zhishilun* and *Lun Dao* was his use of suffixes. Jin added suffixes to terms that, in some cases, already existed as standard translations for Western technical terms. By creating groups of terms that shared the same suffix, Jin signalled that they belonged to one particular aspect, or perspective, of his system of thought. There were at least four suffixes pointing to such groups of terms: *-xiang* 相;[29] *-guan* 觀;[30] *-ti* 體;[31] and *-ran* 然. Regarding the suffix *ran*, Jin was more specific. Traditionally, *ran* served to turn a word into an adverb.[32] Within the context of his ontology, the terms suffixed by *ran* described different aspects of being. For example, Jin distinguished between two worlds: the world of "original being" (*benran* 本然) and of "nature" (*ziran* 自然). The latter was a standard translation, which he deliberately retranslated into English as "itself-so."[33] He regarded the present as "accidental" (*ouran* 偶然).[34] The comprehension of regularities was, for Jin, the comprehension of the "basis of being" (*suoyi ran* 所以然). According to his ontology, logic was "necessary" (*biran* 必然).

Jin did not explain the use of suffixes in his works. However, a self-criticism written in 1958 provides proof—despite his ironic treatment of his ontology—that he created at least the terms ending with "*ran*" inter-dependently. He explained:

In the text *Lun Dao*, I was talking about necessity (*biran*), certainty (*guran* 固然), compellingness (*dangran* 當然), and fitness (*shiran* 適然). In the secondary text,[35] I was even talking about original being (*benran*), the accidental (*ouran*), and the probable (*huoran* 或然). Please note! After talking about so many ways of being, what kind of being (*ran*) did I finally discuss? Strange! Not one.... Regarding concrete facts, *Lun Dao* is an empty tube. There is not the least trace of being. I created such a pile of "basis of [something's] being" (*suoyi ran*), yet there is not the least trace of being. So how can one talk about "reasons; why something is"?[36]

Fourth, although Jin employed traditional idioms, he mostly used pseudo-traditional ones as another form of stylistic device. In his ontology, he imparted the meaning of his key terms to the reader by repeatedly reciting these idioms, almost as though they were ritualistic formulas. Most of them were in literary Chinese and consisted of four characters, for example: "*shi* returns to *li*" (*shi gui yu li* 勢歸於理), and "the production and extinction of particulars" (*shuxiang shengmie* 殊相生滅).[37] Some contained the common Chinese dichotomy of *wu* 無 and *you* 有, such as "*li* is certain" (*li you guran* 理有固然) and "*shi* has no necessary point of arrival" (*shi wu bi zhi* 勢無必至).[38] These phrases have the air of well-established Chinese idioms, but for the most part they were not derived from the traditional textual canon. For example, "*li you guran, shi wu bi zhi* 理有固然，勢無必至" is reminiscent of "*li you guran, shi you changqu* 理有固然，勢有常趣," which appears in Wang Fu's 王符 (ca. 90–165) *Qianfulun* 潛夫論 [The discourses of a recluse].[39] Feng Youlan referred to Jin as "the first to have been good at employing Chinese idioms to express philosophical propositions."[40]

3. Jin's "Play of Concepts"[41]

Writing in the Republican era, Jin was already equipped with a number of standard translations for Western philosophical terms. Some had been adopted from secondary translations produced in Japan. Most of the terms had not yet been standardized, allowing a variety of translations to exist simultaneously, such as *mingxue* 名學 or *luoji* 邏輯 for "logic."[42] Although many Western philosophical works had already been translated into Chinese, there were hardly any bilingual dictionaries for philosophical terms. This gave Jin the freedom to create his own philosophical language.

When reading his textbook on logic, as well as his writings on epistemology and ontology, one can distinguish four different groups of terms in his philosophical language. Standard translations for Western terms appeared in each of his three books, such as *guina yuanze* 歸納原則 for "principle of induction" and *xianshi* 現實 for "realization."[43] Second, he created neologisms, mainly in *Logic,* as he was the first to introduce mathematical logic to the Chinese intellectual world.[44] Third, he seems to have considered some traditional Chinese terms equivalent to Western ones. For example, it is likely that Jin based his term *gongxiang* on Buddhist terminology. This served as his translation for "universal"—an equivalent to the term from the Western, or rather Russell's, dichotomy of the "universal" and "particular."[45]

The fourth, and most interesting group, consists of the terms Jin derived from Chinese tradition, yet without any specific reference to it. Such terms can be found in *Zhishilun* but in greater abundance in *Lun Dao*. With the exception of *dao*, these terms were mainly parts of dichotomies, such as "*li—shi* 理—勢," "*ti—yong* 體—用," and "*ji—shu* 幾—數." In his English essay, Jin used English neologisms to translate some of these, rather than draw from the standard set of Western philosophical terms. *Li* and *shi* therefore became "pattern" and "drift,"[46] while *ji* and *shu* became "occasion" and "pre-ordination." In the latter case, Jin even felt compelled to add the Chinese terms,[47] thus indicating the difficulties he had in finding proper English translations. In *Lun Dao*, Jin presented these Chinese traditional dichotomies as a metaphysical framework for the problem of induction. In the preface, he explained his intentions as follows:

> I know very well that this book has acquired the stigma of having put new wine in old bottles, especially with regard to *wuji* 無極, *taiji* 太極, *ji* 幾, *shu* 數, *li* 理, *shi* 勢, *qing* 情, *xing* 性, *ti* 體, and *yong* 用…. This is because I wanted to transfer the emotion of these nouns to some of the terms in this book.[48]

Jin did not intend to preserve traditional Chinese thought, nor to Westernize it, but rather to draw on its connotations.

4. The Emotional Attachment to Words

To understand Jin's use of terms and stylistic devices derived from Chinese tradition, one must return to his chapter on language in *Zhishilun* and his ideas on "emotional attachment" or "deposit" (*qinggan shangde jituo / yuncang* 情感上的寄託 / 蘊藏). Jin distinguished "words" (*zi* 字) from the "ideas" (*yinian* 意念) and "concepts" (*gainian* 概念) they expressed.[49] Ideas were the precursors of concepts. Both were carefully defined, but in Jin's thought, concepts seem to have gained an almost Hegelian level of absoluteness. Conversely, words could be used with greater liberty.[50] A word had different deposits (*yuncang* 蘊藏), but as an idea, it had a clearly defined "meaning" (*yiyi* 意義). The emotional attachment to a word depended on the individual employing it, as well as on social circumstances such as history, customs, and the environment. Jin saw religious, philosophical, or spiritual emotions as the moving forces behind words. He explained that the Chinese showed reverence towards *dao* 道, *de* 德, *ren* 仁, *yi* 義, and *li* 理, whereas the English felt the same kind of emotions toward the words "Lord" or "God."[51] The connotations of words were derived from one's emotional attachment to them.

According to Jin, the different "connotations" (*yiwei* 意味) of words were dependent on history, circumstances, or the medium through which they were communicated. He illustrated this with the following example:

> ... the emotions that overseas [Chinese] students have regarding the two designations "*Yesu shengdanjie* 耶穌聖誕節" and "Christmas" are completely different. To the first one, they are completely emotionally unattached. To the last, they attach a kind of emotion, but an emotion that has nothing to do with Christian belief. Nevertheless, it is an emotion regarding customs and traditions.[52]

"Sentences" (*juzi* 句子) could also carry connotations. Through the employment of words in different circumstances, they gained connotations that point toward subjective feelings, or the things to which the words referred. Jin's example was the poetic line "*dajiang liu riye* 大江流日夜" (the Yangzi flows day and night). Besides its literal meaning, to Jin, it also conveyed a feeling of nostalgia.[53] Thus, according to Jin, poetry was almost impossible to translate, since it relied heavily on the connotations of words. Therefore, the meaning and connotation in the translation would differ from the original. While scientific texts relied on the meaning of words, poetry relied on connotations.[54] Jin described the translation of philosophical words in the following passage:

> **3. Some philosophical words are easy to translate, and some are not.** Philosophy can be divided into two parts. One part is completely rational; one part is not completely rational. The first is based on analysis and criticism; the second is based on synthesis and creativity. The first is close to science; the second is close to religion.... The first is easy to translate; the second is not easy. Epistemology is rather easy to translate; while *xuanxue* 玄學 or metaphysics is difficult to translate.... The Chinese word "*dao* 道" is, by chance, contained in the Greek "logos." Other languages, such as English, do not seem to have a suitable word. Other [words] such as *tian* 天, *xing* 性, *ming* 命, *ti* 體, *yong* 用, *cheng* 誠, *ren* 仁, *yi* 義, and *li* 禮 have profound connotations; thus the meaning cannot be suitably expressed by other words.[55]

In choosing most of the key terms in his ontology and epistemology from within the Chinese tradition, Jin relied on the emotional attachment of Chinese readers. The problem of induction provided the framework for his texts, and it was within this that Jin's terms attained their definitions. At the same time, they were influenced by existing historical connotations. The same went for the pseudo-traditional idioms introduced above, which Jin presumably created in light of his understanding of emotional attachment. By constructing idioms in the traditional way, he evoked, at least formally, a sense of familiarity. Jin avoided attributing his ideas to past thinkers, not wanting, as he later explained, to "burden them, in the end, with thought that was perhaps untenable."[56] Overall, there are few quotations in Jin's works. The quotations, direct or indirect, that he did have were obviously not meant to imply an affiliation to particular schools of thought in the past.

One might argue that Jin derived these terms from Chinese tradition in order to make Western thought—such as the problem of induction—more accessible to a Chinese audience. This does not seem plausible however, because in his English essay *Tao, Nature and Man,* Jin did not translate these terms using Western terminology. Although he considered *dao* equivalent to *Logos,* as seen above, he still used *dao* instead of choosing a Western term. The emotional attachment Jin ascribed to traditional Chinese words is not easy to grasp, because he did not refer to any specific schools of thought. He was instead rather vague, as will be seen in his answers to the problem of induction.

5. The Problem of Induction According to Jin Yuelin

Although the principle of induction had been introduced to China in the nineteenth century, it became, according to Jin, *en vogue* among Chinese intellectuals after 1911 because it was considered to be the foundation of Western science.[57] He came to discover the problem of induction through his studies of logic. In 1927, Jin outlined, in English, his *Prolegomena*; this would lead to his two main works, *Zhishilun* and *Lun Dao.*[58] In 1928, before starting these projects, he published a detailed critical assessment of Hume's epistemological theory, thereby further laying out the foundations of his later work. He discussed Hume's theory of impression and his views on necessity, as well as cause and effect, while criticizing his notion of induction.[59]

The textbook on logic seems to have taken Jin further in his intellectual development. The last chapter, in particular, can be seen as leading to his other main works, in which he treated the conditions of the deductive and inductive systems.[60] He stressed that with the deductive system, assumptions could be made without the need to prove them outside of the deductive system. The inductive system always relied on verification based on facts (*zhengshi* 證實).[61] In the preface, which he included in *Lun Dao*, he pointed out that Wittgenstein had understood logic to be both a necessity of the outside world, as well as of all possible forms of being and thought.[62]

In his epistemology, Jin dedicated one chapter to the inductive principle. He defined, in English, the inductive principle without indicating the origin of his quotation.[63] However, the definition is almost identical to that provided by Russell in *Our Knowledge of the External World* (1914).[64] Jin identified Hume's problem as one of order.[65] According to Jin, because Hume did not presume a general order independent from the mind, his inductive principle had degraded to the level of an "irrational habit."[66] He agreed with the views of G. E. Moore and Russell on common sense (*changshi* 常識) and assumed the existence of external things (*waiwu* 外物) independent from the mind.[67] In *Zhishilun,* Jin set out two aspects of the problem of induction, asking if: 1) in the future, the world could change such that the principle of induction was no longer applicable, or even false; and 2) whether it could be guaranteed that the future will resemble the past.[68]

The first question emphasizes the validity of the inductive principle as a method. Jin argued, like Russell, that the inductive principle could not be confirmed or renounced through experience, since this would be an inductive generalization.[69] He considered the inductive principle to be the "general principle of reception" (*jieshou zongze* 接受總則) because it allowed any experience of the given always to be categorized through ideas (*yinian* 意念).[70] If the ideas were insufficient, they should be redefined. To illustrate this, Jin gave the example of a black swan; here, the idea of a swan as a white bird no longer applied.[71] There was only one condition under which the principle of induction would become invalid; that is, if time ever stopped.[72] Since such a situation could neither be perceived nor thought of, the invalidity of the principle would never be experienced.[73] For this reason, Jin classified the principle of induction as "*arational a priori*" (*xianyan* 先驗). Throughout his works, he distinguished between *arational a priori* as a necessary condition of experience, and "*rational a priori*" (*xiantian* 先天) as a necessary condition of the possibility of being, such as logical propositions.[74]

The second part of the problem of induction was ontological. This was the question as to whether nature was uniform and followed a certain order, and would proceed according to the same laws in the future. Again, Jin argued, like Russell, that unless laws were based on incorrect judgements in the past, any exceptions to a law in the future could be explained. Even if the expected law did not come into effect, a different law would.[75] In *Zhishilun* and *Lun Dao,* Jin investigated the nature of order, which he perceived as Hume's problem of causality. He chose the term "*li* 理," which was derived from Chinese tradition. Here, this will be translated as "regularity," rather than "order," for several reasons. First, Jin dissociated himself, terminologically, from Hume's notion of order. Second, the term "regularity" reflects the dynamic quality of Jin's term, as will be seen. In opposition to Hume, "*li*" gained metaphysical status and was to be understood as *the* superior order, *the* meta-regularity.

Jin defined regularity in a three-fold manner. "Pure regularity" (*chunli* 純理) reflected the sum of the laws of logic on which being, experience, and thought were based.[76] He laid out the theoretical foundation for this concept in his textbook on logic, while exploring it ontologically in terms of "form" (*shi* 式) in *Lun Dao*. The second kind was the ontological "external regularity" (*wai li* 外理) that he dealt with in *Lun Dao*, which was independent of the perceiving subject. It was the object of the epistemological "inner regularity" (*nei li* 內理), which underlay the process of acquiring knowledge. It depended on the perceiving subject. For Jin, the problem of induction arose because of the tension between the particular and the universal. On the epistemological side, there was the opposition between "theory" and "facts," which Jin expressed using the terms "*li* 理" and "*shi* 事." Jin seems to have borrowed this contrast from Chinese tradition. However, he did not give any indication as to the possible connection with Huayan Buddhism. Feng Youlan also used the *li* and *shi* dyad to discuss the relation between *li* 理 and *qi* 氣, a topic on which he consulted Jin. On the ontological side, there was regularity, which was in opposition to the particular, unpredictable instances in the flow of time. Both were reflected in *Lun Dao* in terms of *li* 理 and *shi* 勢.

6. Epistemology as Reflected in *li* 理 and *shi* 事

Jin divided *Zhishilun* into three parts: experience was covered in chapters 1–5 and reason in chapter 6, while the remainder focused on their inter-relation.[77] He dissociated his epistemology from empirical or idealist approaches, dealing with both by investigating aspects of order as well as facts.[78] Apart from Jin's use of *li* and *shi*, *Zhishilun* was terminologically less interesting than *Lun Dao* since he generally employed standardized neologisms for Western terms. For this reason, it will be discussed only briefly.

In *Zhishilun,* Jin distinguished between three worlds: the world of "facts" (*shishi* 事實, which will be abbreviated to *shi* 事 here), the "natural world" (*ziran shijie* 自然世界), and the "world of original being" (*benran shijie* 本然世界). The first two "have perspective" (*youguan*) whereas the third is "without perspective" (*wuguan*). In analyzing facts and nature, Jin defined the latter as the world of original being having a perspective, which depended on various groups of perception.[79] In this respect, nature typified the world of original being to the extent that it contained all possible objects of perception. However, Jin's use of the term "nature" did not yet involve the element of time.[80] He spoke of nature as a "specific world" (*tebie shijie* 特別世界), which corresponded to the mode or group of perception.[81] The object in the world of nature was the given that differed accordingly. Despite there being differences between subjective perceptions, Jin presupposed an element of the given common to all groups of perception which he named the "realized[82] individual of the world of original being having no perspective" (*wuguande benrande xian-shide geti* 無觀的本然的現實的個體).[83] The world of original being was the pre-condition for experience. Accordingly, Jin classified it, as he had done for the principle of induction, as *arational a priori*.[84] It contained the flow of time as well as a certain amount of order necessary for perception to take place. Both were expressed using the key ontological terms, *li* 理 and *shi* 勢, which will be discussed in the next section.

As quoted above, Jin distinguished the inner and outer parts of regu-larity (*li*). Outer regularity was the ontological part of the world of orig-inal being. It was the object in the process of acquiring knowledge based on epistemological inner regularity, independent from any epistemolog-ical subject. The counterpart to the ontological *shi* 勢 was *shi* 事. It was translated as "the factual" since it represented the totality of all particular facts and, like regularity, gained a metaphysical status. The factual was described in "particular propositions" (*teshu mingti* 特殊命題) that were true. Regularity in the epistemological sense was expressed in "general propositions" (*pubian mingti* 普遍命題).[85]

Jin's key terms in *Zhishilun* were drawn from Chinese tradition; at the same time, they point to neologisms for terms derived from the West. The term "truth" (*zhenli* 真理) contained the term "regularity" (*li*); its counterpart *shi* was included in the terms "fact" (*shishi* 事實) and "event" (*shiti* 事體), which were likewise connected to time.[86] Particular facts could not be repeated, but they contained structures of regularity. Jin believed that in the progress of knowledge, factuality could be derived from regularity,[87] while knowledge concerning regularity could be derived from the factual.[88] Describing their interrelatedness, which comprised "reality" (*shizai* 實在), Jin wrote:

> In the realm of epistemology, in the factual there is regularity (*shi zhong you li* 事中有理), and in regularity there is the factual (*li zhong you shi* 理中有事). This is the difference between studying epistemology and studying logic.[89]

In the case of *li* and *shi*, Jin might have speculated on the emotional attachment of the Chinese intellectual, adding to it connotations from the Chinese context, such as Huayan Buddhism.[90]

Knowledge, which was based on regularity, aimed at comprehension of the regularity of the complete process of being. Jin defined it as an absolute structure comprised of "structures of concepts" (*gainian jiegou* 概念結構), which for him marked a supreme stage in the process of knowledge. Accordingly, Jin's "pattern of ideas" (*yinian tu'an* 意念圖案) represented the less perfect precursor. If patterns were right, they gained the status of structures. These individual structures were seen as parts of the absolute structure.[91] Jin's notion of knowledge was complex and multi-faceted. Within patterns and structures, ideas or concepts were linked. They included propositions that had to be consistent.[92] There were also different groups of knowledge. For example, different sciences had different sets of ideas and patterns with which to receive and arrange (*anpai* 安排) the given. The description of each fact depended on the viewpoint of the subject and the field of knowledge at hand.[93]

Jin understood the acquisition of knowledge to be an infinite process directed towards truth. He had an absolute notion of truth, which he described as being partially, but never completely, attainable:[94]

> True propositions are discrete … they are isolated expressions, not structures of true propositions, and are different from truth. True propositions are

attainable. To have knowledge is thus to have attained true propositions. At the same time, it also means to have attained patterns of ideas, but to have knowledge does not necessarily mean to have attained truth. Truth is the complete structure of concepts or true propositions. In order to attain the complete structure, all aspects of patterns of ideas have to become structures. In addition, an endless number of structures are related together so as to become one complete structure.[95]

Jin acknowledged that this infinite process of acquiring knowledge was constantly progressing.[96] Truth, as a structure of concepts, was equivalent to regularity in both the epistemological and ontological senses.[97]

7. Ontology as Reflected in *li* 理 and *shi* 勢

The ontological *Lun Dao* is Jin's most difficult work. In contrast to his detailed epistemology, in *Lun Dao* his treatment of many philosophical problems was briefer. Jin introduced a number of new terms taken from Chinese tradition, sometimes without elaborating further on their meaning. At times, *Lun Dao* is quite dense, and one gains the impression that towards the end Jin had finished it somewhat hastily.[98] In his ontology, Jin explained the most general conditions for individuation, including human beings and the process of change, as well as the origin and meaning of this process.[99] He laid out the principles of the world of original being, including the two conditions for experience and for the principle of induction. These were regularity in the process of being and time, which he understood not as empty, but as having content that appeared in the continuous transformation of things and events (*shiwu* 事物).[100]

Jin divided his ontology into two halves. First, there was regularity in the process of change, which provided the static conditions for being. The second half described the fleeting existence of constantly changing individuals. The two halves reflected the opposition between the universal and the particular. The first transcended space and time, like all kinds of laws, while the second was situated within a particular space and time. Jin later stated that the flow of time was the main subject in *Lun Dao*.[101] This is very significant, since *Lun Dao* has to be understood as process ontology.[102] For a discussion of Jin's framework of metaphysical terms derived from Chinese tradition, chapters one, seven, and eight are the most important.

In opposition to Hume, Jin defined "regularity" not as "necessary" (*biran*), but as being "certain" (*guran*). Regularity was represented in "universal relations" (*gongxiang di guanlian* 共相底關聯), which were objects in the process of knowledge, as explained above.[103] From the epistemological point of view, they became general laws. To Jin, these laws were not restricted to science but also applied to ethics and aesthetics, as will be seen. The term *shi* 勢 was represented in the "production and extinction of particulars" (*shuxiang shengmie*).[104] It was translated as "situation in process" because Jin considered particular situations always to be in the process of transforming into other ones. Particulars, which were bound to relative time and space, were defined as particular events.[105] The situation in process, and its particulars that had been experienced, were registered as epistemological "facts." The particulars were the causes underlying constant change.[106]

"Regularity is always certain" (*li you guran* 理有固然) because in the process of being, universal laws were always valid. However, there were certain times or points in space in which they did not necessarily come into effect. Therefore, "the situation in process has no necessary point of arrival" (*shi wu bi zhi* 勢無必至). Every particular situation in process had, at each instant, several options with which to proceed. Particular circumstances were never, however, purely accidental, since the options that were present in a certain situation in process always accorded with some kind of law. Jin illustrated his case with the example of someone who had taken lethal poison and who faced numerous possible outcomes. Even if, by chance, such a person was saved and did not die, the law concerning lethal poison had not been proven invalid; rather, a certain prediction had proved to be false. Since a lethal dose of poison will always kill a human being, it may be concluded that the situation had proceeded in a different direction, and another law had come into effect.[107] In *Lun Dao*, Jin again took up Hume's problem by discussing it not in the context of order, but within the framework of terms derived from Chinese tradition:

> When Hume discusses causal relations, he does it in a roundabout way because he encounters the problem of the situation in process that has no necessary point of arrival. Acknowledging that the situation in process has no necessary point of arrival, he then thought that regularity has no certainty. A few years ago, those who engaged in science or those who cherished unlimited hopes regarding science also thought that since regularity was certain the situation in process also had a necessary point of arrival. The problem of the inductive principle is, in part, a matter [related to the fact

that the] situation in process has no necessary point of arrival. The situation in process should not be mixed up with regularity, making [both] one. What is usually meant by "the situation in process has a necessary point of arrival" is that regularity is certain, and not that the situation in process has a necessary point of arrival.[108]

Regularity and the situation in progress were part of the complete process of the transformation of being, or the cosmological process, which Jin called the "process of realization" (*xianshi di licheng* 現實底歷程). Jin's notion of this process was influenced by the theory of evolution, which was well known in China at that time.[109] However, Jin created and used the term "*daoyan* 道演" instead of employing the standard neologism for evolution, "*tianyan* 天演," thereby connecting the meaning of this process to *dao* rather than "Heaven" (*tian*).[110] For Jin, the theory of evolution, in light of *dao*, did not merely apply to human beings or animals, but to all things and events making up the cosmos. He included all options in the process of being. At the same time, *dao* meant that which the cosmos was based upon.

Jin treated *dao* on the basis of its two aspects: "*dao*-one" (*daoyi* 道一) and "*dao*-differentiated" (*daofen* 道分),[111] reminiscent of Zhu Xi's 朱熹 (1130–1200) notion of *li yi fen shu* 理一分殊 (one principle, many particular manifestations). Jin distinguished *dao*-one and *dao*-differentiated in the following way:

> *Dao* is the most eminent concept. *Dao*, which is the most fundamental power, is definitely not empty, is definitely not empty like form (*shi* 式), and is certainly actual.... If we talk about *dao* as it concerns the unity of the myriad [things and events], then it is *dao*-one. If we say that each of the myriad [things and events] has its own *dao*, then it is *dao*-differentiated.... From the point of view of knowledge, the differentiated *dao* (*fenkai lai shuo de dao* 分開來說的道) is extremely important. The objects of research in disciplinary-based learning are each differentiated. From the point of view of human affairs the differentiated *dao* is perhaps even more important. [The sentence] "When he achieves his ambition, he shares [his privileges] with the people; when he fails to do so, he practises *dao* alone"[112] refers completely to the *dao* of human affairs and to the differentiated *dao*. If, however, we think from the point of view of the metaphysical object, then the myriad things are equal. Whether they are short or long, it overcomes any form and discards any quality. There is no other and there is no self. Everything comes into being itself, and dies, but does not cease. That *dao* is *dao* in its unity, the *dao* of *dao*-one.[113]

Apart from the quotation from *Mencius*, Jin did not define *dao* in the light of Chinese tradition but instead remained vague: "... According to my personal opinion, *dao* is evidently not necessarily straight, and not necessarily very narrow. It has a connotation of wideness and generosity. In spite of the term "form" (*shi* 式) being cool, *dao* is not cool."[114]

8. Relative Framework: *Dao*-Differentiated

Jin considered the process of being to be infinite. The *dao*-differentiated represented the basis for the transformation of all things and events in the process of being. It was based on two propositions: "There is no potentiality without form, [and] there is no form without potentiality" (*wu wushi de neng, wu wuneng de shi* 無無式的能，無無能的式). This was the definition of *dao*-differentiated. Jin characterized the two propositions as necessary, and thus (rational) *a priori*, because potentiality was "always there" (*lao shi zai nali* 老是在那裡).[115] He marked his proposition as unique by distancing himself, terminologically, from the similar propositions of Zhu Xi, who stated that "*li* cannot be without *qi*, *qi* cannot be without *li*" (*li bu neng wu qi, qi bu neng wu li* 理不能無氣，氣不能無理); and Aristotle, who stated that "form cannot be without stuff, stuff cannot be without form" (*xing bu neng wu zhi, zhi bu neng wu xing* 形不能無質，質不能無形). Jin did not see necessity as being sufficiently expressed in these propositions. Arguing subjectively, he stated that he did not "feel" the necessity, especially regarding the first part of each sentence. Jin based his impression on the connotation of the terms *"qi"* and "stuff," which he interpreted as the "things" of experience.[116]

Form contained all possibilities, either realized or unrealized, and had to conform to the laws of logic.[117] In the process of being, "potentiality leaves and enters" (*neng you chu ru* 能有出入) possibilities of being, which then become realized. For example, potentiality had "left" the possibility of dinosaurs a long time ago, but during Jin's time, had entered the possibility of aeroplanes.[118] Jin classified this proposition as *arational a priori*, since there was no reason for the constant activity of potentiality.[119] He later described potentiality as "absolutely given."[120] It had no quality but was the basis for the content of time—the particulars on which the constant process of being was founded. In the conclusion to chapter one, Jin defined *dao*-differentiated as "remaining within form, [and] caused by potentiality" (*jushi youneng* 居式由能).[121] In this theorem, which again mimicked traditional idioms, he underlined the logical consistency and dynamic quality of this aspect of his notion of *dao* as infinite.

In the process of being, potentiality was the reason for timeliness and particularity, and form was the basis of universals, which were logically consistent and guaranteed a minimum of constancy. Playing with the two terms, Jin defined both in paragraph 3.9:

> **3.9 Universals are possibilities of individuations; particulars are possibilities of individuations for individuals.** Universals (*gongxiang*) are common and general "qualities" (*xiang* 相) that appear in each individual.... For example, "red" is the universal of each red individual.... Particulars (*shuxiang* 殊相) are in opposition to universals. The "yellow" of this yellow book, and the "red" of this red table, are the particulars we are here talking about. In spite of being qualities (*xiang*), it is unavoidable that they are differentiated (*shu* 殊).[122]

In order to describe the developments in the evolutionary process of *dao*-differentiated, Jin introduced the dichotomy of "*ji* 幾" and "*shu* 數," which drew inspiration from Chinese tradition. As it related to his concepts of the universal and the particular, Jin's term "*ji*" (occasion)[123] stood for change particular to an individual, whereas the term "*shu*" (pre-ordained)[124] stood for changes that concerned a class of individuals. In the case of human beings, it might be pre-ordained that every human being had to die. For Jin, "the pre-ordained is compelling" (*shu suo dangran* 數所當然), thus pointing to an inevitable development. However, neither the particular circumstances in which an individual human being would die, nor the space or period of time in which this would happen, could be predicted—as he showed with his example of someone who had taken lethal poison. Jin marked out particular circumstances through his use of the term "occasion." In the development of an individual "the occasions are fit" (*ji suo shiran* 幾所適然).[125] By choosing the term "*shiran*," he drew a terminological connection to the theory of evolution, even referring to the expression "survival of the fittest" (*shizhe shengcun* 適者生存). Jin went further, considering the development of an individual and stating that if an individual proved to be fit on one occasion, it "gained" (*de* 得) in the process of time, thus surviving.[126]

9. Absolute Framework: *Dao*-One

Jin's ontology was brought to its conclusion in the last chapter of *Lun Dao,* where it obtained its moral turn. It contained an abundance of terms Jin had drawn from Chinese tradition. He constructed a metaphysical framework to explain meaning in the process of being. Jin used the traditional terms "*wuji* 無極" and "*taiji* 太極" to mark the absolute origin and aim of this process. He brought both terms together in the well-known expression "*wuji* yet *taiji*" (*wuji er taiji* 無極而太極), which described *dao*'s second aspect, *dao*-one.[127] He situated the process of being within this absolute framework, which centred on the contrastive conjunction "yet" (*er*).[128] In his definition, Jin laid stress on the "limits" (*ji*) of these terms. He understood *wuji* to be any aspect without limit, and thus the beginning of *dao*. It will be translated here as the "ultimate-less of non-being." As the transcendental beginning of the process of being, it is completely undifferentiated.[129] Jin classified the "ultimateless of non-being" as a "possibility that has to be realized" (*bu neng bu xianshide keneng* 不能不現實的可能), and which, as part of the process of being, could be "conceived" (*siyi* 思議).[130] Through the absolute framework of *wuji* and *taiji,* Jin gave meaning to the transformation of individuals within the *dao*'s evolutionary process.

Jin distinguished between two aspects of the "universal" and "particular," drawing, terminologically, from Chinese tradition. The dichotomy of *xing* and *qing* referred to the inner qualities of individuals. With *ti* and *yong*, he described the relatedness of individuals to the outside world. The first terms of each dichotomy were represented by universals, and the second by particulars. Jin did not provide a detailed definition of *ti* and *yong*, nor did he give any examples. He merely stated that he did not think the meanings of his terms were as broad as in Chinese tradition.[131]

Jin's definitions of *xing* and *qing* were highly subjective and suited to the needs of his philosophy.[132] He proceeded to give examples taken from everyday life. He understood the individual as multi-natured. He drew the picture of a man who was a bank manager, a husband, a lover of arts, and so on. Thus, in the process of unfolding his nature (*jinxing* 盡性), he unfolded the bank manager's nature, the husband's nature, and the lover of art's nature. The particular instances of this process were called *qing*, which here will be translated as "inclination." The process of being was dynamic because the inclinations of individuals were striving to unfold their nature (*qing jin xing* 情盡性). The individual strove, in its different functions in relation to other individuals, to fulfil its roles (*yong qiu ti* 用求體). Again, it could be argued that in using the notion of the unfolding of one's nature he was drawing from the Chinese tradition. There may even be a connection with Mencius, as shown in the following quotation:

> The flow of water downwards,[133] animals running freely about, this is the inclination of a specific body of water striving to unfold its nature, the inclination of specific animals striving to unfold their nature … wind, rain, snow and hail, stars, the sun and the moon all display this phenomenon— of inclinations striving to unfold their nature, and functions striving to fulfil their roles. The unfolding of nature seems to be a principle without any exception.[134]

However, Jin did not give any indication as to whether this was the case:

> I don't dare to say whether the two words *xing* and *qing* were formerly employed in this way or not, but it seems to me a possible mode of employment. Personally, I think that *xing* has always had the connotation of something general, and *qing* the connotation of something particular.[135]

Apart from this vague statement, his definition of the two terms, illustrated by way of the bank manager, was again highly subjective and without any reference to past traditions. In addition, he put them in the context of a Western problem. It seems futile to look further for a connection.[136]

Although Jin granted regularity to the process of being, he defined it as not yet pure. In the beginning of this process, which he described as the ultimate of non-being, regularity was not yet discernable. Moreover, the situation in process, and therefore time, had not yet started.[137] Jin's term "supreme ultimate" (*taiji*) marked the transcendental end of the process in which the striving of the inclinations to unfold their natures, and the functions to fulfil roles, would come to an end. Like the ultimate of non-being, Jin classified the supreme ultimate as a possibility, which had to be realized and which could be thought of.[138] It was the ultimate goal, in which the true (*zhizhen* 至真), the good (*zhishan* 至善), the beautiful (*zhimei* 至美), and the absolute (*zhiru* 至如)[139] became identical in the supreme ultimate. For Jin, the "myriad [things and events would then] revert into one" (*wan guiyu yi* 萬歸於一).[140] It was unattainable. The situation in process and regularity would be completed. Jin described this condition in the following way:

> … in the supreme ultimate, the situation in process is restored to regularity (*shi gui yu li* 勢歸於理). To restore the situation in process to regularity means that regularity, and the situation in process, are united into one (*li shi he yi* 理勢合一). Under this condition…. regularity is pure regularity (*chun li* 純理) and situation in process is pure situation in process (*chun shi* 純勢). During the process of realization, inclinations do not unfold their natures,

and functions do not fulfil their roles. In spite of the situation in process following regularity, it does not reach it completely.... Since the situation in process does not completely reach regularity, it is a situation in process that is unclear. Since regularity is not reached by the situation in process, it is regularity that carries dirtiness.[141]

The ultimate goals of the supreme ultimate might not be attainable at all for human beings. In his last paragraph, Jin reflected on the condition of human beings from a moral point of view. Regarding *dao*'s evolutionary process, in which not all classes of individuals could survive, Jin stated:

[I]n the supreme ultimate, a good number of realizations will be eliminated. In history, it has been inevitable for some wild animals to be eliminated.... I do not dare to say whether the class of human beings will be eliminated. Regarding the class of human beings, I am rather pessimistic. It does not seem to be a problem of whether the class of human beings will later progress. It seems that human beings, as human beings, are impure. Human beings who attain the nature of human beings are nowadays mostly lonely human beings, who, in their isolation, are tragic [and] superfluous [members] of society.... If we look at the class of human beings, there are too many shortcomings to name. I fear that the class of human beings will be eliminated.[142]

If we return to the problem of induction, we may assume that truth can never be attained. Since the process of being never stops, regularity of the complete process will never be clear. The particular transformation cannot be predicted. Thus, each situation in the process has no necessary point of arrival. However, a minimum of regularity will always be certain, since it is a necessary condition of being and experience.

10. Conclusion

Due to his extensive use of traditional Chinese idioms and terms, especially in *Lun Dao*, Jin's work has the "look" and "feel" of Chinese tradition. He also mimicked the traditional style by creating pseudo-traditional idioms. This could be considered the indigenization of the form of philosophical reasoning. Jin used discursive structures borrowed from Chinese and Western thought as a mode of persuasion in his works. He put his theorems into the form of traditional idioms that employed traditional terminology and structural features. By repeatedly quoting these indigenized theorems, he impressed their philosophical meaning upon intellectual readers accustomed to Chinese traditional texts. The features of the Western analytical school support his logical analysis and construction. In his employment of suffixes, Jin probably drew from traditional Buddhist methods of translation, while additionally incorporating standardized Western terms that fit into his system of suffixes.

These traditional Chinese terms were like old bottles into which Jin poured the new wine of Western thought. They became metaphysical terms which allowed for the definitional vagueness he had observed in his analysis of philosophical terms. Did he add new aspects to the problem of induction by choosing the two dyads of *li—shi* 理—事 in the epistemological sense and *li—shi* 理—勢 in the ontological sense? His concrete intentions are difficult to assess. He was more explicit only regarding potentiality and the suffix "*-ran.*" Given this lack of explanation, the interpretation of his metaphysical terms remains highly subjective; they thus become Jin's own private neologisms. His language game remains hidden, understandable only to Jin.

In *Tao, Nature and Man,* Jin had problems retranslating some of the metaphysical terms he had drawn from Chinese tradition into English. It may thus be assumed that he had at least some kind of connotation in mind, which he wanted to add to the philosophical context, and thus the problem of induction. Through his dichotomies, Jin emphasized the interrelatedness, rather than the clearly defined opposition, of the particular and the universal in the process of being and in the process of acquiring knowledge. This also confirms that Jin did not pursue the somewhat nationalistic aim of preserving or developing Chinese traditional philosophy. He instead employed both Western and Chinese elements—terms and discursive structures—from the tool box of world philosophy.[143] In doing so, he added a new perspective to Western thought and Chinese traditional terms. However, regarding the philosophical problems, Western philosophy set the standards and categories for Jin and served as his point of departure. Jin's works may be considered an attempt to take part in the universal discourse of philosophy. He tried to add associative content drawn from Chinese tradition to this universal discourse.

Jin shaped philosophy as an academic discipline institutionally. For the most part, his contribution to academic philosophy was methodological. Feng Youlan referred to Jin's method of logical analysis.[144] In addition, Zhang Dainian stated that in the 1930s, Jin stressed a high theoretical standard, focusing on neo-realism and logical analysis.[145] Liu

Peiyu identified logical analysis, lucid terms, and careful arguments as characterizing the Tsinghua Philosophy Department.[146] Later, Tsinghua University scholars were influential at the Southwestern United University, contributing most of its lecturers.[147]

Jin Yuelin contributed to modern Chinese philosophical discourse, but also to the process of the indigenization of Western philosophical terms. He remained non-political and had only academic objectives. The last chapter of his *Lun Dao* indicates that Jin had a more moralistic point of view when contemplating the future of the human species. However, when considering his works written before 1949 as a whole, it seems that he remained true to his *Prolegomena*. In it, he characterized philosophy as a "form of play," in which every philosopher tried to play, as far as possible, by the rules. As to the aim of a philosopher's life, he stated in his *Prolegomena*:

> We are not concerned with either success or failure, for with us, the result does not count half as much as the process. That is where play is one the most serious activities in life. Other activities often have some axe to grind. Politics is a sphere … in which people aim at wealth. Patriotism is sometimes a matter of economics … but a game of solitaire in a dingy garret is the pure expression of a soul abandoned to the stream of life.[148]

Jin distinguished his understanding of philosophy from what he considered "impure" philosophy. For him, philosophy is based on logical analysis and logical construction, but at the same time it allows for different motivations and outcomes in philosophical research.[149]

Abbreviations of Book Titles

JYLWJ   *Jin Yuelin wenji* 金岳霖文集. Edited by Jin Yuelin xueshu jijinhui xueshu weiyuanhui. 4 vols. Lanzhou: Renmin chubanshe, 1995.

LD   Jin Yuelin. *Lun Dao* 論道. Beijing: Shangwu yinshuguan, 1987.

LJ   Jin Yuelin. *Luoji* 邏輯. Beijing: Sanlian shudian, 1982.

TNM   Jin Yuelin. *Tao, Nature and Man*. In *JYLWJ*, vol. 2, 568–749.

ZSL   Jin Yuelin. *Zhishilun* 知識論. Beijing: Shangwu yinshuguan, 1982.

ZXYJ   *Zhexue yanjiu* 哲學研究.

Notes

1   This chapter is based on my doctoral dissertation on Jin's ontological answer to the problem of induction in *Lun Dao*, which has been published electronically. See Yvonne Schulz Zinda, "'Li' und 'Shi' als ontologische Antwort auf das Humesche Kausalitätsproblem innerhalb des Induktionsproblems in Jin Yuelins Werk Lun Dao" (PhD dissertation, University of Hamburg, 2001); available from http://www.sub.uni-hamburg.de/opus/volltexte/2004/2206/pdf/Dissertation.pdf; Internet. I thank Barry Steben, John Makeham, Carine Defoort, and Thierry Menard for their valuable comments.

2   See his recollections in Hu Qiaomu (1912–1922), "Xiang Jinlao xuexi, bu duan zhuiqiu jinbu" 向金老學習，不斷追求進步 [Learning from Old Jin, unceasingly striving for progress], in *Jin Yuelin de huiyi yu huiyi Jin Yuelin* 金岳霖的回憶與金岳霖 [Jin Yuelin's memories, and remembering Jin Yuelin], edited by Liu Peiyu 劉培育 (Chengdu: Sichuan jiaoyu chubanshe, 1995), pp. 103–104.

3   Zhang Dainian, "Huiyi Qinghua zhexuexi" 回憶清華哲學系 [Remembering the Tsinghua philosophy department], *Xueshu yuekan* 學術月刊 (Shanghai), 8 (1994), pp. 11–12.

4   See Jin Yuelin, *Jin Yuelin wenji* 金岳霖文集 [Complete works of Jin Yuelin], edited by Jin Yuelin xueshu jijinhui xueshu weiyuanhui 金岳霖學術基金會學術委員會, 4 vols. (Lanzhou: Renmin chubanshe, 1995). Hereafter referred to as *JYLWJ*.

5   See Jin Yuelin, *Lun Dao* (Beijing: Shangwu yinshuguan, 1987), hereafter referred to as *LD*; and Jin Yuelin, *Zhishilun* (Beijing: Shangwu yinshuguan, 1982), hereafter referred to as *ZSL*. Drafts of the first three chapters of *Lun Dao*, which Jin later revised, appeared in the journal *Zhexue pinglun* in 1936 (chapters 1 and 2) and in 1937 (chapter 3). See *JYLWJ*, Vol. 2, pp. 41–59; 61–79; 82–103. Jin finished *Zhishilun* in 1948 because he inadvertently left the manuscript containing the first half, comprising about 450 pages, under a bridge after a bomb raid and was thus forced to start anew. Whereas *Lun*

Dao was published in 1940, *Zhishilun* appeared only in 1982—this was due to the tumultuous political conditions which began soon after Jin sent his manuscript to the publisher. See Jin Yuelin, "Wo zhi xiele sanben shu: Bijiao manyide shi 'Lun Dao,' zui hua gongfude shi 'Zhishilun' " 我只寫了三本書：比較滿意的是論道，最花功夫的是知識論 [I only wrote three books: *Lun Dao* was rather satisfying, *Zhishilun* was the most laborious], in *Jin Yuelin de huiyi*, p. 49.

6   See O. Brière, *Fifty Years of Chinese Philosophy, 1898–1950* (London: George Allen & Unwin Ltd., 1956), pp. 85–88. Also see Hu Jun, "Jin Yuelin's Theory of *Dao*," in *Contemporary Chinese Philosophy*, edited by Chung-Ying Cheng and Nicholas Bunnin (London: Blackwell, 2002), pp. 102–125, which is based on his monograph: Hu Jun 胡軍, *Jin Yuelin* 金岳霖 (Taipei: Dongda tushu gongsi, 1993).

7   For example, see Hu Jun's work above. Other monographs include: Qiao Qingju 喬清舉, *Jin Yuelin Xin Ruxue tixi yanjiu* 金岳霖新儒學體系研究 [Research on Jin Yuelin's system of New Confucianism] (Jinan: Qilu chubanshe, 1999); Wang Zongjiang 王宗江 and An Jimin 安繼民, *Jin Yuelin: Xueshu sixiang pingzhuan* 金岳霖學術思想評傳 [Jin Yuelin: An academic (or intellectual) biography] (Beijing: Beijing tushuguan chubanshe, 1998). For an early overview of his works, see Zhou Liquan 周禮全, "Jin Yuelin tongzhi de zhexue tixi" 金岳霖同志的哲學體系 [Comrade Jin Yuelin's philosophical system], *Zhexue yanjiu* 哲學研究 (Beijing) 1 (1984), pp. 16–19, hereafter referred to as *ZXYJ*.

8   Jin Yuelin, "Weiwu zhexue yu kexue" 唯物哲學與科學 [Materialist philosophy and science], in *JYLWJ*, Vol. 2 [1926], p. 210.

9   For example, both Yang Guorong and Hu Weixi treated Jin and Feng Youlan as representatives of Neo-Positivism. See Yang Guorong 楊國榮, *Shizhengzhuyi yu Zhongguo jindai zhexue* 實證主義與中國近代哲學 [Positivism and modern Chinese philosophy] (Taipei: Wunan tushu chuban gongsi, 1995), p. 155; Hu Weixi 胡偉希, *Jin Yuelin yu Zhongguo shizhengzhuyi renshilun* 金岳霖與中國實證主義認識論 [Jin Yuelin and Chinese positivist epistemology] (Shanghai: Renmin chubanshe, 1988); Wang Zongjiang, "Jin Yuelin yu shizhengzhuyi" 金岳霖與實證主義 [Jin Yuelin and positivism], *ZXYJ* 11 (1993), pp. 47–50; Yu Zhenhua 鬱振華, "Jin Yuelin guanxilun yanjiu" 金岳霖關係論研究 [Research on Jin Yuelin's theory of relations], *ZXYJ* 9 (1993), pp. 49–57.

10 Zhang Dainian recalls that in 1936, during one of the two weekly discussions on whether the task of a philosopher was to establish a universal *Weltanschauung* or to analyze scientific problems, Jin stated that he was going to establish a universal *Weltanschauung* (see Zhang Dainian, "Huiyi Qinghua zhexuexi," p. 11).

11 Zhang Dainian, "'Zhongguo xiandai zhexueshi' xu" 中國現代哲學史·序 [Foreword to *History of Modern Chinese Philosophy*], *ZXYJ* 9 (1992), pp. 64–65; Xu Quanxing 許全興 and Chen Zhannan 陳戰難, *Zhongguo xiandai*

zhexueshi 中國現代哲學史 [History of modern Chinese philosophy] (Beijing: Beijing daxue chubanshe, 1992); and Guo Qiyong 郭齊勇, "Xiong, Feng, Jin, He helun" 熊馮金賀合論 [A joint discussion of Xiong, Feng, Jin, and He], *ZXYJ* 2 (1991), pp. 54–62. This division between anti- and non-Marxists has been traced to Xiao Shafu's 蕭萐父 1983 manuscript, "Zhongguo zhexueshi shiliao yuanliu huiyao" 中國哲學史史料源流彙編 [Collection of documents on the course of historical materials on the history of Chinese philosophy]; see Guo Qiyong, "Xiong, Feng, Jin, He helun," p. 54.

12 For example: Chen Weiping 陳衛平, "Zhongguo zhexue jindaihua de yige cemian" 中國哲學近代化的一個側面 [One aspect of the modernization of Chinese philosophy], *ZXYJ* 9 (1986), pp. 30–36; Chen Xiaolong 陳曉龍, "Zai zhishi yu zhihui zhijian" 在知識與智慧之間 [Between knowledge and wisdom], *Zhongguo zhexueshi* 中國哲學史 (Beijing) 4 (1996), pp. 108–114; Liu Zhuanghu 劉壯虎, "Chuanbo xiandai luoji jianli zhexue tixi: Jin Yuelin xueshu shengya jilüe" 傳播現代邏輯建立哲學體系：金岳霖學術生涯記略 [Propagating modern logic to establish a philosophical system: Brief record of Jin Yuelin's academic career], *Beijing Daxue xuebao* 北京大學學報 2 (1998), pp. 144–146; Guo Qiyong, "Xiong, Feng, Jin, He helun"; Feng Youlan 馮友蘭, *Zhongguo xiandai zhexueshi* 中國現代哲學史 [A history of modern Chinese philosophy] (Hong Kong: Zhonghua shuju, 1992), pp. 179–204; Ning Lina 寧莉娜, "Lun Jin Yuelin luoji fangfa de kuajiexing de tezheng" 論金岳霖邏輯方法的跨界性的特徵 [On the characteristics of the cross-over in Jin Yuelin's logical method], *ZXYJ* 1 (2006), pp. 48–52.

13 Fang Songhua 放鬆華, "Jin Yuelin *Lun Dao* zhi Zhongguo zhexue shuxing de yidou" 金岳霖《論道》之中國哲學屬性的疑竇 [Doubt [as to whether] Jin Yuelin's *Lun Dao* belongs to Chinese philosophy], *Xueshu yuekan* 學術月刊 2 (2004), pp. 12–14.

14 His textbook on logic was originally published in 1935. See Jin Yuelin, *Luoji* 邏輯 [Logic] (4th ed.; Beijing: Sanlian shudian, 1982), hereafter referred to as *LJ*. It became part of the Tsinghua curriculum.

15 *ZSL*, p. 830 (4). Jin divided his works into sections. The number of the specific section referred to will be given in parentheses following the page number. Jin's understanding seems contrary to Fu Sinian's conception of language controlling philosophy, as pointed out by Carine Defoort in her chapter in this volume.

16 David Hume (1711–1776), *A Treatise of Human Nature* (2nd ed.; Oxford: Oxford University Press, 1978), p. 421.

17 *ZSL*, p. 419 (4).

18 Zhang Dainian, "Huiyi Qinghua zhexuexi," pp. 11, 13. See also Xiaoqing Diana Lin's chapter in this volume for discussion of some of the Qinghua (Tsinghua) philosophers. Concerning the strong methodological similarities between the otherwise different works of Feng Youlan and Jin Yuelin, see Yvonne Schulz Zinda, "Preliminary Considerations on Two Modern

Approaches to *Li*: Jin Yuelin's *Lun Dao* and Feng Youlan's *Xin Lixue*," *Asian and African Studies* (Ljubljana), 1–2 (2007), pp. 127–140.

19 The following biographical data is based on Liu Peiyu, "Jin Yuelin nianbiao" 金岳霖年表 [Chronology of Jin Yuelin], in *Jin Yuelin de huiyi*, pp. 379–431.

20 Jin Yuelin, "The Financial Powers of Governors," in *JYLWJ*, Vol. 1 [1918], pp. 1–34.

21 Jin Yuelin, *The Political Theory of Thomas Hill Green*, in *JYLWJ*, Vol. 1 [1920], pp. 35–209.

22 His philosophical explorations included texts such as those by Hobbes, Rousseau, Montesquieu, Adam Smith, and Locke, as well as by Kant, Hume, Bradley, and Green. All of these played a significant role in the discussions of the analytical school. In *Zhishilun* and *Lun Dao,* Jin discussed the ideas of the different philosophical branches of idealism, empiricism and the philosophy of science. These included Kant's "*a priori*"; Hume's theory of cause and effect, and his problem of induction; Bradley's internal relations; and the more popular Eddington's *Nature of the Physical World* and Bridgman's *Logic of Modern Physics*, to name but a few.

23 *LD*, p. 4. In his foreword to *Lun Dao*, Jin outlined his philosophical development (pp. 1–18). He seems to have followed Russell, who had also gone through an idealistic phase until 1912, following T. H. Green and then later renouncing him. See Peter Hylton, *Russell, Idealism, and the Emergence of Analytical Philosophy* (Oxford: Clarendon Press, 1990), p. 8. In fact, Jin was preoccupied with Russell's philosophy throughout his life. The manuscript of the monograph which he started in the 1950s and revised several times was published posthumously in 1988 by his students Zhou Liquan and Feng Qi 馮契, under the title *Russell's Philosophy.* See Jin Yuelin, *Luosu zhexue* 羅素哲學 [Russell's philosophy], in *JYLWJ*, Vol. 4 [1988], pp. 454–702.

24 Jin Yuelin, "Feng Youlan *Zhongguo zhexueshi* shencha baogao" 馮友蘭中國哲學史審查報告 [Review of Feng Youlan's *History of Philosophy*], in *JYLWJ*, Vol. 1 [1934], pp. 627–628. In the course of the debate on the legitimacy of Chinese philosophy (2000–2005), Chen Weiping rediscovered "Jin Yuelin's problem," discussing Hu Shi's doubt in the ancient, and Feng Youlan's translation of the ancient, versus the "creative culturalism" of Zhang Dainian. See Chen Weiping, "'Jin Yuelin wenti' yu Zhongguo zhexueshi xueke dulixingde tanqiu" 「金岳霖問題」與中國哲學史學科獨立性的探求 ["Jin Yuelin's Problem" and the search for scientific independence in the history of Chinese philosophy], *Xueshu yuekan* 學術月刊 12 (2005), pp. 11–20.

25 In reaction to C. I. Lewis' article on alternative systems of logic, in two different articles Jin criticised Lewis' pragmatic approach to logical systems. One of Jin's articles appeared in the well-known philosophical journal *The Monist.* See C. I. Lewis, "Alternative Systems of Logic," *The Monist* 4 (1932), pp. 481–307; Jin Yuelin, "Note on Alternative Systems of Logic," in *JYLWJ*, Vol. 1 [1934], pp. 603–606 (it appeared in *The Monist* under the name Y. L. Chin); and Jin Yuelin, "Bu xiangrong de luoji xitong" 不相容的邏輯系統

[Non-coherent logical systems], in *JYLWJ*, Vol. 2 [1934], pp. 607–624. The same opinion can also be found in *LD*, pp. 23–24 (1.5).

26 Regarding Jin Yuelin's work, I prefer to speak of stylistic devices. This is because they are either too singular, as in the case of the suffixes which indicate the influence of Buddhist translation practices, or, in the case of Western philosophical genres, not sufficiently explored to tell us about specific influences. In his work on style in philosophy, Manfred Frank indicates that philosophical texts also bear personal trade-marks and different styles, which are comparable to the genres and styles in literary texts. See Manfred Frank, *Stil in der Philosophie* (Stuttgart: Philipp Reclam Jun., 1992), p. 7.

27 Wittgenstein's *Tractatus* was subsequently translated and published in 1927 in the journal *Zhexue pinglun* (1.5 and 1.6).

28 *ZSL*, p. 90 (1).

29 Within the context of Buddhist terms, the suffix *xiang* describes qualities. It is translated by Soothill as a "distinctive mark, sign," an "indication, characteristic," and a "designation." See W. S. Soothill and L. Hodous, *A Dictionary of Chinese Buddhist Terms* (London: Kegan Paul, Trunch, Trubner & Co., 1937), p. 309. Jin employed the suffix to describe something "without quality" (*wuxiang* 無相), the "universal quality" (*gongxiang* 共相), and the "particular" (*shuxiang* 殊相). In *Tao, Nature and Man*, Jin referred to *neng* as "devoid of quality," which is equivalent to his *wuxiang*. See Jin Yuelin, *Tao, Nature and Man*, in *JYLWJ*, Vol. 2, p. 598; hereafter referred to as *TNM*.

30 The suffix *guan* may have been based on the translation of the Sanskrit term *vipaśyanā*. In the Buddhist context, *guan* is translated as "to look into, to examine, to contemplate" (see Soothill and Hodous, *A Dictionary of Chinese Buddhist Terms*, p. 489). Within the context of Jin's thought, the suffix may be understood to mean "perspective." For Jin, nature "had perspective" (*youguan* 有觀) because it was the subject that added perspective in the process of perception (*ZSL*, p. 733 (1)). This was, however, based on a world "without perspective" (*wuguan* 無觀), which may account for Jin's view that there were external factors independent from perception (*ibid.*, p. 483 (2)). There were "subjective perspectives" (*zhuguan* 主觀) and "objective perspectives" (*keguan* 客觀) (*ibid.*, p. 472 (3)), which at the time were already standard terms used in the translation of Western expressions. For Jin, there were various groups of perceiving subjects. These included human beings, different animal groups, and groups sorted according to sense organs. These groups held a "collective perspective" (*leiguan* 類觀) concerning the same subjects, which was understood as the objective perspective. Individual subjects within a group had an "individual perspective" (*geti guan* 個體觀), which Jin referred to as a subjective perspective (*ibid.*, p. 473 (4)).

31 Jin employed the suffix *ti* to describe an isolated, contained entity. This could be an "individual" (*geti* 個體) or a "concrete entity" (*juti* 具體), which he defined in *Lun Dao* as the precursor to the individual (*LD*, chapter 3). Jin

distinguished "spatial subjects" (*dongxi* 東西) from "temporal entities" (*shiti* 事體) and events (*ZSL*, pp. 600–614). All entities were contained in one "whole entity" (*zhengti* 整體) (*LD*, p. 218 (8.20)), which was equivalent to the universe. At the same time, *ti* was one of the metaphysical key terms in *Lun Dao*, as will be discussed later.

32 W. A. C. H. Dobson, *A Dictionary of the Chinese Particles* (Toronto: University of Toronto Press, 1974), p. 559.

33 Jin Yuelin, "Prolegomena," in *JYLWJ*, Vol. 1 [1927], p. 272.

34 *LD*, p. 164 (6.26).

35 It is not quite clear what Jin meant by "secondary text" (*zhuwen* 注文). However, the terms he mentioned were derived from his epistemology and his ontology.

36 Jin Yuelin, "*Lun Dao* yishu de zong pipan" 《論道》一書的總批判 [General criticisms of the book *Lun Dao*], in *JYLWJ*, Vol. 4 [1958], pp. 186–238.

37 Jin's own translation, as found in *TNM*, p. 676.

38 See, for example, *LD*, p. 201 (8.7); and *ZSL*, p. 512 (3).

39 In *PPTS*, *juan* 8, p. 18.

40 Feng Youlan quoted in the introduction of Zhongguo shehui kexueyuan zhexue yanjiusuo 中國社會科學院哲學研究所, ed., *Jin Yuelin xueshu sixiang yanjiu* 金岳霖學術思想研究 [Studies on Jin Yuelin's academic thought] (Chengdu: Sichuan renmin chubanshe, 1987), p. 1.

41 In his self-criticism, Jin talked about the "play of concepts" (*gainian de youju* 概念的遊劇). See Jin Yuelin, "*Lun Dao* yishu de zong pipan," p. 358).

42 Joachim Kurtz, "Coming to Terms with Logic: The Naturalization of an Occidental Notion in China," in *New Terms for New Ideas: Western Knowledge and Lexical Change in Late Imperial China*, edited by Michael Lackner, Iwo Amelung, and Joachim Kurtz (Leiden: Brill, 2001), pp. 145–175.

43 The Chinese term for "induction" was most likely drawn from the Japanese; see Inoue Tetsujirō 井上哲次郎, *Tetsugaku jii* 哲學字彙 [Dictionary of philosophy] (Tokyo: Tōyōkan, 1884), p. 59. Barry Steben's chapter in this volume shows that the Japanese translation for the term may be traced back to Nishi Amane. In China, it seems to have been employed only since the beginning of the twentieth century. See, for example, Wang Rongbao 王榮寶 and Ye Lan 葉瀾, *Xin Erya* 新爾雅 [New *Erya*] (Shanghai: Mingquanshe, 1903), p. 63. In an early philosophical dictionary we find that *xianshi zhexue* 現實哲學 refers to the German term "Aktualitätsphilosophie." See Fan Bingqing 樊炳清, *Zhexue da cidian* 哲學大辭典 [Dictionary of philosophy] (Shanghai: Shangwu yinshuguan, 1926). This information is derived from the database created by Michael Lackner's project "Chinese as a Scientific Language" at the Universities of Göttingen and Erlangen.

44 Proof that Jin created neologisms comes, for example, from the case of "inversion." Jin continued to employ the English terms "inversion" and "inverse": "[d. 'Inversion'.] I am not sure how best to translate this—one might say that the subject of the original proposition is negated and made

the subject [of the new proposition] so that the new proposition is the 'inverse' of the original proposition" (*LJ*, p. 25).

45 It can only be assumed that Jin created *shuxiang* (particular) to serve in opposition to the term "universal." It was not included in Fan Bingqing's *Dictionary of Philosophy*. However, even if the two Chinese terms did already exist as equivalents for the Western ones, it had not been for long. The original Buddhist connotation was presumably still in the back of the Chinese reader's mind. In Jin's works, the dichotomy should be understood as having a meaning equivalent to the "universal" and "particular" in the ontological sense; more specifically, in the context of Russell's thought.

46 Jin might have borrowed this term from contemporary evolutionary theory. Sewall Wright (1889–1988) employed the term "genetic drift" to describe the phenomenon of random breeding. This explains why the "fittest" might not be represented in subsequent generations of a small population, since features or genotypes can become the norm by pure chance. See Michael Ruse, *The Oxford Handbook of Philosophy of Biology* (Oxford: Oxford University Press, 2008), p. 44.

47 *TNM*, p. 684.

48 *LD*, p. 17.

49 Jin translated both terms into English. See *ZSL*, p. 335 (1).

50 *Ibid.*, pp. 790–791 (3).

51 *Ibid.*, p. 796 (3, 4).

52 *Ibid.*, pp. 800–801 (3).

53 *Ibid.*, p. 810 (2, 3, 4).

54 *Ibid.*, p. 811 (1), 816 (2).

55 *Ibid.*, pp. 816–817 (3).

56 Jin Yuelin, *TNM*, p. 569. During his fellowships at Harvard University and the University of Chicago in 1943, Jin wrote a long essay in English entitled *Tao, Nature and Man*. This contains a number of ideas from his earlier work, *Lun Dao*. However, in *Tao, Nature and Man* Jin formulated these into an abridged version and added a chapter on nature and man.

57 *LD*, p. 2.

58 Jin wrote: "The following chapters intend to deal with a number of idea.... We shall first deal with our notion of facts, then with that of truth. We shall assume the world or at least a part of it to be constantly and continuously changing, and we shall analyse our notion of change. Hence we proceed to a discussion of time, space and motion, and will conclude this book by a disquisition on metaphysics and science" (Jin Yuelin, "Prolegomena," p. 281).

59 Jin Yuelin, "Xiumo zhishilun de piping: Xianyu *Treatise* zhong de zhishilun" 休謨知識論的批評：限於 Treatise 中的知識論 [Criticism of Hume's epistemology: Restricted to the epistemology in *Treatise*] (1928), in *Jin Yuelin de xueshu lunwen xuan* 金岳霖的學術論文選 [Jin Yuelin's selected academic papers], edited by Liu Peiyu 劉培育 (Beijing: Zhongguo shehui kexue

chubanshe, 1990), pp. 195–239. He discussed five topics: 1) ideas (*yixiang* 意像); 2) reality (*shizai* 實在); 3) relations (*guanxi* 關係); 4) experience (*jingyan* 經驗); and 5) theories and facts (*lilun yu shishi* 理論與事實).

60 The textbook is divided into four chapters. In the first two chapters, he described traditional Western logics. He further critically assessed the theories of modern logicians such as Boole, Johnson, and Ladd-Franklin. In the third chapter, he introduced mathematical logic using propositions and calculations taken from Whitehead and Russell's *Principia Mathematica*.

61 Jin used the term *zhengshi* in opposition to the proof within the system (*zhengming* 證明), which was independent of the outside world (*LJ*, pp. 224–225). In his epistemology, he translated the first as "verification" and the latter as "proof" (*ZSL*, pp. 53 (2)).

62 See *LD*, p. 2. This statement can also be found in *LJ*, p. 245 (B).

63 *ZSL*, p. 420 (1).

64 Russell merely added that "there is no instance to the contrary." See Bertrand Russell, *Our Knowledge of the External World* (London: Routledge, 1993), p. 225.

65 *ZSL*, p. 419 (1); He repeated this opinion in an essay written in 1940. See Jin Yuelin, "The Principle of Induction and the A Priori," in *JYLWJ*, Vol. 2 [1940], p. 371.

66 *ZSL*, p. 419 (4).

67 For example, see *ibid.*, pp. 62–63 (A 2).

68 See *ibid.*, p. 421 (4); and Jin Yuelin, "The Principle of Induction and the A Priori," pp. 358, 360. For Russell's position, see Bertrand Russell, *The Problem of Philosophy* (9th ed.; Oxford: Oxford University Press, 1980), pp. 37–38.

69 *ZSL*, pp. 451–452 (1).

70 Jin made a terminological distinction between Hume's concept of "ideas" (意像 *yixiang*), which he considered less abstract, and his own concept of "ideas" (*yinian*), which was similar to that of Russell (see *LD*, p. 4).

71 *ZSL*, pp. 456–457 (2). The example of the black swan and its conclusion can also be found in Bertrand Russell, *The Problem of Philosophy*, pp. 37–38, 41. Whereas Russell stressed probability, Jin placed emphasis on the method of categorization, which made the principle reliable. He argued along the lines of C. I. Lewis, whom he mentioned in his foreword to *Lun Dao*. Hu Jun (*Jin Yuelin*, p. 345) pointed to his *Mind and the World-Order* as a possible influence. In fact, chapters 8 and 11 of this work seem to accord with Jin's attitude. See C. I. Lewis, *Mind and the World-Order: Outline of a Theory of Knowledge* (London: Charles Scribner's Sons, 1928).

72 *ZSL*, pp. 452–453 (2, 3, 4). In an earlier version of the first chapter published in *Zhexue pinglun* in 1936, Jin did not make this distinction (Vol. 2 of *JYLWJ*, pp. 41–59).

73 *ZSL*, p. 450 (2). In his essay published in 1940, he enhanced the status of the principle by stating that when time stopped, the principle would simply be

unable to be applied, yet would still remain valid (Jin Yuelin, "The Principle of Induction and the A Priori," p. 369).

74 *ZSL*, pp. 452–453 (2, 3, 4). Jin employed the English terms in *TNM*, p. 618.

75 *ZSL*, p. 677 (2). This is similar to Russell's arguments. See Bertrand Russell, *Our Knowledge of the External World*, pp. 221, 230; and Bertrand Russell, *The Problem of Philosophy*, p. 38.

76 *LD*, p. 12.

77 *ZSL*, p. 18 (4). The first chapters (1–5) deal with the basis of his epistemology and conditions of perception, treating the idea of the given as the material of perception (chapter 3); the means of perception in the direct level of experience (chapter 4); and the theory of acquaintance (*renshi* 認識) (chapter 5). The following chapters are devoted to the mind's relationship with the outside world, dealing with the process of thought (chapter 6), and the notions of "description" (*mozhuang* 摹狀) and "prescriptions" (*guilü* 規律) (chapter 7). This culminates in a chapter on induction, which Jin introduced as the sole tool of "reception" (*jieshou* 接受) in the gaining of knowledge (chapter 8). Chapter 9 considers nature from an epistemological point of view; chapter 10 deals with the major categories related to the perception of space and time; chapter 11 discusses quality, relation, things, events, and change; chapter 12 takes up cause and effect; and chapter 13 deals with quantity. Jin also describes the realm of facts (chapter 14), the role of language (chapter 15), and the verification of propositions (chapter 16). In chapter 17, he discusses the various definitions of truth.

78 *Ibid.*, p. 18 (4).

79 *Ibid.*, p. 733 (1). As described above, these were comprised of different groups of individuals, as well as modes of perception (such as visual, aural, and so on).

80 *Ibid.*, p. 734 (4).

81 *Ibid.*, p. 733 (1).

82 Jin translated *xianshi* as "realization" or to "realize." See *TNM*, p. 640. Contrary to the conventional meaning of this word, Jin particularly emphasised that *xianshi* was not related to *xianzai*, or something in existence. See *LD*, p. 64 (2.30).

83 *ZSL*, p. 483 (2).

84 *LD*, p. 65 (2.30).

85 *ZSL*, p. 846 (4).

86 *Ibid.*, p. 745 (1).

87 *Ibid.*, p. 849 (4).

88 *Ibid.*, p. 943 (4).

89 *Ibid.*, p. 18 (4).

90 The expression "*shi li bu er* 事理不二" (*shi* and *li* are not divided) may come to mind. See Ciyi 慈怡, ed., *Foguang da cidian* 佛光大辭典 [Great dictionary of Buddhism], 8 vols. (Beijing: Shumu wenxian chubanshe, 1990), pp. 3044–3045). Another Huayan statement which expresses the relationship between

the two terms in a similar way is "*li shi wu ai* 理事無礙" (*li* and *shi* do not obstruct each other). See Dan Lusthaus, "Buddhist Philosophy, Chinese," in *Routledge Encyclopedia of Philosophy*, edited by E. Craig (London: Routledge, 1998). This is also available from http://www.rep.routledge.com/article/ G002SECT8. Accessed 9 September 2009. Unfortunately, Jin did not offer his views on these terms.

91 *Ibid.*, pp. 877–878 (1, 2).

92 *Ibid.*, pp. 346 (3), 951 (3). Jin made a distinction regarding the quality of truth. For him, the emphasis of metaphysical works was on unity; thus their systems of thought had to be coherent (*rongqia* 融洽). Other works, however, such as epistemological ones, had to be consistent (*yizhi* 一致). See *ibid.*, p. 897 (1). Jin translated and discussed both terms in 1935. See Jin Yuelin, "Guanyu zhenjia de yige yijian" 關於真假的一個意見 [An opinion regarding truth and falsehood], in *JYLWJ*, Vol. 2 [1935], p. 21.

93 *ZSL*, pp. 774–776 (section 2, 3).

94 *Ibid.*, p. 952 (4).

95 *Ibid.*, pp. 951–952 (3).

96 *Ibid.*, p. 952 (4).

97 *Ibid.*, p. 878 (2).

98 For example, in the case of the *ti-yong* dyad, he did not extensively define the terms, even in comparison to other Chinese traditional ones—nor did he give any examples to illustrate their meaning.

99 *Lun Dao* is divided into 8 chapters, which discuss the following topics: the logical and metaphysical principles for the constitution of being (chapter 1–2); the static (chapters 3–5) and the dynamic (chapter 6) conditions of the process of being; and the relative (chapter 7) as well as the absolute (chapter 8) framework of the process of realization.

100 *ZSL*, pp. 534 (2), 535 (4). The term "*shiwu*" is an abbreviation of "events" (*shiti* 事體) and "things" (*dongxi* 東西).

101 Jin Yuelin, "*Lun Dao* yishu de zong pipan," p. 209.

102 Jin seems to have taken a similar approach to ontology as Whitehead did in his *Process and Reality*, a revised version of which was published in 1929. He at least knew of Whitehead's work, for he mentioned a Chinese translation by Qu Junong 瞿菊農 (d. 1976) in his article on facts in 1931. He merely made note of the term "*shisu* 事素" as a translation for Whitehead's "event." However, Whitehead does not seem to have had a deep influence on Jin's thought. See Jin Yuelin, "Lun shishi" 論事實 [On facts], in *JYLWJ*, Vol. 1 [1931], p. 503. In the outline of his philosophical development, Jin did not elaborate on Whitehead any further.

103 *LD*, p. 198 (8.5).

104 *Ibid.*, p. 199 (8.5).

105 *Ibid.*, pp. 158–159 (6.22).

106 *Ibid.*, p. 158 (6.21).

107 *Ibid.*, pp. 201–203 (8.7).

108 *Ibid.*, p. 203 (8.7).

109 For example, see James Pusey, *China and Charles Darwin* (Cambridge, MA: Harvard University Press, 1983).

110 *LD*, p. 220 (8.21).

111 Jin's own translation in *TNM*, p. 625. "*Dao*-differentiated" refers to *dao* undergoing a process of infinite division in the world of being. It represents the myriad things and events that are united once more by the "*dao*-one."

112 *Mengzi, juan* 3, B, 2. See also D. C. Lau, trans., *Mencius*, 2 vols. (Hong Kong: Chinese University Press, 1984), Vol. 1, p. 117.

113 *LD*, pp. 17–18.

114 *Ibid.*, p. 41 (1.26).

115 *Ibid.*, p. 24 (1.7).

116 *Ibid.*, p. 25 (1.7).

117 *Ibid.*, pp. 23–24 (1.5)

118 *Ibid.*, pp. 39–40 (1.25).

119 *Ibid.*, pp. 36–37 (1.16).

120 Jin Yuelin, "Shi zhi yuanze" 勢至原則 [The principle of the arrival of *shi*], in *Jin Yuelin de xueshu lunwen xuan* [1943], p. 349.

121 *LD*, pp. 40–41 (1.26).

122 *Ibid.*, pp. 73–75 (3.9).

123 Jin's translation in *TNM*, p. 684.

124 Jin's translation in *ibid.*, p. 689. He understood both as an objective expression of "*yun* 運" and "*ming* 命." See *LD*, pp. 177–178 (7.11). He equated these with "luck" and "fate"—see *TNM*, pp. 689, 694.

125 *LD*, pp. 178–180 (7.12).

126 *Ibid.*, p. 185 (7.18).

127 *Ibid.*, pp. 220–221 (8.22).

128 *Ibid.*, p. 217 (8.18). There was a famous dispute between the Neo-Confucian philosophers Zhu Xi and Lu Jiuyuan 陸九淵 (1139–1193) about how to interpret the conjunction "*er*" connecting "*wuji*" and "*taiji*." Zhu Xi saw in *wuji* a pre-condition to *taiji*, whereas Lu Jiuyuan thought of both as having the same meaning. See Anne Cheng, *Histoire de la pensée chinoise* (Paris: Èditions du Seuil, 1997), pp. 417–418, 475–476. Jin understood the two terms as "simultaneous" conditions for *dao*-one. However, Jin spoke about "*wuji er taiji*" as an "idiom" (*chengyu* 成語). He did not want to delve into the original meaning. See *LD*, p. 217 (8.18). Jin did not even refer to the dispute when discussing his interpretation of the conjunction. This shows that his definitions of the terms had a subjective basis.

129 *Ibid.*, pp. 193–194 (8.3, 8.4).

130 *Ibid.*, p. 197 (8.4).

131 *Ibid.*, pp. 204–205 (8.8).

132 In the case of Xiong Shili, in chapter 6 Thierry Meynard discusses a similar solipsism which resulted from going back and forth between different traditions.

133 There is a similar example in *Mencius*, in which the nature of man is described as being like water, which can flow in different directions. It states, however, that the nature of man is to do good, just as the nature of water is to flow downwards. See *Mengzi, juan* 6, A, 2. and the translation in D.C. Lau, trans., *Mencius*, Vol. 2, p. 223.

134 *LD*, p. 205 (8.9).

135 *Ibid.*, p. 204 (8.8).

136 Another, remarkable point can be made about the term *"xing."* Jin again played with this by placing it in the context of the standardized translations of Western philosophical terms. In chapter 3 of *Lun Dao,* he declared that *xing* had two meanings. The first was "primary quality" (*zhuxing* 主性), which he described in the narrow sense of "nature" (*xing* 性). The second was "secondary quality" (*shuxing* 屬性), which was nature in the wider sense of "quality." Jin continued to introduce both terms as "qualities" (*xingzhi* 性質), which was the technical term for the Western concept of quality. Jin's translation of *shuxing* as qualities and *zhuxing* as nature was presumably not meant to be literal. See *ibid.*, p. 86 (3.22). Otherwise, it is unclear as to why he made a terminological distinction between "qualities" and "quality" (*xingzhi*). He might have intended to distinguish what he considered the epistemological term *shuxing* and the ontological term *zhuxing.* Jin subsequently employed *xing* (nature) when talking about metaphysics and the process of unfolding one's nature, and *xingzhi* (quality) when referring to qualities in an epistemological sense.

137 *Ibid.*, pp. 199–200 (8.6).

138 *Ibid.*, pp. 214–215 (8.17).

139 See W. S. Soothill and L. Hodous, *A Dictionary of Chinese Buddhist Terms*, p. 210. Again, Jin seems to have drawn on the Buddhist connotation.

140 *LD*, pp. 213–214 (8.16).

141 *Ibid.*, pp. 215–216 (8.17).

142 *Ibid.*, pp. 219–220 (8.21).

143 In the case of Xiong Shili, in chapter 6 Thierry Meynard makes the similar observation that Xiong also used traditional Buddhist terms, detaching them from their original meanings to serve in his philosophical explorations.

144 See Liu Peiyu, *Jin Xuelin de huiyi*, p. 392. No further details are provided.

145 Zhang Dainian, "Huiyi Qinghua zhexuexi," pp. 11–12.

146 The first characteristic Liu mentions, which also accords with Jin's work, is that philosophy was not considered "learning" to be subjected to scientific research; rather, it was understood as something to be created. See Liu Peiyu, "Jin Yuelin de weixue" 金岳霖的為學 [Jin Yuelin's scholarly research], *Shandong shifandaxue xuebao (Renwen shehui kexue ban)* 山東師範大學學報 (人文社會科學版) 5 (2003), p. 5.

147 Xie Yong 謝泳, "Xi'nan Lianda de sheli" 西南聯大的設立 [The establishment of the Southwestern University], in *20 shiji Zhongguo zhishifenzi shilun* 20世

紀中國知識份子史論 [On the history of 20th century Chinese intellectuals], edited by Xu Jilin 許紀霖 (Beijing: Xinxing chubanshe, 2005), p. 396.

148 Jin Yuelin, "Prolegomena," p. 282.

149 *Ibid.*, pp. 281–282. He pointed to the example of Bergson, "whose poetry is supposed to take the form of philosophy." He mocks Bergson's "Élan vital [that] has successfully penetrated into the perfumed atmosphere of pink tea parties," and states that his philosophy is regarded by most members of his own profession as vitiated through self-destruction (*Ibid.*, p. 240).

Part III: The Critics' Voices

Chapter 9

Fu Sinian's Views on Philosophy, Ancient Chinese Masters, and Chinese Philosophy[1]

Carine Defoort

"China did not originally have a so-called philosophy. Thank god our people had such healthy habits."[2] This provocative statement, made by Fu Sinian 傅斯年 (1896–1950) in a letter to a good friend, shows the young author in all his self-confidence, originality, and vigour. "Chinese philosophy" had just been created or (re)discovered by his contemporaries as an academic sub-discipline through the study of the nation's ancient masters (*zi* 子). Its creation, guided by major figures such as Hu Shi 胡適 (1891–1962) and Feng Youlan 馮友蘭 (1895–1990), demanded an adaptation of past Chinese thought to a modern Western paradigm, as in other academic fields. This forced adaptation did not, in general, diminish the popularity of the new category of "Chinese philosophy" at the beginning of the twentieth century. But, as Fu Sinian's bold statement shows, there also existed a counter-current which rejected applying the label "philosophy" to the thought of the ancient Chinese masters. Whereas the academic sub-discipline of Chinese philosophy, at Chinese universities, owes its success to the influence of personalities such as Hu Shi and Feng Youlan,[3] Fu Sinian was the first clear and radical voice to oppose it. This resistance, although far from strong enough to stop the emergence of the new discipline, has left its mark on the field. Institutionally, he contributed to the rejection of Chinese philosophy as a field of study at Academia Sinica (Zhongyang yanjiuyuan 中央研究院), and intellectually, he was a forerunner of the contemporary resistance to the identification of ancient Chinese thought with the foreign discipline of philosophy.

Fu Sinian's institutional influence was both direct and indirect. When Academia Sinica was established in 1928, led by Cai Yuanpei 蔡元培 (1868–1940), Cai had planned to include an Institute of Philosophy, but this ultimately did not happen. According to Mou Zongsan 牟宗三

(1909–1995), this change of plan was made under the influence of Hu Shi.[4] Although Hu's *Outline of the History Chinese Philosophy* (*Zhongguo zhexueshi dagang* 中國哲學史大綱) had been a paragon of the newly created discipline in 1919, as we will see below, Hu Shi changed his mind about the label of "Chinese philosophy" under the influence of his former student and close friend Fu Sinian. As the director of the Institute of History and Philology, Fu also directly influenced the rejection of philosophy by insisting on the importance of objective data and neutral facts over reflection and interpretation. Both decisions resulted from a particular view of science and research which Hu Shi and Fu Sinian shared with several other scholars, mostly trained abroad, who were responsible for determining Academia Sinica's policies. Since then, the dominance of this view has frustrated other humanist scholars such as Mou Zongsan,[5] Xu Fuguan 徐復觀 (1903–1982), and Li Minghui 李明輝 (1953–). In the 1960s, Xu Fuguan reported that when he criticized the anti-philosophy tendency at the Institute of History and Philology and suggested the establishment of an Institute for the History of Chinese Thought at Academia Sinica, he was met only with ridicule and abuse.[6] A Preparatory Office of the Institute of Chinese Literature and Philosophy was eventually established in 1989 and formally inaugurated as an Institute in 2002.[7] But the title of this institute (which indicates that it is only half dedicated to philosophy), its research foci, and the experiences of scholars all serve to confirm the Academia Sinica's enduring anti-philosophy stance.[8]

Fu Sinian's second point of contemporary relevance lies in the fact that he was a forerunner of the opinion, increasingly prevalent in contemporary discourse, that ancient Chinese thought should not be lightly subjected to modern Western academic nomenclature and categories. Around the turn of the twenty-first century, the "legitimacy of Chinese philosophy" (*Zhongguo zhexue hefaxing* 中國哲學合法性) became a major topic of debate among scholars. Some felt that ancient Chinese insights were tainted by twentieth-century philosophical neologisms such as "humanism," "realism," "pragmatism," "scepticism," "utilitarianism," "principle," "essence," "definitions," "reason," "truth," "subjective," "objective," "rational," "phenomenon," "inference," "deduction," and so forth. As a result of attempts to make sense of Chinese masters by selective interpretation in the modern philosophical fashion, these masters had become increasingly disfigured, like "feet being forced into small shoes" (*xue zu shi lü* 削足適履).[9] Some scholars also stressed the gap between the merely theoretical business of academic Chinese philosophy and its object of study, namely the Chinese masters, whose reflections were always imbedded in a way of life, self-cultivation, rituals, studies, artistic pursuits, or governmental responsibilities. The desire to "speak for oneself" and "speak about oneself," as Zhang Liwen 張立文 put it, instead of merely applying foreign interpretations to Chinese texts, emerged from these considerations.[10] Fu Sinian's rejection of philosophical jargon—including the term "philosophy"—in the interpretation of ancient Chinese texts went further than a preference for indigenous terms over so-called imperialistically imposed neologisms. As we will see, his concern was not only with intercultural but also inter-temporal misfits. His tentative use of the expression "debaters of policies" (*fangshu lunzhe* 方術論者) for the Warring States masters was meant to avoid the use of Western terms imported from Japan, as well as categories invented in the Han, Song, and Qing dynasties.

1. Methodological Choices and Reflections

During his lifetime, Fu Sinian did not stand alone in his criticism of the category of "Chinese philosophy,"[11] but he was its most radical detractor in Chinese academia, and he has not been adequately studied in this respect.[12] There are obvious reasons for this lacuna. First, since Fu was against the very idea of Chinese philosophy for most of his academic life, he naturally seldom focused on this topic. His interests rather lay with history and linguistics. Therefore, Fu's views on Chinese philosophy have to be collected from the margins of his work: letters, a few articles, introductions to books, and policy statements. Second, perhaps because of this marginal status, his views on Chinese philosophy were not very stable or consistent during the ten years in which he occasionally expressed his thoughts on this topic (mainly between 1918 and 1928). Like the statement quoted at the beginning of this chapter, Fu's remarks on the matter are often somewhat vehement, provocative, and aimed at deconstructing dominant views rather than supporting the construction of a new discipline.

In order to trace the views of this remarkably clever and temperamental scholar during the formative decade of his thought and in the broader context of China's intellectual history, three methodological choices have guided this analysis. First of all, the focus has been deliberately restricted. The present discussion is thus not representative of Fu's whole person—be it as intellectual, administrator, publisher, politician, or academic. Most of his academic achievements, mainly in the fields of history and linguistics, are discussed only in relation to his strong, but infrequently articulated views, on the non-existence of Chinese philosophy.[13] Considering the remarkable evolution of Fu's views, a second decision was made to distinguish three periods: first, his student years at Peking University (1916–1919); then his years spent as a student abroad in London and Berlin (1920–1926); and finally, his return home and assuming academic positions (1927–1929). A third choice was made to concentrate on three topics in particular. This is because Fu's rejection of the category of Chinese philosophy was determined by his insights into two very different fields of study, at least in his eyes: on the one hand, the ancient Chinese masters, with which he was very well acquainted, having been tutored by his grandfather as a child; and, on the other hand, the discipline of philosophy, which he discovered at Peking University thanks to other students[14] and the young professor Hu Shi, who had just returned from the United States. Hence the tripartite division of this presentation of Fu's views: ancient Chinese masters, philosophy, and, finally, Chinese philosophy.

Two more reflections are presented at the outset of this analysis. The first is that, despite Fu's own preference for an objective, scientific approach, it is remarkable how much his own views on these three topics are evaluative, prescriptive, and sometimes emotional. The strong commitment with which he writes is probably due to his personal temperament; to the critical situation of his nation, which had been humiliated by the West and was threatened by Japan; and to his own feelings of responsibility concerning this situation. Therefore, it is worthwhile not only to focus on Fu's *descriptions* of the Chinese masters and of philosophy, but also on his *evaluation* of them. These two aspects, which Charles Stevenson labelled "descriptive meaning" and "emotive meaning,"[15] are, of course, closely related. When, in his youth, Fu portrayed the ancient Chinese masters as producing illogical and ambiguous babble, he did not regard them very highly. Likewise, when he later described German philosophy as a bad habit of the German language, he meant to express his disdain. The changes in his appraisal of Chinese philosophy always involved altering his description and evaluation of the two related entities: the masters and philosophy.

The second reflection is related to the fact that Fu uses the term "philosophy" in at least two different senses. The first is in a factual manner and refers to the enterprise that happens to be labelled as such in academia. This includes the actual topics taught in Western philosophy departments, which are portrayed as being part of a long tradition. His second use of the term was related to what he regarded as its ideal enterprise—"true philosophy"—and that which was associated with it. This distinction does not totally coincide with the previous one between descriptive and emotive meanings: while "true philosophy" is, of course, always mentioned approvingly, the reality that happens to be labelled philosophy is not evaluated consistently by Fu. His evaluation changed depending on which texts he identified as being philosophical during certain periods in his life, and how he felt about the discipline of philosophy at that time.

In the end, they remain complex and sometimes even inconsistent, despite—or because of—their paucity: they never belonged to his core message or formed the focus of his research. Having returned to China after six years abroad, he expressed his final view on the matter in 1928, claiming that philosophy was no more than a by-product of language grown from a specific historical context. Not surprisingly, this view was basically a by-product of Fu's own expertise in philology and history.

2. Fu Sinian as a Peking University Student (ca. 1916–1919)

Fu Sinian was born on 13 February 1896 into a gentry family in Liaocheng 聊城, Shandong province. The household had at one time enjoyed a considerable status but was impoverished during the nineteenth century. Having lost his father at the age of nine, Fu was mainly educated and influenced by his mother and paternal grandfather—two strong characters. At the age of 17, he entered the Preparatory School of the Imperial University (later called Peking University), and in 1916 he was accepted into the Department of Chinese Literature (*Guowen men* 國文門). Thanks to his grandfather's tutoring in the Confucian Classics and his further education, Fu stood out for his knowledge of ancient texts, including those by the masters (*zi*). He was considered a most promising student by classical professors such as Huang Kan 黃侃 (1886–1935) and Liu Shipei 劉師培 (1884–1919).[16]

While not particularly interested in philosophy, Fu Sinian shared a dormitory room with Gu Jiegang 顧頡剛 (1893–1980), who had entered the Philosophy Department (*zhexue men* 哲學門) at the same time. One year later, in 1917, Peking University's new president, Cai Yuanpei, invited Hu Shi to teach the course "History of Chinese Philosophy." Initially, Gu was not very impressed by this young professor who had just returned from studying philosophy with John Dewey. After several classes, however, Gu decided that Hu Shi had an interesting approach. By the end of the year, he had even invited his roommate to attend some lectures. Fu was immediately interested, even though he had some reservations about Hu Shi's knowledge of the ancient Chinese corpus of texts.[17] From then, he attended the class and became a loyal follower and defender of the new teacher. The winds of change were gusting through Peking University. In 1918, Fu Sinian, who was the top student of Chinese literature, became one of the most active members of the New Culture Group, which was critical of the Chinese legacy. Cai Yuanpei and Hu Shi, the two leading figures of the New Culture group, strongly promoted the model of Western philosophy. That same year, Cai also invited Hu to preside over a seminar for MA students in the Philosophy Department.[18] Even though Fu did not attend this particular seminar—he was not a Master's student nor did he belong to the Philosophy Department—he often had opportunities to hear Cai's and Hu's views on philosophy. They not only aroused his interest in philosophy but also shaped his understanding of its content.

As Cai Yuanpei's enthusiastic preface to Hu Shi's *Outline of the History of Chinese Philosophy* pointed out, Hu's new approach to ancient Chinese thought was revolutionary since it was objective towards the different masters, systematic in its account, and based on thorough textual research. Hu Shi thereby combined the Qing tradition of the evidential investigation of texts with the demands of modern science. From John Dewey, he had learned that science does not refer to eternal truth or fixed knowledge but to a specific attitude and methodology, namely to posit bold hypotheses and examine them carefully.[19] But teachers such as Cai and Hu were certainly not Fu's only source of scientific and philosophical knowledge. Through English-language books and the student-organized study society, New Tide (Xin chao 新潮), he was informed about the latest developments in the field of formal logic and mathematics (especially Bertrand Russell), experimental psychology (including behaviourism), psychoanalysis (mainly Freud), and sociology. As Vera Schwarcz has remarked, "*New Tide* intellectuals, thus, were both more philosophical and more psychological in their quest for a scientific worldview than their teachers."[20]

Thanks to the most open-minded teachers at Peking University and to like-minded friends among its student population, Fu Sinian was thoroughly influenced by the university's emphasis on Western sciences combined with Chinese textual research. For him, the ancient corpus stood for his childhood upbringing, whereas philosophy probably represented his independence and critical stance as a university student. His writings as a Peking University student from 1918 onward did not yet explicitly address the adequacy of "Chinese philosophy" as a category but reflected the tension between its two major components: the ancient Chinese masters and philosophy. A selection of three articles from the years 1918 and 1919 will serve to illustrate his views.

2.1   On the Masters

In April 1918, Fu Sinian published "The fundamental error in the world of Chinese academic thought" in the journal of his teachers' generation: *New Youth* (*Xin qingnian* 新青年).[21] The topic of this article was neither philosophy nor the ancient Chinese masters but the backwardness of contemporary Chinese academia: its failure to foster individual, critical, innovative, independent, and logical thought. The cause of this backwardness was, according to Fu, a fundamental yet elusive error, several aspects of which relate to the ancient Chinese masters.

Fu claimed that it was because of the Later Mohist type of argumentation (*bian* 辯) and their use of ancient texts as sources for the legitimation of their views that other masters kept referring to the authority of the past and were more interested in convincing rivals than in finding the truth. He also ridiculed analogical forms of reasoning, such as the maxim that "since there is only one sun in the sky, there is only one king for the people." And this is why, in his eyes, contemporary scholars "make many associations but think little, imagine much but experiment little, and compare much but deduce little."[22] Fu also associated Chinese academia with what he calls "yin-yang specialists"—who influenced many well-known thinkers, including the *ru* scholars—with their wild speculations.[23] Finally, he blamed the "incantation literature," with its vague and powerful statements which characterize much of ancient Chinese thought: "Men such as Confucius, Laozi, and Zisi are generally considered sages. But in the three books, *Change*, *Laozi*, and the *Mean*, the wording is so confused that one word can have various interpretations. Temporarily leaving the *Changes* and the *Mean* aside, the *Laozi* allowed later people to attribute their own views to it: in the Han dynasty 'Huang Lao,' in the Jin dynasty 'Lao-Zhuang.' The same goes for magicians, and Buddhists attributing the 'Transformation of the Barbarians'[24] theory to it.... So, when later people went wrong, it was partly because Laozi's words were confused and ungraspable, and partly because of mistakes they added to it."[25] Thus, for Fu, the failure of academics at that time to explain the thought of these ancient masters was not only their own fault; it was also due to the poor quality of the ancient texts.

Since in this article the Chinese masters are indirectly discussed as the cause of a current problem, they are evaluated negatively. The term philosophy (*zhexue*) seldom occurs, and never as a label of ancient Chinese thought. Fu uses "philosophy" descriptively, as the discipline in which these texts have been emulated or studied, when he claims that "scholars throughout history have continued to nibble at" this worthless correlative talk, as, for example, in philosophy,[26] and when he complains that aspects of the fundamental error now appear in every discipline, for example, "in philosophy, where people take it as their job to preserve the succession of the Way (*daotong* 道統)."[27] He also warns his readers that the fundamental error has to be completely eradicated before one can begin "studying modern Western science, philosophy, or literature."[28] Of these three occurrences of the term philosophy, the first two refer to the actual study of Chinese texts and are criticised; the last refers to the Western discipline and elicits Fu's admiration. The next two articles from this period explicitly discuss philosophy as an ideal, as well as an existing discipline.

2.2 *On Philosophy*

In October of 1918, a letter entitled "A letter from Fu Sinian to the president [of Peking University]: On the mistake of placing the Philosophy Department in the Faculty of Arts" appeared in the journal of his alma mater, *Beijing daxue rikan* 北京大學日刊.[29] The third-year student tried to convince Cai Yuanpei that philosophy did not belong in the Faculty of Arts together with literature and history. According to Fu, because "philosophy is a matter of thinking; literature of feeling," the former, as opposed to the latter, tries to understand events and analyse reality. Therefore, in its content as well as its methodology, philosophy is closer to the natural sciences.[30] Fu urged Cai Yuanpei to move the Preparatory School for Philosophy to the School of Sciences "in order to give the masses the correct idea, and to make professors of the natural sciences interact with philosophers."[31] This change, he predicted, would bring about a spiritual transformation at Peking University.

At this stage in his life, Fu Sinian was so enthusiastic about philosophy that he conflated his ideal view of it with what he saw as the actual philosophical discipline in the West. One of his recurrent arguments was that in Western academia, philosophy is associated with science rather than with literature or history and that "in the West, one has to be good in mathematics to do philosophy."[32] The Chinese masters were not explicitly mentioned, although Fu explained that "the Chinese who study philosophy always work with historical sources. Westerners on the other hand always work with sources in the natural sciences."[33] When making this claim about "the Chinese who study philosophy," Fu may have been thinking of his compatriots studying Western philosophy, but he most probably also had in mind those who had been working on the ancient masters, since they also belonged in Peking University's Philosophy Department.[34] He certainly did not consider the study of ancient Chinese thought to be exemplary philosophy, but he did not explicitly deny it the label either.

In a later article, "Reflections on those in China who nowadays discuss philosophy," Fu Sinian's ideas concerning philosophy were further developed. This article appeared in May 1919 in *New Tide*, the journal that Fu had established in January of that year with some like-minded students.[35] It was no less than a eulogy of philosophy, which in Fu's eyes should properly serve to give one confidence and reveal one's mistakes and prejudices, as well as provide one with a worldview, insight into life, knowledge of oneself and of others, and so on. But unfortunately, in China philosophy was not yet on track:

> What I call the true path of philosophy can certainly not mean the thought of primitive people, nor can it mean the past philosophy that was unable to provide completeness or systematisation, but it must mean contemporary philosophy. To put it even more strictly, it should refer to the new philosophy (*xin zhexue* 新哲學) of the last 30 to 40 years. Because all sorts of systems of old philosophy (*jiu zhexue* 舊哲學), having passed through a great [period of] scientific improvement, have very seldom been able to persist; they can only hope to develop by means of a new system that fits the times.

Fu then explained that "even in the West, philosophy was still dominated by medieval thought and had not yet been baptized by the sciences." Only in the last half century had it first been baptised by the natural sciences, and later by social sciences—from mechanics to biology, to psychology and finally to sociology. The contemporary philosophy which Fu admired so much never competed with these sciences but rather used them as its foundation and represented their current "comprehensive overview" (*huitong de zongji* 會通的總積).[36] For Fu, philosophy contains the reasoning or principles shared by all sciences: it is common thought or basic knowledge. In this sense its scope is the widest. In another sense, however, it is the smallest, since old philosophy had gradually been taken over by the scientific disciplines branching out from it, leaving only metaphysics behind—the sole realm that had not yet been overtaken.[37]

What was implicit in Fu's earlier letter to Cai Yuanpei is explicitly stated here: the discipline that is generally called philosophy, in China as well as in the West, did not correspond to Fu's ideal vision, except for one particular type of thinking that had been entertained for a few decades. But what exactly did Fu have in mind when he referred to the new philosophy "of the last 30 to 40 years"? Having traced the history of Western philosophy from the pre-scientific stage emphasising broad learning to the "critical philosophy" of Hume and Kant, he finally attributed the "the latest victory, which has suppressed Kantian philosophy"[38] to the political thinker Herbert Spencer (1820–1903). Even though Fu believed that one can become a philosopher in any scientific discipline by searching beyond the surface to reveal the commonalities underlying different fields of thought, as did Wilhelm Maximilian Wundt (1832–1920) in psychology and Orrin White (1883–1969) in chemistry, Spencer was accorded the highest praise because he presented a comprehensive philosophy encompassing all the sciences. One major source of inspiration for Fu may have been Hu Shi, who regularly referred to Spencer's *laissez-faire* philosophy in relation to Chinese thought.[39]

A second influence, probably also from Hu Shi, was American pragmatism. Although Hu's teacher, John Dewey, is not explicitly mentioned here, his ideas and terminology pervade the article: Fu insisted that philosophy uses the scientific method, values experience, and eschews abstractions. "Philosophy is a big Hypothesis—the collection of a bundle of hypotheses." Especially in those fields that have not yet been overtaken by science, one should beware of Dogmatism and ideas put forth in terms of the "absolute" and "eternal." It is the task of philosophy to lead these problems towards science and "receive the baptism of Verification."[40] In a slightly earlier book review, Fu referred to William James (1842–1910), whom he associated with realism (*shijizhuyi* 實際主義). The review is of a book (from 1912) by the British pragmatist, Ferdinand C. S. Schiller (1864–1939), criticizing formal logic. Fu argued that "realism is the most sublime product of contemporary thought" and "should be brought to China so that its force can be used to correct China's irrelevant, muddle-headed, and chaotic thought."[41] He criticised formal logic for being too formalistic and irrelevant: "When I hope that the study of logic will come to China, I especially hope for the study of 'true logic.' What I fear most is that harmful logic will come to China. This book by Schiller can function to 'block heresies and open up to the good.' Having read it, one will certainly no longer be seduced by formal logic but will inevitably find the way to logic based on psychology."[42] The new philosophy which Fu had in mind thus included Herbert Spencer, pragmatist philosophers (whom he sometimes labelled "realists"), and most probably also Bertrand Russell's (1872–1970) thought, even though he disagreed with his promotion of formal logic.[43]

What Fu Sinian profoundly disagreed with, and wanted to eradicate thoroughly, was "old philosophy," especially in China: reflections that did not take scientific discoveries into account or, even worse, rejected them. Such scholars, relying on the illusions of their own little niches, could just as well proclaim themselves to be "philosophers" in a small village or in a group of workers, "but it is inappropriate at a university in Beijing to confuse the "Explanation of the Diagram of the Supreme Polarity" ("Taiji tu shuo" 太極圖説), *yin-yang* (陰陽) or *qian-kun* (乾坤) [with philosophy], or in a well-known paper to discuss the fundamental state of the Way (*daoti* 道體), circulation (*xunhuan* 循環), or gradations of energy (*qishu* 氣數)."[44] Fu explains that in the West, such theories belong to a past, pre-scientific, worldview. "Actually I do not deserve to discuss philosophy, but it does no harm to explain this general mistake of considering *yin-yang* and the 'fundamental state of the Way' to be philosophy."[45] According to Fu, modern scientific insights had shown such theories to be simply ridiculous.

In conclusion, in his earliest writings Fu Sinian did not yet thoroughly address the question of whether the ancient Chinese masters ought to be labelled and treated as philosophers. When discussing the masters and philosophy separately he was, of course, aware of their connection because the masters happened to be taught and studied in philosophy departments. He vehemently criticised Chinese traditional thought and was enchanted by modern philosophy. But since Fu used the latter term in two senses—as a fact and as an ideal—he occasionally called the thought of the Chinese masters, and pre-contemporary Western thought, "philosophy." Only in the last article, written in the year he graduated from Peking University, did Fu become more insistent on what he believed deserves to be called "philosophy." Under the influence of Hu Shi and New Tide members, he narrowed his appreciation to one specific type of Western philosophy, namely pragmatism or experimentalism, which relied heavily on the scientific model. Although he occasionally (descriptively) referred to the ancient masters as philosophers,[46] he also suggested that they (prescriptively) do not really deserve this label. As a Peking University student, Fu Sinian did not insist on arguing that Confucius and Laozi were not real philosophers, although he could very well have made this claim.[47] But at that point in his life, he certainly would not have thanked god for his people's healthy habits, as he did a few years later. Although this strong opinion was inspired by his ideal view of contemporary Western thought, it would not survive his encounter with the real West.

3. Fu Sinian as a Student in Europe (1920–1926)

On 2 January 1920, Fu Sinian boarded a ship in Shanghai heading for England. In October he was able to enrol officially at the University College of London University, where he planned to study natural sciences. However, he was convinced by a professor to enrol in experimental psychology and combine under-graduate with post-graduate courses.[48] For this period in Fu Sinian's life, we have no publications to consult. During his Peking University years, Fu had been an extremely prolific writer and seems to have published almost every thought that came into his mind,[49] which he sometimes regretted afterwards.[50] Wang Fan-sen points out that as a Peking University student, "Fu wrote about fifty articles within ten months," many of which were "sparkling pieces on traditional learning … mixed with immature outbursts, but this frame of mind was perhaps typical of such transitional periods."[51] During his six years abroad, Fu hardly published anything and even had to force himself to write letters. His writer's block was caused not only by his self-proclaimed extreme laziness and temporary loss of interest, but also by his increased level of caution. He explained to Hu Shi why he did not feel like writing papers: "Because [I have] some interest in the sciences, I am now very embarrassed about publications with empty talk."[52] To find out what Fu thought about Chinese philosophy we have to rely on his letters, which sometimes, luckily for us, have an academic quality.

Fu Sinian wrote his first letter from England to Hu Shi in the summer of 1920, when he was ready to enrol at the University College. "Hereafter I will focus all my energy on psychology, which will captivate my interest over my whole life."[53] He therefore decided to abandon temporarily the study of philosophy because in his eyes the latter needed a good foundation in scientific knowledge. "I do not select philosophy courses; I think that if I do not have, as a minimal basis, some general insights into the natural and social sciences, studying philosophy first will not produce a good outcome."[54] During his stay in England, Fu does not seem to have returned to philosophy.

In June 1923 he moved to Berlin where he nevertheless enrolled in the Philosophy Department of the Friedrich-Wilhelms-Universität.[55] It was here that he experienced a breakthrough in his thinking about the nature of Chinese philosophy. Between 1924 and 1926, he wrote a very long letter to his previous roommate and friend Gu Jiegang, and in August 1926 he also wrote to Hu Shi just before leaving Germany. These two letters are our major sources for learning about Fu's new thoughts on the matter. To Gu he wrote: "I do not approve of Mr. Hu Shi's designation of the records on Laozi, Confucius, Mozi, and so on as the history of philosophy. China did not originally have a so-called philosophy. Thank god our people had such healthy habits."[56] He expressed almost literally the same view to Hu Shi: "Strictly speaking, China did not have philosophy (thank god for letting our great Han people walk such a healthy path)."[57] This near repetition suggests that he must have been rather pleased with his own provocative insight.

These two letters mark Fu Sinian's emerging interest in the question of whether the ancient Chinese masters ought to be labelled as philosophers. The most remarkable thing is that—using Stevenson's distinction between description and evaluation—his change of opinion hardly meant a change of mind in the former respect: his description of the content of the ancient masters' thought and of philosophy. But his evaluation of both was nevertheless radically new: Fu's criticism of ancient Chinese thought turned into appreciation, whereas his appreciation of Western philosophy was evaporating.

3.1 On Philosophy

What Fu discussed in Germany was actual Western philosophy, more specifically ancient Greek or modern European philosophy, and no longer American pragmatism. This is not surprising, considering the fact that he studied in Europe, unlike Hu Shi, who went to the United States. Moreover, since philosophy had lost much of its appeal for him, he no longer bothered to specify what he actually meant by it—what "true philosophy" was supposed to be. He even began to feel some repugnance toward (Western) philosophy, as he confessed to his teacher:

> When I had just arrived in England, I had the impression that I could read philosophical books, even German philosophy books. Later I found out that I could no longer understand German philosophy, and I found that German philosophy was only some bad habit of the German language. And when I now pick up a book by Hume, I also do not know what he is talking about. All in all, my brains have turned into stone with regard to philosophy. And I am quite pleased with this accomplishment.[58]

In 1920, Fu had decided to study the sciences first, as a preparation for studying philosophy later. But now he felt unable to understand Kant, which then also negatively influenced his interest in non-German philosophy, such as the thought of Hume. Only a few years after his first emotional turn away from the Chinese tradition toward Western philosophy (in 1918), Fu describes a new change in his interests, which he himself merely records but is not yet ready to explain fully. This second change may have had a combination of causes, such as his hurt pride and impatience when discovering his incapacity to understand notoriously difficult texts in a foreign language. A second cause may have been some degree of resentment, felt in the community of Chinese students more generally, towards the inadequacies of the host country. Like many Chinese students studying abroad, most of Fu's social contacts seem to have been with his compatriots, with whom he discussed the situation at home. The rather extreme expression of his disenchantment with Western philosophy was also an overreaction to his previously equally extreme veneration of it. And finally, his new views on Western philosophy may, to some extent, have been due to novel trends in linguistics and a linguistic turn in European philosophy. Ideas associated with the Vienna Circle and logical positivism were emerging, and Ludwig Wittgenstein inspired a fascination with language, whether as a perfect picture of reality (in the early period) or as a tool (in the later period).

Whatever Fu Sinian's experiences were regarding this philosophical trend, we know that he attended courses on new linguistic theories in Berlin. Language was in the air, and so was the idea that philosophical puzzles were caused by linguistic complexities. A few years later, Wittgenstein described philosophy as a "linguistic therapy," a tool "to disentangle ourselves from our self-enveloped confusion—'to show the fly out of the fly bottle.'"[59] Wittgenstein started expressing such ideas most clearly after 1929, when he returned to Cambridge. But already in 1926, Fu explained in a letter to Hu Shi that among the topics discussed by the masters in the late Zhou dynasty, "some were questions caused by the characteristics of the Chinese language (just as Greek metaphysics was the result of the characteristics of the Greek language)."[60] During the next stage in his life, he would further develop this connection between philosophy and language in his academic writings.

3.2   On the Masters

Although Fu had not fundamentally changed his description of the content of ancient Chinese thought, his evaluation of it had changed completely, along with the developments in his evaluation of philosophy. He remained of the opinion that the masters were not really philosophers. This had now become a cause of pride because the Chinese people had been able to avoid this "unhealthy habit." Because of this evolution in his views, Fu was now rather critical of his teacher's influential *Outline of Chinese Philosophy*. According to Fu, not only did it lack the academic quality necessary for it to be a forerunner in the field or the last word on the subject, but the whole enterprise was also flawed by the necessity to force the ancient Chinese texts into the framework of philosophy and make comparisons with Western thinkers. Fu had become convinced that China "at most had something similar to the precursors of Socrates; we did not even really have someone like Plato. As for modern (academic) philosophy, from Descartes, Leibniz, and Kant, it is even more certain that we did not have any of that."[61] Although these statements are expressed in the negative, they do not imply a negative evaluation—that China had missed out on something crucial or valuable. Fu continues with a plea for indigenous terminology: "In contrast, those Chinese who debated policies (*fangshu lunzhe* 方術論者) (I use this term because it is from those times, and not a Western product) mostly discussed practical matters, and most of their questions involved the problems of those days."[62] One wonders what Fu meant by "from those times," since *fangshu* can hardly be considered a term contemporary to the Zhou: it occurs more often in Han texts and, as we will see, Fu was equally suspicious of using Han terminology for the interpretation of Zhou texts.[63] But by denying the indigenous masters' similarity to Western philosophers and by limiting their topics of debate to some contemporary and practical matters, Fu Sinian clearly rejected the application of the label of philosophy to the thought of the ancient Chinese masters. He thereby not only indicated their difference from the actual reality of (Western) philosophy, but also from his ideal view of the more universal or fundamental discipline.

During his six years abroad, Fu's rekindled interest in the Chinese masters was clearer in his mind than his aversion to the Western discipline. Having followed Gu Jiegang's scholarly successes under the guidance of Hu Shi, Fu fantasized about collaborating with his former roommate in the field of ancient Chinese thought. He explained to his teacher: "Now that I have heard that you are considering rewriting the book, I am really very happy. If in the future I have a chance to work with Jiegang, we might also write some chapters in the collection on ancient Chinese thought."[64] Cautious not to label the topic of research "philosophy" but "thought," he lists the four necessary "dogmas" such an enterprise required: avoiding the labels of other times and cultures, such as "philosophy"; treating different historical periods in their own terms; focusing on ancient (pre-Southern Dynasties) times with the disciplines of philology and linguistics; and being aware of the enormous influence of the Han in the interpretation and reconstruction of older periods. The first dogma most explicitly relates to his rejection of the discipline of Chinese philosophy: "If you use terms or frameworks from a later period or of another people to explain them, you will either make inappropriate omissions or add too much. Thus, do not use any later Indian or Western terms or frameworks."[65] Such a statement shows that, at least in theory, Fu was not only in favour of indigenous terms but also warned against intellectual anachronisms.

This letter was written in August of 1926, just a few weeks before Fu met Hu Shi in Paris at the end of his stay in Europe. Hu Shi immediately responded very enthusiastically, making three points. In the second, he expressed his agreement with Fu's suspicion regarding the label "philosophy": "What entangles people most of all is this web that spiders spit out of their belly and in which they entangle themselves. Over the last few years I have done my best to learn to become good at forgetting—for six to seven years I have not taught Western philosophy and have not read Western philosophy books. I have removed quite a lot of the Western spider web, which makes me really happy....[66] I am quite pleased about this because I am a well-known philosophy professor, which makes it rather difficult to remove the bowl from which I eat."[67] During the meeting in Paris, Fu Sinian had a chance to influence his former teacher even more.[68] Afterwards, Hu Shi was reluctant to speak of philosophy: he never completed the two remaining volumes of his *Outline of the History of Chinese Philosophy*, and he returned to Peking University to teach a course on the history of ancient Chinese thought in the Philosophy Department.[69] However, the liberation from his own spider web was not easy, as Sang Bing's detailed analysis of Hu Shi's unending struggle with the label of philosophy shows.[70]

In Fu's last letter to Hu Shi before their meeting in Paris, he constantly refers to Gu Jiegang and the fact that the latter is doing much better in their teacher's eyes. He states, for example, that "recently I have thought of collecting in one long letter all my loose notes, which I have been wanting to write to Jiegang over the last two to three years. When I have finished the draft, I will also send it to you to read." This letter to Gu is our second major source regarding Fu's views on Chinese philosophy while studying abroad.[71] He explains in similar terms, but more thoroughly, his rejection of the category of "Chinese philosophy": "If we call the masters (*zijia* 子家) philosophers, there is a major risk of misunderstanding." Fu believed that different cultures and eras each had their own specific vocabularies: "In general, using new terms for old realities is relatively acceptable for material things because they resemble each other; but for cultural matters it always goes wrong, because they differ, despite [their] apparent similarities. We should now temporarily call these persons (the masters) 'experts of policies' (*fangshujia* 方術家). The term 'thought' should also be seldom used: things of the Han dynasty can generally probably be called 'thought,' but things of the late Zhou should be called 'policies.'"[72] Since Fu rejected not only the application of Western terms to ancient Chinese texts, but also the use of later Chinese nomenclature for earlier periods, he did not even consider the rather abstract "thought" appropriate for the pre-Han reflections on mostly concrete and worldly matters. For the same reason he avoided the use of Han terms for "lineages" such as "*ru jia*" 儒家 and "*dao jia*" 道家 when speaking of the Warring States period.[73] And he would certainly not have followed Feng Youlan's suggestion that Chinese thought could be conveniently labelled using the Qing category of "learning based on normative principles" (*yili zhi xue* 義理之學).[74] Today's research on the different periods of Chinese history would confirm Fu's caution in this respect,[75] although this attitude cannot be pursued to the extreme. Language, by its very nature, consists of terms that function independent of reality in its more concrete form. If this were not the case, and if every specific instance of reality was labelled differently, language would stop functioning completely. Even Fu Sinian continued to use Western terms when speaking about the Chinese tradition, and Han labels to address pre-Han matters, but he advised caution in their use.[76]

In summary, while living abroad, Fu Sinian's major change of mind concerned his evaluation of what he identified as Chinese and Western traditional thought, not of his ideal of philosophy. Therefore, his sustained claim that the ancient masters were not philosophers no longer referred to their failure to live up to the ideal of "true philosophy," but rather to their blessed difference from the European philosophical tradition. The ancient Chinese masters did not resemble the ancient Greek philosophers, and they had even less in common with modern Western philosophy. He thereby pre-empted contemporary concerns about the application of modern and Western categories to ancient Chinese texts.

4. Fu Sinian Back in China (1927–1929)

In the autumn of 1926, Fu Sinian returned home. On 30 October his ship reached Hong Kong, while he was still fervently copying his long letter to Gu Jiegang. At the end of that year, Fu was offered a position as history professor and dean at the Faculty of Letters at Zhongshan University, where he established the Institute for Philology and History in 1927. In 1928, he took part in the establishment of Academia Sinica and became the director of its Institute for History and Philology, a post that he held for 22 years. Whether or not the relation between philology and history changed in his mind—a question that might be prompted by the switch in the Institute's title[77]—it is clear that Fu had finally settled on this double track. In 1929, he moved the Institute to Beiping, and in 1930, he taught history classes at Peking University. These first years back home were very fruitful: he had attracted China's best minds to the Institute and wrote some of his most influential and mature work.[78] As Fu had predicted in his letter to Hu Shi, he now began to spell out all the ideas that had percolated in his mind during his stay abroad. Not surprisingly, the question of "Chinese philosophy" was also touched upon and more than once appeared in the introduction or the first section of a book, as if it was a stubborn obstacle to clear away before undertaking real work.

One influential piece written in 1928 was the "Manifesto for the Work of the Institute of History and Philology," in which he determined the Institute's future policy.[79] As director, Fu Sinian decided that the focus should be on the collection of data and material research, rather than interpretation or popularization. The Institute's first two-year project consisted of nine topics, many of which related to language and history; it did not include philosophy.[80] Axel Schneider characterizes Fu's methodology "as the combination of a very detailed evaluation and reconstruction of historical materials through textual criticism, modelled after the evidential research of the Qianjia school of the Qing period, with an empirical and statistical approach to the texts which Fu claims to have borrowed from modern Western natural sciences and the German school of Ranke's historiography."[81] In both of the Institute's central domains, Fu could rely on a Chinese tradition of expertise in historical records and textual research, as well as on the modern social sciences (specifically positivistic historiography and comparative linguistics). Neither was the case in the field of philosophy, at least in his eyes: as we saw earlier, ancient China had not developed anything resembling Fu's ideal conception of philosophy, and the contemporary discipline which he had come to know in Europe did not fulfil the quasi-scientific expectations that he had of it.

In order to explore Fu's mature view on the question of Chinese philosophy, I mainly focus on one piece: the first section of the "Discussion of the masters of the Warring States," which was written in 1928.[82] This further develops the views he had expressed in earlier letters and which were repeated in later research. For example, Fu's well-known 1940 study of the concepts of "human nature" and "destiny" starts out with a preface in which he largely quotes this particular section, stating that "even though I held this view many years ago, when I think of it today I still pretty much stick with this view."[83] This initial section of the "Discussion of the masters of the Warring States" carries the long title: "About philosophy being a by-product of language; Western philosophy being the by-product of Indo-Germanic languages; Chinese, in fact, being an unphilosophical language; and the Warring States masters also not being philosophers."[84] Although there are no further sub-divisions in the text, its structure is implicitly indicated in this title: more than half of the text is concerned with the nature of Western philosophy. Three shorter sub-sections concerning Chinese matters argue, first, that the Chinese language does not lead to philosophy; second, that the ancient masters were not philosophers; and finally, that they should be studied in their own terms. Thus, in this academic essay, the concept of philosophy finally meets with the Chinese masters. It remains worthwhile, however, to analyse Fu's views on both topics separately.

4.1   On Philosophy

When discussing the nature of philosophy, Fu Sinian clearly has its Indian, Greek, and German forms in mind. These were created by "the three peoples [who], in the whole world and of all times, [are] best known for their philosophy."[85] These three peoples were originally rather barbaric, using simple language and thought. But when they came into contact with a superior culture, their original language could not keep up with the higher level of thought that sprang from this cultural clash. This was the moment at which so-called "philosophical" problems arose. "Since thought arose from culture, but the original form of language remained, and since language can moreover not be separated from thought, an abundance of abstract thought was unconsciously subjected to restrictions by its language. So, having experienced this step, they started coming up with mysterious explanations for specific linguistic forms."[86] For instance, Aristotle's "ten categories" all originated from Greek grammar, such as the distinction between subject and object, cause and result, past and future, complete and incomplete, quantity and quality, concrete and abstract, and so on. "That which is called philosophy is impenetrable Greek."[87] Modern philosophy is even worse. Fu asks why it is so difficult to translate Kantian concepts such as the "*Ding an sich*" and "*Sein* and *Werden*," not only into Chinese, but into other European languages as well. This is also the case for Descartes' "*Cogito ergo sum.*" Fu argues this is because philosophy is controlled by language. "Mathematical thinking, although very different in Chinese and European languages, can be translated perfectly; but philosophical thinking—even though English and German differ from each other no more than dialects do—cannot be translated. So, the fact that philosophy is a by-product is now clear without any need for further proof."[88] Fu even considers the incomprehensibility and mysticism of Chinese Buddhism to be the result of the impossible translation of this Western (Indo-European) philosophy into Chinese.[89] This is, in short, how Fu Sinian seems to have settled the question, but his views leave space for comments and remarks.

First, Fu's over-confident and provocative tone is striking. Although he refers to his opponents only once, in a vague sense which places them in the past, it is clear that he sees himself as fighting against a dominant current. "Some people used to think that the Aryans founded Indian civilization, and that the Greeks founded Mediterranean civilization. But this is the worst mistake among all the major mistakes. When the Aryans went to India, their culture was inferior to that of the half-black indigenes. By adopting the indigenous culture, they rose several levels. The same holds for the Greeks in South-East Europe."[90] Considering the magnitude of this mistake, Fu is happy to report that this erroneous view now belongs to the past, thanks to modern historical insights. But we know that this was not really the case: in the late 1920s philosophy was still respected by many of his colleagues in the West and China alike. Merely a decade before, even Fu Sinian had been among the young intellectuals who venerated it! His own past "mistake," combined with the ongoing success of philosophy under the influence of intellectuals such as Hu Shi and Feng Youlan, was probably the target of Fu's rhetoric. As we will see below, his tone becomes even more vehement and negative when attacking the academic entity he calls "Chinese philosophy."

Second, even though Fu's aversion to philosophy may have been originally caused by his own past veneration of it, by his problems in understanding Kant's work, and by the more general difficulty of translating German philosophy into Chinese, his current view is nevertheless more than merely the result of frustration. As a student, Fu was already convinced of the importance of language,[91] a conviction which probably led him to take classes in linguistics at Berlin University. In another essay written in 1928—which is also an introductory section—he explains the scientific theory behind his reduction of philosophy to a by-product of language.[92] Under the influence of John Watson's behaviourism, Fu argues that thought is the result of language.[93] "People discussing philosophy and psychology have always regarded thought as the inner essence, and language as the outer function; thought as the matter, and language as the tool; language as a way to express thought, and thought as more than language."[94] But Fu claims they were fundamentally wrong: he rejects the commonly held prejudice that people first have thoughts and express them using language only afterwards in order to communicate. In behaviourism, thought amounts to a very silent conversation with oneself; it is the inner retentive habit of language (*nei lian xiguan* 內斂習慣), which predates thinking.[95] Hence, the emotional background of Fu's ideas on philosophy does not necessarily deprive them of scientific value. They remain, however, very far from explaining all instances of Western philosophy through reference to linguistic matters.[96]

There is, thirdly, some dissonance in Fu's sweeping theory. At one point he exclaims that "philosophy should be logical thought, and logical thought should not be restricted to one particular language; it should be as easy to translate as mathematics."[97] This comes as a bit of a surprise in the midst of his characterization of philosophy as a mere by-product of language. But it is clear that he is now suddenly thinking of philosophy as an ideal, a mode of thinking he has apparently not totally relinquished. Although he does not make this distinct use of the term philosophy explicit, Fu's historical analysis of philosophy is meant only for what actually falls under this label, not his ideal view of it. However, Fu's ideal of philosophy as the comprehensive overview of all the sciences that grew out of it, supplemented by the narrow field of metaphysics which was soon to be supplanted by future objective knowledge, was doomed to perish as the result of scientific evolution. Philosophy in the narrow sense (metaphysics) was fated slowly to hand over its objects of study to specific sciences. The survival of "mother" philosophy under the pressure of her own offspring remains a general problem, more specifically for Fu's contemporaries, who valued philosophy exclusively in scientific terms.[98]

A final feature of Fu Sinian's mature vision of philosophy is that he apparently was not as negative about it as his theory would suggest. In 1940, even though he largely quoted this text in the preface to his "Disputation and verification of the ancient glosses on human nature and destiny" as his final statement on the matter, Fu apparently retained some interest in Western philosophy. When, in 1947–1948, he spent more than a year in New Haven, Connecticut, for surgery and recovery, Fu kept a one-hundred page notebook entitled "Notes on Books Bought When Travelling in the United States." The table of contents included items such as "History of Philosophy," "Classical Philosophy," and "Ethics and Religion." The notebook also contained remarks on ancient Greek and Roman works. [99] If Fu Sinian had really been convinced of the fact that philosophy was no more than "helping a fly find its way out of the bottle," as Wittgenstein later put it, there would have been no point in his reading such books, especially not for somebody who was lucky enough to have been brought up speaking the most logical language on earth and hence in a culture devoid of philosophical speculations (see below). This leads us to the second part of his final verdict on the nature of Chinese philosophy.

4.2   On the Masters

After this long historical exposé of philosophy as the by-product of language, in the next three, short sections, Fu Sinian turns to China: its language, the undeserved application of the term "philosophy" to the thought of the masters, and its inherent structure.

Now we can fully understand, and according to Fu, even applaud, his difficulties in grasping the subtleties of Kantian thought as well as his failure to translate it into the Chinese language. Since "philosophy" represents no more than the complex attempts of peoples with relatively backward languages to see and break through their linguistic limitations, it may appear deep and mysterious to them, but for outsiders it is simply incomprehensible. "Since, in terms of logic, Chinese is the most developed language in the world (see the well-known books of Yesibo), it has lost some grammatical complexities and, with its sentence order (Syntax), it seeks to come closer to the demands of logic."[100] Yesibo 叶斯波, to whom Fu refers in passing without giving any further reference, is the Danish linguist Otto Jespersen (1860–1943), who argued that complex morphology was a sign of primitive languages and syntactic simplicity of a more advanced stage of development.[101] Fu praises Chinese for its concreteness and lack of abstraction: "Moreover it is a factual, truthful language, not abundant with abstract nouns. But abstract concepts always have a reality to point at, so they can find a way to be expressed. Since its grammar does not have so much meaninglessness, and its vocabulary, moreover, is not so mysterious, it is only natural that philosophy would not be able to easily emerge from it."[102] This argument is reminiscent of A. C. Graham's study of the difficult Chinese translations of Western reflections on "essence" and "existence," in which he points out that the "dependence of Western ontology on the peculiarities of the Indo-European verb 'to be' is evident to anyone who," like Fu Sinian, "observes from the vantage point of languages outside the Indo-European family."[103] Thus, Graham would have agreed with Fu that Chinese attempts to translate Western philosophical speculations were often wrong-headed and inspired by a mistaken supposition of universality.

Fu then finally turns to the use of the label "philosophy" for the thought of the Chinese masters, the core question of this paper: "If we try to compare all the questions contained in what the West calls learning of the love-of-wisdom with the masters of the Warring States, Qin, and Han, down to the *mingjia* 名家 (logicians, or lineage of names) of the Wei and Jin, and the *lixue* 理學 (learning of principle) of the Song and Ming, [we have to conclude that] a love-of-wisdom theory, such as that of Socrates, existed for the masters until the *lixue* of the Song and Ming. Regarding questions such as those raised by Plato, China at the most had no more than part of it, probably less than half. But as for someone such as Aristotle, there is no one like him at all. And as for something like the modern academic philosophy of the followers of Descartes and Kant, who analyzed one verb to the point of obfuscation, and developed the suffix of one noun into a huge theory...[104] such things had even less influence in China." Significantly, Fu Sinian has, by then, totally abandoned the use of the terms *zhexue* 哲學 and *zhexuejia* 哲學家 in relation to the thinkers he calls "experts of policies." A comparison between the thinkers of both cultures thus shows that "the absence of correspondence is so large, and the correspondence so little, [we have to conclude that] in the thinking on Han soil there originally was no discipline of philosophy in the strict sense of the term."[105] This view is not only opposed to the original view of his teacher, Hu Shi, whom he had been able to influence in Paris in the summer of 1926, but also to the ideas of the equally influential Feng Youlan, with whom Fu never seems to have gone into public debate.[106] The plea against the label of "philosophy" ends with a second, less scientific argument: "The expression 'Chinese philosophy' is originally a vulgar Japanese item.... If we want to find truth in the world, can we afford not to reject this base Japanese product?"[107] Fu Sinian, who came from Shandong, had a strong sense of the Japanese threat, which became ever more pressing while he was writing this work. As many scholars have pointed out, under such conditions, it was hardly possible to separate academic research from political concerns and nationalistic sentiments.[108]

The section ends with a positive alternative: "Well, what are the masters of the Zhou, Qin, and Han dynasties then? The answer is 'experts of policies' (*fangshu jia*)."[109] Referring to the last chapter in *Zhuangzi*, "Tianxia," to *Huainanzi*, and to Mei Cheng's (†140 B.C.) rhapsody "Seven stimuli" (*Qi fa* 七發), Fu points out that this is an indigenous term, just as "philosopher" was invented by the Western lovers-of-wisdom for themselves. If the West felt free to use its own categories to name its own intellectual heritage, then why could China not do the same? But by relying on three Han sources[110] to label the Zhou, Qin, and Han masters all at once, Fu sins against his own dogma concerning the avoidance of anachronisms. Moreover, when further dividing the Warring States masters into three categories, he unreservedly uses the Han term "*Mojia* 墨家"; he even adopts the label "religion" (*zongjiao* 宗教), which was just as much a Japanese import as "philosophy" was. This is not to say that Fu Sinian used terms incautiously or inconsistently, but it shows that even he had to work within the language of his times, despite its traps and inadequacies. Having determined that the Chinese masters were not philosophers, Fu insists on a non-metaphysical reading of Confucianism, in which Xunzi is given priority over the introspective moral reflections of Mencius.[111] It is striking how much Fu Sinian's plea for the use of indigenous terms is still very much informed by the authority of the West: the linguistic theories of Otto Jespersen; the lingering model of a scientifically inspired philosophy; the minimal overlap of Chinese masters with Greek philosophers; and the more striking similarities between the Chinese masters and Western non-philosophers.[112]

After 1928, Fu Sinian largely lost interest in the matter; he had said what he wanted to say and moved on to more interesting research topics. This was his mature view on the nature of the threefold topic of philosophy, Chinese masters, and "Chinese philosophy." But even the view he settled for, and confidently repeated many years later, was not really mature. However much Fu supported scientific neutrality and positivistic research, his theory on the relation between the masters and philosophy, while not at all unfounded or irrational, was to some extent emotional, sweeping, and inconsistent. Not only was there a remarkable evolution in his views over the years, his final opinion also retained signs of a tension between his Chinese identity and Western inspiration. Wang Fan-sen concludes his study of Fu Sinian by remarking that "dilemmas, discrepancies, and contradictions are evident in Fu's mind and writings. He was given the epithet 'a bundle of contradictions' and led a life fraught with tension."[113] In relation to the topic of this chapter, it is remarkable that Fu's description of the masters as un-philosophical is relatively stable. What changes dramatically is his evaluation of this fact: from harsh criticism in 1918 to an appreciation in the 1920s, eventually growing into national pride. What remained constant, even throughout these radical changes, is Fu Sinian's strong temper, his concern for the nation, and—despite all his critical remarks—the Western scientific (mainly historical and linguistic) inspiration even as he pled for the use of indigenous terms. Fu's voice not only lives on in the Academia Sinica and the broader field of human sciences in Taiwan,[114] but also in the more general tendency in contemporary China to speak about the Chinese tradition in Chinese and traditional terms.

Notes

1   I thank Nicolas Standaert and Michael Nylan for their comments on an earlier draft of this chapter.

2   Fu Sinian 傅斯年, "Yu Gu Jiegang lun gu shi shu" 與顧頡剛論古史書 [Discussing ancient history and books with Gu Jiegang], in *Fu Sinian quanji* 傅斯年全集 [Complete works of Fu Sinian], 7 vols., edited by Ouyang Zhe-sheng 歐陽哲生 (Changsha: Hunan jiaoyu chubanshe, 2003), Vol. 1, p. 459. See also below.

3   See Dai Guangming 戴光明, "'Zhongguo (gudai) you wu zhexue' de lishi kaocha" 「中國(古代)有無哲學」的歷史考察 [Investigation of the question of "whether or not (ancient) China had philosophy"], *Guizhou daxue xuebao* 貴州大學學報 24.1 (Jan. 2006), p. 27 and John Makeham, "Hu Shi and the Search for System," in this volume.

4   Mou Zongsan, "Fojiao: Gaishuo" 佛教：概說 [Buddhism: An introduction], in *Siyin shuo yanjiang lu* 四因説演講錄 [Lecture on the four causes] (Shanghai: Shanghai guji chubanshe, 1998), p. 110.

5   "Which country's highest seat of learning does not have a Philosophy Institute?" asked Mou. He went on: "England, Germany and the Soviet Union all have one. The Soviet Union's academy was established by the philosopher Leibniz. The academy on the Mainland was copied from the Soviet Union by Guo Moruo. Hence the Mainland has a philosophy division with very fine subdivisions. Even though he [Guo Moruo] did not understand it himself, its basic capacity to collect material is substantial. How can one explain that Academia Sinica has not had an Institute of Philosophy until today?" (*ibid.*, p. 110)

6   Xu Fuguan, "Xie gei Zhongyang yanjiuyuan Wang yuanzhang Shijie xiansheng de yifeng gongkai xin" 寫給中央研究院王院長世杰先生的一封公開信 [An open letter to Mr. Wang Shijie, president of the Academia Sinica], in *Xu Fuguan wencun* 徐復觀文存 [Collected works of Xu Fuguan] (Taipei: Taiwan xuesheng shuju, 1991), pp. 254–255. This was originally written in June 1968 and published that year in issue 31 of *Yangming zazhi* 陽明雜誌. Two of his final suggestions concern: (1) his criticism of the strong "anti-thought" tendency of the Institute, which smothers scholarship with childish ignorance, and (2) his hope for the establishment of an Institute for the History of Chinese Thought, so that Confucius, Mencius, Zhu Xi, Lu Xiangshan, and Wang Yangming could gain a position next to the "Peking Man" and the "old cave men" in the country's highest academic institution (p. 260). The discipline of archaeology was treated much better at the Institute.

7   See also Wu Wenzhang 吳文璋, "Cong sixiangshi lun zhanhou Taiwan Ruxue de liang da dianxing—Hu Shi he Mou Zongsan" 從思想史論戰後台灣儒學的兩大典型——胡適和牟宗三 [A discussion of Taiwan's two major postwar models for Confucian Studies—Hu Shi and Mou Zongsan—from the viewpoint of the history of thought]. See <http://www.confucius2000.com/

confucian/csxslzhtwrxdlddxhshmzs.htm>. Accessed 1 August 2009. Wu writes that "because of Hu Shi's influence, the highest academic research centre in Taiwan—Academia Sinica—did not have a Philosophy Institute for several decades. Only in the last years was a Preparatory Office of the Institute for Chinese Literature and Philosophy established, which led to a new dawn of free academic thought."

8 According to its own website, the Institute is "devoted to the studies of classical and modern Chinese literature, Chinese and comparative philosophy, and Confucian classics." The four major research initiatives are "Ming-Qing literature, modern literature, Qing classical studies, and contemporary Confucianism." For much of the information about the contemporary situation of philosophy in Taiwan I thank Li Minghui, who holds an appointment in this Institute.

9 For contemporary Chinese scholars using this expression to criticize the use of Western neologisms, see Carine Defoort, "Is 'Chinese Philosophy' a Proper Name? A Response to Rein Raud," *Philosophy East and West* 56.4 (2006), p. 645, note 28. For the legitimacy debate in general, see Joël Thoraval, "De la philosophie en Chine à la 'Chine' dans la philosophie: Existe-t-il une philosophie chinoise?" *Esprit* 201 (1994), pp. 5–38; Carine Defoort, "Is There Such a Thing as Chinese Philosophy? Arguments of an Implicit Debate," *Philosophy East and West* 51.3 (July 2001), pp. 393–413; Carine Defoort, "Is 'Chinese Philosophy' a Proper Name? A Response to Rein Raud"; and Anne Cheng, "Les tribulations de la 'philosophie chinoise' en Chine," in *La pensée en Chine aujourd'hui*, edited by Anne Cheng (Paris: Gallimard, 2007), pp. 159–184.

10 Zhang Liwen, "Zhongguo zhexue de 'Ziji jiang,' 'Jiang ziji'—Lun zouchu Zhongguo zhexue de weiji he chaoyue hefaxing wenti" 中國哲學的「自己講」、「講自己」——論走出中國哲學的危機和超越合法性問題 [Chinese philosophy should "speak for itself" and "speak about itself"—Overcoming the crisis of Chinese philosophy and transcending the legitimacy issue], *Zhongguo renmin daxue xuebao* 中國人民大學學報 18.2 (2003), pp. 2–9. For an English translation, see Zhang Liwen, "Chinese Philosophy Should 'Speak for Itself' and 'Speak about Itself'—Overcoming the Crisis of Chinese Philosophy and Transcending the Legitimacy Issue," *Contemporary Chinese Thought* 37.2 (Winter 2005–2006), pp. 4–21.

11 This opinion was (and still is) not so exceptional among Chinese scholars trained and working in Western philosophy, but they tend not to join the debate on the legitimacy of Chinese philosophy.

12 Two major sources on Fu Sinian's relation to philosophy are Wang Fengqing 王鳳青, "Fu Sinian zhexue sixiang jianlun" 傅斯年哲學思想簡論 [A discussion of Fu Sinian's thoughts on philosophy], *Liaocheng daxue xuebao (zhexue shehuixue ban)* 聊城大學學報 (哲學社會科學版) 3 (2002), pp. 74, 78–80 and Wang Fan-sen 王汎森, *Zhongguo jindai sixiang yu xueshu de xipu* 中國近代思

想與學術的系譜 [The genealogy of modern Chinese thought and scholarship] (Taiwan: Lianjing chuban shiye gufen youxian gongsi, 2005), pp. 336–370.

13   For more information on Fu Sinian in general, see Wang Fan-sen, *Fu Ssu-nien: A Life in Chinese History and Politics* (Cambridge: Cambridge University Press, 2000). For his relations with his contemporaries, see Shi Xingze 石興澤, *Xuelin fengjing: Fu Sinian yu ta tong shidai de ren* 學林風景：傅斯年與他同時代的人 [An academic landscape: Fu Sinian and his contemporaries] (Zhengzhou: Henan renmin chubanshe, 2005).

14   On the influence of other students, more specifically the New Tide (Xin chao 新潮) intellectuals, see Vera Schwarcz, *The Chinese Enlightenment: Intellectuals and the Legacy of the May Fourth Movement of 1919* (Berkeley: University of California Press, 1986), pp. 94–107.

15   See Charles L. Stevenson, "Persuasive Definitions," *Mind* 47 (1938), pp. 331–350, where he deals with "conceptual" and "emotive" meaning; in Charles L. Stevenson, *Ethics and Language* (New Haven/London: Yale University Press, 1944/1972), "conceptual" is replaced by "descriptive."

16   For more detail, see Wang Fan-sen, *Fu Ssu-nien*, pp. 11–54.

17   See Li Chunlei 李春雷, "Cong *Zhongguo zhexue dagang* kan Hu Shi, Fu Sinian zhi jiaoyi" 從《中國哲學大綱》看胡适、傅斯年之交誼 [Looking at the friendship between Hu Shi and Fu Sinian from the *Outline of the History of Chinese Philosophy*], *Huaxia wenhua* 華夏文化 2 (2004), p. 60. For a detailed account of Fu Sinian's introduction to the field of "Chinese philosophy" through Gu Jiegang, see Shi Xingze, *Xueshu fengjing: Fu Sinian yu ta tong shidai de ren*, pp. 5–7.

18   *Feng Youlan xiansheng nianpu chubian* 馮友蘭先生年譜初編 [Preliminary edition of a chronicle of Feng Youlan's life], edited by Cai Zhongde 蔡仲德 (Zhengzhou: Henan renmin chubanshe, 1994), p. 24.

19   For Hu Shi's view on science and Cai's preface, see John Makeham, "Hu Shi and the Search for System," in this volume.

20   Vera Schwarcz, *The Chinese Enlightenment*, p. 105. For the English books that Fu obtained even before Hu Shi's arrival at Peking University, see Wang Fan-sen, *Fu Ssu-nien*, p. 33. For the influence of the other students, see Xiaoqing Diana Lin, *Peking University: Chinese Scholarship and Intellectuals, 1898–1937* (New York: SUNY, 2005), pp. 141–151 and Vera Schwarcz, *The Chinese Enlightenment*, pp. 97–107.

21   Fu Sinian, "Zhongguo xueshu sixiangjie zhi jiben wumiu" 中國學術思想界之基本誤謬 [The fundamental error in the world of Chinese academic thought], in *Fu Sinian quanji*, Vol. 1, pp. 21–28.

22   See *ibid.*, p. 25, where he discussed this as the sixth of the "fundamental error's" seven problematic aspects.

23   *Ibid.*, p. 26–27.

24   *Hua hu* 化胡 is the Daoist theory that Laozi went to the West (India) and converted Buddha.

25   *Ibid.*, p. 27.

26 *Ibid.*, p. 26.

27 *Ibid.*, p. 23.

28 *Ibid.*, p. 28.

29 Fu Sinian, "Fu Sinian zhi xiaozhang han: Lun zhexue men lishu wenke zhi liubi" 傅斯年致校長函：論哲學門隸屬文科之流弊 [A letter from Fu Sinian to the president [of Peking University]: On the mistake of placing the Philosophy Department in the Faculty of Arts] in *Fu Sinian quanji*, Vol. 1, pp. 37–40, reprinted from *Beijing daxue rikan* 北京大學日刊 (October 1918).

30 *Ibid.*, p. 38.

31 *Ibid.*, p. 39.

32 *Ibid.*

33 *Ibid.*

34 Among the professors doing Chinese philosophy at the *Zhexue men* (its name until 1918) were Chen Hanzhang 陳漢章 (1913–1931); Ma Xulun 馬叙倫 (1913 [part-time], 1917–1937 [full time]); Liu Shipei 劉師培 (1917–1919); Hu Shi (1917–1925, 1930–1937; 1946–1948); He Lin 賀麟 (1931–1992); and Xiong Shili 熊十力 (1922–1924, 1925–1926, 1932–1937).

35 Fu Sinian, "Duiyu Zhongguo jinri tan zhexuezhe zhi gannian" 對於中國今日談哲學者之感念 [Reflections on those in China who nowadays discuss philosophy], in *Fu Sinian quanji*, Vol. 1, pp. 239–244, reprinted from *Xin chao* 新潮 1.5 (May 1919).

36 *Ibid.*, p. 240.

37 *Ibid.*, p. 241.

38 *Ibid.*

39 See, for example, Hu Shih, *The Development of the Logical Method in Ancient China* (New York: Paragon Book Reprint Corp., 1922/1968), which is based on his 1917 doctoral thesis; and its further elaboration in *Zhongguo zhexueshi dagang* 中國哲學史大綱 [Outline of the history of Chinese philosophy] (Beijing: Dongfang chubanshe, 1919/1995). Herbert Spencer had also been introduced by Yan Fu 嚴復 (1853–1921) and Yang Changji 楊昌濟 (1871–1920). See, respectively, Vera Schwarcz, *The Chinese Enlightenment*, p. 42 and Xiaoqing Diana Lin, *Peking University*, p. 142.

40 Fu Sinian, "Duiyu Zhongguo jinri tan zhexuezhe zhi gannian," p. 243. The words "Hypothesis," "Dogmatism," and "Verification" are written in English and with capitals in the original.

41 Fu Sinian, "Shi Lei boshi de *Xingshi Luoji*" 失勒博士的《形式邏輯》[Dr. Schiller's *Formal Logic*], in *Fu Sinian quanji*, Vol. 1, pp. 197–201, p. 198. This review was originally published in *Xin chao* 1.3 (March 1919). This view comes relatively close to the line that Vera Schwarcz—wrongly, I believe—attributes to his "Reflections on those in China who nowadays discuss philosophy." See *The Chinese Enlightenment*, p. 103 and p. 322n21: "Formal logic is the foundation of the practical philosophy that we need to borrow and to adopt in China so as to clear the muddleheaded atmosphere prevailing in contemporary Chinese thought." This review shows Fu's

rejection of formal logic, which in his eyes had troubled Western philosophers for more than 1,000 years (p. 199).

42 Fu Sinian, "Shi Lei boshi de *Xingshi Luoji*," p. 199. This review was published in *Xin chao* 1.3. The fact that *Xin chao* 1.2 and 1.4 contained translations of Bertrand Russell's work by Zhang Shenfu 張申府 (1893–1986) may be a reflection of ongoing debates in the student society. Zhang had argued that "philosophy and mathematics had moved closer and closer *in the past forty years*, especially in the domain of formal logic. Formal logic, Zhang argued, was also socially useful." See Vera Schwarcz, *The Chinese Enlightenment*, p. 103 (my italics).

43 Ludwig Wittgenstein's *Tractatus Logico-Philosophicus* (1921) and the logical positivist Vienna Circle (officially launched in 1929 but active in the 1920s) were slightly later.

44 Fu Sinian, "Duiyu Zhongguo jinri tan zhexuezhe zhi gannian," p. 240.

45 *Ibid.*

46 See Fu's 1920 letter to Hu Shi: Fu Sinian, "Zhi Hu Shi" 致胡適 [Letter to Hu Shi], in *Fu Sinian quanji*, Vol. 7, pp. 11–14, p. 13. For another instance, see an article published in the first issue of *Xin chao* (January 1919) in which Fu argues that "in ancient times some philosophers (哲學家 *zhexuejia*) said that man's nature from birth is good." See Fu Sinian, "Wan e zhi yuan" 萬惡之原 [The source of all evil] in *Fu Sinian quanji*, Vol. 1, pp. 104–108, p. 105.

47 Jin Yuelin (1895–1984), a specialist in Western philosophy, did make this claim in the 1930s, in a review of Feng Youlan's first volume, entitled *History of Chinese Philosophy*. See John Makeham's introduction to this volume.

48 Fu Sinian, "Zhi Hu Shi," pp. 11–14, p. 13.

49 According to a bibliography of Fu's important writings in *Fu Sinian xuanji* 傅斯年選集 [Selected works of Fu Sinian], edited by Yue Yuxi 岳玉璽, Li Quan 李泉, and Ma Liangkuan 馬亮寬 (Tianjin: Tianjin renmin chubanshe, 1996), pp. 380–393, he published 36 articles in the years 1918 and 1919, and only two in the period between 1920 and 1926; both were published in 1920. Hence, even these two pieces were written before he left China.

50 For an expression of regret, see the editorial in the August 1919 issue of *Xin chao* in which he reflects on the journal's first seven months. Fu Sinian, "*Xin chao* zhi huigu yu qianzhan"《新潮》之回顧與前瞻 [*Xin chao*'s past and future], in *Fu Sinian quanji*, Vol. 1, pp. 290–297, p. 294.

51 Wang Fan-sen, *Fu Ssu-nien*, p. 33.

52 Fu Sinian, "Zhi Hu Shi," p. 13. In August of 1926, in a letter to Hu Shi he wrote that he had enough ideas for three dozen publications, but that he wanted to wait until he had returned home before starting to write them down. See Fu Sinian, "Zhi Hu Shi [1926]," pp. 36–43, p. 43.

53 *Ibid.*, p. 12.

54 *Ibid.*, p. 13.

55 *Fu Sinian wenwu ziliao xuanji* 傅斯年文物資料選輯 [A selection and compilation of Fu Sinian's cultural materials], edited by Wang Fan-sen 王汎森 and Du Zhengsheng 杜正勝 (Taipei: Academia Sinica, 1995), p. 53. Fu also took courses in anthropology, Sanskrit, and general linguistics.

56 Fu Sinian, "Yu Gu Jiegang lun gu shi shu," pp. 445–473, p. 459.

57 Fu Sinian, "Zhi Hu Shi [1926]," p. 38.

58 *Ibid.*, p. 42.

59 See David Edmonds and John Eidinow, *Wittgenstein's Poker: The Story of a Ten-Minute Argument between Two Great Philosophers* (New York: Harper Collins, 2002), pp. 231, 230, who quote Wittgenstein's analogy of the fly: "What is your aim in philosophy?—To show the fly the way out of the fly-bottle." See Ludwig Wittgenstein, *Philosophical Investigations,* translated by G. E. M. Anscombe (Oxford: Basil Blackwell, 1958/1984), p. 103, n. 309.

60 Fu Sinian, "Zhi Hu Shi [1926]," p. 38.

61 *Ibid.*, p. 38.

62 *Ibid.*

63 The term *fangshu* 方術 was much more current in the Han, where it seems to refer to expertise and techniques. The three sole occurrences which might have been considered from the Warring States period are in *Xunzi* 荀子: "Yao wen 堯問"; *Zhuangzi* 莊子: "Tian xia 天下"; and *Hanfeizi* 韓非子: "Wai chu shuo zuo shang 外儲說左上," where it rather refers to policies used to advise the ruler. The occurrence in *Xunzi*'s last chapter is questionable (Knoblock does not even translate it), and Fu Sinian dated the *Zhuangzi* collection to the Han. See Fu Sinian, "Zhanguo wenji zhong zhi pianshi shuti: Yige duanji" 戰國文籍中之篇式書體：一個短記 [The forms of writings of Warring States sources: A short note), in *Fu Sinian quanji*, Vol. 3, pp. 17–21, p. 18. This piece was written between 1929 and 1930.

64 Fu Sinian, "Zhi Hu Shi [1926]," p. 38.

65 *Ibid.*, pp. 38, 40–41.

66 As a somewhat paradoxical example he adds: "Like Descartes, I only remember his being 'good at doubting.' That is all I teach about him; all his other dogmas I have long forgotten." It is striking that as a confirmation of his success in forgetting Western philosophy, Hu Shi nevertheless quotes a Western philosopher, quickly adding that he has forgotten all Descartes' other ideas.

67 Hu Shi, "Zhi Fu Sinian" 致傅斯年 [Letter from Hu Shi to Fu Sinian], in *Hu Shi quanji* 胡适全集 [Complete works of Hu Shi], 44 vols., edited by Ji Xianlin 季羨林, Hefei: Anhui jiaoyu chubanshe, 2003, Vol. 23, pp. 498–500, p. 499. This was written on 24 August 1926.

68 See Wang Fan-sen, *Zhongguo jindai sixiang yu xueshu de xipu*, pp. 337–339.

69 See Wu Wenzhang, "Cong sixiangshi lun zhanhou Taiwan Ruxue de liang da dianxing," p. 2. Wu also recounts the humiliation Mou Zongsan underwent in 1932 when he suggested to Hu Shi, then dean of the department, that Mou work on Chinese metaphysics.

70 Sang Bing 桑兵, "Heng kan cheng ling ce cheng feng: Xueshu shicha yu Hu Shi de xueshu diwei" 橫看成嶺側成峰：學術視差與胡适的學術地位 [Views from different perspectives: Academic perspectives and Hu Shi's position in China's academia], *Lishi yanjiu* 歷史研究 5 (2003), pp. 35–42.

71 Fu Sinian, "Yu Gu Jiegang lun gu shi shu," pp. 446–473. The letter was very long, and Fu had not finished copying it when his ship arrived in Canton. Gu Jiegang waited one year for it to be completed and finally published it as it was (p. 473), which made Fu Sinian very angry. It is partly included in *Gushi bian* 古史辨 [Disputing ancient history], Vol. 2, edited by Gu Jiegang 顧頡剛 (Taibei: Landeng wenhua, 1926–1941/1987), pp. 288–301.

72 Fu Sinian, "Yu Gu Jiegang lun gu shi shu," p. 459.

73 *Ibid.*, p. 460. See also Fu Sinian, "Zhi Hu Shi [1926]," p. 41.

74 See Feng Youlan 馮友蘭, *Zhongguo zhexueshi* 中國哲學史 [History of Chinese philosophy], Vol. 1 (Shanghai: Shenzhou guoguangshe, 1931), pp. 7–8. Feng argued that, at least in theory, a Chinese label could just as well be applied to Western philosophy. But with his historical approach, Fu even denied the appropriateness of using one Chinese term for all historical periods. For Feng's use of *yili zhi xue* as a general Chinese (and possible universal) category, see John Makeham's introduction to this volume.

75 For the debate among contemporary scholars on the inappropriateness of applying Han categories to Warring States thought, see for example Mark Csikszentmihalyi and Michael Nylan, "Constructing Lineages and Inventing Traditions through Exemplary Figures in Early China," *T'oung Pao* 89 (2003), pp. 59–99.

76 Fu Sinian, "Yu Gu Jiegang lun gu shi shu," p. 460. In this letter, written between 1924 and 1926, Fu speaks of the "proto-dao-branch" (*gu dao zong* 古道宗) and "proto-ru-branch" (*gu ru zong* 古儒宗) instead of *daojia* 道家 and *rujia* 儒家.

77 On the switch from the Institute for Philology and History to the Institute for History and Philology, see Wang Fan-sen, *Fu Ssu-nien*, pp. 66–67. Cai Yuanpei had apparently planned an Institute of Psychology, which was to be headed by Fu, but the latter persuaded Cai to found an Institute for History and Philology instead.

78 He wrote many pieces in 1928, some of which were only published in the year of his death (1950).

79 Fu Sinian, "Lishi Yuyan Yanjiusuo gongzuo zhi zhiqu" 歷史語言研究所工作之旨趣 [Manifesto for the work of the Institute of History and Philology], in *Fu Sinian quanji*, Vol. 3, pp. 3–13. See also Wang Fan-sen, *Fu Ssu-nien*, pp. 55–97, who also shows (p. 66) that this manifesto was largely planned during Fu's years abroad.

80 Fu Sinian, "Lishi Yuyan Yanjiusuo gongzuo zhi zhiqu," p. 11.

81 Axel Schneider, "Between Dao and History: Two Chinese Historians in Search of a Modern Identity for China," *History and Theory: Studies in the Philosophy of History*, 35.4 (December 1996), p. 69.

82 Fu Sinian, "Zhanguo zijia xulun" 戰國子家敘論 [Discussion of the masters of the Warring States], in *Fu Sinian quanji*, Vol. 2, pp. 249–304. This was written in 1928 but published in 1950.

83 Fu Sinian, "Xing ming guxun bianzheng xun" 性命古訓辯證訓 [Disputation and verification of the ancient glosses on human nature and destiny], in *Fu Sinian quanji*, Vol. 2, pp. 499–666, p. 508. Although published in 1940, this piece was largely drafted before 1937.

84 Fu Sinian, "Lun zhexue nai yuyan zhi fuchanpin; Xiyang zhexue ji Yindu Ri'erman yuyan zhi fuchanpin; Hanyu shi fei zhexue de yuyan; Zhanguo zhuzi yi fei zhexuejia" 論哲學乃語言之副產品，西洋哲學即印度日耳曼語言之副產品，漢語實非哲學的語言，戰國諸子亦非哲學家 [About philosophy being a by-product of language; Western philosophy being the by-product of Indo-Germanic languages; Chinese, in fact, being an unphilosophical language; and the Warring States masters also not being philosophers], in *Fu Sinian quanji*, Vol. 2, pp. 251–254.

85 *Ibid.*, p. 251.

86 *Ibid.*

87 *Ibid.*, p. 252.

88 *Ibid.*

89 *Ibid.*, p. 251.

90 *Ibid.*

91 As a student he had defended the importance of language in relation to thought. See, for example, the debate with Gu Jiegang on the relation between language and thought in *Xin chao* 1.4 (April 1919) in Fu Sinian, "Fu Sinian da Gu Chengwu" 傅斯年答顧誠吾 [Fu Sinian answers Gu Chengwu], in *Fu Sinian quanji*, Vol. 1, p. 237. See also Vera Schwarcz, *The Chinese Enlightenment*, pp. 78–79.

92 Fu Sinian, "Zhongguo gudai wenxue shi jiangyi" 中國古代文學史講義 [Lecture on the history of ancient Chinese literature], in *Fu Sinian quanji*, Vol. 2, pp. 12–133. The first part of the "Fanlun" 泛論 [General discussion] is entitled "Sixiang he yuyan: Yige wenxue jieshuo" 思想和語言：一个文學界説 (Thought and language: A definition of literature], pp. 12–15. This lecture was drafted in 1928 at Zhongshan University and published in 1950 at National Taiwan University.

93 Fu refers to John Watson, *Psychology from the Standpoint of a Behaviourist* (Philadelphia and London: Lippincott Company, 1919) and John Watson, *Behaviourism* (London: Kegan Paul, 1931). In *Psychology from the Standpoint of a Behaviourist*, Watson considers behaviourism to be "a true and legitimate field for experimental study of our human material. It must be experimental and we must some time have laboratories" (p. 8).

94 Fu Sinian, "Zhongguo gudai wenxue shi jiangyi," p. 12.

95 Fu Sinian's own theory on the origin of philosophy as proposed in his "Discussion of the masters of the Warring States" does however suggest that, after a culture clash, we are able to think independently of language since he

    sees philosophy as the attempt to reconcile more abstract thought with a less cultivated language.

96   Wang Fan-sen also notes the influence of Wilhelm von Humboldt (1767–1835) on Fu's ideas concerning the relation between thought and language. See Wang Fan-sen, *Fu Ssu-nien*, p. 134. For the influence of behaviourism on Chinese students, see Xiaoqing Diana Lin, *Peking University*, p. 143–151.

97   Fu Sinian, "Lun zhexue nai yuyan zhi fuchanpin," p. 252. This view is in line with that of Jin Yuelin, who believed that, although the content of thought is reliant upon language, it is also independent from language. See Yvonne Schulz Zinda's chapter, "Jin Yuelin's Ambivalent Status as a 'Chinese Philosopher,' in this volume.

98   For a contemporaneous debate in the USSR, see, for example, Werner Meissner, *Philosophy and Politics in China: The Controversy over Dialectical Materialism in the 1930s*, translated from German (1986) by Richard Mann (London: Husts & Company, 1990) on the debate between mechanical materialism (science outstrips philosophy) and dialectical materialism (philosophy retains a dominant role above science). For an example of contemporary reflections on philosophy (as a problem-solving discipline) in relation to science (providing knowledge of the world), see Brian Leiter, *The Future for Philosophy* (Oxford: Clarendon, 2004), pp. 3–6, 11–17.

99   *Fu Sinian wenwu ziliao xuanji*, p. 153.

100   Fu Sinian, "Lun zhexue nai yuyan zhi fuchanpin," pp. 252–253.

101   Fu also supports his view by making reference to "the many examples" given by "previous people." See *ibid.*, pp. 251–252. However, he does not provide any of these specifically. I thank Ge Zhaoguang 葛兆光 for helping me identify Yesibo as Otto Jespersen. On Jespersen and the Chinese language, see Otto Jespersen, *Progress in Language: With Special Reference to English* (Amsterdam & Philadelphia: John Benjamins Publishing Company, 1993), pp. 80–111 and Robert Kern, "Otto Jespersen and Chinese as the Future of Language," in *Orientalism, Modernism, and the American Poem* (Cambridge: Cambridge University Press, 1996), pp. 111–114.

102   Fu Sinian, "Lun zhexue nai yuyan zhi fuchanpin," p. 253.

103   A. C. Graham, *Disputers of the Tao: Philosophical Argument in Ancient China* (La Salle: Open Court, 1989) p. 406. For the general argument, see pp. 406–414. Graham argues that the philosophical problem of distinguishing essence from existence was caused by language, and that the Chinese translations needlessly invented neologisms to make a point which could not (and need not) be made in Chinese.

104   Fu explains between brackets: "Such as the fact that the concept of Cangality (*sic*) arises under the influence of the concept of the Instrnmental (*sic*) or Ablative position of the words." See *ibid.*, p. 253. I must admit that this explanation is not totally clear to me. I also do not know whether the mistakes in English are Fu Sinian's or the editor's.

105 *Ibid.*, p. 253. One wonders to what extent, in Fu's opinion, pre-Aristotelian philosophy was also determined by language, and what the implications of this are for its correspondence with Chinese thought.

106 We know from *Feng Youlan xiansheng nianpu chubian* (p. 80) that in 1929 Fu Sinian presented Feng Youlan with a draft version of this book and that, in the same year, Feng Youlan finished writing a draft of the first volume of his *Zhongguo zhexueshi*, which he gave to "teachers and friends" for comments, including perhaps Fu Sinian. No record is preserved of Fu Sinian's explicit response to Feng's work. On the non-relation between Fu and Feng, see Carine Defoort, "Fu Sinian in the Mirror: His Non-Existing Debate with Feng Youlan," paper presented at the First Workshop on The Formation and Development of Academic Disciplines in Twentieth-Century China (Canberra, December 2007).

107 Fu Sinian, "Lun zhexue nai yuyan zhi fuchanpin," p. 253.

108 This is a central idea in both Vera Schwarcz's *The Chinese Enlightenment* and Wang Fan-sen's *Fu Ssu-nien*.

109 Fu Sinian, "Lun zhexue nai yuyan zhi fuchanpin," p. 253.

110 The term *fangshu* 方術 (not *fangshujia* 方術家) occurs once in *Zhuangzi*, but, as mentioned above, Fu dated the book (but not necessarily the writing of the separate chapters) to the Han. The term occurs once in *Huainanzi* 淮南子, and once in Mei Cheng's 枚乘 *Qifa* (in its last fragment), where it explicitly refers to men such as Zhuang Zhou, Wei Mou, Yang Zhu, Mo Di, Kongzi, Laozi, and Mengzi.

111 See Fu Sinian, "Xing ming guxun bianzheng xun," pp. 499–666. At the end of his life, as the president of National Taiwan University, Fu returned to Mencius. See Wang Fan-sen, *Fu Ssu-nien*, pp. 126–139.

112 Fu Sinian, "Lun zhexue nai yuyan zhi fuchanpin," pp. 253–254. Fu argues that the Warring States masters closely resemble the clients of patrons in seventeenth and eighteenth-century Europe, who were not considered philosophers either.

113 Wang Fan-sen, *Fu Ssu-nien*, p. 197.

114 Personal communication (letter of July 2009) from Li Minghui. Li also indicated that Fu Sinian's most direct influence was on the Academia Sinica: Li confirms the complaints of Xu Fuguan and Mou Zongsan, noted above, that there is a very strong current at Academia Sinica against (Chinese) philosophy. But Fu Sinian also indirectly, through his connection with Hu Shi, influenced the human sciences with his preference for textual studies over philosophical reflection.

Chapter 10

Marxist Views on Traditional Chinese Philosophy Pre-1949[1]

Yvonne Schulz Zinda

At the beginning of the twentieth century, discussions arose regarding the appropriate methodology to be applied in the historiography of Chinese philosophy. Were Western categories suitable to describe Chinese traditions? More specifically: Could *dao* 道 be equated with the Western term "philosophy"?[2] Western-orientated scholars such as Hu Shi 胡適 (1891–1962) and later Feng Youlan 馮友蘭 (1895–1990) made the first efforts at writing a history of Chinese philosophy. Beijing (Peking) University, Qinghua (Tsinghua) University, and later South-Western United University became centers for academic philosophy modeled after institutions in Europe and America. In the 1930s and 1940s, Chongqing and Yan'an established themselves as centers for Marxist studies. Chinese Marxists started to work on the history of Chinese philosophy relatively late. In 1940, the journal *Zhexue* 哲學 included a bibliography of Marxist works of philosophy published in China before 1940. Among the ten works listed under the section "History of philosophy," Zhao Jibin's 趙紀彬 (1905–1982) *Zhongguo zhexueshi gangyao* 中國哲學史綱要 (1939) is the only work on Chinese philosophy.[3] Earlier attempts had been made to place traditional Chinese thought into a Marxist framework. In the mid-thirties, Marxist-oriented scholars started to reflect upon the historiography of traditional Chinese philosophy. Ye Qing 葉青 (penname of Ren Zhuoxuan 任卓宣 [1896–1990]) edited a two-volume *Hu Shi pipan* 胡適批判 [Hu Shi criticism][4] in 1933 and Li Da 李達 (1890–1966), the first systematic interpreter of Marxism, also criticized Hu Shi's work from a Marxist point of view.[5]

Various studies have dealt with different aspects of the introduction of Marxism.[6] As yet, little attention has been paid to the Marxist conception of traditional Chinese philosophy in the Republican era (1911–1949).

Due to the lack of secondary sources and the abundance of primary material on this subject, this chapter provides an overview of the early roots of Marxist-oriented historiography of this subject. The sources selected for this study are those that attempted to put traditional Chinese philosophy or thought as a whole into a Marxist framework. They can be arranged in two phases. The first phase is the application of Marxism to the historiography of Chinese philosophy in the mid-1930s, as represented in the works of Li Shicen 李石岑 (1892–1934), Fan Shoukang 范壽康 (1895–1982), Chen Zhongfan 陳鐘凡 (1888–1982), and the early Zhao Jibin. The second is the consolidation of Marxism in the 1940s in the works of the Chongqing school represented by Hou Wailu 侯外廬 (1903–1987) and the later Zhao Jibin. In the 1950s, Hou Wailu's *Zhongguo sixiang tongshi* 中國思想通史 [General history of Chinese thought] became the standard work and was republished in the 1980s by Renmin chubanshe. Zhao Jibin and the historian Du Guoxiang 杜國庠 (1889–1961) became the co-editors of the first volume that appeared in 1949 along with all of the subsequent volumes.

The first section of this chapter, "Importing Marxism into China," introduces translations and transmitters of Marxism. Since Marxist historiography on philosophy integrates social, political, and economic issues, the analysis of traditional Chinese philosophy cannot be separated from other debates.[7] This statement especially applies to the major debate on Chinese social history that took place among left-wing intellectuals and in the Marxist community in the 1930s; this will be briefly outlined. Then the centers as well as the major journals of Marxist scholarship in the philosophical discipline are identified. In the second and third sections, "Pioneers in Marxist historiography of philosophy" and "Consolidation: The Works of Hou Wailu and Zhao Jibin," selected historiographical works are introduced, focusing on issues concerning the form and periodization of Chinese philosophy and the selection and categorization of Chinese philosophers. It is divided into two periods: the pioneers and the consolidation of Marxist scholarship. The conclusion summarizes the development of Marxist academic historiography of philosophy.

1. Importing Marxism to China

The earliest mention of socialism seems to have been in Yan Fu's 嚴複 (1854–1921) essay "Yuan qiang" 原強 [On power] written in 1895.[8] Xiong

Yuezhi claims that Marx and his theory were first introduced in 1899 in a translation from Benjamin Kidd's (Xiede 頡德) work under the title of *Datongxue* 大同學 [Study on the great unity].[9] In 1908, *Tianyi bao* 天義報—a newspaper established by anarchist groups in Japan—first published parts of Marx's *Communist Manifesto* and Engels' foreword to the 1888 English edition. It is based on Japanese translations from 1904 and 1906.[10] In the beginning, intellectuals informed themselves through Chinese translations of Japanese translations as well as original writings on Marxism.[11] Kawakami Hajime 河上肇 (1879–1946) was the most influential Japanese translator of Marxist works and was widely read by Chinese Marxist intellectuals. Not only Li Dazhao 李大釗 (1889–1927) but also Guo Moruo 郭沫若 (1892–1978) acknowledged his works.[12] Two translations of Akizawa Shūji's works are also mentioned in the 1940 bibliography. Zhao Jibin referred to one of them, *Dongyang zhexueshi* 東洋哲學史 [History of Eastern philosophy], as a major influence on his *Zhongguo zhexueshi gangyao*.

Chenshan Tian has linked the influx of Marxism with the Chinese students studying Western learning (*xixue* 西學) in Japan after China's defeat in the Sino-Japanese War in 1895. Marxism, socialism, and the idea of dialectics were introduced as part of Western learning.[13] The earliest, most prominent transmitter was probably Liang Qichao 梁啟超 (1873–1929), who had to flee to Japan after the Hundred Days' Reform in 1898. He established two journals, *Qingyibao* 清議報 [The China discussion] in 1899 and the *Xinmin congbao* 新民叢報 [New people's miscellany] in 1902. Drawing on Japanese sources, he even developed a personal style in introducing Western philosophical and political theory.[14] This "Liang Qichao-style" or "new style" influenced later generations. For example, leading figures in the May Fourth Movement of 1919 such as Hu Shi and Chen Duxiu 陳獨秀 (1879–1942), Guo Moruo, and even Mao Zedong 毛澤東 (1893–1976) were influenced by it.[15] In the early 1900s Liang Qichao outlined Kang Youwei's ideal of utopia as "socialism."[16] Not surprisingly, the understanding of such novel terms was neither consistent nor clear. In the beginning, terms such as "socialism," "Marxism," "anarchism," and "democracy" were intermingled.[17] Japanese sources had a further impact on immediate understanding through translation, especially of technical terms.[18]

In 1927, translations of Marxist works by Marx, Engels, Lenin, and Stalin suddenly increased. Stalin's works in particular were rendered into Chinese between 1934 and 1937.[19] In May 1938 the C[hinese]

C[ommunist] P[arty] Central Academy for Marxism-Leninism (Zhonggong zhongyang Malie xueyuan 中共中央馬列學院) was created in Yan'an as the first official organ with the task of translating a canon of Marx's and Lenin's works.[20] By the 1930s, the understanding of Marxism had consolidated. Huang Jiande contends that between 1928 and 1930 approximately forty titles of Marx's and Engels' works were published for the first time in Chinese. A contemporary source claimed that 50% of the 400 social science books published during this same period related to Marxism or dialectical materialism. Translations were undertaken of Russian, Japanese, and German writings on Marxist philosophy, including works by Kawakami Hajime, G. Plekhanov, and A. M. Deborin along with texts by younger Soviet Marxists.[21] The main transmitter of Marxist thought in China, Ai Siqi (1910–1966), translated (with Zheng Yili) M. Mitin's (1901–1987) essay, "Dialectical Materialism," under the significantly different title of *Xin zhexue dagang* 新哲學大綱 [Outline of new philosophy] in 1936. They revised it in 1938 and reprinted it several times.[22] Both Ai and Zheng had trained in Japan. However, some of this second generation of translators had also studied in the West and therefore had a more direct access to the original works. For example, Hou Wailu, who translated Marx's *Das Kapital*, had studied in Paris (1927–1930) and lived for a time in Russia.

Hegel provided another point of entry to the study of Marxism. It was not only right-wing or Western-orientated philosophers such as He Lin 賀麟 (1902–1992) who took notice of Hegel's idealism but also Marxist Chinese scholars. Ai Siqi's main opponent, Ye Qing, published a collection of studies by well known scholars such as He Lin and Zhang Junmai 張君勱 (1886–1969) on Hegel titled *Heige'er* 黑格爾 commemorating his anniversary with an appendix on Feuerbach.[23] From their studies of Hegel, Marxists such as Li Da, Wu Liangping 吳亮平 (1908–1986), Shen Zhiyuan 沈志遠 (1902–1965), Zhang Ruxin (1908–1976), Chen Weishi 陳唯實 (1913–1974),[24] and Ai Siqi posited dialectical materialism as the basis for the New Philosophy, which became equivalent to Marxist theory.[25] The Chinese pioneers of Marxist philosophy were Qu Qiubai 瞿秋白 (1899–1935), Ai Siqi, and Li Da. According to Nick Knight, they emphasized politics as well as philosophy. The latter two contributed to translating Marxist texts, which received much attention from Mao Zedong.[26]

From 1931 until 1936 Chinese Marxists were heavily influenced by discussions in Soviet New Philosophy. Three works were central: M. Mitin et al., *Outline of New Philosophy* (originally, *Dialectical*

Materialism); his *Dialectical and Historical Materialism*; and M. Shirokov and A. Aizenberg et al., *A Course on Dialectical Materialism.*[27] In these works Knight identified six themes that created the basis for the Chinese Marxists' interpretation of dialectical materialism. Some of these aspects are directly related to the historiography of philosophy. First, it is the materialist ontology that recognizes the two tendencies of materialism and idealism in the development of philosophy. They are determined by the answer to the basic question of the relation between reality and consciousness. Materialists hold that reality determines human consciousness. It follows Hegel's dialectical premise but rejects his notion of an absolute being; and it affirms that change is neither at random nor accidental. Change takes place according to a pattern of affirmation and negation. The identity of opposites is the premise for existence and for development in this dialectical process. Knowledge is reflected in the brain of the subject. The process of knowledge is developmental, going through stages. Knowledge production relies on different social practices, of which production and class struggle are the most important.[28] This shows a broader understanding of the historical process that is not limited to theory and philosophy.

1.1   Debates on Chinese History and Philosophy

The split between the Guomindang (GMD) and CCP due to the GMD assault on Shanghai Communists and worker unions in 1927 led to an increasingly critical attitude among the intellectuals and sparked an interest in Marxist theory. This resulted in "the controversy on China's social history" among Marxist-oriented intellectuals between 1928 and 1937.[29] It was part of an international debate which had started earlier in the Soviet Union and Japan. The points of discussion were the nature of contemporary (pre-communist) Chinese society and the Marxist periodization of Chinese history.[30] During this period Marxist thought in China matured.[31] In the mid-1930s—towards the end of the "controversy on China's social history"—the first academic efforts were made to write a history of Chinese philosophy using a Marxist framework. This subject is also closely related to the historiography of Chinese philosophy. Most of the early histories mentioned so far began by explaining the historic periods before delving into the history of philosophy or intellectual history. As Arif Dirlik has pointed out, most Marxist historians had a complex conception of historical explanation as an "interaction of forces immanent in the socioeconomic structure."[32]

In his early analysis Benjamin Schwartz identified three groups in this debate, each differing on the interpretation of the main "mode of production"[33] in Chinese history. The first group are the protagonists of capitalist theory who argue that all material evidence points to the fact that the capitalist mode of production already existed in early China.[34] The second group are the protagonists of feudalism, who identify feudalism with individual landlordism. This group took the state as a derivative feature of the superstructure.[35] The third group are the protagonists of the Asiatic mode of production. They were fewer in China than in the Soviet Union. For Marx, water control was crucial to the Asiatic mode, as a variant of other modes of production. Among the historians of Chinese philosophy Hou Wailu proposed this last model.[36]

Dirlik identifies three dominant groups in academic Marxism after 1933. Two of them are also relevant to the historiography of philosophy: scholars such as Zhou Gucheng 周穀城 (1898–1996; Chongqing Fudan University) who employed historical materialism in an eclectic way; and a group of (Yan'an) scholars such as Jian Bozan 剪伯贊 (1898–1968), Fan Wenlan 範文瀾 (1893–1979), and He Ganzhi 何干之 (1906–1969) whose views became dominant after 1949. They adopted the so-called five-stage view of history: 1) primitive communism, 2) slavery, 3) feudalism, 4) capitalism, and 5) socialism. This became orthodoxy among communists after Stalin approved the *History of the Communist Party of the Soviet Union*, which appeared in 1938. Dirlik shows that historians of the China Historical Research Association (Zhongguo lishi yanjiuhui 中國歷史研究會) reached consensus on the five-stage theory as represented in Fan Wenlan's *Zhongguo tongshi jianpian* 中國通史簡篇 [Abridged general history of China], published in 1947. Although Fan Wenlan was the editor, it was a joint production of several historians and sponsored by the Association.[37] Some of the following histories of philosophy also adopted this five-phase-model. Among the intellectuals who participated in these debates, Schwartz distinguished those driven by politics and those who were merely looking for an explanatory tool.[38] This observation applies as well to Marxist thinkers in the realm of philosophy centered on Yan'an and Chongqing.

1.2 Centers and Journals

After the outbreak of the Sino-Japanese War two centers of Marxist historiography and New Philosophy emerged in Yan'an and Chongqing. In 1937 a number of famous historians flocked to Yan'an. Among them were Wu Yuzhang 吳玉章 (1878–1966), Fan Wenlan, He Ganzhi, Yin Da 尹達 (1906–1983), Tong Dong 佟冬 (1905–1996), and Ye Huosheng 葉蠖生 (1904–1990). That same year, Fudan University moved to Chongqing and only went back in 1946. A year later, after the Guomindang had left, Chongqing became the second center hosting well-known Marxist-scholars such as Guo Moruo, (temporarily) Jian Bozan, Hou Wailu, Deng Chumin 鄧初民 (1889–1981), Du Guoxiang, Hu Sheng 胡繩 (1918–2000), Ji Wenfu 稽文甫 (1895–1963), Wu Ze 吳澤 (1913–2005), and Zhao Jibin. According to Huang Jing each group developed its own style. Chongqing scholars preferred the history of ancient Chinese society and thought.[39] In Yan'an the Zhonggong Zhongyang Malie Xueyuan was divided into two branches representing their different tasks: the education of cadres and the translation of the Marxist canon.

On 30 September 1938, an article appeared in *Jiefang zhoukan* 解放週刊 [Liberation weekly] announcing the establishment of the Yan'an New Philosophy Association (Yan'an xin zhexueshe 延安新哲學社). Among the initial members were Ai Siqi, Chen Boda 陳伯達 (1904–1989), and Zhou Yang 周揚 (1908–1989); after the establishment of the PRC they all became important figures in academic politics, but not in academia. In the Association's statutes, members proclaimed their commitment to apply the lessons learnt from the anti-Japanese war, as well as the best theoretical achievements from inside and outside China, "to promote the most oustanding elements in the traditions of the Chinese nation."[40] Following Mao's call for a study competition within the party on the sixth plenary session of the sixth Party committee in October 1938, various study groups were established. Mao created his personal philosophy study group (*zhexue xiaozu* 哲學小組), which included Ai Siqi, He Sijing 何思敬 (1896–1968), Yang Chao 楊超 (1905–?) not known, and Chen Boda as members.[41] The most important figure in Marxist theory was Mao's close assistant, Ai Siqi, who illustrated Marxist theory through examples and sayings drawn from daily life. Knight suggests that Ai's strength was "to elaborate through simplification."[42] Ai's main work is *Dazhong zhexue* 大眾哲學 [Philosophy for the masses], first published in 1938 and reprinted several times. However, he also wrote for other readers. For example, *Zhexue xuanji* 哲學選集 [Philosophy selection] is based on extracts from the three Soviet works mentioned above, as well as *Shehuixue dagang* 社會學大綱 [Outline of sociology].[43]

The Yan'an New Philosophy Association sought to integrate universal truths with the practice of Chinese revolution. It did not pursue the scholarly undertaking of categorizing and evaluating traditional Chinese thought in order to write a history. Mao Zedong Thought was officially adopted as the guiding principle at the seventeenth Party congress in 1945. Knight observed that: "Once 'Mao Zedong Thought' was established as Party ideology, the Yan'an Philosophy Association outlived its purpose, or at least its title. The task of its philosophers and theorists henceforth was no longer the dissemination of the New Philosophy (under that name, at least) but the elaboration of Mao's philosophical thought."[44] Earlier on, the same process of homogenization had taken place in the Zhonggong zhongyang Malie xueyuan. In July 1941 it was renamed the Malie yanjiuyuan 馬列研究院 (Marx-Lenin Research Institute); the following month it became the Zhongyang yanjiuyuan 中央研究院 (Central Research Institute) marking the transition to a central academic party instrument.[45]

The explorations into traditional Chinese philosophy undertaken by most Yan'an scholars should be read against this political background. Ai Siqi concentrated his efforts on the sinification of Marxism rather than the application of Marxist terms to Chinese tradition. In 1934 he wrote an essay called "Analysis of the Term 'the Mean.'"[46] Despite the title, Ai did not intend to write a scholarly work on Chinese philosophy. Rather it should be understood—according to Chenshan Tian's description—as "a strand of Chinese Marxism that draws on the Chinese tradition and that overcomes some of the difficulties that have attended Western Marxism." This form of Marxism is found in the writings of Mao Zedong and Qu Qiubai.[47] Acknowledging that the mean is a universal, Ai compared it to Hegel's ethical notion of quality (*zhiliang* 質量). He attached what he later called "mean-ism" to the Confucian ethical system and identified it as metaphysics. He did not yet apply the division of idealism and materialism to this traditional notion, but he described the Confucian ethical system of mean-ism employing such terms as "abstract"[48] and "absolute ideals."[49] These two terms point already to the attributes of idealism in the Marxist value-system. Ai characterized "the mean" as a "conservative ideology."[50] In opposition to mean-ism he identified Hegel's ethics as close to materialism.[51]

Another example is an early essay by Chen Boda on filial piety (*xiao* 孝). He essentialized filial piety as good relations and tried to accommodate it within the communist conception of new society.[52] The Chongqing historian Hu Sheng later wrote an essay titled "Lun cheng" 論誠 [On sincerity] with a similar political intention. It too is not a scholarly analysis of the past but rather emphasises the future of China, as his concluding paragraph shows. After discussing this traditional Chinese term, Hu Sheng continued: "From what has been said above, one can see that the meaning of the term 'sincerity' is not something which deserves to be fully affirmed. The problem is that it cannot be simply turned into an abstract, absolute dogma but has to be explained in terms of real, concrete, practical life. From the praxis of the present experience of anti-fascist battle, sincerity should mean to us: in the anti-fascist lineup every country and every power should regard and treat one other with sincerity."[53]

In Yan'an, Marxist academic work developed under Mao Zedong; in Chongqing Zhou Enlai 周恩來 (1898–1976) led academic life.[54] Yan'an academic research was largely influenced by Soviet historical scholarship. After the translation of Stalin's *Liangong (bu) dangshi jianming jiaocheng* in 1938 and successively published in Yan'an's *Jiefang zhoukan*, Mao praised it as an historical as well as a theoretical work and recommended it for study in 1939.[55] Chongqing scholar Hou Wailu disagreed with Stalin's theory in this work that productive forces and relations of production constituted the productive mode of society. In following Marx's *Das Kapital*, Hou stated that the productive mode is derived from the particular material of production and particular labour forces, both of which are determined by history.[56]

Being at the political center, Yan'an Marxists sought to popularize New Philosophy and educate the masses. They emphasized the study of Marxism and further research into historical materialism. The study of history was directly related to the practical issues of the revolutionary course. Work on China's general history as well as modern history was always consistent with Mao's theories and the undertakings of the CCP. In contrast, the Chongqing historians were more focused on scholarship. Their emphasis on antiquity—as represented by Guo Moruo, Jian Bozan, and Hou Wailu—was a consequence of their direct involvement in the debates on social history. Another reason was that after arriving in Chongqing the Marxist historians had to keep a low profile by taking up their former research on antiquity during the White Terror. Guo Moruo wrote his *Shi pipanshu* 十批判書 [Ten critical essays] (1945); Jian Bozan was dedicated to Qin and Han studies; and Hou Wailu studied ancient Chinese society.[57] Hou Wailu, Zhao Jibin, and Du Guoxiang were the leading scholars in the field of the history of philosophy and intellectual history in the 1940s and 1950s.

Before the establishment of the Marxist journals in the 1930s, *Xin qingnian* 新青年 [New youth] was one of the main sources of intellectual debates involving different political views in Republican China. Chen Duxiu founded the journal with Li Dazhao and others. Li Dazhao's two most famous essays, which in 1950s PRC historiography are referred to as a major turning point in modern Chinese history, were published in 1918 in *Xin qingnian*.[58] Between 1934 and 1937, Ai Siqi edited the journal *Dushu shenghuo* 讀書生活 [Intellectual life], which attracted attention from the beginning of the debate between himself and Ye Qing.[59] The Yan'an branch of the Yan'an New Philosophy Association published *Zhongguo wenhua* 中國文化 [Chinese culture], and the Chongqing branch launched *Lilun yu xianshi* 理論與現實 [Theory and reality] in 1939. In Shanghai, two other journals appeared. In 1940 *Zhexue yuekan* 哲學月刊 [Philosophy monthly] was launched, its goal being the study and dissemination of Marxism. It ceased after one year when the Japanese invaded the Concessions.[60] The other was *Zhexue zazhi* 哲學雜誌 [Philosophy magazine], which included discussions on and translations of Soviet Marxists such as A. A. Zhdanov (1896–1948), whose definition of philosophy became standard in the 1950s.[61]

At the end of the nineteenth century the notion of Marxism was still vague and even confused with other Western terms of political theory. Marxist works and terms entered China through Japanese scholarship and translations. In the 1920s and the early 1930s, a wave of returnee Chinese students from Japan and the West contributed to the greater influence of Marxist works. With a better grasp of foreign languages, their translations became more accurate. Some were direct translations of the Marxist canon from Western languages and Russian. These prepared the way for Marxist scholarship in the mid-1930s. The scholarship can be divided into political and academic, corresponding with the two centers of Yan'an and Chongqing. Yan'an scholars occupied themselves with the sinification of Marxism as well as with the establishment of Mao Zedong Thought. Traditional Chinese philosophy became an instrument to secure the future of China. Scholars in Chongqing took a more scholarly approach, dedicating their studies to Chinese antiquity. One of the reasons for this development was that the GMD still dominated the political environment. Journals publishing the results of Marxist studies were established in the 1930s. Whereas Yan'an scholars became influential party officials in the 1950s, it was the Chongqing scholars who laid the foundation for the academic field of the historiography of Chinese thought.

2. Pioneers in Marxist Historiography of Philosophy

2.1 Li Shicen

Published in 1935, Li Shicen's[62] *Zhongguo zhexue shijiang* 中國哲學十講 [Ten lectures on Chinese philosophy][63] was based on lectures he had given in the summer of 1932 at the Fujian Provincial Education Bureau. He employed dialectical materialism as the guiding thought and leading method to study Chinese philosophy. In his lectures he followed neither a chronological, dynastic order nor the format of Masters Studies (*zhuzixue* 諸子學), where each thinker and each school was presented separately. He mostly discussed different schools of thought under a central theme or a certain characteristic. In his first lecture, he compared Chinese and Western philosophical traditions while stressing the universal character of philosophy. His other lectures dealt with Confucian ethical views, the practical spirit of the Mohists, Daoist cosmology, the dialectics and formal logic of the School of Names, philosophy of the doctrine of the Mean, Chan philosophy, the school of principle, the monism of *ti—yong* 體—用, and the philosophy of nature.

Li divided Western and Chinese philosophy into three eras almost within the same time frame, with Chinese philosophy starting a hundred years earlier (he does not indicate when Chinese or Western philosophy started). The first is one of growth (China: up until the third century B.C.; the West up until the fourth century B.C.); the second of transformation (China: third century B.C to the seventeenth century; the West: fourth century B.C. to seventeenth century) and the third of development (China and the West: seventeenth century until today).[64] Li characterized the first stage in China as essentially feudal. After the Spring and Autumn and Warring States periods, commercial and capital development followed. However, although feudalism had major setbacks, its system of landowners exploiting farmers prevailed and even intensified due to the development of commercial capital and the demand for luxury goods by landowners. This was reflected in the philosophy of the time and in two strands of thought: safeguarding feudalism and anti-feudal thought.[65] Li selected exemplary Chinese thinkers and compared them to Greek philosophers.[66] He described Chinese feudalism as unique because it was combined with a patriarchal system which placed aristocrats above agricultural society.[67]

Li designated the second era as starting from the beginning of the Qin dynasty and lasting until the beginning of the Qing dynasty. After the Qin and Han dynasties, he saw the particular patriarchal function of Chinese feudalism increasing, encouraged by the Mohists' concepts of ghosts and heaven (*tiangui guannian* 天鬼觀念). Following the convergence of Chinese society with religion, all three teachings became religions. For Li, this was why Buddhism and the three teachings "rode bridle to bridle" right from the beginning.[68] He also directly compared phenomena and currents in the Chinese and Western philosophical traditions. The first phenomenon is the blending of Confucianism and Buddhism on the one hand, and Hellenism and Hebrewism on the other, showing how religion substantially changed philosophy. In the following section, he compared the Neo-Confucian schools of Zhu Xi 朱熹 (1130–1200) and Wang Yangming 王陽明 (1472–1529) with those of Thomas Aquinas (ca. 1225–1274) and John Duns Scotus (ca. 1266–1308). Because each pair of philosophers distanced themselves from the philosophy of the former phase, Li linked this to the aggravation of feudalism in social history.[69]

The third phase extends from the Qing dynasty to the present. He identified "renaissance" as a common feature of Chinese and Western thought. He also saw in pre-Qin and Greek thought progressive elements of "doubting antiquity" and the search for evidence, which he defined in a relationship of cause and effect. Qing scholars went backwards from Song to Han sources (Han Learning), and from Han Learning to Masters Studies. Western scholarship, from Hume to Spencer, proceeded from mythology to metaphysics to science. Although the directions were different, Li granted both a similar spirit.[70]

Li then compared the traditions from the perspectives of dialectics, materialism, and dialectical materialism. Although both have strong similarities due to their social disposition—the existence of a ruling class that exploited its subjects—they started out differently. While the West was organized into a slave-owning society, China lived under feudal and patriarchal rule.[71] Li turned the number of dialectical elements into the yardstick for great thinkers. For the Confucians, he detected such elements particularly in *Zhongyong* 中庸 (*Doctrine of the Mean*) and *Yizhuan* 易傳 (Commentary on *Book of Change*). In the case of the early Daoists, he found *Laozi* 老子 and *Zhuangzi* 莊子 to be rich in dialectical thought. Li further listed the School of Names and their contradictory and anti-contradictory dialectics. He attributed some elements of dialectics to the Mohists. Later Neo-Confucianism drew from the dialectical outlook of Chan Buddhism but their standpoint rested in the "abyss of idealism."[72]

In his conclusion, Li acknowledged that "[m]ost Chinese thinkers knew how to employ dialectics, but they did not clearly and consciously regard dialectics as a method, much less apply it to the history of knowledge and epistemology. They knew how to employ dialectics in order to explain cosmology, but seldom did they know that dialectics in itself is a cosmology."[73]

In terms of materialist thought as defined by Marxist theoretician G. V. Plekhanov (1857–1918), Li Shicen saw little evidence of it in Chinese tradition since it mostly followed idealism. He merely pointed out that Laozi and Daoism were the most progressive currents in Chinese antiquity. For this reason Li also negated any dialectical materialism in the Chinese tradition.[74]

2.2 Fan Shoukang

Like Li Shicen, Fan Shoukang also published philosophy lectures he had given at Wuhan National University during his appointment there in 1930.[75] However, in contrast to Li, Fan arranged his lectures as a history of philosophy. While writing this work, Fan exchanged views with pioneers in the historiography of Chinese philosophy, such as Liang Qichao, Hu Shi, and Feng Youlan, whom he thanked in the early editions.[76] The work is comprised of six chapters, arranged chronologically, beginning with the pre-Qin period that he classified as Masters Studies. Apart from Han dynasty thinkers, Fan dedicated no separate sections to individual thinkers.

In a later foreword written one year before he died, Fan acknowledged that at that time he was deeply interested in Adam Smith's *On Wealth* and in Karl Marx's *Das Kapital*. Whereas Li Shicen only looked for dialectical elements, Fan attempted to describe Chinese thinkers of different historical periods based on Marx's notions of materialism and dialectical materialism.[77] Fan did not regard history as being created out of human free will; instead, he believed in a developmental history which takes "the necessary course of evolution." He also followed the Marxist view that granted human society the power to influence the course of events. According to this "new conception" he put forward three basic principles in studying history.[78]

First, he stated that the evolutionary process of human society is unending. He described two relationships that appear when humans exploit nature: humans towards nature and humans among themselves. The former is reflected in the notion of productive forces (*shengchan zhuli* 生產諸力; *Produktivkraefte*) and the latter in that of relations of production (*shengchan zhu guanxi* 生產諸關係; *Produktionsverhaeltnisse*), which, through their contradictions, comprise material life.[79] Second, the development of society depends on economic movements. Its different stages are thus in accordance with the development of productive forces.[80] The third principle spells out the relationship between existence and consciousness of society that Fan translated into the opposition of idealism (*guannianlun* 觀念論) and materialism (*weiwulun* 唯物論), adding the relationship of theory and practice. He stressed the dialectical materialist conception that the materialist world exists independent of our perception and that social consciousness follows social reality.[81] This shows Fan's complex understanding of history as influenced by social and economic factors.

After briefly introducing the reader to these principles, Fan then divides Chinese history according to Marxist historical conceptions into five stages.[82] He classified 1) the period before the Yin dynasty (?–1765 B.C.) as primitive communism without any documents; 2) the Yin dynasty (1764–1121 B.C.) as a slave-owning system; 3) the Zhou dynasty (1120–247 B.C.) as feudalism in which historians and diviners were the philosophers; 4) the period from Qin to the Opium Wars (246 B.C.–A.D. 1839) as a simple commercial economic system; and 5) from the Opium Wars to the present (1840–1935) as the capitalist period.[83] In spite of this periodization he divided his work on Chinese philosophy into six chapters, attributing to each an essential feature: 1) the pre-Qin (before 246 B.C.) schools of Confucians, Daoists, Mohists, the school of Names, and the Legalists (Masters Studies); 2) Han dynasty (206 B.C.–A.D. 220) (canonical studies); 3) Wei, Jin, and Northern and Southern dynasties (220–581) (Dark Learning [*xuanxue* 玄學]); 4) Sui and Tang dynasties (589–907) (Buddhist Learning); 5) Song to Ming dynasties (960–1644) (canonical studies) and 6) Qing dynasty (1622–1911) (canonical studies).

The division does not seem to support Fan's proclaimed notion of history as following a necessary course of evolution, since canonical studies recur. Fan named the dialectical concepts of *Yijing* 易經 (*Book of Change*) as the product of the feudal period which began at the turning point between the Yin and Zhou dynasties. He considered the Spring and Autumn and the Warring States periods as the most fecund for producing different schools. However, he shared Li Shicen's view that the next stage of the Qin was, philosophically speaking, a failure. He held socio-economic and political developments—such as the introduction of private landownership and the first Qin emperor's policy of keeping the people ignorant—responsible for philosophical currents. The Han dynasty aggravated the situation by turning Confucianism into ortho-doxy and rejecting all other schools.[84] Han thought was based on resur-recting antiquity and reverence for the king, and it was thus advantageous to Han emperors. Fan maintained that from the Han to the Qing dynas-ties, although the three schools of Confucianism, Daoism, and Buddhism "distrusted each other like relatives," they all supported imperial rule. He saw this as the reason for the slow development of productive forces and the unchanging relations of production during these many centuries and to be reflected in the philosophical ideology (*guannian xingtai* 觀念形態, translated by Fan as "Ideologie").[85]

For Fan, the New Text School is representative of the period after the Opium Wars in which the Western impact resulted in another turning point in thought based on the economic transition from handcrafts to mechanized industry. Likewise, Fan points out that the Qing Gongyang scholars were not only influenced by the thought of the Spring and Autumn period but even more by Western philosophical ideas such as liberty, equality, and compassion.[86] At the end of his introduction, he envisioned a future internationalized Chinese philosophy which had overcome its roots to the point of severing any ties with the past and which developed as part of world philosophy:

> Whether it is Confucianism, Buddhism, or Daoism, we cannot make use of any one of them for the establishment of a future, new Chinese thought. This is not only because the three schools were produced based on former productive relations, but also because only at that time were they able to serve kings and emperors. Now China has already become a China of the world. Due to the development of productive forces, the present economic world system is collapsing. In consequence, the world of thought is presently

also in a phase when the old is being substituted for the new. So in my opinion, the establishment of new Chinese thought is probably also the establishment of new world thought.[87]

2.3 Chen Zhongfan

Cai Shangsi 蔡尚思 (1905–2008) had originally planned to edit a series with Chen Zhongfan called *Zhongguo sixiangshi* 中國思想史 [History of Chinese thought]. His *Zhongguo sixiang yanjiufa* 中國思想研究法 [Method for the study of Chinese thought] was to be the first volume. Apparently they never realized their ambition.[88] In his foreword to *Zhongguo sixiang yanjiufa*, he described several reasons for the compilation of his book. Among them are the problems of categorization and poor methodology in the existing scholarship typically used in gathering material. The book is divided into seven chapters and deals with methods of research, collecting material, and the scope and selection of materials. It was widely received since it includes five forewords in addition to the author's own introduction.[89] The most detailed and, in terms of Marxism, most interesting foreword is that by Chen Zhongfan from 1936. It is included here because Chen briefly outlined the history of Chinese philosophy.

At the beginning of his foreword Chen quoted Plekhanov's *The Development of the Monist View of History* (1895), defining the difference between idealism (*guannianlun*) and materialism. He praised Cai Shangsi for adopting neither empty idealism nor mechanical materialism or a harmonized synthesis of both. Chen explained basic Marxist terms such as the relations of production, productive forces, and superstructure.[90] Similar to Fan Shoukang, he first divided the Chinese history of social development according to the relations of production into five phases.[91] Economically, Chen classified the Zhou as "feudal," understanding the term not only as a superstructure but also as mode of production. He characterized the phase from Qin to Qing as autocratic and proto-capitalist.[92] In addition to the political, legal, and cultural superstructures, Chen saw the economic basis reflected in the consciousness of these five phases.[93]

Again like Fan Shoukang, his analysis of Chinese thought had a different emphasis, identifying only four periods of thought. Neglecting the first two (pre-Yin and Yin dynasty), Chen arranged the feudal phase from Western Zhou to Qing into four sub-phases. The philosophical discussions after the Spring and Autumn period revealed the contradictions that appeared in the phase between the two Zhou (Eastern and Western) to the installment of the feudal system. Chen perceived the Qin and Han dynasties (246 B.C.–A.D. 220) as the "darkest age," triggering the Yellow Turbans Rebellion.[94] He classified the Wei and Jin dynasties (220–420) as a semi-feudal age and Song to Qing (960–1911) as a late phase of semi-feudalism.[95] In sum, he painted a less pessimistic picture of the development of traditional Chinese thought than Li Shicen and Fan Shoukang.

Chen identified some of the pivotal points when philosophy overcame the past and led to a new phase. These included, for example, the "skeptic" Wang Chong 王充 (ca. 27–ca. 97), Chan Buddhism, the "utilitarians" Ye Shi 葉適 (1150–1223) and Chen Liang 陳亮 (1143–1194) of the Song dynasty, and the practical learning (*shixue* 實學) of the Ming dynasty.[96] These turning points are used as proof in Chen's dialectical conception of history.

2.4   *Zhao Jibin*

Zhao Jibin—who belonged to the Chongqing branch of the Yan'an New Philosophy Association[97]—was one of the first to write a history of Chinese philosophy from a Marxist perspective.[98] In his foreword to the 1939 *Zhongguo zhexueshi gangyao* he announced that "this book is the first work of Chinese materialist history," apologizing at the same time for its possible shortcomings. This work seems to be a more conscious effort in which Zhao reflected upon the general difficulties of writing a history of Chinese philosophy. He followed the Marxist view of a complex historiography, relating the history of the development of society and of science to the history of materialism, which for him was equivalent to philosophy. Since he considered both fields still to be in their early phase, he relied on the Japanese materialist Akizawa Shūji for his introductory chapter. He referred to Guo Dingtang's 郭鼎堂 (penname of Guo Moruo) *Xian Qin tiandao guannian zhi fazhan* 先秦天道觀念之發展 [The development of the pre-Qin concept of the Heavenly Way] as a second source. Another, more general problem Zhao recounted was that the traditional texts were not easily accessible to youth if not sufficiently explained. Authenticity posed another difficulty for the texts. Zhao feared that, although he had tried to write an introductory work, the essays were too long and not written in a popular style. [99]

In tracking down dialectical as well as materialist factors, Zhao argued against two "prejudices" which deny the existence of materialism and dialectics in Chinese tradition. He named Hegel and Hartmann as representatives of those who even deny any philosophical tradition in China at all. He disagreed with Ranke, who excluded China as a unique case from universal developments.[100] Zhao defined philosophy as a synthesis of nature, society, and thought. Like Li Shicen and Chen Zhongfan, he considered philosophy to be a universal category necessarily produced in the progress of mankind. That China in its social development surpassed the phase of the slave-owning society was further proof of its having a philosophical tradition. In spite of particular forms, the basic categories underlying all philosophies were for Zhao idealism and materialism. He stated that the development from religion to philosophy and the continuous philosophical process is dialectical.[101] Zhao Jibin, similar to Fan Shoukang, understood philosophy as a particular form of ideology determined by economic and social factors, to which Zhao added the scientific as a third factor. All three are interrelated and determine each other: 1) productive forces and relations of production; 2) socio-political organization, that is the nature of class relations and their form; and 3) positivistic science, especially natural science.[102]

While claiming the universal character of Chinese philosophy, Zhao also acknowledged its particularity and urging that it should neither be denied nor exaggerated. To this end, he described three features of traditional Chinese philosophy. First, in China the development of materialism and dialectics was not complete. He identified the beginning of dialectics with the concept of "*yi* 易" in *Yijing*, and the beginning of materialism in the teaching of the five phases. Materialism became part of Laozi's systematic thought. Xunzi further developed the materialism and atheism of Yang Zhu but was circumscribed due to the Confucian notion of rites.[103] As had Chen Zhongfan, Zhao attributed a significant role to Wang Chong, even though he was eventually unable to create systematic materialist thought because he clung to naturalism. In spite of these early roots, Chinese materialism did not reach the quality of Democritus's atomic theory. Consequently, Zhao reasoned that natural science did not develop in China.[104] The second feature can be seen in Laozi's philosophy of human life, which Zhuangzi later turned into idealism. Zhao also saw this represented in Buddhist and Confucian concepts, although neither teaching had positive and scientific content.[105] For Zhao, as for both Li and Fan, the third and most distinctive feature of Chinese philosophy is that its development stagnated at the beginning in the Han dynasty.[106] Zhao did not restrict the history of philosophy to materialism but included the battle of materialism against idealism and the resulting dialectics and materialism. He closely related philosophy to social relations and social practice, turning everyday life into a factor that determines the character of philosophy.[107] After Sun Yat-sen, the May Fourth movement, the 1925/1927 revolution, and the import of materialism and dialectics, Chinese philosophy became part of world philosophy.[108]

The eighteen chapters of Zhao's *Zhongguo zhexueshi gangyao* are grouped into five parts. After the introduction on the development of Chinese society, science, and philosophy, Zhao continued with Masters Studies in part two, analyzing the thought of Laozi, Confucius, Mozi, Xunzi, and their disciples, as well as the School of Names. He classified Laozi, Mozi, and Xunzi as the materialists of Chinese antiquity and then described the three stages in the development of canonical studies. Canonical studies began with Han-dynasty thought. Zhao focused on the "religious idealist" Dong Zhongshu 董仲舒 (2nd century B.C.) as well as the "materialist" Wang Chong and then on Buddhism in the following dynasties. During the Song and Ming dynasties canonical studies entered its second phase with a new emphasis on elements of dialectical materialism associated with figures such as Zhou Dunyi 周敦頤 (1017–1073) and Zhang Zai (1020–1077). In addition, he described the idealism of Zhu Xi and the subjective idealism of Wang Yangming. Zhao saw the third stage climaxing in two waves of Qing criticism of the Wang Yangming School, leading eventually to the decline of canonical studies under imperialist invasion. In contrast to his other chapters, he did not focus on single philosophers. In the last subsection, he ended his analysis with the materialist and dialectical elements in Sun Yat-sen's empiricism.

Zhao divided the history of Chinese philosophy into Masters Studies and canonical studies, with modern thought being represented by Sun Yat-sen's empiricism. However, at the same time he employed other classifications recounting the three great philosophical traditions in China—Daoism, Confucianism, and Buddhism—to which he applied the Marxist categories of materialism and idealism, as well as subcategories in the case of individual philosophers. For instance, he categorized the two Cheng brothers as "idealist monists," while identifying the dialectical materialism inherent in their principle (*li* 理) and material-force (*qi* 氣) dualism. In his introductory chapter, Zhao further added to the confusion, dividing the development of Chinese philosophy into four stages and covering even the most recent events: 1) Masters Studies during the Spring and Autumn and Warring States periods to the Qin and its slave-owning society; 2) from Han to Tang as the turning point in canonical studies; 3) Song to the beginning of Qing; and 4) from the reign of Wenzong (or Xianfeng, beginning in 1851) to 1937.[109]

The studies outlined above all take a universal view of philosophy which they applied to traditional Chinese thought. They followed the complex Marxist understanding of history, including social and economic factors, as well as scientific factors as indicated by Zhao, in order to describe the history of Chinese thought. They evaluated it according to materialist and dialectical elements. Although they differ in their periodization schemes, they all considered the pre-Qin as a positive and creative phase. They regarded developments immediately after this more or less negatively, as a step backwards and as setting in place conditions which affected the subsequent development of Chinese philosophy. The end of the Qing, under the impact of Western thought, represented another major turning point. Fan, Chen, and Zhao shared a concern for the fate of China and a future vision for China to which they directly or indirectly saw their work as contributing. However, whereas Chen believed in the notion of using the philosophical heritage to serve a future China, Fan followed a radical anti-traditionalist path of rejecting the past. With the explorations of Chen and Zhao, the classification became more diverse and individualized.

3. Consolidation: The Works of Hou Wailu and the Later Zhao Jibin

3.1 *Hou Wailu*

Hou Wailu's *Zhongguo sixiang tongshi* 中國思想通史 [General history of Chinese thought][110] is adapted to the form of the "general history" that the new materialist conception adopted in order to describe the complex causal relations in historical development. The Marxist conception of history differed from the approach of "naïve positivists" such as Fu Sinian 傅斯年 (1896–1950), president of the Institute of History and Philology at the Academia Sinica, who emphasized textual criticism and refrained from interpretation.[111] While studying in Paris (1927–1930), Hou started to translate Marx's *Das Kapital*. The ten years of translation work enabled

Hou to reflect on how Marxism can be applied to Chinese ancient history. Later, in 1943, he published his thoughts in *Zhongguo gudian shehui lun* 中國古典社會論 [Discussions of classical Chinese society].[112] In 1932, the first volume of his translation appeared. Hou continued the work with Wang Sihua 王思華 (1904–1978), who later became member of the Yan'an New Philosophy Association.[113] Hou's studies were not restricted to the field of philosophy but also included intellectual history and early works on social history.[114]

Hou Wailu's *Zhongguo sixiang tongshi* is considered a milestone in Marxist historiography. Hou did not belong to the Yan'an group but was based in Chongqing. The first volume was published in 1947 and republished several times after the establishment of the PRC. The second volume, in two parts, appeared in 1950, the third in 1951. All volumes were revised and republished in 1957. According to his assistant, Zhang Qizhi, the fourth volume took a long time to write since during the day academics had to participate in various study groups as part of the Anti-Rightist Campaign. It appeared only in 1959. Although it was the standard work on the history of Chinese thought in the 1950s, Hou Wailu was tacitly already seen as heretical (*yiduan* 異端). According to Zhang Qizhi, Hou disagreed with Mao's opinion that Chinese antiquity had a system of private ownership. In the major discussion of the historiography of Chinese philosophy which occurred in 1957, he either did not take part or his paper was not included in the volume published afterwards.[115]

In much the same way as Zhao Jibin and Fan Shoukang, Hou understood philosophy—like science, art, logic, ethics, and religion—to be part of ideology.[116] Hou agreed with his contemporaries on the three aspects of the concept of *dao*. First, the traditional Chinese scholarly notion of *dao* is that of a *Weltanschauung* in which philosophy was the theoretical form of expression. He considered philosophical problems as inherent to every thought.[117] Second, *dao* is a kind of logical thinking that serves as a method to explain philosophical viewpoints, such as that developed by Hu Shi.[118] Third, *dao* is social consciousness,[119] a view obviously connected with the Marxist practice of including social factors in the notion of philosophy. In his foreword to *Zhongguo sixiang tongshi*, Hou stressed that the history of Chinese thought follows universal laws, denying that there is a special Eastern way of thought. Nevertheless, he conceded that Chinese thought had unique characteristics within the universal framework of dealing with life and changing reality. Hou, similar to Chen Zhongfan, aimed at "critically inheriting tradition."

The first volume is divided into three main parts and seventeen chapters. In the first part he addresses some general features of the Yin and two Zhou dynasties, relating political, religious, and social aspects. The second part is dedicated to Confucius and Mozi. The third, which is on the Hundred Schools, is the longest: Laozi; the subjective idealism of Zhuangzi; the metaphysical thought of Mencius; Hui Shi's 惠施 (3rd century B.C.) relativist and Gongsun Long's 公孫龍 (3rd century B.C.) absolutist sophistry; later Mohist epistemology and logic and the synthesizer Xunzi; the tragic history of the Legalists; and a general summary on the downfall of antiquity.

3.2 Zhao Jibin

In 1948 Zhao Jibin published *Zhongguo zhexue sixiang* 中國哲學思想 [Chinese philosophical thought].[120] In comparison to his earlier work, here he appears more moderate. Previously he had argued in a more general way, relating the particular features of traditional Chinese philosophy to the stages of its development. Similar to Hou, he became more specific and less mechanical in applying Marxist principles in this later work. Keeping his dialectical view of the history of philosophy, he followed Western universal models in dividing Chinese philosophical thought into three periods: 1) antiquity (starting with the Spring and Autumn period and the Hundred schools [from about 720 B.C.]; 2) the Middle Ages from Han to the beginning of Ming [220–1368]; and 3) modernity from the beginning of Ming to the Republican era [1368 on].[121]

Zhao identified three unique features of Chinese philosophical thought. The first is the style of the wise man (*xianren zuo feng* 賢人作風), which he likened to the Western notion of charisma and associated with the charisma of the wise (*zhizhe qixiang* 智者氣象). In the West, thinkers such as Plato and Aristotle, and later Spinoza (1632–1677) and Leibniz (1646–1716), were mainly concerned with philosophical problems such as the relation of thought and existence, the origin of the cosmos, and epistemology or method. In contrast, he characterized Chinese thinkers as not being concerned with philosophy, but rather with lifelong education, because they were interested in problems of ethics and politics. However, he also saw rare examples of the Western charisma of the wise model in the works of Mozi, Xunzi, and Wang Chong that led to accomplishments similar to those achieved in the West in regard to cosmology, epistemology, and logic. In logic, he mentioned names such as Hui Shi and

Gongsun Long. However, these currents remained hidden due to the prevailing orthodox thought. Only through the renaissance of Masters Studies during the enlightenment of the Qing dynasty did the situation gradually change.[122]

The second feature is the notion of former sage kings (*xianwang guannian* 先王觀念). Zhao stated that although the Chinese philosophers of antiquity and the Middle Ages had inquired into this historical notion, they did not question it. Only modern philosophers such as Tan Sitong and Sun Yat-sen negated it more strongly than the authors of *Mozi* and *Han Feizi*.[123] The third unique aspect was an attitude associated with canonical studies (*jingxue taidu* 經學態度). According to Zhao, this attitude, which prevailed from the time of Confucius, is "to transmit but not to create." Consequently, scholars only dared to comment upon the canonical works but not to study or criticize them. Zhao saw this as the result of the historical notion of the former sage kings.[124]

At the end of his introduction, Zhao summed up the reasons for these features of Chinese thought. Comparing the period of the Yin and Zhou dynasties to ancient Greece, like Hou Wailu he argued that, contrary to Greece, China had not developed a model of the revolutionary way but instead followed the path of reforms under the guidance of the aristocracy. This had economic as well as political consequences. For example, he argued that economically, the production of iron was not developed, and politically, there was no freedom and thus the clan system was not overthrown. Philosophically, it meant that no private, independent philosophical schools were established, thus inhibiting private writing and discussion.[125] Furthermore, the aristocrats saw reforms as a means to protect the old social system from crisis. Due to frequent crises, only political and ethical problems were considered, and both knowledge of nature and speculative philosophy was thus neglected. No philosophical thought or natural science was able to develop.[126] Ethics was of a religious character and therefore became the instrument of the ancient kings of Zhou. The Spring and Autumn period prolonged the reformism. The frame of thought of the early Confucians was based on the style of the wise man, and the notion of former sage kings sprang from clan system consciousness. Zhao linked *Mozi*, *Xunzi*, and *Han Feizi* to the abolition of the clan system and the establishment of private ownership of land in the early Warring States period. In turn, he saw the revival and development of the clan system in the third century B.C. as marking the start of the Middle Age. The need to control thought produced the attitude of canonical studies as a third feature of Chinese political thought.[127]

In his introduction, Zhao also talked about the method of studying Chinese philosophical thought. As in his earlier work, he referred to two misunderstandings of Chinese philosophy, blaming them on the style of the wise man. The first is that China did not have philosophy; Hegel attributed this to its lack of freedom and Hartmann to its writing system. Zhao argued that although China may not have been as systematic in philosophical reasoning and may not have treated all philosophical problems as such, it posed questions, had its own technical terms and ways of reaching conclusions, and employed categories in the same way as systematic philosophy.[128] He called on researchers of Chinese philosophy to study the standpoint and the method of Chinese philosophical thought. The standpoint would provide the *Weltanschauung*; the method would reveal the epistemology.[129] The second misunderstanding is different from the one in his earlier work, namely that Chinese philosophy was a philosophy of human life. In his earlier work, Zhao himself had pointed to this as a particular feature of traditional Chinese philosophy. Now he stated instead that this was a theory that had been developed only recently by the promoters of national essence and newly formulated after the First World War. Zhao attributed the lack of systematic philosophical works to the style of the wise man in which the focus was on ethics as well as politics. In contrast to the West, where philosophy and science became independent of each other, in China they remained an undifferentiated whole.[130] In the West, science created the basis for philosophical system:

> Because the West employed the revolutionary method in creating ancient society, philosophy and science could appear at the same time. Because of its reformism in antiquity, China did not develop science. Thus it fell behind the West and philosophical thought was based upon the style of the wise man. Because of the lack of a scientific basis, Chinese philosophy is anthropocentric, starting from inner reflections in looking for the origins of the cosmos. This led to the mysticism of Dark Learning, even [to the point of] neglecting ethical and political problems and thus becoming religious Dark Learning. Scholars at the end of the Ming and the beginning of the Qing opposed Neo-Confucianism and showed an interest in natural sciences. The Gongyang School as well as Zhang Taiyan's system also included categories of natural sciences. They had already begun the process of abolition of the style of the wise man.[131]

Beyond Hou Wailu's scholarly concentration on the past, Zhao also envisioned a future development for Chinese thought. In order to complete the modernization of Chinese philosophy Zhao urged that the elimination of the style of the wise man, already started by former generations, be continued. He further emphasized the need to acknowledge the relation between the concepts of the "former sage kings" and "restoration," while pointing out that the reverence for the former sage kings did not always amount to restoration (*fugu* 復古). Similar to Chen Zhongfan, he argued for the critical reception of China's philosophical heritage. He criticized Feng Youlan for merely repeating the words of the former generations and thus not contributing to the progress of Chinese philosophy. As an example he cited Feng's *Zhongguo zhexueshi* [History of Chinese philosophy]. Although he agreed with Feng's interpretations in general, Zhao did not accept his view that the commentaries to the classics in each period are like "children growing up." True to his dialectical approach, Zhao thought that commentaries adopted an oppositional attitude to the original classics. He saw them not as a continuation, but as the negation, of the "attitude associated with canonical studies"—that is, transmitting but not creating—and that their contribution has to be acknowledged in the study of philosophy.[132]

4. Conclusion

Notions of Marxism first entered China at the end of the nineteenth century via Japan. In the 1920s and the 1930s translation work intensified, probably due to the establishment of the CCP in 1921. It took until the mid-1930s until Marxism entered the academic field, when the major debates on New Philosophy and—more important for this study—on the nature of Chinese history and social history took place. At this time, Marxists also took the first steps in conceptualizing and studying traditional Chinese thought. Two centers of Marxist scholarship arose. In Yan'an scholars emphasized the political mission to sinify Marxism and to establish Mao Zedong Thought as party ideology. In the process this group employed parts of traditional Chinese philosophy as an instrument to achieve these aims. In contrast, Marxist scholars in Chongqing took a more scholarly attitude and analyzed traditional Chinese thought.

From the beginning, the history of Chinese philosophy was understood in the Marxist style as a complex history that embraced social, economic, and political factors. The pioneers of the 1930s had not yet established a firm periodization for Chinese thought. They employed different periodization schemes, emphasizing different social, economic, and political factors. Marxist scholars also took note of and even incorporated the formats of the first Western-style historiographers of Chinese philosophy such as Zhang Taiyan, Hu Shi, and Feng Youlan. These early Marxist scholars adhered to the values of materialism and dialectics while acknowledging the battle between idealism and materialism. As academic work matured, Marxism was consolidated in the works of the later Zhao Jibin and Hou Wailu and became more homogenous, more detailed, and less mechanical. Eventually, the Chongqing school represented in Hou Wailu's *Zhongguo sixiang tongshi*, co-edited with Zhao Jibin and Du Guoxiang, became authoritative in the field of the history of Chinese philosophy. They laid the foundation for the academic discipline in the PRC and dominated this field during the 1950s.

Notes

1   I thank John Makeham for his great support in writing up this article.

2   Fang Guanghua 放光華, Hou Qie'an 侯且岸, and Zhang Maoze 張茂澤, *Zhongguo xiandai xueshu sixiangshi lunji* 中國現代學術思想史論集 [Collected essays on the intellectual history of modern Chinese scholarship] (Xi'an: Shaanxi renmin daxue chubanshe, 2003), pp. 534–535.

3   The other nine works brought together by the editorial board of the journal were: Ai Siqi 艾思奇, *Xiyang zhexueshi jiaocheng* 西洋哲學史教程 [Course in Western philosophy]; Akizawa Shūji 秋澤修二, *Xiyang zhexueshi* 西洋哲學史 [History of Western philosophy], translated by Xiong Deshan 熊得山; Akizawa Shūji, *Dongyang zhexueshi* 東洋哲學史 [History of Eastern philosophy], translated by Liu Zhizhi 劉執之 and Wang Yaosan 汪耀三; Debolin 德柏林 (A. M. Deborin), *Jindai zhexueshi* 近代哲學史 [History of modern philosophy], translated by Lin Yixin 林一新; unattributed, *Bianzhengfa weiwulun rumen* 辯證法唯物論入門 [Introduction to dialectical materialism], translated by Lin Boxiu 林伯修; Lubo'er 盧波爾 (I. K. Luppol), *Wu da zhexue sichao* 五大哲學思潮 [Five great philosophical currents], translated by Li Shengu 李申穀; Zhang Ruxin 張如心, *Su E zhexue chaoliu gaiguan* 蘇俄哲學潮流概觀 [Outline of Soviet and Russian currents]; Li Zhongrong 李仲融, *Xila zhexueshi* 希臘哲學史 [History of Greek philosophy]; and Zhang Ruxin, *Zhexue gailun* 哲學概論 [Outline of philosophy]. In *Zhexue* 哲學 5 (1940), p. 694.

4   Ye Qing, *Hu Shi pipan*, 2 vols. (Shanghai: Xinken, 1933).

5   O. Brière, *Fifty Years of Chinese Philosophy, 1898–1950* (London: George Allen & Unwin Ltd., 1956), pp. 76–77.

6   See for example Nick Knight, ed., *Mao Zedong on Dialectical Materialism: Writings on Philosophy, 1937* (Armonk: M. E. Sharpe, 1990); Arif Dirlik, *The Origins of Chinese Communism* (New York: Oxford University Press, 1989); Helmut Martin, *Kult und Kanon: Entwicklung und Entstehung des Staatsmaoismus, 1935–1978* (Hamburg: Institut für Asienkunde, 1978); Arif Dirlik, ed., *Critical Perspectives on Mao Zedong's Thought* (Atlantic Highlands, NJ: Humanities Press, 1987); Werner Meissner, *Philosophie und Politik in China: Die Kontroverse über den Dialektischen Materialismus in den Dreißiger Jahren* (München: Wilhelm Fink Verlag, 1986).

7   The debate over the New Philosophy and dialectical materialism (which began in 1934 and reached its climax in the period from 1936/37 to 1939) was another major controversy among the left-wing intellectuals. However, the debate was mainly concerned with European and Russian Marxists. See Brière, *Fifty Years of Chinese Philosophy*, p. 83.

8   Li Yu-ning, *The Introduction of Socialism into China* (New York: Columbia University Press, 1971), pp. 3–4.

9   Xiong Yuezhi 熊月之, *Xixue dongjian yu wan Qing shehui* 西學東漸與晚清社會 [*The Dissemination of Western Learning and the Late Qing Society*] (Shanghai: Shanghai renmin chubanshe, 1994), p. 417.

10 The first Japanese translation of *Kommunistisches Manifest, Kyōsantō sengen* 共產黨宣言, excluding the third chapter, was produced by Kōtoku Shūsui 幸德秋水 and Sakai Toshihiko 堺利彥 who translated it from the English. It appeared in 1904 in *Heimin shinbun* 平民新聞 [Newspaper of the common people]. Sakai published the third chapter in 1906, in *Shakai-shugi kenkyū* 社會主義研究 [Socialist studies]. See Wolfgang Lippert, *Entstehung und Funktion einiger Chinesischer Marxistischer Termini: Der Lexikalisch-Begriffliche Aspekt der Rezeption des Marxismus in Japan und China* (Wiesbaden: Franz Steiner Verlag, 1979), pp. 79–80.

11 For a bibliography of Chinese translations of Japanese sources on socialism, see Yoshihiro Ishikawa, "Chinese Translations from Japanese of Works on Socialism, 1919–1922," translated by Joshua Fogel, in *Sino-Japanese Studies* 16.2 (2009), pp. 14–35.

12 Lippert, *Entstehung und Funktion einiger Chinesischer Marxistischer Termini*, pp. 75, 90.

13 Huang Jiande 黃見德 et al., *Xifang zhexue dongjianshi* 西方哲學東漸史 [A history of Western philosophy's eastward advance] (Wuhan: Wuhan daxue chubanshe, 1991), p. 476; Y. T. Wu, "Movements among Chinese Students," in *China Christian Year Book* 17 (Shanghai: Christian Literature Society, 1931), p. 265. Both sources are cited in Chenshan Tian, "The Development of Dialectical Materialism in China," in *History of Chinese Philosophy*, edited by Bo Mou (London: Routledge, 2009), p. 516.

14 Lippert, *Entstehung und Funktion einiger Chinesischer Marxistischer Termini*, pp. 60–61.

15 Sanetō Keishō 實藤惠秀, *Chūgokujin Nihon ryūgakushi* 中国人日本留学史 [History of Chinese students in Japan] (Tokyo: Kuroshio shuppan, 1960), pp. 343–344. Cited in Lippert, *Entstehung und Funktion einiger Chinesischer Marxistischer Termini*, p. 61.

16 Hao Chang, *Chinese Intellectuals in Crisis: In Search for Order and Meaning (1890–1911)*, (Berkeley: University of California Press, 1987), p. 61.

17 Tian, "The Development of Dialectical Materialism in China," p. 516. According to Edward X. Gu: "Alongside a variety of socialism [*sic*] the idea of populistic democracy had become a major theme in modern Chinese ideologies since 1910, and by 1919 it had become a major role in the political stage of Chinese revolution and modernization." (Edward X. Gu, "Who was Mr. Democracy? The May Fourth Discourse of Populist Democracy and the Radicalization of Chinese Intellectuals (1915–1922)," *Modern Asian Studies* 3 (2001), p. 620.

18 For a detailed analysis of Chinese translations of Marxist terms and their Japanese origins, see Lippert, *Entstehung und Funktion einiger Chinesischer Marxistischer Termini*. In this study Lippert traces the route of translation from Western languages via Japanese to Chinese. Later on, some Japanese translations were replaced by alternative Chinese translations. Lippert contends that some translations of Western terms—such as *sixiang* 思想,

ziben 資本, and *renmin* 人民—were originally imported from China to Japan and reintroduced in a Marxist framework through Japanese sources (p. 393).

19   Zhang Jinglu 張靜廬, *Zhongguo chuban shiliao* 中國出版史料 [Historical documents on publishing in China], supplement to *Zhongguo xiandai chuban shiliao* 中國現代出版史料 [Historical documents on publishing in modern China] (Beijing: Zhonghua shuju, 1957), pp. 447–475. Cited in Arif Dirlik, *Revolution and History: Origins of Marxist Historiography in China, 1919–1937* (Berkeley: University of California Press, 1978), p. 44n79.

20   Wang Yafu 王亞夫 and Zhang Hengzhong 章恒忠, eds., *Zhongguo xueshujie dashiji (1919–1985)* 中國學術界大事記 (1919–1985) [Great events in Chinese academia (1919–1985)] (Shanghai: Shanghai shehui kexueyuan, 1988), p. 102.

21   Tian, "The Development of Dialectical Materialism in China," p. 523.

22   Miding 米丁 (M. Mitin) et al., *Xin zhexue dagang*, translated by Ai Siqi and Zheng Yili 鄭易裡 (Shanghai: Shenghuo dushu xinzhi, 1949).

23   Brière, *Fifty Years of Chinese Philosophy*, pp. 75, 130.

24   Chen Weishi included an additional chapter on Chinese philosophy in his work *Tongsu bianzhengfa* 通俗辯證法 [Accessible dialectics], first published in 1936 and reprinted several times even after the GMD government had banned it. See Tian, "The Development of Dialectical Materialism in China," p. 526). In 1936 Chen Weishi also published an article on the dialectical thought in *Yijing*, *Laozi*, and *Zhuangzi*. He considered these to be the representative texts of rich dialectical thought in early Chinese philosophy. Although still simplistic and unsystematic, he defended the dialectical thought he found in these texts as being limited by social conditions and low scientific standards. See Chen Weishi, "Guanyu *Yijing* he *Lao Zhuang* de bianzhengguan" 關於易經和老莊的辯證觀 [On the dialectical perspectives of *Yijing*, *Zhuangzi*, and *Laozi*] (1936), in *Chen Weishi wenxuan* 陳唯實文選 [Selected writings of Chen Weishi] (Guangdong: Guangdong renmin chubanshe, 1986), p. 9.

25   Tian, "The Development of Dialectical Materialism in China," p. 525.

26   Nick Knight, *Marxist Philosophy in China: From Qu Qiubai to Mao Zedong, 1923–1945* (Dodrecht: Springer, 2005), pp. 6. For a detailed discussion on these philosophers see Nick Knight, *Marxist Philosophy in China*; Joshua A. Fogel, *Ai Ssu-ch'i's Contribution to the Development of Chinese Marxism* (Cambridge, MA: Council on East Asian Studies, Harvard University Press, 1987).

27   They are listed in the 1940 bibliography with the following data: Miding 米丁 (Mitin), *Bianzheng weiwulun yu lishi weiwulun* 辯證唯物論與歷史唯物論 [Dialectical materialism and historical materialism], translated by Shen Zhiyuan 沈志遠 (n.p.: Zhongshan wenhua jiaoyuguan, 1936); Aisenbao 愛森堡 (Aizenberg) et al., *Bianzhengfa weiwulun jiaocheng* 辯證法唯物論教程 [A course in dialectical materialism], translated by Li Da 李達 and Lei

Zhongjian 雷仲堅 (Shanghai: Bigengtang, n.d.). Knight lists different publishers for these works.

28   Nick Knight, *Marxist Philosophy in China*, p. 76.

29   Dirlik, *Revolution and History*, p. 45.

30   Benjamin Schwartz, "A Marxist Controversy on China," *Far Eastern Quarterly* 13.2 (Feb. 1954), pp. 143–153. According to Schwartz, the controversy referred to Marxism refracted by the Leninist interpretation.

31   Dirlik, *Revolution and History*, p. 45.

32   *Ibid.*, p. 9.

33   The terminology used for the idea of "mode of production" remained ambiguous in Marxist writings. On the one hand, it can be seen as a basis for social and political arrangements, yet on the other, it also functions as a model of economic organization that develops throughout the course of history. Marx described five modes of production: "Asiatic mode (primitive communal form of production), ancient (based on slavery), feudal (based on serfdom), capitalist (based on wage labour), communist (based on communal ownership of the means of production)." David Walker and Daniel Gray, *Historical Dictionary of Marxism* (Lanham, MD: The Scarecrow Press, 2007), pp. 219–220.

34   Schwartz, "A Marxist Controversy on China," p. 146.

35   *Ibid.*, pp. 147–150. The official theorists of the communist party line such as Li Lisan 李立三 (1899–1967) and Bo Gu 博古 (1907–1946; = Qin Bangxian 秦邦憲) were among this group.

36   *Ibid.*, pp. 150–151. Representatives of this group are He Ganzhi and Li Jizi.

37   Dirlik, *Revolution and History*, pp. 221. A textbook version appeared in 1938 in China: Liangong (bu) zhongyang teshe weiyuanhui 聯共（布）中央特設委員會, ed., *Sulian gongchangdang (bu) lishi jianming jiaocheng* 蘇聯共產黨（布）歷史簡明教程 [A short course in the history of the Communist Party in the Soviet Union] (Moscow: Waiguowen shuji chubanju, 1938). It became the standard work of reference in academic historical studies in the 1950s and was republished several times.

38   Schwartz, "A Marxist Controversy on China," p. 145.

39   Huang Jing 黃靜, "Kangzhan shiqi Chongqing Makesizhuyi shijia dui gudai shehuishi he sixiangshi de yanjiu" 抗戰時期重慶馬克思主義史家對古代社會史和思想史的研究 (Studies by Chongqing-based Marxist historians during the Anti-Japanese War on early social history and intellectual history), *Shixueshi yanjiu* 史學史研究 3 (2005), p. 26.

40   "Xin zhexuehui yuanqi" 新哲學會緣起 [Origins of the New Philosophy Association], cited in Lu Guoying 盧國英, *Zhihui zhi lu: Yidai zheren Ai Siqi* 智慧之路：一代哲人艾思奇 [The road of wisdom: Philosopher of a generation Ai Siqi] (Beijing: Renmin chubanshe, 2006), p. 233.

41   Wang Liang 王良, "Yan'an Xin Zhexuehui shiliao jieshao, er" 延安新哲學會史料介紹，二 [Introduction to the historical materials of the Yan'an New

Philosophy Association—part 2), *Mao Zedong zhexue sixiang yanjiu dongtai* 6 (1984), p. 1.

42 Knight, *Marxist Philosophy in China*, p. 218.

43 This might be the work of Li Da that Mao called the first textbook on Marxism-Leninism written by a Chinese (Wang Yafu and Zhang Hengzhong, *Zhongguo xueshujie dashiji*, p. 99). Although it was first published in 1937, one year after Ai Siqi's work, Ai might have already read the manuscript that seems to have circulated in 1935. Chenshan Tian, *Chinese Dialectics: From Yijing to Marxism* (Oxford: Lexington, 2005), p. 115.

44 Nick Knight, *Marxist Philosophy in China*, p. 213.

45 Li Weihan 李維漢, "Yan'an zhongyang yanjiuyuan de gongzuo he zhengfeng yundong" 延安中央研究院的工作和整風運動 [The work of the Yan'an Central Research Institute and the rectification campaign], in *Zhongyang yanjiuyuan huiyilu* 中央研究院回憶錄 [Recollections of the Central Research Institute], edited by Wen Jize 溫濟澤 et al. (Changsha: Zhongguo shehui kexue chubanshe, 1984), pp. 6, 7.

46 Ai Siqi, "Zhongyong guannian de fenxi" 中庸觀念的分析 [Analysis of the concept of the Mean], in his *Xin zhexue lunji* 新哲學論集 [Collection of essays on New Philosophy], (Shanghai: Duzhe shufang, 1936), pp. 89–103.

47 Tian, "The Development of Dialectical Materialism in China," p. 527.

48 Ai Siqi, "Zhongyong guanniande fenxi," p. 96.

49 *Ibid.*, p. 94.

50 *Ibid.*, p. 103.

51 *Ibid.*, p. 100.

52 Chen Boda, "Guanyu xiao" 關於孝 [On filial piety], in *Zhongguo wenhua* 中國文化 1 (1930), pp. 4–8. Mao shared the same interest, and even a pride, in traditional Chinese thought but combined it with his political mission. Chen Boda had sent all his papers on traditional Chinese philosophy to Mao Zedong. In a letter he wrote in 1939 Mao congratulated Chen on his paper, "Mozi zhexue sixiang" 墨子哲學思想 [Mozi's philosophical thought], saying that his great achievement was that he had found the Chinese Heraclitus but also criticized him. See Chen Xiaonong 陳曉農, *Chen Boda zuihou koushu huiyi* 陳伯達最後口述回憶 [Chen Boda's final recollections] (Hong Kong: Xingke'er, 2007), pp. 63–64.

53 Hu Sheng, *Ziyou yu lixing* 自由與理性 [Liberty and reason] (Shanghai: Huaxia shudian, 1946), p. 144.

54 Hou Wailu, *Ren de zhuiqiu* 韌的追求 [In pursuit of tenacity] (Shanghai: Sanlian shuju, 1985), p. 123, cited in Hong Renqing 洪認清, "Kangzhan shiqi Yan'an yu Chongqing Makesizhuyi shixue de quyu tese" 抗戰時期延安與重慶馬克思主義史學的區域特色 [The regional characteristics of Yan'an and Chongqing Marxist historiography during the Anti-Japanese War period], *Sanming xueyuan xuebao* 三明學院學報 1 (March 2006), p. 68.

55 Mao Zedong, *Mao Zedong wenji* 毛澤東文集 [Mao Zedong's collected writings], Vol. 3 (Beijing: Renmin chubanshe, 1991), cited in Hong Renqing, p. 72.

56 Hou Wailu, *Ren de zhuiqiu*, p. 227, cited in Hong Renqing, "Kangzhan shiqi Yan'an yu Chongqing Makesizhuyi shixue de quyu tese," p. 72.

57 Huang Jing, "Kangzhan shiqi Chongqing Makesizhuyi shijia," pp. 29–30.

58 "Shumin de shengli" 庶民的勝利 [Victory of the masses] and "Bu'ershen-weizhuyi de shengli" 布爾什維主義的勝利 [The victory of Bolshevism] both appeared in the 15 October 1918 issue of *Xin qingnian*.

59 Brière, *Fifty Years of Chinese Philosophy*, p. 78.

60 *Ibid.*, p. 35.

61 For example Yuesefu 約瑟夫 (Joseph [Stalin]), Jiluofu 基洛夫 (Kirov), and Cidanuofu 慈達諾夫 (Zhdanov), "Guanyu *Jindaishi gangyao* de jidian yijian" 關於《近代史綱要》的幾點意見 [Some views on *Outline to Modern History*], translated by Zheng Dai 鄭岱, *Zhexue zazhi* 哲學雜誌 1 (1930), pp. 34–37.

62 After studying in Japan, Li Shicen became professor of philosophy at various universities. His travels to Germany and France in 1928 inspired him to compare Oriental and Occidental philosophies. In his early years, Li was a follower of Nietzsche and of Bergson's philosophy of life. His later *Zhexue dagang* 哲學大綱 [Outline of philosophy] and the lectures discussed here were dominated by his new belief in Marxist dialectics. He was, as Brière remarked, a man of transition and typical of many Chinese intellectuals at that time. See Brière, *Fifty Years of Chinese Philosophy*, p. 22.

63 Li Shicen 李石岑, *Zhongguo zhexue shijiang* (Shanghai: Shijie shuju, 1935), reprinted in *Li Shicen xueshu lunshu* 李石岑學術論述 [Scholarly writings of Li Shicen], edited by Qiu Zhihua 邱志華 (Hangzhou: Zhejiang renmin chubanshe, 1998), pp. 3–398.

64 *Ibid.*, pp. 4–5.

65 *Ibid.*, p. 5.

66 He created the following groupings of Chinese and Greek philosophers: 1) Confucians: Confucius and Socrates; Mencius and Plato; Xunzi and Aristotle; 2) Mohists: Mozi and Parmenides; Hui Shi, Gongsun Long and Zeno; 3) Daoists: Zhuangzi, Laozi and Heraclitus; Yang Zhu and Protagoras.

67 *Ibid.*, p. 6.

68 *Ibid.*, pp. 18–19.

69 *Ibid.*, pp. 19–21.

70 *Ibid.*, pp. 22–24.

71 *Ibid.*, p. 25.

72 *Ibid.*, pp. 26–27.

73 *Ibid.*, p. 27.

74 *Ibid.*, pp. 29–31.

75 Fan Shoukang went to study in Japan in 1913, eventually obtaining his PhD in education and philosophy in 1923. He worked as a translator for Shanghai Commercial Press and became interested in Marxism. In 1945 Fan was part of the committee for taking over the (Japanese) Imperial University in Taipei that later was renamed National Taiwan University. See Ou Suying 歐素瑛, "Gongxian zhege daxue yu yuzhou de jingshen—Tan Fu Sinian yu

Taiwan Daxue shizi zhi gaishan" 貢獻這個大學於宇宙的精神——談傅斯年與臺灣大學師資之改善 [Contributing higher education to the world—Fu Sinian and the improvement of instructors at Taiwan University], *Guoshiguan xueshu jikan* 國史館學術集刊 6 (2007), p. 209.

76 Fan Shoukang, "Fuyin tiji" 複印題記 [Dedication], no pagination, in Fan Shoukang, *Zhongguo zhexueshi tonglun* 中國哲學史通論 [Expositions on the history of Chinese philosophy] (Shanghai: Kaiming shudian, 1938).

77 Fan Shoukang, *Zhongguo zhexueshi tonglun* 中國哲學史通論 [Expositions on the history of Chinese philosophy] (Beijing: Shenghuo, dushu, xinzhi sanlian shudian, 1983], pp. 1–3.

78 Fan Shoukang, "Xulun" 緒論 [Foreword], in *Zhongguo zhexueshi tonglun* 中國哲學史通論 (Beijing: Shenghuo, dushu, xinzhi sanlian shudian, 1983), p. 5.

79 *Ibid.*, pp. 6–7.

80 In a diagram Fan organised the history of society and the productive forces into five stages: 1) primitive communism; 2) a slave-owning system when the productive forces developed; 3) feudalism based on agricultural productive forces; 4) a system of labour and money lending or proto-capitalism (or simple merchandise economic system); and 5) new society or capitalism based on mechanised industry. (*Ibid.*, p. 15)

81 *Ibid.*, p. 15.

82 *Ibid.*, p. 20.

83 *Ibid.*, p. 22.

84 *Ibid.*, p. 23.

85 *Ibid.*, p. 23.

86 *Ibid.*, p. 24.

87 *Ibid.*, p. 26.

88 Cai Shangsi was an historian who later criticized Hu Shi in the literary field. After 1949 he continued his study of traditional Chinese philosophy, as seen by his *Zhongguo chuantong sixiang zong pipan* 中國傳統思想總批判 [General criticism of traditional Chinese thought] (Shanghai: Dangdai chuban gongsi, 1950). Chen Zhongfan entered the Department of Philosophy at Peking University in 1914 and stayed on after his graduation. Later he taught literature at various universities. See *Guoxue wanglu* 國學網路 [National Studies Net], http://www.guoxue.com/master/chzhf/chzhf.htm, accessed 12 December 2009. After the establishment of the PRC he also contributed to the anti-Hu Shi campaign.

89 Cai Shangsi, *Zhongguo sixiang yanjiufa* (Shanghai: Shangwu yinshuguan, 1940). In *Minguo congshu* 民國叢書 [Collection of Republican-era books] (Shanghai: Shanghai shudian, 1989), Vol. 3, p. 1.

90 Chen Zhongfan, "Xu wu" 序五 [Foreword five], in Cai Shangsi, *Zhongguo sixiang yanjiufa*, pp. 2–4.

91 *Ibid.*, pp. 6–7.

92 *Ibid.*, p. 8.

93 *Ibid.*, p. 9.

94   *Ibid.*, p. 13.

95   *Ibid.*, p. 13.

96   *Ibid.*, p. 19.

97   Zhao Jibin, who later took the penname of Xiang Linbing 向林冰, was exposed to Marxism-Leninism early on and became a member of the CCP in 1926. Together with Ai Siqi he translated Mitin's work. He engaged in revolutionary activities and taught at various universities. In 1946 he went to Shanghai Dongwu 東吳 University where he became professor. Hou Wailu engaged Zhao along with Chen Jiakang 陳家康 (1913–1970) and Du Guoxiang in writing *Zhongguo sixiang tongshi* 中國思想通史. In 1949 Zhao became the director of the school of literature at Shandong University. See San Mu 散木, "Zhexuejia Zhao Jibin de rensheng gushi" 哲學家趙紀彬的人生故事 [The life story of the philosopher Zhao Jibin], *Dangshi bolan* 黨史博覽 1 (2007), pp. 54–55.

98   Zhao Jibin, *Zhongguo zhexueshi gangyao*, in *Zhao Jibin wenji* 趙紀彬文集 [Collected works of Zhao Jibin], Vol. 1, edited by Zheng Han 鄭涵 (Zhengzhou: Henan chubanshe, 1985). It was originally published by Shenghuo shudian 生活書店 in 1939. Others have identified Lü Zhenyu's 呂振羽 (1900–1980) *Zhongguo zhengzhi sixiangshi* 中國政治思想史 [History of Chinese political thought] as the first Chinese intellectual history to employ a Marxist standpoint, conception, and method. However, the first to have systematically worked on intellectual history were Guo Moruo, Hou Wailu, and Du Guoxiang. See Huang Jing, "Kangzhan shiqi Chongqing Makesizhuyi shijia," p. 28.

99   Zhao Jibin, *Zhongguo zhexueshi gangyao*, p. 13.

100   *Ibid.*, p. 15.

101   *Ibid.*, pp. 16–17.

102   *Ibid.*, p. 17.

103   *Ibid.*, pp. 23–24.

104   *Ibid.*, p. 24.

105   *Ibid.*, pp. 24–25.

106   *Ibid.*, pp. 25–26.

107   *Ibid.*, pp. 26–27.

108   *Ibid.*, p. 27.

109   *Ibid.*, p. 55.

110   Hou Wailu, *Zhongguo sixiang tongshi* 中國思想通史 [General history of Chinese thought], Vol. 1 (Shanghai: Xinzhi shudian, 1947). Du Shousu 杜守素 (penname of Du Guoxiang) and Ji Xuanbing 紀玄冰 (penname of Zhao Jibin) are given as the two other editors, but the foreword is by Hou Wailu.

111   Dirlik, *Revolution and History*, pp. 12–13. On Fu Sinan's methodology, see Carine Defoort's chapter in this volume.

112   Zhang Qizhi 張豈之, "Yuanjian zhuoshi de yinluzhe—lüelun Hou Wailu xiansheng dui Zhongguo sixiangshi, zhexueshi yanjiu de zhuoyue gongxian" 遠見卓識的引路者——略論侯外廬先生對中國思想史、哲學史研究的卓越貢獻

[Farsighted pioneer—brief discussion of Hou Wailu's outstanding accomplishments regarding intellectual history and research into the history of philosophy], in *Jinian Hou Wailu xiansheng bainian danchen zhuanji* 紀念侯外廬先生百年誕辰專集 [Special collection [of essays] in honour of the hundredth anniversary of the birth of Hou Wailu], edited by Zhang Qizhi 張豈之 (Guilin: Guangxi shifandaxue chubanshe, 2003), p. 237.

113 Fang Guanghua et al., *Xiandai xueshu sixiangshi lunji*, p. 532. For a list of Hou Wailu's works refer to *Jinian Hou Wailu*, pp. 368.

114 Hou Wailu's *Zhongguo gudian shehui lun* and *Zhongguo gudai sixiang xueshuoshi* 中國古代思想學說史 [History of early Chinese intellectual doctrines] were published in 1943. In 1944, the first volume of his *Zhongguo jinshi sixiang xueshuoshi* 中國近世思想學說史 [History of early-modern Chinese intellectual doctrines] was published (Chongqing: Sanyou shudian).

115 *Zhongguo zhexueshi wenti taolun zhuanji* 中國哲學史問題討論專輯 [Special edition on problems in the history of Chinese philosophy], edited by *Zhexue yanjiu* bianjibu 哲學研究編輯部 [Editorial board of *Zhexue yanjiu*] (Beijing: Kexue chubanshe, 1957).

116 Hou Wailu and Luo Keting 羅克汀, *Xin zhexue jiaocheng* 新哲學教程 [Course in New Philosophy] (Shanghai: Xinzhi shudian), p. 1.

117 Fang Guanghua et al., *Zhongguo xiandi xueshu sixiangshi lunji*, p. 536–537.

118 *Ibid.*, p. 538.

119 *Ibid.*, p. 540.

120 Zhao Jibin, *Zhongguo zhexue sixiang* 中國哲學思想 [Chinese philosophical thought] (n.p.: Zhonghua shuju, 1948), in *Minguo congshu*, Vol. 2, p. 5.

121 *Ibid.*, pp. 2–3.

122 *Ibid.*, pp. 4–5.

123 *Ibid.*, pp. 6–7.

124 *Ibid.*, p. 7.

125 *Ibid.*, p. 8.

126 *Ibid.*, p. 8.

127 *Ibid.*, p. 9.

128 *Ibid.*, p. 10.

129 *Ibid.*, p. 11.

130 *Ibid.*, pp. 11–13.

131 *Ibid.*, p. 13.

132 *Ibid.*, pp. 15–16.

Epilogue

Inner Logic, Indigenous Grammars, and the Identity of *Zhongguo zhexue*[*]

John Makeham

The views of the scholars examined in this volume are not only of intellectual-historical significance—they also throw into relief how "*Zhongguo zhexue*" is understood today. In this Epilogue, I argue that whereas earlier generations of internal participants in the formation of Chinese philosophy as an academic discipline acknowledged that "Chinese philosophy" was a product of the complex interaction between internal and external agencies, and that one or more non-Chinese philosophical traditions were essential to articulating China's philosophical past, influential modern commentators have instead argued that paradigms and norms derived from the West, in particular,[1] are not only inappropriate to the articulation of China's philosophical heritage but also fundamentally hegemonic. I also draw attention to the influence of what I call the "inner logic" paradigm—which emphasizes the continued agency and relevance of the past in the present—as developed, especially, by intellectual historians of China on contemporary Chinese views of China's philosophical heritage. I maintain that this paradigm has contributed to the conferral of methodological legitimacy on so-called epistemological nativism: the idea that the articulation and development of China's philosophical heritage must draw exclusively on the endogenous paradigms and norms of China's indigenous heritage.[2]

---

[*] I am grateful to Barry Steben for constructive feedback on several drafts of this Epilogue.

1. The Trend to Epistemological Nativism

Prominent contemporary Chinese philosopher, Chen Lai 陳來 (now at Tsinghua University where he heads the recently revived National Studies Research Institute), relates how Feng Youlan 馮友蘭 (1895–1990) contrasted two knowledge systems: Chinese *yili zhi xue* 義理之學 (learning based on normative principles) and Western philosophy. (Feng understood *yili zhi xue* as encompassing Wei-Jin *xuanxue* 玄學, Song-Ming *daoxue* 道學, and Qing dynasty *yili zhi xue*.) Feng proposed two possible paths to reconciling these two systems with one another: either adopt the standards of Western philosophy as the overarching framework and select those aspects of Chinese *yili zhi xue* which correspond with the standards of Western philosophy and call it Chinese philosophy; or simply adopt the standards of *yili zhi xue* as the overarching framework and call it Chinese *yili zhi xue*. (Feng even proposed the possibility of writing a history of Western *yili zhi xue* based on the standards of Chinese *yili zhi xue*.)[3] Chen Lai, however, maintains that because Feng adopted the former approach, the integrity of the holistic character of *yili zhi xue* was compromised, with some crucial elements having been rejected on the grounds that they did not conform to the standards of so-called Chinese philosophy. Chen, in turn, proposed a third alternative: treat traditional Chinese *yili zhi xue* as Chinese philosophy and bypass the need to limit the parameters of Chinese philosophy strictly in accord with Western notions of philosophy. Chen further notes that, in fact, ever since the appearance of Feng's seminal history of Chinese philosophy, studies in the history of Chinese philosophy have in fact taken this approach: "On the one hand, in theory, scholars of the history of Chinese philosophy have endorsed [the principle of] taking the content of Western philosophy as standard; on the other hand, they have actually adopted Chinese *yili zhi xue* as the scope of their studies."[4] In other words, for Chen, it is the "inner dynamics" of Chinese philosophy that have enabled it to persist into the present.

Over the past decade, however, a more widely-shared critical perspective has emerged about the deleterious consequences of using Western analytical frameworks. A growing number of Chinese academics have argued that "Western philosophy" has yet to acknowledge "the legitimacy" of Chinese philosophy and to engage it as an equal partner in dialogue.[5] They have further insisted that the articulation and development of China's philosophical heritage must draw exclusively on the endogenous paradigms and norms of China's indigenous heritage, and that paradigms and norms derived from the West, in particular, are not only inappropriate but fundamentally hegemonic and/or ill suited to China's "conditions." Discussion of these and related issues reached a watershed with the publication of two influential essays—one at the end of 2001 and one early in 2002—by two prominent Chinese scholars of Chinese philosophy.[6] These essays marked the beginning of a period of debate and discussion focused on the topic of "the legitimacy of Chinese philosophy."

In the very opening passage of the first volume of his *Zhongguo zhexueshi*, Feng Youlan proclaimed that one of the main tasks in writing a history of Chinese philosophy is as follows: "From all the various types of learning in Chinese history, select and provide a narrative account of those aspects which can be named according to what is called philosophy in the West."[7] Contemporary scholar, Renmin University philosopher Zhang Liwen 張立文, provides the following critique of Feng's proposal:

> Such a narrative account would inevitably lead to the dismemberment of the various forms of traditional Chinese learning, that is, to the disintegration and smashing into pieces of China's various branches of learning which together constitute an organic whole, by picking out "those aspects which can be named according to what is called philosophy in the West," discarding those aspects which cannot, and then reassembling [what is left]. The outcome of such a reassembly would ... bring to an end the living existence of Chinese learning, thought, or philosophy. It would be just like in *Zhuangzi* where, in order to repay Hundun for his kind hospitality, Shu and Hu chiseled seven holes in Hundun [so he would be] just like them, but when the seven holes were completed, Hundun died.[8]

In a similar vein, Chen Shaoming 陳少明 (Philosophy Department, National Sun Yat-sen University), writes:

> In many textbook-style writings, once traditional thought has been subjected to the analytical framework of Western philosophy, the inherent integrity of the meaning of traditional thought becomes dislocated and completely unrecognizable. In this way, there is a total disconnect between the feeling one gets from reading the canonical writings and from reading textbook interpretations.... In these formulaic narratives of the histories of philosophy [found in textbooks] Chinese concepts are often used to draw far-fetched analogies with Western philosophical categories and Chinese classics are imperceptibly transformed into examples illustrating [principles of] Western philosophy.[9]

Jing Haifeng 景海峰 (Philosophy Department, Shenzhen University) has been one of the most trenchant critics of Chinese attempts to ape Western models of philosophy. For Jing, the institutionalization of philosophy as an academic discipline has meant that so-called Chinese philosophy has effectively become little other than Western-style philosophy with a Chinese mask. He complains that despite the developments over the past century in the study of Chinese philosophy, as well as the professionalization and institutionalization of the discipline, Chinese philosophy remains insubstantial and devoid of real content.[10]

Even more dramatic is the assessment of Taiwanese philosopher Lin Anwu 林安梧 (at the time appointed at Taiwan Normal University):

> The current state of affairs with research on Chinese philosophy in Taiwan (and indeed on both sides of the Taiwan Strait) is such that even those scholars who regard Chinese philosophy highly still regard Chinese philosophy as a passive object of their research. Having overlooked the fact that "she" is a living, vital formation, at every opportunity they say that they are researching Chinese philosophy from the perspective of some Western philosopher. I call this situation the "prostitute-client mentality." Some adopt a Thomist perspective, some a Kantian perspective, some a Hegelian perspective, some a Marxist perspective, some an existentialist perspective, some a phenomenological perspective, some a hermeneutic perspective.... This way of approaching Chinese philosophy is not a dialogue of equals but an act of violence. It is as if Chinese philosophy was a prostitute and Western philosophy a mob of clients.[11]

Less lurid, but making essentially the same point, is Yu Dunkang's 余敦康 (Chinese Academy of Social Sciences) assessment that "Neo-Kantianism, Neo-Hegelianism, and New Pragmatism are all alike in that they fruitlessly employ Chinese materials to prove fundamental Western theories; they are all replications of various Western intellectual movements on Chinese soil rather than the inherent development of Chinese thought itself."[12]

Often such critical views have been accompanied by a more optimistic assessment of what this new-found "subjective autonomy" now makes possible. Jing Haifeng, for example, maintains that although concerns about the "legitimacy" of Chinese philosophy seem to indicate a sense of crisis, in fact they are more representative of an awakening. In Jing's words, it is an awakening on the part of contemporary Chinese intellectuals to the lack of a subject position they hold in the meta-narrative of their own national thought.[13] Other commentators are similarly optimistic. Wei Changbao 魏長寶, for example, regards the legitimacy issue to be linked to the process of Chinese philosophy's long march toward "rationalization," a term he employs as shorthand for the distancing of Chinese philosophy from its vassal-like association with Western philosophy. According to Wei, Chinese philosophy is now in a position to challenge its hitherto inferior and dependent relation with Western philosophy. Taking up this challenge will further promote the rationalization of Chinese philosophy and enhance its unique profile.

For Wei, the study and development of Chinese philosophy must not be guided by the paradigms of "Western philosophy" but rather by endogenous theoretical discourses. In the past, Western philosophical issues and paradigms were adopted as the standards for constructing Chinese philosophy. Although "the Western model" contributed greatly to the development of specialization and to the discipline's modernization, this has been at the cost of appreciating the unique problematics, structure, and character of Chinese philosophy. "Reflection on and discussions of the 'legitimacy' issue presage a change in the contemporary study of Chinese philosophy, as the focus of attention moves from 'philosophy' to 'China'; as the focus of attention moves from 'Chinese philosophy' in the sense of the establishment of a discipline to 'Chinese philosophy' in the sense of cultural representation…. We must endeavor to return to Chinese philosophy's own theoretical contexts and problematics so as to establish the subjective autonomy or self-determination of Chinese philosophy and to promote the indigenization (*bentuhua* 本土化) … of Chinese philosophy."[14]

In addition to this trend towards so-called indigenization, a closely related concern has been that Chinese thought and scholarship should occupy a position as benchmark or standard when conducting research into Chinese philosophy. Wang Zhongjiang 王中江 (Chinese Academy of Social Sciences) provides the following overview:

> Corresponding to the strengthening of people's identification with Chinese history and tradition since the 1990s, everyone has been deeply disturbed by the adverse effects caused by the use of Western paradigms to explain Chinese learning. As people began to entertain doubts about the customary method of using Western philosophical paradigms and concepts to investigate Chinese philosophy, some people began to waver even about the term "Chinese philosophy," which has long been in currency as a representative aspect of "Chinese learning".… "Simplistic, forced analogies" and "misreading" may merely be problems of detail, but concealing or

sacrificing Chinese philosophy's intrinsic "problematics," "ways of thinking," and "inner structures and goals" causes systemic harm. This is at least part of the reason for the sympathetic and welcoming reception in China of [Paul A.] Cohen's "China-centered perspective" and [Edward] Said's "Orientalism." This is also a background factor for why some of us have called for the "indigenization" (本土化) of Chinese scholarship, or for returning to a Chinese linguistic context, or even using classical Chinese to speak.[15]

Such notions as "inherent development," "endogenous theoretical discourses," "unique problematics," and "inner structures and goals" suggest a shared paradigm. I will return to this point in the third part of this Epilogue.

2. The Views of Early "Internal Participants"

What were the views of scholars who participated in creating the academic discipline of Chinese philosophy on the question of the relationship between non-Chinese philosophy and Chinese philosophy? Among Hu Shi's 胡適 (1891–1962) older contemporaries and colleagues in the Peking University Philosophy Department there was a well-entrenched view that China had its own independent philosophical tradition. This view clearly dates back at least to the founding of the Philosophy Department.

One advocate, Liang Shuming 梁漱溟 (1893–1988), developed a cultural philosophy (*wenhua zhexue*) based on an engagement with three philosophical traditions, as set out in his 1922 publication, *Dong-Xi wenhua ji qi zhexue* 東西文化及其哲學 [Eastern and Western cultures and their philosophies]. According to Liang, there are three attitudes or directions a culture and its corresponding philosophy (metaphysics/ontology/philosophy of life, epistemology, and ethics) can take. It can focus on resolving the problems presented by the natural world (as in the case of the West); it can concentrate its attention on the issues raised by relationships between people (as in the case of China); or it can give its primary attention to the question of the "self" (as in the case of India). Liang believed that the first of these was the most basic and the third the most advanced. The second was an intermediate position. As Thierry Meynard demonstrates in chapter 6, Liang was attempting to reveal fundamental differences and incompatibilities between these cultures, not influences and commonalities.

In his 1929 general history of Chinese philosophy, Zhong Tai 鍾泰 (1888–1979) objected to Hu Shi's use of Western philosophy as a framework for understanding Chinese philosophy. Insisting that the latter should be understood on its own terms, he argued that "Chinese and Western learning each have their own systems, and if one is forced to conform to the other, the true meaning of each will be lost." On this premise he justified using terms found in the original texts as the basis for his own exegesis, rather than employing introduced concepts. (These views had in fact already been expressed by Fu Sinian 傅斯年 (1896–1950), as Carine Defoort shows in her chapter in this volume.[16]) The major difference between Zhong and Fu on this matter is that Fu did not acknowledge that Chinese philosophy—as distinct from Chinese thought—had ever existed.) Zhong further explained: "In this book I have employed the genre of the historical biography to relate the true purport of accounts recorded in former texts. Hence, when reviewed from beginning to end, the origins and flow of the history of Chinese philosophy are set out in detail, making it possible to distinguish how it differs from the history of Western philosophy."[17] Zhong Tai thus represents an unambiguous expression of the view that Chinese and Western philosophy are fundamentally different and that if the concepts or historical divisions of Western philosophy are applied to Chinese philosophy, this will have a deleterious and distorting effect on the latter.

In contrast to Zhong Tai, Xie Wuliang 謝無量 (1884–1964) in his 1916 *Zhongguo zhexueshi* 中國哲學史 [History of Chinese philosophy] clearly expressed the view that philosophy/*zhexue* was a general category, which he referred to as *daoshu* 道術 (techniques of the way);[18] and that different traditions—philosophy, *zhexue*, and Buddhist *yixue* 義學 (doctrinal learning)—were but localized expressions of *daoshu*. A variation of this view is evident in different expressions of a commitment to an overarching global philosophy, a goal already made explicit in Nishi Amane's 西周 (1829–1897) writings, with roots in Comte's positivism, as Barry Steben shows in chapter 1. Another variation is the Marxist view—represented in this volume by the scholars discussed in chapter 10—that all philosophy is global philosophy so long as it is refracted through the prisms of materialism and dialectics.

As with other "Tsinghua school" philosophers of the 1930s, including Feng Youlan and Zhang Dainian 張岱年 (1909–2004), Jin Yuelin 金岳霖 (1895–1984) sought to contribute to a global philosophy. In chapter 8 Yvonne Schulz Zinda draws attention to the fact that when Jin was writing his ontology, he stated that he intended to create a universal *Weltanschauung*, and in "his appraisal of Feng Youlan's work he stated that philosophy should not be confined to national boundaries, but discussed in a broader, more general context. He seemed to cherish hopes for progress towards a universal philosophy. In the case of logic, Jin repeatedly argued … in favor of a universal logic."

Jin's writings, however, suggest an ambiguous relationship with traditional Chinese thought. Although Jin employed traditional Chinese terms as key metaphysical concepts to address the problem of induction and in his epistemology used terms derived from both Chinese and Western traditions, he did so with minimal reference to traditional Chinese contexts. The overwhelming impression is that to the extent Jin did recognize a Chinese philosophical tradition, he sought to appropriate concepts and terms from the Chinese past in order to address problems highlighted in Western philosophy. Thus, Xiaoqing Diana Lin argues in her chapter, "For Jin, logic constituted the essence of the world, but this logic was based on concepts coined to reflect Chinese thought, although now situated in a larger, universal framework."

There remains, however, a real question as to whether Jin did, in fact, acknowledge a Chinese philosophical tradition, given the influential distinction he drew between "Chinese philosophy" and "philosophy in China,"[19] a distinction which highlights the tension between the universalist claims of theory (typically seen as "Western" in origin) and the particularity of local cultural identity. In his 1930 evaluation of the prepublication version of the first volume of Feng Youlan's *Zhongguo zhexueshi*, Jin outlined the following distinction:

> Nowadays the trend is to treat European philosophical problems as general philosophical problems. If the problems discussed by the pre-Qin masters are the same as those discussed in European philosophy, then those problems are philosophical problems…. Philosophy has both substance and form, problems and method. If the substance and the form of a particular type of thought are both the same as the substance and the form of philosophy in the general sense (*pubian zhexue* 普遍哲學), then that type of thought is philosophy. If, however, the substance and the form of a particular type of thought both differ from the substance and form of philosophy in the general sense, then it is rather questionable that that type of thought is a type of philosophy. To have the substance of philosophy but to lack its form, or to have its form but to lack the substance of philosophical thought—both cases present a problem for the historian of philosophy. The term "Chinese

philosophy" is such a problem. Is the so-called history of Chinese philosophy the history of Chinese philosophy or is it the history of philosophy in China?... Writing a history of Chinese philosophy comes down to an issue of basic attitude. There are two such basic attitudes. One attitude regards Chinese philosophy to be a particular type of learning within National Studies (*guoxue* 國學). This attitude does not necessarily prompt a question of similarity with or difference from philosophy in the general sense. The other attitude regards Chinese philosophy to be philosophy that is discovered in China.[20]

For Jin, the contrast is between, on the one hand, "Chinese philosophy" understood as a localized, culturally specific phenomenon that has no generic connection with some more generalized notion of philosophy and, on the other hand, the selective "discovery" of elements of this more generalized notion of Philosophy in the context of historical China. (Jin subsequently proceeded to voice a mild criticism of Feng for failing to adopt a particular philosophical position in his exposition of the history of philosophy in China.) Although Jin's philosophical writings reveal an ambiguous relationship with traditional Chinese thought, in the above passage "Chinese philosophy" (as distinct from "Philosophy discovered in China") is not subsumed within the category of Philosophy, and so the application of the principles derived from Philosophy have no proper application in the case of what is called "Chinese philosophy." In other words, only those aspects of traditional Chinese thought which correspond to aspects of Philosophy in the general sense (which just happens to be based exclusively on norms adopted in Western traditions) can be deemed to be "philosophy."

Jin was not the first to voice this distinction. As Carine Defoort shows in chapter 9, Fu Sinian maintained that "The ancient Chinese Masters did not resemble the ancient Greek philosophers; they had even less in common with modern Western philosophy.... Fu Sinian rejected the label of philosophy for the ancient Chinese Masters [and] thereby implicitly suggested that philosophy concerns more universal and abstract matters." Although Jin, unlike Fu, is not generally portrayed as representative of a counter-current which rejects the very idea of "Chinese philosophy"—and ironically, thus helped to sharpen its profile—his distinction between "Chinese philosophy" and "Philosophy in China" has provided ammunition for those who have sought to make such a distinction.

In his major study published in 2003, *Zhu Xi de lishi shijie: Songdai shi dafu zhengzhi wenhua de yanjiu* 朱熹的歷史世界——宋代士大夫政治文化的研究 [The historical world of Zhu Xi: Investigations into the political culture of Song scholar-officials], Yu Yingshi used Jin's distinction to challenge the "legitimacy" of studying aspects of so-called Song-dynasty *daoxue* 道學 and *lixue* 理學 thought as philosophy rather than studying them from the perspective of the discipline of history. Yu's underlying position is that the ultimate goal of Song *daoxue* thinkers (in particular, Zhu Xi 朱熹 [1130–1200]) was political, not philosophical, and that to ignore this is to miscontrue the true significance of *daoxue* discourse. His critique, however, begins with an attack on what he sees as the contrived nature of "Chinese philosophy":

> Generally speaking, when modern scholars of the history of philosophy study *daoxue*, just as Jin Yuelin[21] stated, first and foremost "they take European philosophical questions as general philosophical questions," and next treat *daoxue* "as philosophy discovered in China." As to the significant disparity between various interpretations of *daoxue*, this is due to the fact that each researcher adopts a different European philosophical system. With this as the basis for selection, the research of historians of philosophy inevitably focuses on the various discussions of *daoti* 道體 [fundamental state of the way] by *daoxue* thinkers, because this is the sole component [of *daoxue* thought] that can pass muster as "philosophy."[22]

Yu complains that the "history of philosophy" approach has led to *daoxue*'s being "abstracted" from the broader context of Song *ruxue* and also to the abstraction of *daoti* from the context of *daoxue*. The upshot of this is that the actual "historical world"—or more specifically, the "political culture"—in which *daoxue* protagonists operated has been ignored.[23]

In the preface to his 1919 publication, *Zhongguo zhexueshi dagang* 中國哲學史大綱 [An outline of the history of Chinese philosophy], Hu Shi outlined a sequence of rise, decline, assimilation, and renaissance in the history of Chinese philosophy from ancient until modern times. The centerpiece of the renaissance was Masters Studies' securing independence from Classical Studies. Hu credited the Han Learning philologists of the Qing dynasty with making this breakthrough possible: "Only with the efforts made by the Han Learning specialists in matters of evidential learning, collation, and the glossing of old terms could those classical texts and masters texts just manage to be read."[24] Writing later in his autobiography, however, Hu revealed that it was Dewey who "helped me [to understand] Chinese classical learning (*gudian xueshu* 古典學術) of the past several thousand years—in particular of the past three hundred years—as well as the methods of Chinese historians, such as *kaojuxue* 考據學 and *kaozhengxue* 考證學 (evidential scholarship)." As I argue in chapter 5, it was Dewey's genetic method that especially stimulated Hu's understanding, encouraging him to identify the internal threads of China's philosophical past.

Feng Youlan was both a philosopher and an intellectual historian. His representative philosophical writings were published individually between 1938 and 1946 and subsequently collectively published under the title of *Zhen Yuan liu shu* 貞元六書 [Purity descends, primacy ascends: Six books]. In chapter 7 of this volume, Hans-Georg Moeller describes *Zhen Yuan liu shu* as a work that "on the one hand, conceives of itself as a continuation of the entire history of Chinese philosophy, and, on the other hand, attempts to contribute to a new world philosophy that gives equal consideration to the whole range of Western philosophy." Similarly, Feng's representative history, *Zhongguo zhexueshi* (1931, 1934), is not just a history of Chinese philosophy; it also provides important insights into Feng's own philosophical thought.

As with many Chinese philosophers in the first half of the twentieth century, Feng's interest in philosophy started with his introduction to logic. Unlike Hu Shi, however, he did not seek to excavate an indigenous logic from early Chinese philosophical writings. Instead, he saw logic as providing a method: "The permanent contribution of Western philosophy to Chinese philosophy is the method of logical analysis.... It gives the Chinese people a new way of thinking.... It is the method, not the ready-made conclusions of Western philosophy, that is important."[25] And just as his philosophical predecessors had accorded logic a privileged role in telling the story of Chinese philosophy, so too Feng emphasized the need for system. Indeed, writing at the very end of his life, Feng opined that the single most important contribution of Hu Shi's *Zhongguo zhexueshi dagang* was to have provided Chinese philosophy with a "formal system." Nevertheless, like Hu Shi, Feng did not believe that Chinese philosophy was in fact devoid of its own inherent system. To this end, he had long distinguished "formal" (*xingshi* 形式) system and "real" (實質) system:

> It may be admitted that Chinese philosophy lacks formal system; but if one were to say that it therefore lacks any real system, meaning that there

is no organic unity of ideas to be found in Chinese philosophy, it would be equivalent to saying that Chinese philosophy is not philosophy, and that China has no philosophy. The earlier Greek philosophy also lacked formal system.... Although Chinese philosophy, formally speaking, is less systematic than that of the West, in its actual content it has as much system as does Western philosophy. This being so, the important duty of the historian of philosophy is to find within a philosophy that lacks *formal* system, its underlying *real* system.[26]

As he explained with reference to his own philosophical system, New Principle-centered Learning (*xin lixue* 新理學) or New Metaphysics, the term "new" refers to his intention not merely to provide a continuation (*jiezhe jiang* 接著講) of Principle-centered Learning, but to develop it critically (*zhaozhe jiang* 照著講).[27] Now, although earlier figures such as Zhang Binglin 章炳麟 (Taiyan 太炎) (1869–1936) can (retrospectively) also be credited with having contributed to the development of Chinese philosophy as an academic discipline by developing their own creative hermeneutics, it is perhaps with Feng Youlan that for the first time a Chinese philosopher self-reflexively asserted that creative interpretation is in fact a contribution to the development of Chinese philosophy; that the task of modern scholars of Chinese philosophy is not merely the recovery of its past. Accordingly, Feng treated the history of Chinese philosophy as a philosophical topic, maintaining that there was no clear dividing line between studying the history of philosophy and creating philosophy as long as one "carried the discussion forward" and did not just rehearse earlier philosophies.[28] Hans-Georg Moeller's following comment is apposite: "Hegel's philosophical notion of the history of philosophy had a profound impact on Feng Youlan's writings on the history of Chinese philosophy in the 1920s and 1930s. It could thus be argued that Feng's attempt to identify the 'spirit' of Chinese philosophy, and to see his own philosophy as its very culmination, follows very closely in the footsteps of Hegel—and is thus not very endogenous."

Strongly influenced by Anglo-American New Realist philosophy—which characterizes reality as logical—Feng sought to defend his own metaphysical system against the challenges posed by the pro-empiricist, anti-metaphysical approach to philosophy championed by the Vienna Circle philosophers. Feng compared the significance of his own meta-physical system with Kant's belief that his *Critique of Pure Reason* had found a "middle way" between the subjectivism of poor metaphysics and Hume's scepticism and provided metaphysics with a renewed legitimacy.

As for the methodology employed in Feng's metaphysics, Moeller describes it as consisting of "a transformation of the Chinese philosophical—and, in particular, the Neo-Confucian—vocabulary into concepts, and thus its 'rationalization,' so that it becomes compatible with contemporary Western philosophical discourse." In short, both in Feng's attempts to provide traditional Chinese philosophy with a formal system and in his endeavour to develop his own philosophical system, the role of Western philosophy was crucial.[29]

A similar perspective on the centrality of Western philosophy in the articulation of China's philosophical past had been expressed by Wang Guowei 王國維 (1887–1927) already in 1903 when he wrote that that the only way for China's philosophical legacy to be promoted and developed was by means of a thorough understanding of Western philosophy. "Philosophy is a type of learning that has always existed in China…. Our ancient books, however, are loosely organized and lacking in structure; or they are damaged and incomplete. Although they contain truth, it is not easy to find. When compared to the splendid systematization (*xitong* 系統) and orderly formation of Western philosophy, there is no hiding which tradition of philosophy is formally superior."[30] Finally, perhaps the most direct and mechanical application of Western theory to the "systematization" of China's philosophical past is Marxist historiography.

Western philosophy was not the only non-Chinese tradition to be applied to the articulation of China's past. As had Liang Shuming, Xiong Shili 熊十力 (1885–1968) consciously attempted to create a new philosophy. In Xiong's case, this was done by drawing selectively on past Chinese texts and thinkers. Athough Xiong's writings fitted the systematic, analytical form of modern philosophy, and opened the door for a modern reinterpretation of Confucian concepts, that analytic form was indebted to Yogācāra philosophy, not to Western philosophy.[31] Thus, although Xiong clearly did recognize the existence of an endogenous philosophical tradition in China—one associated in particular with the Lu-Wang tradition of Neo-Confucian philosophy—he drew on Buddhist philosophical paradigms to shape his creative transformation of the Chinese tradition. He was less concerned about recovering the past than about constructing his own metaphysical system that drew on selective aspects of that past, a project which, incidentally, he never finished.

Significantly, although he was profoundly influenced by Yogācāra philosophy, his own philosophical system is a critique of Yogācāra.

Despite appropriating important terms, concepts, and problematics from Yogācāra philosophy (strongly mediated through its Chinese interpretation), as well as Madhyamaka philosophy and Sinitic traditions of Buddhist thought, Xiong Shili went on to develop these elements into his own onto-cosmology: a metaphysics in which the primary ontological realm of the "Fundamental Reality" (*benti* 本體) transforms and permeates all things such that nounenal reality and phenomena cohere as an undifferentiated whole. Xiong's onto-cosmology was influenced by both Confucian and Buddhist teachings. He was particularly inspired by the view found in the *Book of Change* that the cosmos is perpetually and vigorously changing. By and large, it was in reaction to the notion of a quiescent and unchanging Fundamental Reality (which Xiong associated with certain Buddhist views) that spurred his embrace of the philosophy of change and process he found in the *Book of Change*. He also subscribed to the notion of Mind as being originally enlightened, a view common to several Sinitic systems of Buddhist thought—Tiantai, Huayan, and Chan—influenced by the *Dasheng qixin lun* 大乘起信論 (*Mahāyānaśrāddhotpāda-Śāstra*; *The Awakening of Faith in Mahāyāna*).

As with Xiong, Zhang Taiyan also drew substantially from Yogācāra philosophy (albeit, necessarily a Sinitic-inflected understanding of it). Zhang's attitude to Western philosophy might seem ambivalent. After all, he saw the concepts of ontology, epistemology, and logic as essential to any philosophical system. However, it should be borne in mind that his interest was not in the terms but in the concepts underlying those terms, and there is little doubt he saw Chinese, Indian, and Western philosophical traditions as all operating with these concepts. In fact, Zhang was highly critical of Western philosophy, remarking that "Although Western philosophy is incisive in the written word, its [perspectives] still remain at the level of imagination, not yet verifiable by the mind, and quite baseless. Western philosophy is still not even able to measure up to Song learning, and the theories proposed by Western philosophers are actually quite at odds with one another." Instead, his allegiances were with Yogācāra philosophy, which he regarded as being characterized by organized, systematized thought and concepts. It was an intellectual resource which could be co-opted to counter the challenges posed by the logic, philosophy (then including psychology), and science of the West. As I argue in chapter 3, he believed *yinming* 因明 (Buddhist logic) enabled the recovery of the true meaning of certain pre-Qin writings on logic and reasoning in a way that Western philosophy could not.

In sum, this survey of the views of a range of scholars who participated in creating the academic discipline of Chinese philosophy reveals
that the great majority of them held the view that one or more non-
Chinese philosophical tradition was crucial to the articulation and development of China's philosophical heritage. Variations of this widely held
view were shared by Wang Guowei, Zhang Taiyan, Hu Shi, Xiong Shili,
Feng Youlan, and He Lin 賀麟 (1902–1992),[32] among many others. For
Marxist scholars, of course, materialism and dialectics were essential to
the articulation of China's philosophical past. Jin Yuelin's position,
however, is ambivalent. On the one hand, Western philosophy has no
bearing on the tradition of "Chinese philosophy" (which he did not
regard as genuine philosophy), yet, on the other hand, by definition
"philosophy in China" was tied to the paradigms and norms of Western
philosophy.

3. Inner Logic

Over the past three decades, a different paradigm from that proposed by
Levenson (cited in the Introduction) has emerged in historical studies of
China which emphasizes the continued agency and relevance of the past
in the present. This approach has been variously formulated by intellectual historians of China. In one early study, *Crisis of Chinese Consciousness: Radical Antitraditionalism in the May Fourth Era* (1979), Lin Yu-
sheng identifies a "cultural-intellectualistic approach" in the thinking of
two generations of May Fourth intellectuals which was grounded in deep-
seated cultural norms. Lin describes the "cultural-intellectualistic
approach" as stressing "the necessary priority of intellectual and cultural
change over political, social and economic changes. It implied a fundamental belief that cultural change was the foundation for all other necessary changes." He argues that this "cultural-intellectualistic approach"
was so powerful and pervasive that the Chinese intelligentsia of both
generations were not necessarily conscious "that their views were influenced by a deep-seated traditional Chinese cultural predisposition"
which "infiltrated into the minds of members of the first two generations
of intelligentsia and led them to maintain their belief in the power and
priority of ideas."[33] Lin further insists that the cultural-intellectualistic
approach was shared "by the different schools of postclassical Confucian
philosophers through time" and that this "indicates a distinctive
predisposition of postclassical Confucian culture: a monistic and

intellectualistic way of thinking, which approaches moral and political problems by stressing the power and priority of fundamental ideas."[34] Central to this intellectualism—the idea that intellectual doctrines determine the course of history—was "the stress placed on the function of the inward moral and/or intellectual experience of the mind,"[35] the origins of which Lin traces to the writings of the classical thinkers Mencius and Xunzi. Lin's book was translated into Chinese in 1988.

In his 1984 critique of the "Western impact—Chinese response" thesis (of which Levenson is often seen to be representative[36]), set out in *Discovering History in China*, Paul A. Cohen wrote: "The enormous potency that Levenson invested in the Western impact caused him not only to date prematurely the point in time at which Western ideas penetrated from the periphery to the center of Chinese concern but also to exaggerate the degree to which, once such penetration occurred, earlier Chinese concerns became moribund.... The fact is, with the arrival of the West, Levenson no longer took the *inner dynamics* [my emphasis] of [the Chinese intellectual] world seriously."[37]

Cohen's *Discovering History in China* was translated into Japanese in 1988 and into Chinese in 1989. At the time, the Japanese intellectual historian of late imperial China, Mizoguchi Yūzō 溝口雄三, showed considerable enthusiasm for it.[38] He had been developing a similar methodology through his own studies of late imperial Chinese history. Mizoguchi's "China as method"[39] emphasizes the inherent continuity of key traditional concepts and paradigms and the importance of recognizing the central role of endogenous transformations in Chinese modern history. It was in part inspired as a critical response to Takeuchi Yoshimi's 竹内好 (1910–1971) "Asia as method" (*hōhō toshite no Ajia* 方法としてのアジア) thesis.[40] In contrast to Takeuchi's argument that the Other (China and the West) has had an inalienable role in the construction of (Japanese) self-identity, Mizoguchi's "China as method" thesis argues that the endogenous developments in Chinese history—rather than foreign interventions—have been decisive in shaping the course of modern Chinese history. Many of Mizoguchi's books and articles have been translated into Chinese.[41]

Hao Chang is another prominent intellectual historian who publishes in Chinese and whose English-language writings have been widely translated into Chinese. In his 1987 study, *Chinese Intellectuals in Crisis: Search for Order and Meaning, 1890–1911*, he wrote: "Apart from cultural identity, there was another channel through which tradition continued to impinge on the minds of Chinese intellectuals. This is what may be called 'internal dialogues.' By 'internal dialogues,' I refer to intellectual discussions of a specific nature that went on in the Chinese tradition over the centuries." Chang relates that these internal dialogues "must be recognized as important channels through which tradition made its influence felt" on the minds of a generation of "transition era" late-Qing dynasty intellectuals.[42]

Over the past two decades, American-based intellectual historian, Yu Yingshi (Yu Ying-shih) 余英時, has also developed a related thesis about the role of endogenous developments in Chinese intellectual history. In commenting on the shortcomings of Zhang Taiyan's and Hou Wailu's 侯外廬 (1903–1987) respective accounts of the rise of so-called Qing learning, Yu remarked:

> Irrespective of whether it is a political explanation, an economic one, or a politically-motivated one that objects to the doctrines of Principle-centered Learning, in all cases appeal is made to external factors to account for the changes in scholarship and thought. By failing to pay attention to the internal developments of intellectual history, the life-force of intellectual history is overlooked…. Hence, apart from external factors we should also particularly discuss the internal development of intellectual history. I refer to this as inner logic (*neizai lilu* 內在理路). That is, every particular intellectual tradition has its own set of problems/issues that require ongoing interpretation. Some of these problems/issues are solved on a temporary basis, some remain unsolved. Some are considered important at some given time but later are no longer considered so, the succession proceeding without end. Within this there is a thread (*xiansuo* 綫索) that can be followed.[43]

One final example is Thomas Metzger's *A Cloud across the Pacific: Essays on the Clash between Chinese and Western Political Theories Today* (2005) in which he identifies an "epistemological optimism" common to Chinese Marxism, "Sunism" [Three principles of the people], modern Confucian humanism, and Chinese liberalism. At the heart of this optimism he finds the metaphysical claim that humans can use intuition or dialectical reasoning to attain knowledge of, or even become one with, an ineffable ultimate reality that governs the natural world, history, and ethical life. Metzger traces the ideological grounding of this epistemological optimism to "the Confucian and Neo-Confucian tradition."[44]

The inner dynamics/inner dialogue/inner logic paradigm has been a dominant thread[45] in contemporary claims that the articulation and development of China's philosophical heritage must draw exclusively on China's indigenous paradigms and norms. Indeed, implicitly and explicitly, this paradigm has also served to confer methodological legitimacy on so-called epistemological nativism.[46] Other factors in China conducive to this attitude towards the past include the indigenization trend in a number of the social sciences, the rise of National Studies since the mid-1990s,[47] and a growing cultural nationalism evident in many parts of the Chinese academy.[48]

The contrast with the view widely shared by earlier generations of internal participants in Chinese philosophy's formative development—that exogenous philosophical traditions and/or theoretical constructs were crucial to the articulation and development of China's philosophical heritage—is stark. Whereas those earlier generations acknowledged that "Chinese philosophy" was a product of the complex interaction between internal and external agencies, influential modern commentators seem to believe that the clock can somehow be turned back, that a pristine Chinese philosophy (or "techniques of the way")[49] can be recovered, reclaimed, and developed.[50]

Recently, Hong Kong-based Chinese philosopher, Shun Kwong-loi, has drawn attention to the consequences of the modern default practice of using Western concepts and frameworks for doing comparative work between Chinese and Western philosophies, noting that "while we see frequent deployment of Western philosophical frameworks in the study of Chinese thought, we rarely encounter the reverse phenomenon, namely, the deployment of Chinese philosophical frameworks in the study of Western thought." And while acknowledging that the use of Western philosophical concepts can help highlight certain features of Confucian thought related to ethical issues,[51] Shun further insists that "Chinese ethical traditions themselves have rich insights into the ethical experiences of human beings that are conveyed through concepts distinctive of these traditions. Viewing Chinese thought from the perspective of Western philosophical conceptions will not do full justice to these insights." Yet, can China's intervening philosophical legacies of the immediate past—Japanese, Indian, European, American, and so forth—be bracketed and ignored? Do these legacies not also serve to transform the past?[52] Indeed, are not contemporary Chinese conceptions of just what is "philosophical" inevitably shaped by this more immediate philosophical legacy? If the answer to these questions is in the affirmative, then this would seem to complicate the claim that "[i]t is by studying

Chinese ethical thought on its own terms that we can bring out its more distinctive ideas, which can then be fleshed out and developed without being shaped by agendas set by Western philosophical discussions."[53]

4. Coda

Hu Shi's case is particularly intriguing as we consider the explanatory value of the inner dynamics/inner dialogue/inner logic paradigm in relation to the formation of Chinese philosophy. As I show in chapter 5, for Hu, the internal threads of China's philosophical past were revealed through discrete, isolatable chains of causes and effects which had their origins in the writings of the pre-Qin masters and which subsequently shaped the parameters of the development of the Chinese philosophical tradition. In his understanding of the history of Chinese philosophy, Hu distinguished two threads (*xiansuo* 線索), external and internal: "Internal threads" refers to "a kind of method, a philosophical method, the foreign name of which is logic." He explained that he sought "to grasp the logical method (名學方法) … of each philosopher or each school of thought. I take this to be the central topic of the history of philosophy." For Hu, these "internal threads" reveal a logical sequence, a causal relationship, between one historical event and another.

As it happens, this bears an uncanny similarity to Yu Yingshi's notion of an inner logic which he too contrasts with external influences and which also provides a thread (*xiansuo* 線索) enabling one to trace the internal developments of China's intellectual history. Yu explains that he employs the concept of inner logic not to displace the explanatory role of "external influences" but rather to defend "the autonomy of intellectual history":

> Figures associated with Song-Ming Principle-centered Learning as well as Qing-dynasty evidential scholars engaged in *rujia* classical studies. Without doubt, they belonged to the same tradition of research. Not only did they deal with the same classical documents, they were confronted with the same question: in the early classics, to what did *dao* and related principal concepts refer? This was a question internal to the *ruxue* tradition, with its own internal demands for development and transformation, and was not necessarily closely connected to external influences.

Yu is at pains to point out that he did not seek to posit "inner logic" and "external influences" to be in opposition. He insists, however, that "if research in intellectual history attends merely to external influences and fails to penetrate deeply into 'inner logic,' it will fail to reveal fully the twists and turns of intellectual history and will even 'reject the fundamental in pursuit of the peripheral.'... 'Inner logic' and 'external influences' each have their own field of application. If pursued independently, then the merits of each will be evident; if pursued in combination, then each will suffer."[54] "Only by focusing on the unique course and shape of Chinese historical changes, I am convinced, can we hope to see more clearly how that great cultural tradition moved from stage to stage driven, mainly if not entirely, by its internal dynamics."[55]

Chen Shaoming 陳少明 is surely correct to see parallels between Yu's internal/external distinction and sociologist Karl Mannheim's (1893–1947) "intrinsic interpretation"/"extrinsic interpretation" distinction.[56] As noted above, Yu's formulation of the notion of "inner logic" also shares unambiguous similarities with notions such as "inner dynamics" (Cohen) and "inner dialogue" (Chang), and together these three notions contribute to a shared paradigm. Yet the parallels with Hu Shi's notion of internal and external threads, in which internal threads are characterized in terms of a "logical method," strike me as unusually compelling, suggesting that in the early phase of the formation of Chinese philosophy as an academic discipline, essentially the same paradigm had already been employed as a tool in the recovery and articulation of China's philosophical heritage.[57] Crucially, however, even though Hu argued for the existence of an inner logic in China's philosophical past, he further insisted that Western philosophy was crucial to uncovering and articulating that inner logic. For Hu, Western philosophy—channeled most immediately via John Dewey—had proved essential to identifying the inner threads of China's philosophical past.

Notes

1   For these scholars, it seems that other philosophical traditions—say Japanese or Indian—are of little relevance.

2   So-called *bentu* 本土 (indigenous/local) or *benwei* 本位 (China-based) perspectives on Chinese philosophy.

3   Feng Youlan, *Zhongguo zhexueshi* 中國哲學史 [A history of Chinese philosophy], Vol. 1 (Shanghai: Shangwu yinshuguan, 1934), pp. 7, 8.

4   Chen Lai, "Guanyu 'Zhongguo zhexue' de ruogan wenti qianyi" 關於「中國哲學」的若干問題淺議 [Some superficial remarks on several problems concerning Chinese philosophy], first published in *Jiang-Han luntan* 江漢論壇 7 (2003). Online version <http://www.guoxue.com/ws/ShowArticle. asp?ArticleID=882>, accessed 15 December 2004.

5   Discussion of these and related issues was widespread between 2001 and 2006 and described under the rubric of "the legitimacy of Chinese philosophy" (*Zhongguo zhexue de hefaxing* 中國哲學的合法性). On this topic, see Carine Defoort, "Is There Such a Thing as Chinese Philosophy? Arguments of an Implicit Debate," *Philosophy East and West* 51.3 (July 2001), pp. 393–413; "Is 'Chinese Philosophy' a Proper Name? A Response to Rein Raud," *Philosophy East and West* 56.4 (2006), pp. 625–660. Three issues of *Contemporary Chinese Thought* 37.1–3 (2005–2006) are devoted to translations of representative articles on the topic of the legitimacy of Chinese philosophy.

6   The two essays are Zheng Jiadong 鄭家棟, "'Zhongguo zhexue' de 'hefaxing' wenti" 「中國哲學」的「合法性」問題 [The problem of the "legitimacy" of "Chinese" philosophy] in *Zhongguo zhexue nianjian 2001* 中國哲學年鑒, edited by the Chinese Philosophy Institute, Chinese Academy of Social Sciences (Beijing: Zhexue yanjiu zazhishe, 2001) and unnamed interviewer, "'Zhongguo zhexue' yanjiu de tiaozhan: Fangtan Chen Lai jiaoshou" 「中國哲學」研究的挑戰——訪談陳來教授 [The challenges facing the study of "Chinese philosophy": An interview with Professor Chen Lai], *Zhexue dongtai* 哲學動態 3 (2002), pp. 2–5.

7   Feng Youlan, *Zhongguo zhexueshi*, Vol. 1, p. 1.

8   Zhang Liwen, "Zhongguo zhexue de 'Ziji jiang,' 'jiang ziji'—Lun zouchu Zhongguo zhexue de weiji he chaoyue hefaxing de wenti" 中國哲學的「自己講」、「講自己」——論走出中國哲學的危機和超越合法性的問題 [Chinese philosophy's self-account and account of itself—Finding a way out of the crisis of Chinese philosophy and overcoming the problem of legitimacy], *Zhongguo renmin daxue xuebao* 中國人民大學學報 2 (2003), p. 3.

9   Chen Shaoming, "Chongti 'Zhongguo zhexue' de zhengdangxing" 重提「中國哲學」的正當性 [Once more on the appropriateness of "Chinese philosophy"], *Jiang-Han luntan* 江漢論壇 7 (2003), p. 34.

10   Jing Haifeng, *Zhongguo zhexue de xiandai quanshi* 中國哲學的現代詮釋 [A modern interpretation of Chinese philosophy] (Beijing: Renmin chubanshe, 2004), pp. 210, 241–247 *passim*.

11 Lin Anwu, "Dangqian Taiwan zhexuejie geng da de wenti zai sangshi zhu-tixing de hao wu xingjue" 當前臺灣哲學界更大的問題在喪失主體性的毫無省覺 [A bigger problem facing today's Taiwan philosophy scene concerns the total lack of awareness about the loss of subjective autonomy], in Wang Yingming 王英銘, ed., *Taiwan zhi zhexue geming* 臺灣之哲學革命 [Taiwan's philosophical revolution] (Taipei: Shuxiang wenhua shiye youxian gongsi, 1998), p. 237.

12 Yu Dunkang, "Zhongguo quanshixue shi yizuo qiao" 中國詮釋學是一座橋 [Chinese hermeneutics is a bridge], *Zhongguo quanshixue* 中國詮釋學 1 (2003), p. 247.

13 Jing Haifeng, *Zhongguo zhexue de xiandai quanshi*, p. 210.

14 Wei Changbao, "Zhongguo zhexue de 'hefaxing' xushi ji qi chaoyue" 中國哲學的「合法性」敍事及其超越 [The narrative of Chinese philosophy's "legitimacy" and how to overcome it], *Zhexue dongtai* 哲學動態 6 (2004), pp. 7–9, passim.

15 Wang Zhongjang "'Fanshi,' 'shendu guandian,' yu Zhongguo zhexue 'yanjiu dianfan'" 「範式」、「深度觀點」與中國哲學「研究典範」 ["Paradigms," "profound perspectives," and "research models" for Chinese philosophy], *Jiang-Han luntan* 江漢論壇 7 (2003), pp. 26, 27.

16 These views have by no means been relegated to the past. In his *Mencius and Early Chinese Thought* (Stanford: Stanford University Press, 1997), pp. 11–12, Kwong-loi Shun explains that he tried to avoid the use of Western philosophical terms in a study directed to understanding the perspectives of early Chinese thinkers.

17 Zhong Tai, *Zhongguo zhexueshi* 中國哲學史 (Beijing: Dongfang chubanshe, 2008; originally published in 1929), p. 1.

18 Xie Wuliang, *Zhongguo zhexueshi* (Taipei: Taiwan Zhonghua shuju, 1967), p. 1.

19 At the same time, Feng Youlan used the terms *Zhongguo di zhexue* 中國底哲學 and *Zhongguo de zhexue* 中國的哲學 to draw a similar distinction.

20 Jin Yuelin, "Shencha baogao" 審查報告 [Appraisal report], pp. 2, 5, appended to the first volume of Feng Youlan's *Zhongguo zhexueshi*.

21 Jin's comments were actually passed in respect of Feng Youlan's trailblazing *Zhongguo zhexueshi*.

22 Yu Yingshi, *Zhu Xi de lishi shijie: Songdai shi dafu zhengzhi wenhua de yanjiu* 朱熹的歷史世界：宋代士大夫政治文化的研究 [The historical world of Zhu Xi: Investigations into the political culture of Song scholar-officials], 2 vols. (Taipei: Yunchen, 2003), Vol. 1, pp. 33–34.

23 For a response to Yu's challenge, in which I argue that his critique is actually directed at New Confucian interpretations of Neo-Confucian thought as philosophy, see my introduction to *Dao Companion to Neo-Confucian Philosophy* (Springer: New York, 2010), pp. xxxv–xli.

24 Hu Shi, *Zhongguo zhexueshi dagang*, in *Hu Shi xueshu wenji: Zhongguo zhexueshi* 胡適學術文集：中國哲學史 [Collected essays of Hu Shi's scholarship:

History of Chinese philosophy], 2 vols., edited by Jiang Yihua 姜義華 (Beijing: Zhonghua shuju, 1998), Vol. 1, Preface p. 13.

25 Feng Youlan, *A Short History of Chinese Philosophy*, edited by Derk Bodde (New York: The Free Press, 1996/1948), pp. 329–330.

26 Fung Yu-lan (Feng Youlan), *A History of Chinese Philosophy*, translated by Derk Bodde, Vol. 1 (Princeton University Press, 1973/1937), p. 4. A decade later (1948), Marxist intellectual historian Zhao Jibin 趙紀彬 (1905–1982) was still making the same point. As Yvonne Schulz Zinda relates in chapter 10: "Zhao argued that although China may not be as systematic in philosophical reasoning and may not treat all philosophical problems as such, similar to other philosophies in the world, it posed questions, had its own technical terms and ways of reaching conclusions, and employed categories in the same way as systematic philosophy."

27 Feng Youlan, *Xin lixue* 新理學 [New Principle-centred learning], originally published in 1938, in *Zhen Yuan liu shu* 貞元六書 [Purity descends, primacy ascends: Six books], 2 vols. (Shanghai: Huadong shifan daxue chubanshe, 1996), Vol. 1, p. 5.

28 Echoes of this are found in the following comments by Chen Lai: "If one studies only Zhu Xi's thought and does not study the thought of Yi T'oegye 李退溪 (1501–1570), Yi Yulgok 李栗谷 (1536–1584), or Itō Jinsai 伊藤仁齋 (1627–1705), then one would be unable to appreciate the possibilities inherent in developing all facets of the logic contained in Zhu Xi's philosophical system; be unable to appreciate all the possibilities that Zhu Xi's philosophical system has in terms of its being susceptible to challenges; and be unable to appreciate the possibilities for multiple developments in Zhu Xi Learning." See his *Dong Ya ruxue jiu lun* 東亞儒學九論 [Nine essays on East Asian *ruxue*] (Beijing: Sanlian shudian, 2008), pp. 3–4.

29 For a more general account of how "Tsinghua philosophy faculty members found a rationale to link Chinese and Western learning via a logical approach through reliance on New Realism," see Xiaoqing Diana Lin's essay in this volume.

30 Wang Guowei, "Zhexue bianhuo" 哲學辨惑 [Disputing confusions about philosophy] (1903), in *Wang Guowei zhexue meixue lunwen jiyi* 王國維哲學美學論文輯軼 [Edited collection of Wang Guowei's lost essays on philosophy and aesthetics], compiled by Fo Chu 佛雛 (Shanghai: Huadong shifandaxue chubanshe, 1993), pp. 5–6.

31 This is not to suggest that Xiong was opposed to the study of Western philosophy. In 1935 he even argued that if a new Chinese philosophy was to be developed in China, equal effort had to be made in working on both Chinese philosophy and Western philosophy. (Xiong regarded Buddhist philosophy as indigenized or Sinicized philosophy.) See his "Wei zhexue nianhui jin yi yan" 為哲學年會進一言 [A recommendation to the annual meeting of the Chinese Philosophy Association], in *Shili lunxue yu jilüe* 十力論學語輯略 [Edited collection of Xiong's Shili's discussions on scholarship],

in *Xiong Shili quanji* 熊十力全集 [Complete writings of Xiong Shili], Vol. 2 (Wuhan: Hubei jiaoyu chubanshe, 2001), p. 300.

32 For He Lin's view that "the spirit of Confucian learning would be strengthened by absorbing ideas from the West," see Xiaoqing Diana Lin's chapter in this volume.

33 Lin Yu-sheng, *Crisis of Chinese Consciousness: Radical Antitraditionalism in the May Fourth Era* (Madison: University of Wisconsin Press, 1979), pp. 26, 29, 28, 50.

34 *Ibid.*, p. 48.

35 *Ibid.*, p. 38.

36 The impact-response formulation had already been clearly formulated in Ssu-yu Teng and John K. Fairbank, *China's Response to the West, a Documentary Survey 1839–1923* (Cambridge, MA: Harvard University Press, 1954).

37 Paul A. Cohen, "Moving beyond 'Tradition and Modernity'" was first published in 1984 as the second chapter in Cohen's *Discovering History in China: American Historical Writing on the Recent Chinese Past* (New York: Columbia University Press). I have used the reprint in his *China Unbound: Evolving Perspectives of the Chinese Past* (London: Routledge Curzon, 2003), p. 61.

38 Barry Steben, who studied under Mizoguchi's supervision in the early 1990s, relates that "[Prof.] Mizoguchi was very much enamoured of Cohen's book, saying that it jibed with his own methodology, and he had me read it both in English and Japanese and give a lecture on it in Japanese to his grad students at Daitō Bunka University" (personal communication).

39 Mizoguchi Yūzō, *Hōhō toshite no Chūgoku* 方法としての中国 [China as method] (Tokyo: Tōkyō Daigaku shuppankai, 1989).

40 Takeuchi Yoshimi, *Hōhō toshite no Ajia*, in *Shisōshi no hōhō to taishō: Nihon to Seiō* 思想史の方法と対象—日本と西欧, edited by Takeda Kiyoko 武田清子 (Tokyo: Sōbunsha, 1961). The essay was one in a series of lectures given at International Christian University in Tokyo by Takeuchi, Maruyama Masao 丸山真男, Ōtsuka Hisao 大塚久雄, and others. On Takeuchi's "Asia as method" thesis, see Tetsuo Najita and H. D. Harootunian, "Japan's Revolt against the West," in *Modern Japanese Thought*, edited by Bob Tadashi Wakabayashi (Cambridge: Cambridge University Press, 1998), pp. 268–270.

41 Mizoguchi's *Hōhō toshite no Chūgoku* was translated into Chinese twice: once in China in 1996 and once in Taiwan in 1999.

42 Hao Chang, *Chinese Intellectuals in Crisis: Search for Order and Meaning, 1890–1911* (Berkeley: University of California Press, 1987), pp. 9, 10. This book was translated into Chinese in 1988.

43 Yu Yingshi, "Qingdai sixiangshi de yige xin jieshi" 清代思想史的一個新解釋 [A new interpretation of Qing intellectual history], in his *Zhongguo sixiang chuantong de xiandai quanshi* 中國思想傳統的現代詮釋 [Modern interpretations of Chinese intellectual traditions] (Nanjing: Jiangsu renmin chubanshe, 1991, p. 209. (This essay is not included in the original Taiwan edition of this book [Taipei: Lianjing chuban shiye gongsi, 1987).

44 Thomas Metzger, *A Cloud across the Pacific: Essays on the Clash between Chinese and Western Political Theories Today* (Hong Kong: Chinese University Press, 2005), p. 673. Curiously, three decades before this, in his *Escape from Predicament: Neo-Confucianism and China's Evolving Political Culture* (New York: Columbia Press, 1977)—in similarly emphasizing the decisive and ongoing influence of the traditional roots of China's transformative visions of modernization—Metzger was careful to temper this claim with the observation that interplay with Western ideas was crucial. And in 1980 he wrote: "Of course the position at stake is not that the Chinese found this dynamic orientation simply within their tradition, but rather that it arose through the interplay in their minds between a powerful indigenous 'tension' and certain important impressions made by the Western impact." See Metzger, "Author's Reply," *Journal of Asian Studies* 39.2 (1980), p. 282.

45 This is not altogether surprising given the availability in translation of books written by leading exponents of the paradigm, as detailed above.

46 I borrow this term from a paper by Arif Dirlik, "*Guoxue*/National Learning in the Age of Global Modernity," *China Perspectives* 1 (2011), p. 4.

47 See John Makeham, "The Revival of *Guoxue*: Historical Antecedents and Contemporary Aspirations," *China Perspectives* 1 (2011), pp. 14–21.

48 See John Makeham, *Lost Soul: "Confucianism" in Contemporary Chinese Academic Discourse* (Cambridge, MA: Harvard University Asia Center, 2008).

49 For example, Zhang Xianglong 張祥龍 has proposed that, because China does not possess philosophy in the Western sense of the term, Chinese philosophy should therefore be referred to as "Chinese learning" (*Zhongxue* 中學) or "old Chinese learning" (*Zhongguo de guxue* 中國的古學) or even "techniques of the way" (*daoshu* 道術). Zhang Xianglong, *Cong xianxiangxue dao Kong Fuzi* 從現象學到孔夫子 [From phenomenology to Confucius] (Beijing: Shangwu yinshuguan, 2001), p. 190; Zhang Xianglong, "'Zhongguo zhexue,' 'daoshu,' haishi kedaoshuhua de guangyi zhexue?" 「中國哲學」、「道術」還是可道術化的廣義哲學? ["Chinese philosophy," "techniques of the way," or a broad sense of philosophy that accommodates the techniques of the way?], *Zhexue dongtai* 哲學動態 6 (2004), pp. 11.

50 For two recent views from Taiwan which buck this trend, see Li Minghui 李明輝, "Xingsi Zhongguo zhexue yanjiu de weiji: Cong Zhongguo zhexue de 'zhengdangxing wenti' tanqi" 省思中國哲學研究的危機——從中國哲學的「正當性問題」談起 [Reflections on the crisis of Chinese philosophy: Beginning with Chinese philosophical studies' "problem of legitimacy"], *Sixiang* 思想 9 (2008), pp. 171, 172. Similar sentiments are expressed by Lin Yuehui 林月惠 in her article in the same issue, "Zouxiang duibi shiyu de Zhongguo zhexue yanjiu: Cong jiben nengli de xunlian tanqi" 走向對比視域的中國哲學研究：從基本能力的訓練談起 [Chinese philosophical studies moving towards a contrast of horizons: Beginning with an account of basic training], *Sixiang* 9 (2008), pp. 211–220. I am grateful to Zhang Jinzhi for alerting me to these two articles.

51 Shun distinguishes two goals in the study of early Chinese thought: "understanding the perspective of an early Chinese thinker and drawing out its implications for contemporary practical and philosophical concerns." As he explains, in his own work he has sought to avoid the use of Western terms in studies "directed to understanding the perspectives of early Chinese thinkers, while leaving it open that the use of such terms might have a place in other kinds of study with different goals." Shun Kwong-loi, "Studying Confucian and Comparative Ethics: Methodological Reflections," *Journal of Chinese Philosophy* 36.3 (2009), p. 455.

52 On this point, see, for example, Prasenjit Duara, *Rescuing History from the Nation: Questioning Narratives of Modern China* (Chicago: University of Chicago Press, 1995), p. 76.

53 Shun Kwong-loi, "Studying Confucian and Comparative Ethics," pp. 456–457, 476.

54 Yu Yingshi, *Lun Dai Zhen yu Zhang Xuecheng* 論戴震與章學誠 [Dai Zhen and Zhang Xuecheng] (Taipei: Sanmin shuju, 1996), preface to revised edition, pp. 2, 3, 4.

55 Yu made this comment on the occasion of receiving the John W. Kluge Prize at the Library of Congress, 5 December 2006. See <http://www.loc.gov/today/pr/2006/06-A07.html>. Accessed 25 September 2007.

56 Chen Shaoming, "Zhishi puxi de zhuanhuan: Zhongguo zhexueshi yanjiu fanli lunxi" 知識譜系的轉換——中國哲學史研究範例論析 [The transformation of intellectual genealogies: Analysis of research paradigms from the history of Chinese philosophy], *Xueren* 學人 30 (1998), pp. 175–176; Karl Mannheim, *The Ideological and Sociological Interpretation of Intellectual Phenomenon* (New York: Oxford University Press, 1971), pp. 116–131.

57 They also suggest the influence of Hu on Yu.

Index